ZAGAT®

World's Top Restaurants

Fourth Edition

Covering 1,404 Restaurants in 58 Cities
From the Diner's Point of View

Published and distributed by
Zagat Survey, LLC
4 Columbus Circle
New York, NY 10019
T: 212.977.6000
E: world@zagat.com
www.zagat.com

ACKNOWLEDGMENTS

We thank Hugo Arnold, Alicia Arter, Jeanine Barone, Jelena Bergdahl, Olga Boikess, Nikki Buchanan, Evee Cho, Bill Citara, Sholto Douglas-Home, Claudia Eilers, Victoria Elmacioglu, Jeanette Foster, Judy Witts Francini, Maria Pilar Gallas, Rona Gindin, Barbara Goerlich, Eric Grossman, Jony Gruitjers, Katrin Gygax, Meesha Halm, Jennifer Hattam, Florian Holzer, Valerie Jarvie, Tina Kanagaratnam, Marty Katz, Aina Keller, Michael Klein, Hyejin Kwon, Sharon Litwin, Alec Lobrano, Maria Francesca LoDico, Cecilia Lundgren, Eric Lyman, Lucy Mallows, Gail Mangold-Vine, Nan McElroy, Stacey McLeod, Lori Midson, Eileen Wen Mooney, David Nelson, Jan Norris, Tim and Heather Pawsey, Joe and Anna Pollack, Svend Rasmussen, Mike Riccetti, Heidi Knapp Rinella, Sara Rosso, Joanna Sanecka, Shelley Skiles Sawyer, George Semler, Merrill Shindler, Valerie Stivers, Eryn Swanson, Jan Ghane Tabrizi, Suzy Taher, Alice Van Housen and Angie Wong as well as the following members of our staff: Brian Albert, Sean Beachell, Maryanne Bertollo, Danielle Borovoy, Reni Chin, Larry Cohn, Bill Corsello, Nicole Diaz, Carol Diuguid, Kelly Dobkin, Alison Flick, Jeff Freier, Curt Gathje, Michelle Golden, Matthew Hamm, Justin Hartung, Marc Henson, Anna Hyclak, Aynsley Karps, Rus Kehoe, Cynthia Kilian, Natalie Lebert, Mike Liao, Vivian Ma, Caitlin Miehl, James Mulcahy, Polina Paley, Josh Rogers, Emily Rothschild, Amanda Spurlock, Chris Walsh, Jacqueline Wasilczyk, Yoji Yamaguchi, Sharon Yates, Anna Zappia and Kyle Zolner.

The reviews in this guide are based on public opinion surveys. The ratings reflect the average scores given by the survey participants who voted on each establishment. The text is based on quotes from, or paraphrasings of, the surveyors' comments. Phone numbers, addresses and other factual data were correct to the best of our knowledge when published in this guide.

Our guides are printed using environmentally preferable inks containing 20%, by weight, renewable resources on papers sourced from well-managed forests. Deluxe editions are covered with Skivertex Recover® Double containing a minimum of 30% post-consumer waste fiber.

SUSTAINABLE FORESTRY INITIATIVE
Certified Sourcing
www.sfiprogram.org
SFI-00993

ENVIROINK™

The inks used to print the body of this publication contain a minimum of 20%, by weight, renewable resources.

Contents

Ratings & Symbols

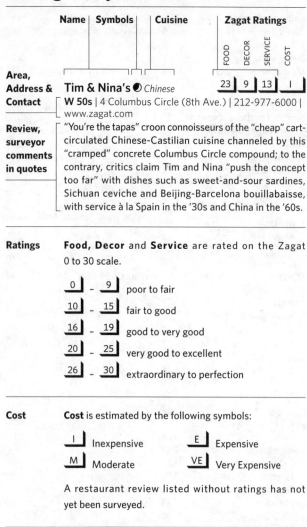

	Name	Symbols	Cuisine	Zagat Ratings			
				FOOD	DECOR	SERVICE	COST

Area, Address & Contact

Tim & Nina's ◑ *Chinese*   23 | 9 | 13 | I

W 50s | 4 Columbus Circle (8th Ave.) | 212-977-6000 | www.zagat.com

Review, surveyor comments in quotes

"You're the tapas" croon connoisseurs of the "cheap" cart-circulated Chinese-Castilian cuisine channeled by this "cramped" concrete Columbus Circle compound; to the contrary, critics claim Tim and Nina "push the concept too far" with dishes such as sweet-and-sour sardines, Sichuan ceviche and Beijing-Barcelona bouillabaisse, with service à la Spain in the '30s and China in the '60s.

Ratings

Food, Decor and **Service** are rated on the Zagat 0 to 30 scale.

0	– 9	poor to fair
10	– 15	fair to good
16	– 19	good to very good
20	– 25	very good to excellent
26	– 30	extraordinary to perfection

Cost

Cost is estimated by the following symbols:

I	Inexpensive	E	Expensive
M	Moderate	VE	Very Expensive

A restaurant review listed without ratings has not yet been surveyed.

Symbols

◑	serves after 11 PM
Ⓢ̶	closed on Sunday
Ⓜ̶	closed on Monday
⊘	no credit cards accepted

About This Survey

This fourth edition of our **World's Top Restaurants Survey** covers 1,404 outstanding eateries in 58 major markets across Asia, Europe and North America. Like all our guides, this one is based on input from thousands of avid local consumers. Our editors have synopsized this feedback, highlighting representative comments (in quotation marks within each review). To read full surveyor comments – and share your own opinions – visit **ZAGAT.com,** where you will also find the latest restaurant news, special events, deals, reservations, menus, photos and lots more, **all for free.**

ABOUT ZAGAT: In 1979, we started asking friends to rate and review restaurants purely for fun. The term "user-generated content" had yet to be coined. That hobby grew into Zagat Survey; 33 years later, we have over 375,000 surveyors and cover airlines, bars, dining, fast food, entertaining, golf, hotels, movies, music, resorts, shopping, spas, theater and tourist attractions in over 100 countries. Along the way, we evolved from being a print publisher to a digital content provider, e.g. **ZAGAT.com** and **Zagat To Go** mobile apps (for iPad, iPhone, Android, BlackBerry, Windows Phone 7 and Palm webOS). We also produce marketing tools for a wide range of blue-chip corporate clients. And you can find us on Twitter (twitter.com/zagat), Facebook, Foursquare and just about any other social media network.

UNDERLYING PREMISES: Three simple ideas underlie our ratings and reviews. First, we believe that the collective opinions of large numbers of avid consumers are more accurate than those of any single person. (Consider that our surveyors visit restaurants regularly year-round, anonymously – and on their own dime.) Second, food quality is only part of the equation when choosing a restaurant, thus we ask our surveyors to rate food, decor and service separately and report on cost. Third, since people need reliable information in an easy-to-digest, curated format, we strive to be concise and we offer our content on every platform – print, online and mobile. Our Top Food by City (pages 7-10) and Most Popular by City (pages 11-14) lists are also designed to help you quickly choose the best place anywhere in the world.

JOIN IN: To improve our guides, we solicit your comments – positive or negative; it's vital that we hear your opinions. Just contact us at **nina-tim@zagat.com.** We also invite you to join our surveys at **ZAGAT.com.** Do so and you'll receive a choice of rewards in exchange.

New York, NY
November 9, 2011

Nina and Tim Zagat

What's New

Like every sector of the global economy, the restaurant industry has seen some tough times in recent years, e.g. an increase in the cost of ingredients. But luckily for diners, that hasn't translated into a significant rise in menu prices. In the U.S. this last year, the per-meal average rose a slight 0.8% (over the past three years, the average rise has been 1.4%). In Tokyo, the per-meal average has actually fallen 2.3%. London bucks that trend with an average that's climbed a hefty 6.3%, though that obviously hasn't put a damper on things: Londoners are dining out 2.4 times a week (up from 2.2 previously). Meanwhile, Tokyo survey-ors are eating out 3.8 times a week (up from 3.3 previously) and the U.S. average remained 3.1. Healthy patronage aside, spending habits have changed in the past few years. Not only are diners mindful of the overall price level of the restaurants they choose, but to save money they're also skipping hard liquor, first courses and desserts.

WORLDLY PLEASURES: The globalization of each city's fine-dining scene continues apace, with an ever-increasing range of variety and creativity. Such diversity is evidenced in many top-rated places, e.g. **Gargantua** in Frankfurt (French/Mediterranean), **Varanda** in Lisbon (French), **Mario** in Moscow (Italian) and **Allegro** in Prague (Italian/Mediterranean), to name just a few. And as China continues to grow and diversify, so too does its roster of restaurants; among the top five places in the Chinese cities we survey, you'll find upscale ren-ditions of Indian, Italian, French and even Brazilian cuisines.

BIG NAMES: Despite the fiscal climate, there's been an upsurge of pricey debuts, many helmed by top toques. Examples include London's **Dinner by Heston Blumenthal,** featuring the eponymous chef's unique Modern British fare; Boston's **Menton,** where local celeb Barbara Lynch's French-Italian creations rank as the city's most expensive; Chicago's **Next,** Grant Achatz's daring Eclectic, whose price depends on the day and time (but is always high); Seoul's **Clock16,** an elegant European with a veteran NYC chef; and Paris' second branch of **L'Atelier de Joël Robuchon.** Interestingly, when asked about the influence of celebrity chefs, about 38% of surveyors say they're more likely to dine at a restaurant associated with one; 56% say that has no effect.

TECH EFFECTS: In every market, the internet as a reservations tool is gaining ground, and more and more fans are following their fa-vorite restaurants and chefs via social-media platforms. However, most respondents say the digitalization of dining shouldn't extend to the table, deeming texting, tweeting, emailing and talking on the phone while at the table "rude and inappropriate" (they're more for-giving of occasional picture-taking).

LEANING GREEN: All over the world, surveyors are seeking out restaurants whose ingredients lean "green." In the U.S., 67% feel it's important that the food they eat is local, organic and/or sustainably raised, while 57% say that they would even pay more for it.

New York, NY
November 9, 2011

Nina and Tim Zagat

Top Food by City

ASIA

BEIJING

- **27** Made in China
- **26** Taj Pavilion
- Alameda
- **25** Beijing Da Dong
- Danieli's

HONG KONG

- **28** Lung King Heen
- Sushi Hiro
- **27** Gaddi's
- Petrus
- L'Atelier de Joël Robuchon

SEOUL

- **26** Ristorante Eo
- **25** Continental

- Malta Tuna
- Sushi Hyo
- Sushi Cho

SHANGHAI

- **28** Hanagatami
- **26** Guyi Hunan
- Vedas
- Jean Georges
- Din Tai Fung

TOKYO

- **29** Kyoaji
- Restaurant Bacar
- **28** Burgaz Ada
- **27** Raku-tei
- Gyuzo

CANADA

MONTRÉAL

- **28** Milos
- La Chronique
- Toqué!
- **27** Le Jolifou
- Le Club Chasse

TORONTO

- **29** Sushi Kaji
- **27** Chiado/Senhor Antonio

- Terra
- Scaramouche
- Scaramouche Pasta

VANCOUVER

- **28** La Belle Auberge
- Vij's
- Cioppino's
- **27** Le Crocodile
- Tojo's

EUROPE

AMSTERDAM

- **28** Ron Blaauw
- **27** Yamazato
- Van Vlaanderen
- La Rive
- **26** Bordewijk

ATHENS

- **29** Spondi
- **27** Varoulko
- **26** Matsuhisa Athens
- Milos
- Papadakis

BARCELONA

- **28** Cinc Sentits
- **27** Passadis del Pep
- Hofmann
- Cal Pep
- Neichel

BERLIN

- **26** VAU
- **24** Lorenz Adlon
- Maxwell
- Gabriele
- **23** Alt Luxemburg
- Die Quadriga*

---

* Indicates a tie with restaurant above

BRUSSELS

28 Comme Chez Soi
Bruneau
27 La Truffe Noire
Sea Grill
26 Le Passage

BUDAPEST

28 Baraka
Vadrózsa
25 Kacsa
24 Gundel
Fausto's

COPENHAGEN

28 Noma
27 Era Ora
Restaurationen
26 Søllerød Kro
Kong Hans Kælder

DUBLIN

27 Thornton's
Patrick Guilbaud
26 Seasons
25 L'Ecrivain
One Pico

FLORENCE

27 Enoteca Pinchiorri
26 Fuor d'Acqua
La Giostra
Taverna del Bronzino
Cibrèo

FRANKFURT

25 Gargantua
Villa Rothschild
Osteria Enoteca
24 Restaurant Français
Goldman

GENEVA

29 Dom./Châteauvieux
26 Auberge du Lion d'Or
25 Patara
Le Tsé-Fung
24 Le Floris

HAMBURG

25 Haerlin
Seven Seas*
Henssler & Henssler
24 Atlantic
23 Jacobs

ISTANBUL

26 Borsa
25 Istanbul Culinary Institute
Develi
Seasons
Tugra

LISBON

26 Varanda
25 O Mercado do Peixe
Gambrinus
Restaurante 100 Maneiras
Bocca

LONDON

29 Ledbury
28 Pied à Terre
Dinings
Le Gavroche
Hunan

MADRID

27 DiverXo
Santceloni
Zalacaín
La Terraza del Casino
Viridiana

MILAN

28 Il Luogo/Aimo e Nadia
27 Sadler
Joia
26 D'O
Il Teatro

MOSCOW

25 Mario
24 Palazzo Ducale
23 Café Pushkin
Cantinetta Antinori
22 Vogue Café

MUNICH

27 Tantris
25 Vue Maximilian
Schuhbeck's
Boettner's
24 Königshof

PARIS

28 Taillevent
Le Cinq
Guy Savoy
L'Astrance
Pierre Gagnaire

PRAGUE

- 26 Allegro
- 25 Aquarius
- V Zátiší
- Essensia
- 24 U Zlaté Hrušky

ROME

- 26 La Pergola
- La Rosetta
- 25 Felice a Testaccio
- Vivendo
- Antico Arco

STOCKHOLM

- 28 Wedholms Fisk
- 27 Oaxen Skärgårdskrog
- Mathias Dahlgren
- F12
- 26 Lux Stockholm

VENICE

- 26 Osteria alle Testiere
- Fortuny
- 25 Club del Doge
- Al Covo
- Corte Sconta

VIENNA

- 28 Steirereck
- 26 Imperial
- 24 Demel
- Eisvogel
- Walter Bauer

WARSAW

- 25 Dom Polski
- 24 La Rotisserie
- Rózana
- 23 Rubikon
- U Kucharzy

ZURICH

- 27 Rico's
- 26 Pavillon
- Lindenhofkeller
- 25 Wirtschaft
- 24 Restaurant

UNITED STATES

ATLANTA

- 29 Bacchanalia
- 28 Quinones Room
- Aria
- McKendrick's
- Bone's

BALTIMORE

- 28 Charleston
- Volt
- 27 Prime Rib
- Samos
- Di Pasquale's

BOSTON

- 29 O Ya
- 28 Oleana
- La Campania
- Neptune Oyster
- Lumière

CHICAGO

- 29 Les Nomades
- Alinea
- Schwa
- 28 Arun's
- Topolobampo

DALLAS/FT. WORTH

- 29 Bonnell's
- 28 Saint-Emilion
- French Room
- Cacharel
- Pappas Bros.

DENVER/MTN. RESORTS

- 28 Fruition
- Frasca
- Matsuhisa
- Splendido
- Mizuna

HONOLULU

- 28 Sushi Sasabune
- Hiroshi
- Alan Wong's
- La Mer
- 27 Chef Mavro

HOUSTON

- 28 Le Mistral
- Kanomwan
- Pappas Bros.
- Mark's
- 27 Da Marco

KANSAS CITY

29 Justus Drugstore
28 Bluestem
Michael Smith
27 Oklahoma Joe's
Le Fou Frog

LAS VEGAS

28 Joël Robuchon
Todd's Unique Dining
Steak House
Raku
Sen of Japan

LOS ANGELES

29 Matsuhisa
28 Angelini Osteria
Asanebo
Mélisse
Urasawa

MIAMI

29 Naoe
28 Palme d'Or
Zuma
Palm
27 Il Gabbiano

NEW ORLEANS

28 Bayona
Stella!
Brigtsen's
27 Clancy's
Royal China

NEW YORK CITY

29 Le Bernardin
Daniel
28 Per Se
Bouley
Jean Georges

ORLANDO

28 Victoria & Albert's
4 Rivers
27 Del Frisco's
Jiko
California Grill

PALM BEACH

28 Marcello's La Sirena
Chez Jean-Pierre
27 11 Maple St.
Captain Charlie's
Café L'Europe

PHILADELPHIA

28 Vetri
Fountain
Birchrunville Store
Amada
Gilmore's

PHOENIX/SCOTTSDALE

28 Kai
Binkley's
Quiessence
Noca
27 Barrio Cafe

SAN DIEGO

29 Market
28 Sushi Ota
Hane Sushi
27 Wine Vault
Addison

SAN FRANCISCO BAY AREA

29 Gary Danko
French Laundry
28 Cyrus
Manresa
Aubergine

SEATTLE

28 Cafe Juanita
Paseo
Mashiko
Spinasse
Herbfarm

ST. LOUIS

28 Niche
27 Stellina
Sidney St. Cafe
Trattoria Marcella
Tony's

WASHINGTON, DC

29 Marcel's
Inn at Little Washington
Komi
28 CityZen
Rasika

Most Popular by City

ASIA

BEIJING
1. Alameda
2. Din Tai Fung
3. Made in China
4. Beijing Da Dong
5. CourtYard

HONG KONG
1. Felix
2. Yung Kee
3. Gaddi's
4. Nobu
5. Spoon by Alain Ducasse

SEOUL
1. Ganga
2. Gassra
3. Woolaeoak
4. Little Saigon
5. Yongsusan

SHANGHAI
1. M on the Bund
2. Jean Georges
3. T8
4. Din Tai Fung
5. Simply Thai

TOKYO
1. Kyubey
2. Ukai-tei
3. Shotai-en
4. Din Tai Fung
5. Tsurutontan

CANADA

MONTRÉAL
1. Au Pied de Cochon
2. Toqué!
3. L'Express
4. Gibbys
5. Moishe's

TORONTO
1. Canoe
2. Scaramouche
3. North 44°
4. Ruth's Chris
5. Auberge du Pommier

VANCOUVER
1. Vij's
2. Keg Steakhouse
3. Blue Water
4. Le Crocodile
5. Chambar

EUROPE

AMSTERDAM
1. D'Vijff Vlieghen
2. Dylan
3. La Rive
4. Christophe'
5. De Kas

ATHENS
1. Matsuhisa Athens
2. Balthazar
3. Spondi
4. Electra Roof Garden
5. GB Corner*
6. Milos*

BARCELONA
1. 7 Portes
2. Botafumeiro
3. Cal Pep
4. El Asador
5. Comerç 24

BERLIN
1. VAU
2. Borchardt
3. Lorenz Adlon
4. Margaux
5. Bocca/Bacco

BRUSSELS
1. Comme Chez Soi
2. Aux Armes de Bruxelles
3. Belga Queen
4. La Maison du Cygne
5. L'Ecailler du Palais Royal
6. L'Ogenblik*
7. Sea Grill*

BUDAPEST

1. Gundel
2. Kacsa
3. Café Kör
4. Centrál Kávéház
5. Spoon Café*

COPENHAGEN

1. Krogs Fiskerestaurant
2. Era Ora
3. Le Sommelier
4. Café Victor
5. Restaurationen*

DUBLIN

1. Patrick Guilbaud
2. Shanahan's
3. Seasons
4. Tea Room
5. Eden

FLORENCE

1. Cibrèo
2. Enoteca Pinchiorri
3. Cantinetta Antinori
4. Il Latini
5. Alle Murate

FRANKFURT

1. Apfelwein Wagner
2. Holbein's
3. Edelweiss
4. Gargantua*
5. Aubergine

GENEVA

1. Auberge du Lion d'Or
2. Le Relais/l'Entrecôte*
3. Brasserie Lipp
4. Dom./Châteauvieux
5. Les Armures

HAMBURG

1. Jacobs
2. Doc Cheng's
3. Haerlin
4. Rive
5. Cox

ISTANBUL

1. Seasons
2. Tugra
3. Laledan
4. Ulus 29
5. Develi

LISBON

1. A Casa
2. Restaurante 100 Maneiras
3. Varanda
4. Tavares Rico
5. Gambrinus

LONDON

1. Wolseley
2. Gordon Ramsay/68 Royal
3. J. Sheekey
4. Nobu London
5. Ivy

MADRID

1. Casa Lucio
2. Botín
3. Zalacaín
4. Café de Oriente
5. Teatriz

MILAN

1. 10 Corso Como
2. Armani/Nobu
3. Cracco
4. Trattoria Milanese
5. Antica Trattoria

MOSCOW

1. Café Pushkin
2. Galereya
3. Shinok
4. Scandinavia
5. Cantinetta Antinori

MUNICH

1. Tantris
2. Dallmayr
3. Königshof
4. Käfer-Schänke
5. Lenbach
6. Schuhbeck's*

PARIS

1. Taillevent
2. L'Atelier de Joël Robuchon
3. Le Grand Véfour
4. Alain Ducasse
5. La Tour d'Argent

PRAGUE

1. Kampa Park
2. Allegro
3. Bellevue
4. U Modré Kachnicky
5. V Zátiší

Vote at ZAGAT.com

ROME

1. La Pergola
2. Sora Lella
3. Ambasciata d'Abruzzo
4. Dal Bolognese
5. Giggetto

STOCKHOLM

1. Operakällaren
2. F12
3. Wedholms Fisk
4. Berns Asian
5. Sturehof*

VENICE

1. Harry's Bar
2. Corte Sconta
3. Al Covo
4. Fiaschetteria Toscana
5. Terrazza Danieli

VIENNA

1. Demel
2. Steirereck
3. Imperial
4. Korso bei der Oper
5. DO & CO

WARSAW

1. Belvedere
2. Dom Polski
3. Oriental
4. Qchnia Artystyczna
5. Santorini*

ZURICH

1. Kronenhalle
2. Rico's
3. Widder
4. Brasserie Lipp
5. Pavillon

UNITED STATES

ATLANTA

1. Bacchanalia
2. Bone's
3. Buckhead Diner
4. Rathbun's
5. Canoe

BALTIMORE

1. Woodberry Kitchen
2. Charleston
3. Volt
4. Cinghiale
5. Prime Rib

BOSTON

1. Legal Sea Foods
2. Abe & Louie's
3. Craigie on Main
4. Blue Ginger
5. Oleana

CHICAGO

1. Frontera Grill
2. Alinea
3. Topolobampo
4. Charlie Trotter's
5. Gibsons

DALLAS/FT. WORTH

1. Abacus
2. Fearing's
3. Del Frisco's
4. French Room
5. Stephan Pyles

DENVER/MTN. RESORTS

1. Frasca
2. Sweet Basil
3. Rioja
4. Mizuna
5. Elway's

HONOLULU

1. Alan Wong's
2. Roy's
3. La Mer
4. Chef Mavro
5. Duke's Canoe Club

HOUSTON

1. Da Marco
2. Mark's
3. Tony's
4. Pappas Bros.
5. Pappadeaux

KANSAS CITY

1. Fiorella's Jack Stack
2. Arthur Bryant's
3. Oklahoma Joe's
4. Lidia's
5. Bristol

LAS VEGAS

1. Bouchon
2. Aureole
3. Picasso
4. Mon Ami Gabi
5. Joe's Sea/Steak/Crab

LOS ANGELES

1. Spago
2. Bazaar/José Andrés
3. Angelini Osteria
4. Osteria Mozza
5. Pizzeria Mozza

MIAMI

1. Joe's Stone Crab
2. Michael's Genuine
3. Prime One Twelve
4. Michy's
5. Il Gabbiano

NEW ORLEANS

1. Commander's Palace
2. Galatoire's
3. Bayona
4. August
5. Acme Oyster

NEW YORK CITY

1. Le Bernardin
2. Gramercy Tavern
3. Peter Luger
4. Union Square Cafe
5. Eleven Madison Park

ORLANDO

1. Seasons 52
2. Victoria & Albert's
3. California Grill
4. 4 Rivers
5. Del Frisco's

PALM BEACH

1. Café Boulud
2. Abe & Louie's
3. Kee Grill
4. Seasons 52
5. Bonefish Grill

PHILADELPHIA

1. Amada
2. Buddakan
3. Le Bec-Fin
4. Osteria
5. Vetri

PHOENIX/SCOTTSDALE

1. P.F. Chang's
2. Binkley's
3. T. Cook's
4. Lon's/Hermosa
5. Fleming's

SAN DIEGO

1. George's Ocean Terrace
2. Sushi Ota
3. In-N-Out
4. Market
5. Donovan's

SAN FRANCISCO BAY AREA

1. Gary Danko
2. Boulevard
3. French Laundry
4. Slanted Door
5. Chez Panisse

SEATTLE

1. Wild Ginger
2. Dahlia Lounge
3. Canlis
4. Cafe Juanita
5. Rover's

ST. LOUIS

1. Sidney St. Cafe
2. 1111 Mississippi
3. Niche
4. Annie Gunn's
5. Tony's

WASHINGTON, DC

1. Zaytinya
2. 2 Amys
3. Central Michel Richard
4. Citronelle
5. Inn at Little Washington

ASIA
RESTAURANT
DIRECTORY

Beijing

TOP FOOD RANKING

	Restaurant	Cuisine
27	Made in China	Chinese
26	Taj Pavilion	Indian
	Alameda	Brazilian/European
25	Beijing Da Dong	Chinese
	Danieli's	Italian
	Din Tai Fung	Chinese
	Hatsune	Japanese
	Comptoirs de France	French
	Feiteng Yuxiang	Chinese
24	Pure Lotus	Vegetarian
	Liqun Roast Duck	Chinese
	Sichuan Provincial	Chinese
23	CourtYard	Eclectic
	Morel's	Belgian/French
	Haiku by Hatsune	Japanese
	Cafe Sambal	Malaysian
	South Beauty*	Chinese
	Crystal Jade Palace	Chinese

Alameda *Brazilian/European*   26 | 20 | 22 | M

Chaoyang | Nali Mall | Sanlitun Beijie (bet. Sanlitun Xiliujie & Sanlitun Xiwujie) | (86-10) 6417-8084

Trendy types generate the "buzz" at Beijing's Most Popular restaurant, a "bustling" Brazilian-European venue whose crowd syncs up with the "chic" Chaoyang setting and "consistently excellent", "constantly changing" "contemporary cuisine"; overall, it's "hard to find better", especially when you factor in the "gracious" service and "steal" of a lunch.

Beijing Da Dong *Chinese*   25 | 17 | 18 | M

Chaoyang | Tuanjiehu Beikou, Dongsanhuan Lu, Bldg. 3 (Changhong Qiao) | (86-10) 6582-2892

Dongcheng | Nanxincang International Tower | 22 Dongsishitiao (bet. Chaoyangmen Beidajie & Chaoyangmen Beixiaojie) | (86-10) 5169-0329

Dongcheng | Jinbao Dasha | 88 Jinbao Jie, 5th fl. (bet. Chaoyangmennei Dajie & Jianguomennei Dajie) | (86-10) 8522-1234

"Spectacular Peking duck" that fans call "the best, hands down" is what this popular chainlet is prized for; the other Chinese fare is "satisfying" too, so it's no wonder backers say they're "worth the trip"; P.S. the Nanxincang Int'l Tower Dongcheng location features a glassed-in kitchen, and the Jinbao and Chaoyang settings are equally "modern."

Cafe Sambal ● *Malaysian*   23 | 20 | 21 | M

Dongcheng | 43 Doufuchi Hutong (Jiugulou Dajie) | (86-10) 6400-4875 | www.cafesambal.com

Deemed the "perfect neighborhood hangout", this hip, rustic, "mellow" Malaysian in Dongcheng dishes up "excellent", spicy and less fiery fare

---

* Indicates a tie with restaurant above

	FOOD	DECOR	SERVICE	COST

paired with "warm" service; an added attraction is the nearby Houhai Lake, around which pre- or post-dinner strolls are not uncommon.

Comptoirs de France *French* | 25 | 22 | 24 | I |

Chaoyang | Huairun International Apartments | 12 Jiangtai Lu, Bldg. 5, 1st fl.
(bet. Fangyuan Xi Lu & Jiangtai Lu) | (86-10) 5135-7645
Chaoyang | East Lake Villas | 35 Dongzhimenwai Dajie (Xindong Lu) |
(86-10) 6461-1525 ⊄
Chaoyang | 4 Ritan Bei Lu (bet. Chaoyangmenwai Dajie & Guanghua Lu) |
(86-10) 8562-3355 ⊄
Chaoyang | Riviera Plaza | 5 Laiguangying Dong Lu, 2nd fl.
(bet. Jingcheng Gaosu & Jingmi Lu) | (86-10) 8470-2347 ⊄
Chaoyang | Central Park Pl. | 89 Jianguo Lu, Bldg. 15 (Zhenzhi Lu) |
(86-10) 6530-5480
Shunyi | Europlaza | 99 Yuxiang Lu (bet. Huoshayu & Xinyuan Xi Lu) |
(86-10) 8046-6309 ⊄
www.comptoirsdefrance.com

"So hard to choose" say surveyors of all the "decadently tasty", "visually appealing" breads, croissants and sandwiches at these "oases of deliciousness" opened by the son of a French bread-baking family who charges prices that equal Beijing's No. 1 Bang for the Buck; the East Lake location is somewhat spacious, and the Shunyi spot has a terrace.

CourtYard, The *Eclectic* | 23 | 26 | 24 | VE |

Dongcheng | 95 Donghuamen Dajie (bet. Beichizi Dajie & Nanchizi Dajie) |
(86-10) 6526-8883 | www.courtyardbeijing.com

"As good as any top NYC restaurant", this "magical" "remodeled courtyard house" in Dongcheng boasts "spectacular" panoramas of "the Forbidden City and its moat" from a "cool" interior with high ceilings, mirrored walls and "modern Chinese art"; the Eclectic cuisine, laying "Asian riffs on mostly Western food", is "expensive" but "worth it."

Crystal Jade Palace *Chinese* | 23 | 22 | 20 | M |

Chaoyang | The Place | 9 Guanghua Lu, 4th fl. (Dongdaqiao Lu) |
(86-10) 6587-1228
Dongcheng | Malls at Oriental Plaza | 1 Dong Chang'an Jie
(bet. Dongdan Beidajie & Wangfujing Dajie) | (86-10) 8515-0238
www.crystaljade.com

Fans applaud the "variety" served up at this Dongcheng Chinese (with a Chaoyang sib) filled with "lovely" antiques; not only is it "well run", but the lunchtime dim sum is "the best", so "what more could you ask for?"

Danieli's *Italian* | 25 | 23 | 26 | VE |

Chaoyang | St. Regis Beijing | 21 Jianguomenwai Dajie (Ritan Lu) |
(86-10) 6460-6688, ext. 2440 | www.stregis.com

"Superb" service (voted Beijing's No. 1), a "lavish" selection of "high-quality" (and "expensive") Italian cuisine and a "tremendous wine list" make this a "perfect special-occasion destination" in Chaoyang's St. Regis Beijing; the rustic dark-wood decor plus dim lighting "combines casual comfort with elegant outings."

Din Tai Fung *Chinese* | 25 | 18 | 20 | M |

Chaoyang | 24 Xinyuan Xili Zhong Jie (bet. Xindong Lu &
Zuojiazhuang Xijie) | (86-10) 6462-4502
Chaoyang | Shin Kong Pl. | 87 Jianguo Lu, 6th fl. (bet. Dongsanhuan Zhonglu &
Jintai Lu) | (86-10) 6533-1536

(continued)

(continued)

Din Tai Fung

Haidian | Dangdai Shangcheng | 40 Zhongguancun Nandajie, 7th fl. (bet. Beisanhuan Xi Lu & Zhizhuyuan Lu) | (86-10) 6269-6726 www.dintaifung.com.cn

The "outstanding", "perfectly light" soup dumplings are "little pieces of heaven" say allies of this "bright, airy" Chaoyang-Haidian Chinese chainlet hosting "huge" crowds; "quick", "attentive" service only increases the "good-value" factor; P.S. the upstairs kids' room at Xinyuan Xili Zhong is "a plus."

Feiteng Yuxiang   *Chinese*   25 | 17 | 15 | I

Chaoyang | Yanhua Yuan | 24 Jianguomenwai Dajie (southwest of Jianguomen Bridge) | (86-10) 6515-9600 ⊞

Chaoyang | The Place | 9 Guanghua Lu, North Bldg., 4th fl. (Dongdaqiao Lu) | (86-10) 6589-5588

Chaoyang | A3 Xinyuan Nanlu (northwest of Yansha Bridge) | (86-10) 8455-2333

Chaoyang | Huatongxin Hotel | Chunxiu Lu (bet. Gongti Beilu & Xingfucun Zhonglu) | (86-10) 6415-3764 ⊞

Xicheng | Chengming Dasha | 2 Xizhimen Nandajie, 2nd fl. (bet. Pinganli Xi Dajie & Xizhimenwai Dajie) | (86-10) 5190-1778 www.ftyx.com

It's the "famed" shui zhu yu ('water-cooked fish', a misnomer since the fish is actually cooked in a lot of oil) that brings accolades to this Chaoyang and Xicheng chain that, aside from its signature dish, cooks up other "consistently good", reasonably priced Sichuan-style fare for a hip, young clientele; snaring one of the sunken booths is a challenge – the place is "popular" and reservations are taken only at Xinyuan Nanlu.

Haiku by Hatsune ● *Japanese*   23 | 24 | 21 | E

Chaoyang | Block 8 | 8 Chaoyang Gongyuan Xilu (bet. Liangmaqiao Lu & Nongzhanguan Nanlu) | (86-10) 6508-8585 | www.hatsunesushi.com

Located in the nightlife district near Chaoyang Park's west gate, this Japanese venture from Alan Wong (of Hatsune) is home to "amazing" cocktails, "flawless" sushi and "wonderful" cooked fare; the sparse space, set off in white and oak tones, draws local and foreign patrons, just about all of them ultrafashionable.

Hatsune   *Japanese*   25 | 22 | 21 | M

Chaoyang | Village at Sanlitun | 19 Sanlitun Lu, 3rd fl. (Gongti Beilu) | (86-10) 6415-3939

Chaoyang | Heqiao Bldg. C | Jia 8 Guanghua Dong Lu, 2nd fl. (bet. Jintai Lu & Zhenzhi Lu) | (86-10) 6581-3939

Marrying a "slick" setting with "unique" fare, this second-floor address in Chaoyang is acclaimed for its "fresh", "addictive" "American-style" sushi ("throw authenticity to the wind, and you'll love it"); it's a "lunchtime favorite" too, thanks to the "great" deals; N.B. the Sanlitun branch set in a glitzy shopping complex features an aquatic theme complete with a waterfall.

Liqun Roast Duck ⊞ *Chinese*   24 | 9 | 13 | M

Dongcheng | 11 Beixiangfeng Hutong (Qianmen Dongdajie) | (86-10) 6705-5578

As the pictures in the corridors attest, everyone from Anthony Bourdain to Al Gore has sampled the famously "fabulous" duck roasted at this taste of the "real China" located in "what's left of" a "historic hutong" in Dongcheng (it's also known for "silky", "translucent" pancakes and "unhelpful service"); the "grease on the walls", "makeshift tables" and general "dilapidation" may prove "too authentic" for some, but "for the adventuresome", it's "quite the experience"; P.S. credit cards not accepted.

Made in China *Chinese*　　　　　27 | 26 | 24 | E

Dongcheng | Grand Hyatt Beijing | 1 Dong Chang'an Jie (bet. Dongdan Beidajie & Wangfujing Dajie) | (86-10) 8518-1234, ext. 3608 | www.beijing.grand.hyatt.com

"Popular with tourists", but "far from a trap", this "elite" eatery in Dongcheng's Grand Hyatt serves the "best Peking duck in the whole wide world" – or so say surveyors who've voted all of the "outstanding" "fancified" Northern Chinese fare the No. 1 Food in Beijing; a dash of "fun" is added to the "stylish", "stunning setting" with multiple "glass-walled" kitchens to view, which you won't be able to enjoy unless you "reserve well ahead" (and while you're at it, put in your duck order); P.S. your local "friends will be shocked by the price tag."

Morel's ●Ⓜ *Belgian/French*　　　23 | 14 | 18 | M

Chaoyang | 5 Xinzhong Jie (Gongti Beilu) | (86-10) 6416-8802 | www.morelsgroup.com

Cross the street from Workers' Indoor Arena in Chaoyang and, voilà, "you're in a small Brussels bistro" where "authentic Belgian" and French tastes abound in dishes like "succulent mussels", "juicy steak" and "awesome waffles", all "well worth the money" (and they're "not even that expensive!"); the decor strikes some as "corny" and space is "cramped", but the "fabulous beer selection" obliterates protests; P.S. the Liangmaqiao sibling has closed.

Pure Lotus　　　　　　　　　24 | 23 | 22 | M
Vegetarian *Vegetarian*

Chaoyang | 12 Nongzhanguan Nanlu (bet. Chaoyang Gongyuan Lu & Dongsanhuan Beilu) | (86-10) 6592-3627
Chaoyang | Holiday Inn Lido | 6 Jiangtai Lu (Fangyuan Xi Lu) | (86-10) 6437-6688

"How can this not be meat?" ask "amazed" carnivores when they taste what these monk-run Chaoyang veggie venues "accomplish": "intriguing", "inventive" dishes served in "stimulating artistic preparations"; with stone statues, prayer wheels and incense, the "temple"-like Holiday Inn Lido locale is the more ornate, but both are completely "serene" and blessed with servers who "genuinely care."

Sichuan Provincial　　　　　24 | 11 | 12 | I
Government Restaurant ⊅ *Chinese*

Dongcheng | 5 Gongyuan Toutiao (Jianguomennei Dajie) | (86-10) 6512-2277

"Have your last meal in Beijing" at this "real slice" of Sichuan life in Dongcheng, because "you won't get anything this authentic until your next trip" (the "fresh chile oil makes all the difference" in the "zingingly tasty" dishes); you'll have to "wait for ages" to get into the "chaotic", pink-plastic-tablecloth-bedecked "government building", but it's "worth" it for "some of the best", "cheapest" fare to be found.

	FOOD	DECOR	SERVICE	COST

South Beauty *Chinese* — 23 | 20 | 19 | M

Chaoyang | Kerry Centre Mall | 1 Guanghua Lu (Dongsanhuan Zhonglu) | (86-10) 8529-9458

Chaoyang | China World Mall | 1 Jianguomenwai Dajie (Dongsanhuan Zhonglu) | (86-10) 6505-0809

Chaoyang | Henderson Ctr. | 18 Jianguomenwai Dajie (Beijingzhan Jie) | (86-10) 6518-7603

Chaoyang | Sunshine Plaza | 68 Anli Lu (Zhi Zhonglu) | (86-10) 6495-1201

Chaoyang | Fangheng Shopping Mall | Futong Dong Dajie, 6th Zone, Unit 4, 3rd fl. (bet. Guangxun Nandajie & Huajiadi Jie) | (86-10) 8478-5315 ⊅

Chaoyang | Pacific Century Pl. | Jia 2 Gongti Beilu (bet. Dongsanhuan Beilu & Sanlitun Nanlu) | (86-10) 6539-3502

Dongcheng | Dongfang Yinzuo/Kenzo Building | 48 Dongzhimenwai Dajie, 4th fl. (bet. Dongzhimennei Dajie & Xindong Lu) | (86-10) 8447-6171

Haidian | Info Tech Park | 2 Kexueyuan Nanlu, Tower A (bet. Beisihuan Xi Lu & Zhichun Lu) | (86-10) 8286-1698

Xicheng | Shuncheng Fandian | 26 Jinrong Jie, 1st fl. (bet. Fuchengmennei Dajie & Wudinghou Jie) | (86-10) 6622-8989

www.southbeautygroup.com

"With branches all over" China, this "popular", "dependable" chain's specialty is "spicy", "top-class Sichuan cuisine" with "bold, bright flavors"; "each one has different decor" – from "highly stylish" baroque to "innovative" "modern" minimalism – but all have plenty of private rooms that "work for large" business groups (and "professional service" to match).

Taj Pavilion, The *Indian* — 26 | 21 | 25 | M

Chaoyang | Holiday Inn Lido | 6 Jiangtai Lu, 3rd fl. (Fangyuan Xi Lu) | (86-10) 6436-7678

Chaoyang | China Overseas Plaza North Tower | 8 Guanghua Dongl (Dongsanhuan Zhonglu) | (86-10) 6505-5866

Shunyi | Europlaza | 99 Yunxiang Lu, 2nd fl. (bet. Houshayu & Xinyuan Xi Lu) | (86-10) 8046-3238

www.thetajpavilion.com

"Absolutely the best Indian food" in Beijing can be found at these "ideally located" Chaoyang destinations (with a Shunyi outpost) whose "gracious" owner not only ensures the "consistency" of the "high-quality" fare, but "adds warmth" to the already "fantastic" service; the Holiday Inn Lido branch feels "authentic" with candlelight illuminating the intricate wood carvings on the wall, while the Europlaza iteration is "nice and bright."

Hong Kong

TOP FOOD RANKING

	Restaurant	Cuisine
28	Lung King Heen	Chinese
	Sushi Hiro	Japanese
27	Gaddi's	French
	Petrus	French
	L'Atelier de Joël Robuchon	French
26	Fook Lam Moon	Chinese
	Morton's	Steak
	Nadaman	Japanese
	Da Domenico	Italian
	Yan Toh Heen	Chinese
	Man Wah	Chinese
	Spring Moon*	Chinese
25	Mandarin Grill & Bar	Eclectic
	Caprice	French
	One Harbour Road	Chinese
	Nobu	Japanese
	Steakhouse Winebar + Grill	Steak

Café Gray Deluxe *American/European*   - | - | - | VE

Admiralty | Upper House at Pacific Pl. | 88 Queensway, 49th fl. (Justice Dr.) | (852) 3968-1106 | www.cafegrayhk.com

The meticulous chef Gray Kunz is in residence at this dining room on the top floor of the Upper House Hotel in Admiralty overseeing his signature dishes – hybrids of European and American fare – that ring up a somewhat less-costly price tag than his fans are used to (about $500 per head for dinner, $250 for lunch); the contemporary setting done up in subdued browns and blues features panoramic views and a big open kitchen, plus a bar area.

Caprice *French*   25 | 27 | 26 | VE

Central | Four Seasons | 8 Finance St. (Connaught Rd.) | (852) 3196-8860 | www.fourseasons.com

"One of the most beautiful" restaurants in Hong Kong is the Four Seasons' French in Central, where you "enter through carved doors" onto a "glass walkway lit from below" and arrive in an "elegant" room with "glorious views" of Victoria Harbour; add "impeccable" service from an "attentive" staff", "exquisite" Gallic cuisine from chef Vincent Thierry (ex Le Cinq in Paris) and an "epic" wine list, and you have a "wonderful", albeit "expensive", place for "special occasions"; N.B. it also features an extensive cheese cellar.

Da Domenico 🗷 *Italian*   26 | 14 | 15 | VE

Causeway Bay | Sunning Plaza | 8 Hoi Ping Rd. (Hysan Ave.) | (852) 2882-8013

"Simple but top-notch" Italian cooking and a "cult"-like following heavy on "tycoons and celebrities" are the claim to fame of this Causeway Bay scenester; everything down to the salt is "freshly flown in"

---

* Indicates a tie with restaurant above

	FOOD	DECOR	SERVICE	COST

from Italy – a mark of "authenticity" that's reflected in its "astronomical" prices – and while the "small" quarters are decidedly "down-to-earth" and the service "limited", nothing seems to stifle its "snob appeal."

Felix *Continental*

| 21 | 27 | 23 | VE |

Tsim Sha Tsui | The Peninsula | Salisbury Rd., 28th fl. (Nathan Rd.) | (852) 2315-3188 | www.hongkong.peninsula.com

Philippe Starck makes his mark in Hong Kong via this "lavish" "hipster" (voted Hong Kong's Most Popular restaurant) atop Tsim Sha Tsui's Peninsula Hotel, where "jaw-dropping" 360-degree vistas of the harbor and city skyline meet "sexy" modern design with "stunning" results – and prices to match; maybe it's mostly about the "over-the-top atmosphere" and "beautiful-people" crowd here, but those who can focus on the Continental cuisine say it's "delicious"; P.S. "don't forget to check out" the "spectacular" men's WC, as well as the "must-visit" upstairs bar.

Fook Lam Moon *Chinese*

| 26 | 16 | 21 | VE |

Tsim Sha Tsui | 53-59 Kimberley Rd. (bet. Carnarvon & Observatory Rds.) | (852) 2366-0286

Wan Chai | Newman House | 35-45 Johnston Rd. (Luard Rd.) | (852) 2866-0663

www.fooklammoon-grp.com

"Some of the best Cantonese food you can find in Hong Kong" comes out of the kitchen of this "old-school" Wan Chai institution (with a Tsim Sha Tsui sibling) known for its "to-die-for dim sum" and luxury specialties ("shark's fin soup, abalone", etc.); "upscale" prices and a "tycoon and *tai tai*"–heavy clientele have earned it the nickname the "millionaire's canteen", where "you must go with a regular" or service "can be lacking", but still to most surveyors it "doesn't get much better than this."

Gaddi's *French*

| 27 | 26 | 29 | VE |

Tsim Sha Tsui | The Peninsula | Salisbury Rd. (Nathan Rd.) | (852) 2315-3171 | www.hongkong.peninsula.com

"Time stands still" (in a good way) at this "old-world", chandelier-bedecked "jewel box" in Tsim Sha Tsui's Peninsula Hotel, a "European palatial"–style "landmark" that's "as fancy and classically French as can be found in Hong Kong"; the "world-class" fare and decor are surpassed only by the near-"perfect" "formal" service (Hong Kong's No. 1 in this Survey), and while such "not-to-be-missed" experiences come at a "stiff price", the "rich-and-famous" types who dine here swear it's "worth every cent"; P.S. for "extraordinarily special occasions", book the chef's table in the kitchen.

L'Atelier de Joël Robuchon *French*

| 27 | 27 | 26 | VE |

Central | The Landmark | 11 Pedder St., 4th fl. (Queen's Rd.) | (852) 2166-9000 | www.robuchon.hk

"Spend your children's inheritance" for a "fabulous experience" at this Robuchon production in Central, where you "sit at the counter and watch the show" unfold in the open kitchen, which produces a tasting menu of "superbly executed", "modern" French cuisine in "small portions", paired with one of the "best wine lists in town"; "beautiful, yet subdued" decor graces the "impressive" space, and the service is "excellent."

	FOOD	DECOR	SERVICE	COST

Lung King Heen Chinese
28 | 24 | 24 | E

Central | Four Seasons | 8 Finance St. (Connaught Rd.) | (852) 3196-8880 | www.fourseasons.com

"Everything from the menu is well executed" at this Chinese housed in the Four Seasons Hotel in Central (voted Hong Kong's No. 1 for Food), where "innovative", "top-notch" Cantonese cuisine and an "excellent selection" of "scrumptious" dim sum are paired with an eclectic, China-centric wine list, while "amazing views of the harbor" serve as a backdrop to the "pretty", contemporary room accented with silver and glass; it's "expensive", but the consensus is that the experience is "worth it."

Mandarin Grill & Bar Eclectic
25 | 24 | 27 | VE

Central | Mandarin Oriental, Hong Kong | 5 Connaught Rd. (Ice House St.) | (852) 2825-4004 | www.mandarinoriental.com

A "sure winner every time", this "expense-account" Eclectic in Central's Mandarin Oriental is a "class act", where the "attentive" staff has "everything down pat" and the kitchen turns out "excellent" fare, including the "freshest sashimi and oysters"; the "addition of windows was a tremendous improvement" to the "classic", "elegant" dining room, although a few prefer the old "formal club" setting to the present "glass, chrome and marble" look.

Man Wah Chinese
26 | 24 | 26 | VE

Central | Mandarin Oriental, Hong Kong | 5 Connaught Rd. (Ice House St.) | (852) 2825-4003 | www.mandarinoriental.com

"Still worth a visit" after more than 40 years ("if you have the money"), this "old standby" in the Mandarin Oriental in Central delivers "superb" "traditional" Cantonese cuisine and "excellent" service in an "elegant" room with a "spectacular view of the harbor"; while a few fault the chef for "unimaginative" cooking, it's the "favorite" "upmarket Chinese" of many others.

Morton's of Chicago Steak
26 | 22 | 25 | VE

Tsim Sha Tsui | Sheraton Hong Kong | 20 Nathan Rd. (Salisbury Rd.) | (852) 2732-2343 | www.mortons.com

For a "taste of America" in Tsim Sha Tsui, carnivores commend this outpost of the chophouse chain in the Sheraton that cronies contend is a "step above most locations in the U.S.", thanks to "excellent" steaks and seafood, a "well-balanced wine list" and "prompt", "professional" service; the "clubby, sophisticated" setting and a "first-class view of the skyline" are "icing on the cake", and though the tabs are "hefty", many feel it's "worth it."

Nadaman Japanese
26 | 20 | 25 | VE

Admiralty | Island Shangri-La at Pacific Pl. | 88 Queensway, 7th fl. (Supreme Court Rd.) | (852) 2820-8570
Tsim Sha Tsui | Kowloon Shangri-La | 64 Mody Rd. (bet. Chatham Rd. & Mody Ln.) | (852) 2733-8751
www.shangri-la.com

A crowd of mostly "old-money" and "business clientele" gravitates to this "fabulous", "pricey" outpost of a venerable Tokyo-based Japanese chain in Admiralty's Island Shangri-La Hotel (with a Tsim Sha Tsui branch at the Kowloon Shangri-La) for "amazing", "masterful" kaiseki courses, including "excellent" Wagyu beef, and "impeccable" service; the space, a modern take on "traditional" decor from Japan, includes sushi and teppanyaki counters and a private tatami room.

Nobu ● *Japanese* 25 | 24 | 23 | VE

Tsim Sha Tsui | InterContinental Hong Kong | 18 Salisbury Rd. (Ave. of Stars) | (852) 2313-2323 | www.hongkong-ic.intercontinental.com

A "solid" addition to Nobu Matsuhisa's global "empire", this Tsim Sha Tsui outpost offers "outstanding" "nontraditional" Japanese, including a chef's menu that "always has something special" and "fresh", "super" sushi; a "stellar" harbor view is the backdrop to the Rockwell Group–designed space, which features an undulating ceiling and bamboo-embedded terrazzo walls, while the service is "quick and efficient."

One Harbour Road *Chinese* 25 | 24 | 26 | VE

Wan Chai | Grand Hyatt Hong Kong | 1 Harbour Rd. (Convention Ave.) | (852) 2584-7722 | www.hongkong.grand.hyatt.com

"Impeccable" service, "high-quality" Cantonese fare (including "excellent" dim sum) and a "wonderful" space with a "spectacular view of the harbor" win raves for this Chinese in the Grand Hyatt in Wan Chai; it's "expensive", but that's "the price you pay" for "one of the best fine-dining places on Hong Kong Island."

Petrus *French* 27 | 26 | 27 | VE

Admiralty | Island Shangri-La at Pacific Pl. | 88 Queensway, 56th fl. (Supreme Court Rd.) | (852) 2820-8590 | www.shangri-la.com

"Expensive, but worth it" according to *amis*, this haute French in the Island Shangri-La in Admiralty showcases "top-notch" toque Frederic Chabbert's "inventive" cuisine with an "amazing" wines; the "helpful staff" provides "impeccable" service while "jaw-dropping views" of Victoria Harbour complement the room that some find "romantic", others a bit "gaudy"; while the tabs might approach the "Chinese GDP", most agree it's the "right place" to "impress a date or client."

Spoon by Alain Ducasse ● *French* 23 | 25 | 25 | VE

Tsim Sha Tsui | InterContinental Hong Kong | 18 Salisbury Rd. (Ave. of Stars) | (852) 2313-2323 | www.hongkong-ic.intercontinental.com

"Superb" food, "impeccable" service and a "breathtaking view of the harbor" make this "chic" French export in Tsim Sha Tsui's Intercontinental Hotel "a must for the total experience"; although some call the "eclectic" menu a bit "odd" (with "small portions"), and wish that star chef "Alain would visit more often", most appreciate the "attention to detail and quality", recommending it for "impressing clients" on your "expense account" or for a "very special date"; P.S. "take a seat before 8 PM to enjoy the light show on the harbor."

Spring Moon *Chinese* 26 | 25 | 27 | VE

Tsim Sha Tsui | The Peninsula | Salisbury Rd. (Nathan Rd.) | (852) 2315-3160 | www.hongkong.peninsula.com

"Sublime" is the word on this "traditional" Cantonese in Tsim Sha Tsui that diners say "sets the standard for Chinese cuisine" across the country, with favorites including "fabulous dim sum" and "heavenly" Peking duck; its "exceptional Peninsula service", "classic art deco design" and "fine tea menu" further elevate the experience, making it well worth the "expensive" tab; N.B. jacket suggested.

	FOOD	DECOR	SERVICE	COST

Steakhouse Winebar + Grill *Steak*   25 | 24 | 26 | VE

Tsim Sha Tsui | InterContinental Hong Kong | 18 Salisbury Rd. (Ave. of Stars) | (852) 2721-1211 | www.hongkong-ic.intercontinental.com

Carnivores tout this "expense-account" hotel chophouse in Tsim Sha Tsui the "coolest yet hottest steakhouse in Hong Kong", which offers patrons "multiple choices" of steak knives, mustards and salts to complement the "unbelievable" cuts of meats from the Americas, Australia and Japan (including "Kobe beef to die for") and "fabulous salad bar"; oenophiles "love" the wine bar serving some 270 labels, and "proper" service enhances the "warm" ambiance in the otherwise "masculine" setting.

Sushi Hiro *Japanese*   28 | 18 | 21 | VE

Causeway Bay | Henry House | 42 Yun Ping Rd., 10th fl. (Pak Sha Rd.) | (852) 2882-8752
Causeway Bay | Henry House | 42 Yun Ping Rd., 11th fl. (Pak Sha Rd.) | (852) 2808-4110
Tsim Sha Tsui | Toy House | 100 Canton Rd. (bet. Gateway Blvd. & Haiphong Rd.) | (852) 2377-9877
www.sushihiro.com.hk

It's "definitely one of the best sushi restaurants in town" declare diners about this find on two floors of a Causeway Bay office building and in Tsim Sha Tsui serving "ultrafresh fish" that keeps it "popular among a Japanese clientele"; the minimally decorated setting is relaxed but formal enough for a business meal, and most agree the "expensive" tab is "reasonable" considering the "excellent" quality – plus "lunch is a great deal"; P.S. be sure to "book ahead."

Yan Toh Heen *Chinese*   26 | 26 | 28 | VE

Tsim Sha Tsui | InterContinental Hong Kong | 18 Salisbury Rd. (Ave. of Stars) | (852) 2313-2323 | www.hongkong-ic.intercontinental.com

"Magnificent in every way", this Chinese in Tsim Sha Tsui's Intercontinental Hotel is "true decadence", offering "top-notch" service, "splendid" Cantonese cuisine, including some of the "best dim sum in the world", and an "elegant, beautiful" space featuring "jade place settings" and "amazing" views of the harbor; not surprisingly, "you'll pay through the nose", but "oh, is it worth it."

Yung Kee *Chinese*   23 | 14 | 17 | M

Central | 32-40 Wellington St. (D'Aguilar St.) | (852) 2522-1624 | www.yungkee.com.hk

A "classic Hong Kong establishment", this "famous" Central landmark (circa 1942) is a "must-try for visitors", serving "generous" portions of "wonderful" "traditional" Cantonese cuisine, including "out-of-this-world" roast goose and "perfectly done" preserved eggs, that "packs in the crowds"; the scene gets "hectic" in the "large", "bright" space that can accommodate "families and large groups", but you "don't come here for the ambiance or service."

Seoul

TOP FOOD RANKING

	Restaurant	Cuisine
26	Ristorante Eo	Italian
25	Continental	French
	Malta Tuna	Japanese
	Sushi Hyo	Japanese
	Sushi Cho	Japanese
	Kiku	Japanese
	Palsun	Chinese
24	Yamamoto	Japanese
	Ariake	Japanese
	Pierre Gagnaire	French
	A Table	French
23	Myongwolgwan	Korean
	A Coté	French
	Sushi Moto	Japanese
	Bamboo House	Korean
	Mi Piace	Italian

A Coté *French*   23 16 24 VE

Gangnam-gu | 422-6, Dogok 2-dong | (82-2) 577-1044
Francophiles fawn over the "seamless French cuisine" at this reservation-only Gangnam-gu destination that's expensive but delivers "excellent", "creative" country-style fare "for the price"; though it's a bit "hard to find" and has unremarkable decor, the "attentive, diligent" service (sometimes by the chef himself) adds to its "charm."

Ariake *Japanese*   24 23 23 VE

Jung-gu | The Shilla Seoul, fl. 2 | 202, Jangchung-dong 2-ga | (82-2) 2230-3356 | www.shilla.net
One of "Korea's leading Japanese restaurants", this "delightful" destination in Jung-gu's Shilla Seoul Hotel serves "to-die-for" sushi ("better than what you get in Japan") that "everyone should try at least once"; "excellent service" and a "chic, minimalist" interior add to the "comfortable vibe", making it a "popular hangout for celebrities" and others who don't mind "paying a bunch" for a memorable meal.

A Table 🅍 *French*   24 16 20 E

Jongno-gu | 104-8, Palpan-dong | (82-2) 736-1048
Each course exhibits "delicacy and wit" at this bistro in Jongno-gu offering "well-prepared" fare that's "great for a newcomer to French cuisine"; "you won't get in without a reservation", "parking can be difficult" and the "extremely cozy" space means "you can hear the conversation at the next table", but even critics are appeased by the "thoughtful explanations of the dishes by the handsome chef" at your table.

Bamboo House 🅍 *Korean*   23 20 21 VE

Gangnam-gu | Bamboo House Bldg. | 658-10, Yeoksam-dong | (82-2) 566-0870 | www.bamboohouse.or.kr
"The taste merits the high price" for "melt-in-your-mouth" Korean dishes prepared at this "conservative" favorite of visiting VIPs in the

"center of Seoul" in Gangnam-gu; the privacy afforded by the multi-room interior suits "small exclusive meetings", while the distinctive roof garden will make you "wish it were your own."

NEW Clock16 European

| - | - | - | VE |

Gwangjin-gu | Sheraton Grande Walkerhill Hotel, fl. 16 | 21, Gwangjang-dong | (82-2) 450-4516 | www.sheratonwalkerhill.co.kr

This elegant European on the 16th floor of the Sheraton Grande Walkerhill boasts an eclectic array of robust dishes by veteran NYC chef Justin Toth, such as Spanish jamón, Bourgogne-style escargot and chicken prepared using the sous-vide method; with a bar on the mezzanine level and live piano music, it's perfect for a formal dinner or cocktails with a spectacular view of the Han River and Mt. Acha.

Continental French

| 25 | 22 | 26 | VE |

Jung-gu | The Shilla Seoul, fl. 23 | 202, Jangchung-dong 2-ga | (82-2) 2230-3369 | www.shilla.net

Serving some of the "best French food in Seoul", this "extraordinary" institution on the 23rd floor of the Shilla Seoul in Jung-gu, rated No. 1 for Service and French cuisine in the city, earns a hearty "two thumbs-up" from "people who know the real" cuisine; the "palacelike" decor and "great view of Namsam" make for a "romantic" setting, and the "friendly" staff offers service commensurate with the high-end tabs.

Ganga Indian

| 20 | 19 | 17 | M |

Gangnam-gu | Gujeong Bldg., fl. 2 | 610-5, Sinsa-dong | (82-2) 3444-3610
Gangnam-gu | GS Tower, fl. B1 | 679, Yeoksam-dong | (82-2) 2005-0610
Gangnam-gu | Geumgang Tower, fl. B1 | 889-13, Daechi-dong | (82-2) 3468-4670
Jung-gu | Seoul Finance Center, fl. B2 | 84, Taepyeongno 1-ga | (82-2) 3783-0610
Seocho-gu | Samsung Electronics Bldg., fl. B1 | 1320-10, Seocho-dong | (82-2) 2055-3610
Yeongdeungpo-gu | Dure Bldg., fl. 1 | 24, Yeouido-dong | (82-2) 782-3610
www.ganga.co.kr

This "pioneering", "high-quality" Indian chain, voted the Most Popular restaurant in Seoul, is credited with "influencing many Koreans" to embrace subcontinental cuisine thanks to specialties such as "flavorful, creamy", "addictive" curries and "to-die-for" tandoori chicken accompanied by "different kinds of naan"; the ambiance has an "upscale" feel, but some would like to see the prices downscaled, the service bolstered and the menu freshened with "new developments."

Gassra ● Japanese

| 20 | 15 | 15 | I |

Gangnam-gu | 817-11, Yeoksam-dong | (82-2) 558-3838
Jung-gu | Jaewon Bldg., fl. 3 | 2-1, Myeong-dong 2-ga | (82-2) 774-3690
Jung-gu | Seoseoul Bldg., fl. B1 | 59-21, Myeong-dong 1-ga | (82-2) 775-3690
Jung-gu | Myeongdeok Bldg., fl. 1 | 87-4, Myeong-dong 2-ga | (82-2) 779-3690
Yeongdeungpo-gu | Star Bldg., fl. B1 | 44-6, Yeouido-dong | (82-2) 782-6576
www.gassra.com

"Affordable", "delicious" and sometimes "impressive" Japanese bar bites can be found at this izakaya mini-chain that's pleasant for "spending time with a friend on a winter night drinking sake" and sampling different plates; some say it's developed an unfortunate "franchise feel" and warn "don't expect great service", but most consider it a "good deal" overall.

Kiku *Japanese*
25 | 11 | 16 | VE

Yongsan-gu | 301-162, Ichon 1-dong | (82-2) 794-8584

Despite its "shabby, unremarkable exterior", customers "run like crazy" to this "small", pricey neighborhood sushi bar in Yongsan-gu for "authentic", "super-fresh" fish of the "highest quality"; the lunch menu is an "excellent bargain", and though some grumble that "regulars get special treatment from the chef", that might be the best reason to become a regular.

Little Saigon *Vietnamese*
21 | 14 | 13 | I

Gangnam-gu | Galleria Dept. Store, fl. B1 | 494, Apgujeong-dong | (82-2) 3449-4143

Gangnam-gu | 535-11, Sinsa-dong | (82-2) 518-9051 ◗

Gangnam-gu | Miseung Bldg., fl. 1 | 640-1, Sinsa-dong | (82-2) 547-9050 ◗

Seocho-gu | 1309, Seocho-dong | (82-2) 532-5420 ◗

"One bowl of pho, and your hangover is gone" guarantee guests who savor the "spicy seasoning" and "richly flavored broths" at these cheap, "jam-packed" Vietnamese "noodle havens"; despite "bare walls", frequent "lines" and iffy service, they're "casual, comfy places to bring friends" – especially for late-night eats, since most are open till 3:30 AM (except for the Galleria branch).

Malta Tuna *Japanese*
25 | 13 | 20 | VE

Gangnam-gu | Dolce Tower, fl. 2 | 891-48, Daechi-dong | (82-2) 508-7861

"Premium tuna" is the star at this "expensive but definitive" Gangnam-gu sashimi bar, rated Seoul's No. 1 for Japanese cuisine, that "can't be beat" for "unique cuts" of the specialty fish, supported by "tasty", "charming" side dishes; the decor is "nothing special", but the chef's "sincere", "very personal" approach to service seals the deal.

Mi Piace *Italian*
23 | 18 | 19 | E

Gangnam-gu | Samyeong Bldg., fl. 1 | 97-22, Cheongdam-dong | (82-2) 516-6317

"All the pastas are excellent", but the "unique" "sea urchin spaghetti is highly recommended" at this destination for "impressive" yet moderately priced Italian fare in Gangnam-gu; enthusiasts add that the "delightful" fresh flower arrangements will make you "feel as warm inside" as the food, but just be aware that "reservations are a must" as it's very popular.

Myongwolgwan *Korean*
23 | 18 | 22 | VE

Gwangjin-gu | Annex to Sheraton Grande Walkerhill Hotel | 21, Gwangjang-dong | (82-2) 450-4595 | www.sheratonwalkerhill.co.kr

Customers commend the high "quality of the beef" at this pricey longtimer in Gwangjin-gu, rated No. 1 for Korean cuisine in Seoul, serving charcoal-fired barbecue that's "as good as it gets", along with "incomparable" short rib soup (known to "sell out early") and "Supex" kimchi (its famous house brand); set amid traditional *hanok*-style surroundings in the annex to the Sheraton Grande Walkerhill, it's a "relaxing" place with a "pleasant" view of the Hangang River and service by a "superior staff."

	FOOD	DECOR	SERVICE	COST

Palsun *Chinese*

| 25 | 20 | 23 | VE |

Jung-gu | The Shilla Seoul, fl. 2 | 202, Jangchung-dong 2-ga |
(82-2) 2230-3366 | www.shilla.net

This "high-class" institution (since 1979) in Jung-gu's Shilla Seoul ho-tel, voted Top Chinese restaurant in our Seoul Survey, is widely viewed as "the most trustworthy Chinese restaurant in Korea" – and is "even famous in China" – for "haute" cuisine that's a favorite of diplomats, executives and other "opinion makers"; the art-adorned interior is contemporary, and "like the Shilla, it has the best service", so guests agree it "lives up to its name."

Pierre Gagnaire à Séoul ⊠ *French*

| 24 | 24 | 24 | VE |

Jung-gu | Lotte Hotel Seoul, New Bldg., fl. 35 | 1, Sogong-dong |
(82-2) 317-7181 | www.pierregagnaire.co.kr

Widely regarded as one of "the best French restaurants" in Seoul, as well as one of the most expensive, this Jung-gu offshoot of chef Pierre Gagnaire's highly rated, eponymous Parisian provides "superb", "very creative" food that represents "the acme of French modern cuisine"; the dining room, frequented by "foodies", celebrities and captains of industry, is "absolutely gorgeous", as are the "views of the city at night", making for a "memorable" experience that's "worth the money – at least once."

Ristorante Eo Ⓜ *Italian*

| 26 | 21 | 25 | VE |

Gangnam-gu | 99-11, Cheongdam-dong, fl. 2 | (82-2) 3445-1926

The "rare, real Italian restaurant in Korea", this "most cherished" Cheongdam-dong choice – voted No. 1 for Food in our Seoul Survey – exhibits the chef's "professional touch" in the preparation and presentation of "classic" dishes, "accentuated by the use of seasonal ingredients"; newly relocated to the second floor, it's still quite small but boasts "impressive hospitality", so while tabs are "expensive" it's "worth it", and lunch is a relative bargain – "you won't believe you're getting haute cuisine for the price"; N.B. its spin-off, Gourmet Eo, is lo-cated in the same building.

Sushi Cho *Japanese*

| 25 | 23 | 24 | VE |

Jung-gu | The Westin Chosun Seoul, fl. 20 | 87, Sogong-dong |
(82-2) 317-0373 | www.echosunhotel.com

This ritzy house of "real sushi" at the Westin Chosun Seoul in Jung-gu is dubbed a "national treasure" by loyalists who love its "butter"-like cuts of fish and the "excellent texture" of the rice, complemented by an "impressive" sake selection; yes it's very "expensive", but every-thing from the exceptional service to the sushi bar itself, carved from a 350-year-old hinoki tree, makes for a special experience.

Sushi Hyo *Japanese*

| 25 | 19 | 21 | VE |

Gangnam-gu | Yuhyeon Bldg., fl. 1 | 21-16, Cheongdam-dong |
(82-2) 545-0023
Guro-gu | Mario Tower, fl. 1 | 222-12, Guro 3-dong | (82-2) 890-8400 ⊠
Jongno-gu | Somerset Palace Seoul, fl. 2 | 85, Susong-dong |
(82-2) 730-5396
Seocho-gu | Seocho Tra Palace, fl. 2 | 1327-26, Seocho-dong |
(82-2) 521-3594

Featured in the popular Japanese manga *Shota No Sushi*, master chef Hyo-Ju An opens up a "new world" of "indescribable" creations at these refined, pricey places that some consider "the pinnacle" of sushi in Seoul; admirers assure that once you "take a seat at the bar of chef An" (who usually resides at the Cheongdam-dong branch) "you won't be able to enjoy sushi anywhere else" – and you may even be inspired to become "more successful so you can enjoy" it every day.

Sushi Moto *Japanese*   23 | 19 | 19 | VE

Gangnam-gu | 79-11, Cheongdam-dong | (82-2) 514-1812 | www.sushimoto.co.kr

"You can feel the chef's passion" in every "creative" dish at this "high-priced" but "impressive" sushi house in Gangnam-gu; while some of the cuisine "may be challenging to those new to Japanese food", everyone can appreciate the "cozy atmosphere" enhanced by "pretty" "tatami rooms, Japanese tableware and a garden."

Woolaeoak *Korean*   22 | 11 | 12 | M

Gangnam-gu | 983-13, Daechi-dong | (82-2) 561-6121
Jung-gu | 118-1, Jugyo-dong | (82-2) 2265-0151
www.xn--9d0bz8qk7l3pa98cozb.kr

In business since 1946, this inexpensive Korean with locations in Gangnam-gu and Jung-gu delights diners with its "delicacy from the North" – "legendary", "savory" cold buckweat noodles – as well as "tender", "artful" bulgogi; just "don't expect fine service" and be ready for a "loud, crowded" space that "feels more worn-out than comfy", but "long lines" attest to the quality of the food.

Yamamoto Sushi *Japanese*   24 | 18 | 19 | VE

Gangnam-gu | Tower Palace, Sports Ctr. Vantt, fl. 1 | 469-29, Dogok-dong | (82-2) 2057-0053
Gangnam-gu | Owon Bldg., fl. 1 | 93-12, Cheongdam-dong | (82-2) 548-2031

Fans exclaim "hurray" for the "outstanding", "super-fresh" fish at these "understandably high-priced" sushi houses in Gangnam-gu where "all of the menu items show the personal touch" of star chef-owner Yamamoto Sadao; the small spaces are "cramped" and the look is a bit "dated", but the food alone attracts a devoted following, so plan ahead as it's "hard to get a reservation."

Yongsusan *Korean*   17 | 18 | 18 | E

Jongno-gu | 118-3, Samcheong-dong | (82-2) 739-5599
Jongno-gu | 148, Wonseo-dong | (82-2) 743-5999
Jung-gu | Seoul Finance Center, fl. B1 | 84, Taepyeongno 1-ga | (82-2) 771-5533
Seocho-gu | Acrovista Arcade, fl. B1 | 1685-3, Seocho-dong | (82-2) 591-9674
Seocho-gu | 83-16, Banpo-dong | (82-2) 596-0335
Songpa-gu | 58-17, Songpa-dong | (82-2) 425-4674
www.yongsusan.co.kr

Opened in 1984, this chain of "upscale *hangeongsik*" restaurants specializes in classic, "well-seasoned" Gaesung cuisine (based on recipes saved by founder Sang-Ok Choi) that's "perfect for treating the elders"; the decor varies from branch to branch, and while it's not cheap and groups tend to make it "quite loud on weekends", "friendly" service smoothes out the meal.

Shanghai

TOP FOOD RANKING

	Restaurant	Cuisine
28	Hanagatami	Japanese
26	Guyi Hunan	Chinese
	Vedas	Indian
	Jean Georges	French
	Din Tai Fung	Chinese
25	Kitchen Salvatore Cuomo	Italian
	Palladio	Italian
	T8	Eclectic
	Crystal Jade	Chinese
	Danieli's	Italian
	South Beauty 881	Chinese
	Yi Café	Eclectic
	Bukhara Grill	Indian
	Vegetarian Lifestyle*	Chinese/Vegetarian
24	Di Shui Dong	Chinese
	Jade on 36	French
	Nan Xiang	Chinese
	South Beauty	Chinese
23	1221	Chinese

Bukhara Grill Indian   25 | 20 | 23 | M
Gubei/Hongqiao | 3729 Hongmei Lu (Yan'an Xi Lu) |
(86-21) 6446-8800 | www.bukhara.com.cn
Granted, it's "a bit far" from the center of town in the expat enclave of
Gubei, but this "consistently excellent", "family"-friendly Indian is
"worth the trip" for its "delicious, authentic" dishes and "professional,
friendly" staff; a pleasant bar/lounge on the ground floor broadcasts
sporting events on a giant flat-screen.

Crystal Jade Chinese   25 | 19 | 19 | M
Huaihai/Xintiandi | South Block Xintiandi | Ln. 123 Xingye Lu,
House 6-7, 2nd fl. (Madang Lu) | (86-21) 6385-8752 ●
Jing An | Westgate Plaza | 1038 Nanjing Xi Lu, 7th fl. (Jiangning Lu) |
(86-21) 5228-1133
www.crystaljade.com
"Popular" is the word for this "always packed" Singapore chain import
where the Cantonese-Shanghainese fare is "excellent" and "affordable";
"don't be put off by the shopping-mall settings" – it's beside the point
once they roll out their "delicious" dim sum and "sublime" dumplings.

Danieli's Italian   25 | 24 | 25 | E
Pudong | St. Regis | 889 Dongfang Lu, 39th fl. (Weifang Lu) |
(86-21) 5050-4569, ext. 6370 | www.stregis.com
Although "a little out of the way", this "elegant" Italian in the St. Regis
Hotel is worth seeking out for an "impressive business dinner" owing
to its "sublime" cooking and "fabulous view" of Pudong from its 39th-
floor perch; sure, "you'll definitely pay for it", but economizers tout the

---

* Indicates a tie with restaurant above

"reasonable" set-menu lunch and Sunday brunch, a "well-kept secret" featuring free-flowing champagne.

Din Tai Fung *Chinese*   26 | 17 | 21 | M

Gubei/Hongqiao | Peace Sq. | 18 Shuicheng Lu (Hongqiao Lu) | (86-21) 6208-4188
Huaihai/Xintiandi | South Block Xintiandi | Ln. 123 Xingye Lu, House 6 (Huangpi Lu) | (86-21) 6385-8378 ●
Huangpu | 168 Fangbang Zhong Lu (Zhoujin Lu) | (86-21) 6334-1008 ⑤ M
Jing An | Shanghai Ctr. | 1376 Nanjing Xi Lu (Xikang Lu) | (86-21) 6289-9182
Pudong | World Financial Ctr. | 100 Century Ave. (Dongtai Lu) | (86-21) 6877-6886 ⑤ M
www.dintaifung.com.tw

"Some of the best dumplings in the Far East" turn up at this "favorite" Taiwanese chain serving "street food in restaurant settings", notably that "addictive" *xiaolongbao* that will "keep your mouth watering"; add in "quality service" and "modern" if "simple" decor, and it's no surprise that many say dining here is "mandatory for Shanghai newcomers."

Di Shui Dong ● *Chinese*   24 | 11 | 13 | I

Luwan | 56 Maoming Nan Lu (Changle Lu) | (86-21) 6253-2689
Xuhui | 5 Dongping Lu (Hengshan Lu) | (86-21) 6415-9448

"Cheap and tasty", this "popular" Xuhui and Luwan duo serves "excellent" Hunan cuisine to a crowd of "locals and expats"; for some, the "alarmingly casual" settings may be too "downscale" and the acoustics too "boisterous", but a "big menu" brimming with "delicious" options and a "smiling if harried" staff help distract.

Guyi Hunan *Chinese*   26 | 12 | 15 | M

Jing An | 87 Fumin Lu (Julu Lu) | (86-21) 6249-5628

"If you like it spicy", check out this "fiery hot" Hunan outlet in in Jing An that's "popular with locals" who "keep a few bottles of beer handy" to "cool their throats"; it's a "bustling, noisy" scene with "prices that are a throwback to the '50s", so naturally "ridiculous lines" and "long waits" come with the territory.

Hanagatami *Japanese*   28 | 21 | 26 | VE

Jing An | Portman Ritz-Carlton | 1376 Nanjing Xi Lu (Xikang Lu) | (86-21) 6279-8888, ext. 5898 | www.ritzcarlton.com

What just might be the city's "best sushi bar" lies in this Japanese "marvel" in Jing An's Portman Ritz-Carlton that also offers kaiseki, teppanyaki and a variety of sakes in a "comfortable", sophisticated space done up with plenty of light wood and screen dividers; maybe you'll wind up paying "higher-than-Japan" prices, but this "excellent" place does take Top Food (and Top Service) honors in the Shanghai Survey.

Jade on 36 *French*   24 | 26 | 24 | VE

Pudong | Pudong Shangri-La | 33 Fucheng Lu, 36th fl. (Huayuanshiqiao Lu) | (86-21) 6882-8888 | www.jadeon36.com

The "food is as spectacular" as the "stunning", picture-postcard views of the Bund from this glamorous 36th-floor aerie in the Pudong Shangri-La Hotel, where the French dishes are served in pricey, prix fixe-only menus; "impeccable service" and "inspirational" decor via Adam Tihany enhance the "crème de la crème" mood, leading many to swoon "does it get any better than this?"

	FOOD	DECOR	SERVICE	COST

Jean Georges *French* `26` `27` `26` `VE`

Huangpu | Three on the Bund | 3 Zhongshan Dong Yi Lu, 4th fl. (Guangdong Lu) | (86-21) 6321-7733 | www.jean-georges.com

"Impress the boss or the wife (or both)" at Jean-Georges Vongerichten's "wow"-inducing French "splurge", a "world-class experience" set in Huangpu's "sophisticated" Three on the Bund complex; look for "exceptional" New French cooking, "attentive service", a "must-see" Michael Graves setting that includes a "million-dollar view" of the river and, of course, "money-is-no-object" pricing; N.B. Nougatine, the chef's more casual, less-expensive eatery, is a popular draw in the bar area.

Kitchen Salvatore Cuomo *Italian* `25` `23` `21` `E`

Pudong | 2967 Lujiazui Xi Lu (Fenghe Lu) | (86-21) 5054-1265 | www.ystable.co.jp

The eponymous Naples-born chef brings his Japanese franchise to Shanghai via this "authentic Italian" set along the river in Pudong with an "absolutely spectacular view of the Bund"; the "modern" menu (including some of the "best pizza" in the city) lives up to the "exceptional" setting, as does the "attentive staff."

M on the Bund *Continental/Eclectic* `21` `25` `23` `VE`

Huangpu | 5 Zhongshan Dong Yi Lu, 7th fl. (Guangdong Lu) | (86-21) 6350-9988 | www.m-onthebund.com

Swells seeking the "chic side of Shanghai" tout this circa-1999 Bund "trailblazer" that's still a "place to be seen" thanks to a "delicious" Continental-Eclectic menu, "knock-your-socks-off" river views from its outdoor terrace and the Glamour Bar downstairs that some call an even "better scene"; sure, a few critics carp "you're paying for the address" not the "unspectacular" food, but then again, this "institution" was voted Shanghai's Most Popular restaurant.

Mr & Mrs Bund *French* `-` `-` `-` `VE`

Huangpu | Bund 18 | 18 Zhongshan Dong Yi Lu, 6th fl. (Nanjing Dong Lu) | (86-21) 6323-9898 | www.mmbund.com

Avant-garde chef Paul Pairet turns out molecular creations (as he famously did at his former Jade on 36 post) at this Huangpu fine-dining oasis in a former bank building with high ceilings and dramatic columns, where sophisticated diners select from the New French menu's impressive assortment; the wine list is similarly expansive, offering 32 kinds by the glass and encouraging pairing with each course.

Nan Xiang *Chinese* `24` `13` `14` `I`

Old Town | Yu Gdn. | 85 Yuyuan Lu (adjacent to the Bridge of Nine Turnings) | (86-21) 6355-4206 | www.nanxiangrestaurant.com

"Be prepared to push and shove" for a taste of the "heavenly" soup dumplings (*xiaolongbao*) at this "tourist"-heavy Shanghainese triplex opposite Yu Garden; while the crowds can be "unbearable" at the ground-floor take-out counter, the more comfortable upper floors offer sit-down dining with "better service" but "higher prices."

Palladio *Italian* `25` `23` `25` `VE`

Jing An | Portman Ritz-Carlton | 1376 Nanjing Xi Lu (Xikang Lu) | (86-21) 6279-7188 | www.ritzcarlton.com

"Exactly what you would expect from a restaurant in the Ritz-Carlton", this Jing An "special-occasion" Italian offers "flawless food" (from a wood-burning oven–equipped kitchen), "great service" and, "of course, high prices"; swanky decor incorporating Palladian arches and columns and an "exceptional wine list" make it a natural for everything from power lunches to romantic suppers.

Restaurant Martín *Spanish*   — | — | — | VE

Xuhui | Xujiahui Park | 811 Hengshan Lu (Yuqing Road) | (86-21) 6431-9811 | www.restaurantmartin.com.cn

Bring a splurge-ready credit card to acclaimed Spanish chef Martín Berasategui's first overseas outpost – the elevated prices at this eatery in a historic villa in leafy Xujiahui Park match his status as a culinary heavyweight; the high ceilings, hardwood floors and silk drapes of the majestic rooms are as decadent as the San Sebastian-style fine-dining tasting menus, while the garden patio is perfect for summer evening wine and tapas.

Simply Thai *Thai*   21 | 19 | 18 | M

Gubei/Hongqiao | No. 28, Ln. 3338 Hongmei Lu (Hongxu Lu) | (86-21) 6465-8955

Huaihai/Xintiandi | North Block Xintiandi | 159 Madang Lu (Xingye Lu) | (86-21) 6326-2088 ◑

Xuhui | 5C Dongping Lu (Hengshan Lu) | (86-21) 6445-9551 www.simplylife-sh.com

"Nicely decorated" with "enchanting outdoor areas", this Thai chain dishes out "quite authentic" grub for on-the-go types seeking a "quick fix"; though foes feel they've "run out of steam", citing "overpricing" and "rushed" service, diehards claim they successfully "bring back memories of Thailand."

South Beauty *Chinese*   24 | 23 | 18 | M

Gubei/Hongqiao | Shanghai City Ctr. | 100 Zunyi Lu (Tianshan Lu) | (86-21) 6237-2885

Jing An | CITIC Plaza | 1168 Nanjing Xi Lu, 3rd fl. (Shaanxi Bei Lu) | (86-21) 5292-5331 ⓈⓂ

Luwan | Times Sq. | 99 Huaihai Zhong Lu, 5th fl. (Pu'an Lu) | (86-21) 6391-0100

Pudong | Super Brand Mall | 168 Lujiazui Xi Lu (Fucheng Lu) | (86-21) 5047-1817

Xuhui | 28-1 Taojiang Lu (Hengshan Lu) | (86-21) 6445-2581 www.southbeautygroup.com

"Not for the timid", this Beijing-based chain specializes in "fiery hot" "modern Sichuan" cooking ("leave your tongue at home") hailing from Southwest China; the staff "really tries", and thanks to the "rich flavors", "hip settings" and "classy" vibes, they're a natural for "showing off to foreign guests."

South Beauty 881 *Chinese*   25 | 27 | 17 | E

Jing An | 881 Yan'an Zhong Lu (Shaanxi Nan Lu) | (86-21) 6247-1581 | www.southbeautygroup.com

This "splashy" Jing An branch of the fast-growing chain offers "terrific" Sichuan dishes in a "beautiful" setting incorporating two buildings: an "elegantly renovated" period mansion and an ultramodern glass-lined garden house; the menu's heavy on seafood – and very spicy and rather pricey – but it's the glamorous old Shanghai vibe that draws in the movers, the shakers and the deep-pocketed "out-of-towners."

	FOOD	DECOR	SERVICE	COST

T8 ◐ *Eclectic* — 25 | 27 | 23 | VE

Huaihai/Xintiandi | North Block Xintiandi | Ln. 181 Taicang Lu, House 8 (Huangpi Nan Lu) | (86-21) 6355-8999 | www.t8shanghai.com

"High style" is alive and well at this "magical" Xintiandi "class act", one of the "most decorated" places in town where the "elegant" setting complete with a "fun" open-fronted glass kitchen is matched by a "fancy" fusion menu of Eclectic dishes, an "interesting wine list" and service that runs as "smoothly as a Swiss clock"; ok, it's "definitely not cheap", but that doesn't seem to faze its many fans one bit.

1221 *Chinese* — 23 | 17 | 21 | M

Changning | 1221 Yan'an Xi Lu (Fanyu Lu) | (86-21) 6213-6585

"Targeted to foreigners", this chic Changning Shanghainese is a "popular expatriate hangout" where the homestyle offerings may be "slightly tailored to non-Chinese palates" but are still plenty "authentic"; hidden "at the end of an alley", it's "not so easy to find" but worth seeking out for its "friendly service" and overall "good value."

Vedas *Indian* — 26 | 22 | 21 | M

Xuhui | 550 Jianguo Xi Lu (Wulumuqi Lu) | (86-21) 6445-8100 | www.vedascuisine.com

The unbeatable recipe of "great food" and "good prices" keeps the trade brisk at this much admired Xuhui French Concession Indian that seals the deal with a spacious, classy setting that avoids the usual curry house decor clichés; a moodily lit bar area is ideal for pre-dinner drinks, while those hoping for entertainment with their meal can peer through a glass partition into the kitchen to see the chefs in action.

Vegetarian Lifestyle *Chinese/Vegetarian* — 25 | 16 | 17 | I

Gubei/Hongqiao | 848 Huangjincheng Dao (Shuicheng Nan Lu) | (86-21) 6275-1798

Huaihai/Xintiandi | 77 Songshan Lu, 1st fl. (Huaihai Zhong Lu) | (86-21) 6384-8000

Jing An | 258 Fengxian Lu (Nanjing Xi Lu) | (86-21) 6215-7566 www.jujubetree.com

"Traditional" Chinese dishes mainly "prepared with vegetables" fill out the menu of this "pleasant" mini-chain where they do a good enough job to "fool the most discernable carnivore" while supplying real "value for your money"; P.S. in keeping with the overall "healthy" mindset, the "no-smoking rules are strictly enforced" here.

Yi Café ◐ *Eclectic* — 25 | 22 | 21 | E

Pudong | Pudong Shangri-La | 33 Fucheng Lu (Huayuanshiqiao Lu) | (86-21) 6882-8888, ext. 210 | www.shangri-la.com

"Eat yourself silly" at this bustling, "something-for-everyone" Eclectic buffet in the Pudong Shangri-La Hotel, where the walk-through layout is designed to replicate a public market equipped with "multiple food stations" drawn from around the globe; there is also an "impressive array of desserts" as well as a candy counter geared toward small fry.

Tokyo

TOP FOOD RANKING

	Restaurant	Cuisine
29	Kyoaji	Japanese
	Restaurant Bacar	French
28	Burgaz Ada	Turkish
27	Raku-tei	Tempura
	Gyuzo	Yakiniku
	Ristorante Hamasaki	Italian
	La Blanche	French
	Cuisine[s] Michel Troisgros	French
	Sazanka	Steak/Teppanyaki
	Shima	Steak
	Ristorante Aso	Italian
	L'Assiette Blanche	French
	Les Saisons*	French
	Le Manoir d'Hastings	French
26	Les Creations de Narisawa	French
	Hommage	French
	Sushi Mizutani	Sushi

Burgaz Ada ●🛇Ⓜ️ *Turkish*   28 | 25 | 26 | E

Azabu-Juban | Azabu-Rokudo, 3rd fl. | 3-7-4 Azabu-Juban (Azabu-Juban) | Minato-ku | (81-3) 3769-0606 | www.burgazada.jp

This Azabu-Juban Turkish will "open your eyes" to the "exciting", "alluring" flavors of Ottoman court cuisine, with its "perfect blend of spices" and "Eastern and Western accents" that "pack a punch" and "can only be described as delicious"; "warm", "friendly" service and a "cozy", "exotic" space complete the picture.

Cuisine[s] Michel Troisgros *French*   27 | 23 | 24 | VE

Nishi-Shinjuku | Hyatt Regency Tokyo, 1st fl. | 2-7-2 Nishi-Shinjuku (Tochomae) | Shinjuku-ku | (81-3) 5321-3915 | www.troisgros.jp

"Contemporary French cuisine at its finest" can be found at Michel Troisgros' establishment in the Hyatt Regency Tokyo, where the "creative", "subtle" dishes resemble "works of modern art" and are enhanced by some "lovely wine pairings"; what's more, the service is "pleasant and not overbearing", while the open kitchen "whets your appetite" and the "woody" interior makes you feel like you're in a "mountain villa."

Din Tai Fung *Chinese*   18 | 12 | 11 | M

Nihonbashi | Nihonbashi Takashimaya, main bldg., fl. B2 | 2-4-1 Nihonbashi (Nihonbashi) | Chuo-ku | (81-3) 3246-4768 Ⓜ️

Higashi-Shinbashi | Caretta Shiodome, fl. B2 | 1-8-2 Higashi-Shinbashi (Shiodome) | Minato-ku | (81-3) 5537-2081 Ⓜ️

Tamagawa | Tamagawa Takashimaya SC, south bldg., 9th fl. | 3-17-1 Tamagawa (Futago-Tamagawa) | Setagaya-ku | (81-3) 5797-3273 Ⓜ️

Sendagaya | Takashimaya Times Sq., 12th fl. | 5-24-2 Sendagaya (Shinjuku) | Shibuya-ku | (81-3) 5361-1381 Ⓜ️

---

* Indicates a tie with restaurant above.

(continued)

Din Tai Fung

Nishi-Ikebukuro | Ikebukuro Tobu Spice, 13th fl. | 1-1-25 Nishi-Ikebukuro (Ikebukuro) | Toshima-ku | (81-3) 5957-7811
www.d.rt-c.co.jp

Fans of this "famous" Taiwan-based dim sum chain "can't get their fill" of the steamed signature *xiaolongbao*, which also go into "robust" soups, although some purists who've been to the "original restaurant in Hsinchu" find the local versions "wanting"; while service "varies by location", it strikes many as "disappointing overall", but on the plus side, it's "easy to dine alone" in the casual, "cafeteria-style" spaces.

Gyuzo Ⓜ⇗ *Yakiniku*

27 | 12 | 18 | M

Nukui | 3-10-2 Nukui (Fujimidai) | Nerima-ku | (81-3) 3970-2257

Occupying a "minor plot of land" near Fujimidai Station, this "always packed" yakiniku spot offers "unbelievable value", with a menu of Grade A-5 (top grade) Wagyu beef, including "unusual cuts", which you can tuck into "with gusto"; fans also approve of the "brisk" service, and while the digs may look like a "cheap chain", they're always "tidy."

Hommage Ⓜ *French*

26 | 18 | 21 | E

Asakusa | 4-43-4 Asakusa (Asakusa) | Taito-ku | (81-3) 3874-1552

Francophiles are "amazed" to find this relative "bargain" French on the "outskirts of Asakusa", where the "creative", "refined" cuisine "reflects the chef's personality" and offers a "revelation in every bite"; the "kimono-clad" hostess provides "warm", "attentive" service, while the space, which it's occupied since September 2009, is "roomy and comfortable"; the "main complaint – it's tough to get a reservation."

Kyoaji ⓈⓂ⇗ *Japanese*

29 | 21 | 24 | VE

Shinbashi | 3-3-5 Shinbashi (Shinbashi) | Minato-ku | (81-3) 3591-3344

Sure, it's "tough for newcomers to get in" and the prices are "sky-high", but this Shinbashi eatery, voted Tokyo's No. 1 for Food, represents "Japanese cuisine at its finest", offering "subtle" yet "profound" flavors in dishes that are "flawless"; the "amiable" chef-owner regales you with "enjoyable conversation", making the food "taste even better", so "whether at the counter or in a private room, it's all good."

Kyubey *Sushi*

25 | 21 | 22 | VE

Kioicho | Hotel New Otani, Garden Tower, lobby | 4-1 Kioicho (Akasaka-Mitsuke) | Chiyoda-ku | (81-3) 3221-4144
Kioicho | Hotel New Otani, main bldg., lobby | 4-1 Kioicho (Akasaka-Mitsuke) | Chiyoda-ku | (81-3) 3221-4145
Ginza | 8-7-6 Ginza (Shinbashi) | Chuo-ku | (81-3) 3571-6523 Ⓢ
Toranomon | Hotel Okura Tokyo, main bldg., 5th fl. | 2-10-4 Toranomon (Kamiyacho) | Minato-ku | (81-3) 3505-6067
Nishi-Shinjuku | Keio Plaza Hotel | 2-2-1 Nishi-Shinjuku (Tochomae) | Shinjuku-ku | (81-3) 3344-0315
www.kyubey.jp

"Not conventional, but not too quirky" is how fans describe the "artistic", "flawless" "bite-size" sushi at this Ginza institution (and its hotel outposts), voted Tokyo's Most Popular restaurant; despite its "lofty reputation", the service is "friendly" and the atmosphere "inviting", especially the "clean", "elegant" four-story original location with "multiple sushi counters."

	FOOD	DECOR	SERVICE	COST

La Blanche *French*

27 | 17 | 20 | VE

Shibuya | Aoyama Pony Heim, 2nd fl. | 2-3-1 Shibuya (Omotesando) | Shibuya-ku | (81-3) 3499-0824

Foodies' "hearts race" over the "haute" French cuisine at this Shibuya "institution" that eschews "simplicity" and emphasizes "excellent preparations" and "extraordinary, elaborate combinations"; "friendly" but "not overbearing" service enhances the experience, and the only gripe is about the "lack of space between tables."

L'Assiette Blanche *French*

27 | 17 | 22 | E

Shirokane | Pearl Shirokane | 3-2-2 Shirokane (Shirokane-Takanawa) | Minato-ku | (81-3) 5420-6720

"Haute French cuisine at bistro prices" helps many get over the "inconvenient" location of this Shirokane eatery showcasing "subtle", "meticulously crafted" fare, with the "outstanding seafood and game-in-season" getting special praise; service is "attentive without being overbearing" and the "simple" room provides "ample space between tables" (perhaps because there "aren't many" of them), making it a "good special-occasion place."

Le Manoir d'Hastings *French*

27 | 18 | 19 | VE

Ginza | MST Bldg., fl. B1 | 6-5-1 Ginza (Ginza) | Chuo-ku | (81-3) 3248-6776

At his "admirable" Ginza "wonderland", chef Yasuo Igarashi creates "superb" French fare that's "full of surprises", and insiders advise you can "really appreciate it" when you "order à la carte"; the "low-key, courteous" service also wins praise, although some feel it "doesn't live up to the food", and many are cool to the space, which they describe as "cramped" and "ordinary."

Les Creations de Narisawa Ⓢ *French*

26 | 24 | 23 | VE

Minami-Aoyama | 2-6-15 Minami-Aoyama (Aoyama 1-chome) | Minato-ku | (81-3) 5785-0799 | www.narisawa-yoshihiro.com

Fans "salute the boundless creativity" of chef Yoshihiro Narisawa, which is evident in his "beautifully presented", "innovative contemporary" French cuisine that "never disappoints" at this Minami-Aoyama establishment, a "first-rate" destination for a "special occasion"; the "stylish" location "resembles a spaceship on the outside", and the staff generally provides "steady, reliable" service, but regulars say "watch out for the rookie servers."

Les Saisons *French*

27 | 25 | 27 | VE

Uchisaiwaicho | Imperial Hotel Tokyo, main bldg. | 1-1-1 Uchisaiwaicho (Hibiya) | Chiyoda-ku | (81-3) 3539-8087 | www.imperialhotel.co.jp

"Magnificent food and magnificent service" are what make this "flawless" French the "face of the Imperial Hotel" in the minds of many; surveyors salute the "subtle sensibilities" of chef Thierry Voisin, whose "thoroughly modern" presentations are "spectacular", and also applaud the "diligent", "top-notch" staff and a space that's "neither ostentatious nor chic", just "comfortable and lovely."

Raku-tei Ⓜ⊅ *Tempura*

27 | 21 | 20 | VE

Akasaka | Akasaka Music Inn | 6-8-1 Akasaka (Akasaka) | Minato-ku | (81-3) 3585-3743

This Akasaka institution serves "tempura as it's meant to be", and devotees declare it a "national treasure" for its "incredible frying techniques" that "bring out the flavor of every item", wrapped in a coating that's "light but not insipid" – in a word, "perfection"; the "classy" digs are always "immaculate" and the veteran husband-and-wife team makes you "comfortable" with "warm" service, but some regulars fret that they "don't seem to be grooming any successors" and wonder "how much longer they'll keep it going."

Restaurant Bacar ⊠ French — 29 | 17 | 21 | E

Shoto | Ville Shoto | 2-14-5 Shoto (Shinsen) | Shibuya-ku | (81-3) 6804-7178 | www.restaurant-bacar.com

The "best of its class" is what devotees dub this "tiny", "casual" French bistro in a residential section of Shoto, where many are left "speechless" by the "incredible value" of the ¥5,250 dinner course menu, featuring "exceptional" dishes such as a "unique" take on Italian bagna cauda made with "crab offal"; though it's essentially a "one-man show", the service is "brisk" and "flawless" and while the room is "cozy", the limited space makes reservations all the more precious.

Ristorante Aso Italian — 27 | 26 | 25 | VE

Daikanyama | 29-3 Sarugakucho (Daikanyama) | Shibuya-ku | (81-3) 3770-3690 | www.aso-net.jp

One of "Tokyo's elite Italians", this upscale ristorante near Daikanyama Station is "worth every yen", delighting "the eyes as well as the palate" with "creative presentations" of "impressive" fare; the "dreamy" "retro Western-style" building boasts "beautiful" decor and a "lovely" garden, while the "considerate" staff "makes you feel at home."

Ristorante Hamasaki ⊠ Italian — 27 | 23 | 26 | VE

Minami-Aoyama | Sun Light Hill Aoyama | 4-11-13 Minami-Aoyama (Omotesando) | Minato-ku | (81-3) 5772-8520

"Consistently perfect", the "sophisticated" Italian food at this "always full" Minami-Aoyama eatery is arguably the "best in the country"; the service is nearly as "wonderful" thanks to chef Ryuichi Hamasaki, who "never fails to greet each table", and his "self-effacing" staff, while the "pretty" room and "relaxing" vibe also seem to "reflect his personality."

Sazanka Steak/Teppanyaki — 27 | 20 | 27 | VE

Toranomon | Hotel Okura Tokyo, main bldg., 11th fl. | 2-10-4 Toranomon (Kamiyacho) | Minato-ku | (81-3) 3505-6071 | www.hotelokura.co.jp

"Typical of the Hotel Okura", the "first-class", "quintessentially Japanese" service at this Toranomon "teppanyaki king" leaves diners "fully gratified" and earns Tokyo's No. 1 Service honors; "even jaded steakhouse regulars on expense accounts" "rave" about the Wagyu beef and are "more than happy with even the cheapest course option", not to mention the "fine" wine list; by comparison, many feel the setting is "nothing to get too excited about."

Shima ⊠M Steak — 27 | 15 | 22 | VE

Nihonbashi | Nihonbashi MM Bldg., fl. B1 | 3-5-12 Nihonbashi (Nihonbashi) | Chuo-ku | (81-3) 3271-7889

"Beautifully marbled" beef and "top-notch preparations" are par for this Nihonbashi steakhouse, which is also known for its "take-out sandwiches" and "marvelous garlic rice"; the husband-wife team provides "wonderful" service, and while some find the counter seating "cramped", most "feel good" about the "classy clientele."

Shotai-en ● *Yakiniku*   25 | 16 | 15 | M

Machiya | AN Machiya Heights 102 | 1-20-9 Machiya (Machiya) | Arakawa-ku | (81-3) 5901-2929 Ⓜ
Machiya | 8-7-6 Machiya (Machiya) | Arakawa-ku | (81-3) 3895-2423
Ginza | Cheers Ginza, 9th fl. | 5-9-5 Ginza (Ginza) | Chuo-ku | (81-3) 6274-5003 Ⓜ
Shiba-Daimon | Park Side Shiba-Daimon, 1st fl. | 1-7-4 Shiba-Daimon (Daimon) | Minato-ku | (81-3) 5733-5025 Ⓜ
Shinbashi | Shinbashi Park Bldg., 2nd fl. | 2-3-4 Shinbashi (Uchisaiwaicho) | Minato-ku | (81-3) 6908-4529

It's "all good" at this Machiya-based yakiniku chain where the meat's "so fresh you can eat it raw" at prices that make it an "incredible value"; the original location set in a "renovated" house is full of "retro charm", while its various outposts are "well kept" and "suitable for dates."

Sushi Mizutani Ⓩ⌦ *Sushi*   26 | 20 | 20 | VE

Ginza | Juno Bldg., 9th fl. | 8-2-10 Ginza (Shinbashi) | Chuo-ku | (81-3) 3573-5258

"Pleasing to the eye as well as the palate", the "artistic" sushi at this Ginza specialist is some of the "best in Japan" according to fans, who laud the "superb" seafood and "zesty" seasoned rice as "outstanding"; there's a "unique buzz" to the "large, relaxing" digs, and the "good-humored" proprietor is as "agreeable" as ever.

Tsurutontan *Noodle Shop*   18 | 15 | 12 | I

Marunouchi | Tokyo Tokia Bldg., fl. B1 | 2-7-3 Marunouchi (Tokyo) | Chiyoda-ku | (81-3) 3214-2626
Roppongi | Roppongi 3-chome Bldg., 1st fl. | 3-14-12 Roppongi (Roppongi) | Minato-ku | (81-3) 5786-2626 ●
Kabukicho | Tsunamoto Bldg., fl. B1 | 2-26-3 Kabukicho (Shinjuku) | Shinjuku-ku | (81-3) 5287-2626 ●

Tsurutontan Kinsho-ro ● *Noodle Shop*

Roppongi | Roppongi 3-chome Bldg., 2nd fl. | 3-14-12 Roppongi (Roppongi) | Minato-ku | (81-3) 5786-2626
www.tsurutontan.co.jp

"Creative, Kansai-style" udon is the specialty of this chain where the "huge bowls" of "chewy" noodles are so "modestly priced" you feel like "you're getting a three-for-one deal"; the "cool" digs are "relaxing", but the "constant lines" aren't, according to critics, who also describe the staff as frequently "flustered"; the Kabukicho branch and both Roppongi locations are open through the night until 8 AM.

Ukai-tei *Steak/Teppanyaki*   24 | 25 | 24 | VE

Ginza | Jijitsushin Bldg., 1st fl. | 5-15-8 Ginza (Higashi-Ginza) | Chuo-ku | (81-3) 3544-5252
Akatsukicho | 2-14-6 Akatsukicho (Hachioji) | Hachioji-shi | (81-42) 626-1166
Jingumae | Omotesando Gyre Bldg., 5th fl. | 5-10-1 Jingumae (Meiji-jingumae) | Shibuya-ku | (81-3) 5467-5252 Ⓜ
www.ukai.co.jp

Whether it's the Hachioji original with its "magnificent garden", the "stately" Ginza branch or "spacious" Jingumae sib, you can't go wrong for a special occasion at this steak/teppanyaki chain with "gorgeous" interiors; diners with "discriminating tastes" find the offerings "wonderful" and served "flawlessly", and while "pricey", most agree it's "worth it."

CANADA
RESTAURANT
DIRECTORY

Montréal

TOP FOOD RANKING

	Restaurant	Cuisine
28	Milos	Greek/Seafood
	La Chronique	Eclectic/Québécois
	Toqué!	Québécois
27	Le Jolifou	French/Mexican
	Le Club Chasse	Eclectic/Québécois
	Européa	French
	Laloux	French
	Ferreira Café	Portuguese/Seafood
26	Au Pied de Cochon	French/Québécois
	Au Cinquième Péché	French
	Chez L'Épicier	Eclectic/French
	laurie raphaël	French/Québécois
	Jun i	Japanese
	Le Locale	French
25	Moishe's	Steak
	Garde Manger	Eclectic/Seafood
	Leméac	French
	Aix Cuisine du Terroir	Québécois
	XO, Le Restaurant	Eclectic/French
	La Colombe	French
24	L'Express	French
	Queue de Cheval	Seafood/Steak
	L'Atelier	Québécois

Aix Cuisine du Terroir *Québécois* `25 | 24 | 24 | E`

Old Montréal | Hotel Place d'Armes | 711, Côte de la Place d'Armes (rue St-Jacques) | 514-904-1201 | www.aixcuisine.com

"Adventurous" but "not over the top" describes the cuisine at this "*très chic*" Québécois in an Old Montréal boutique hotel where seasonal dishes are enhanced by "gorgeous" presentations and a "knowledgeable" sommelier at the ready with pairings; customers congregate on the rooftop terrace, in the trendy lounge or in the "romantic" dining room with service that is always "attentive" and "personable."

Andiamo Ⓢ *Mediterranean/Seafood* `- | - | - | M`

Downtown | 1083, Côte du Beaver Hall (bet. rue de la Gauchetière O. & boul. René-Lévesque) | 514-861-2634 | www.andiamo.ca

Star chef Jérôme Ferrer (Européa) goes back to his Catalan roots at this more casual Downtowner serving a seafood-focused Mediterranean menu with an emphasis on simple preparations and organic ingredients; the sunny ambiance takes a cue from seaside resorts, which feels appropriate for sipping well-priced wines from Italy, France and Spain; P.S. now open for lunch and dinner Wednesdays to Saturdays.

Au Cinquième Péché Ⓢ Ⓜ *French* `26 | 22 | 24 | E`

Plateau Mont-Royal | 330, ave. du Mont-Royal Est (rue Drolet) | 514-286-0123 | www.aucinquiemepeche.com

The name refers to the fifth deadly sin (gluttony), and indeed it would be a crime to miss this "intimate" Plateau bistro, a "best-kept secret"

FOOD DECOR SERVICE COST

offering chef Benoît Lenglet's "vibrant", midpriced French fare crafted from "market-fresh" ingredients; the checkered floors, blackboard menus and open kitchen give it a "cozy" feel, as do the "warm and engaging" servers who greet you like you're a guest in their "home"; P.S. save room for the "exquisite" desserts.

Au Pied de Cochon ●Ⓜ *French/Québécois*   26 20 23 E
Plateau Mont-Royal | 536, ave. Duluth Est (ave de Chateaubriand) | 514-281-1114
Cabane à Sucre
Au Pied de Cochon Ⓜ *French/Québécois*
St-Benoît de Mirabel | 11382, Rang de la Fresnière (bet. Montée Robillard & Montée Rochon) | 450-258-1732
www.restaurantaupieddecochon.ca

"Gastronomy" meets "gluttony" at this "sublime" Plateau "foodie" "destination" - Montréal's Most Popular restaurant - where *enfant terrible* chef-owner Martin Picard turns out a "heart-stoppingly delicious" French-Québécois menu heavy on the foie gras; "it's tight, but cozy" in the "bustling" wood-heavy space with an open kitchen, and though prices and service are a sore spot for some, it remains a "one-of-a-kind" "indulgence" that's worth experiencing, even if you have to eat "nothing but salad the next day"; P.S. Picard now also operates an authentic Québec sugar shack in the Lower Laurentians (about 45 minutes from Downtown Montréal), which is open February-April and serves a hearty brunch.

Bar & Boeuf Ⓢ Ⓜ *French*   - - - E
Old Montréal | 500, rue McGill (rue Notre-Dame O.) | 514-866-3555 | www.baretboeuf.com

At this Old Montréal bistro, rising Québécois chef Alexandre Gosselin puts an Eclectic spin on French classics, using market-fresh ingredients in specialties like his daily changing tartares with housemade pickles; the bi-level space exudes the understated grandeur of an old-time cruise ship, complete with tufted walls, porthole mirrors and an opulent bar.

Chez L'Épicier *Eclectic/French*   26 23 24 E
Old Montréal | 311, rue St-Paul Est (rue St-Claude) | 514-878-2232 | www.chezlepicier.com

Groupies "can't stop raving" about this "culinary gem" in Old Montréal where chef Laurent Godbout's "clever" French-influenced Eclectic creations are crafted from local ingredients and set down by a "knowledgeable" staff; the chicly renovated storefront with stellar street views gives it a "charming" feel, as does an "adorable" boutique onsite vending jams, olive oils and other "gourmet" provisions.

Européa *French*   27 24 26 VE
Downtown | 1227, rue de la Montagne (rue Ste-Catherine O.) | 514-398-9229 | www.europea.ca

"It's not just dinner, it's an *experience*" assert acolytes of chef Jérôme Ferrer's Downtown destination where classic French cuisine is "brilliantly prepared", "served with wit and panache", and best appreciated in a "long and luxurious" 10-course tasting menu with "well-thought-out" wine pairings; the overall vibe is "lovely" and "sophisticated", with "impeccable" service capping a "memorable" evening.

	FOOD	DECOR	SERVICE	COST

Ferreira Café *Portuguese/Seafood*   27 | 24 | 24 | VE

Downtown | 1446, rue Peel (rue Ste-Catherine O.) | 514-848-0988 | www.ferreiracafe.com

"Haute" Portuguese cooking is the hook at this "transporting" Downtown fixture famed for its "exquisite" "fresh fish" paired with "outstanding" wines and ports; the handsome Mediterranean-style setting decked out with blue-and-white ceramic tiles pulls in an equally "beautiful" clientele, while a "caring", "efficient" staff ensures a "pleasant" time, no matter how "packed" or "noisy" it gets.

Garde Manger ●M *Eclectic/Seafood*   25 | 20 | 21 | E

Old Montréal | 408, rue St-François-Xavier (rue St-Paul O.) | 514-678-5044

"Showstopping" Eclectic dishes (including an "out-of-this-world" lobster poutine) take center stage at this moderately priced Old Montréal eatery helmed by "dynamic" TV chef Chuck Hughes; a "pleasant" staff increases the appeal, although the "energetic" atmosphere boasts "rock concert"–worthy decibels that can detract – "for calmer" dining, "go early"; P.S. children under 18 not allowed.

Gibbys *Seafood/Steak*   24 | 21 | 23 | E

Old Montréal | Youville Stables | 298, pl. d'Youville (rue St-Pierre) | 514-282-1837 | www.gibbys.com

"Nostalgia" rules at this "legendary" Old Montréal "mainstay" set in a "charming" 18th-century stable where "tourists" and "well-dressed families" munch on "huge", "tender" steaks and "stellar" seafood set down by a "polite" staff; despite a few murmurs that it's "ordinary" and "expensive" to boot, most leave "satisfied"; P.S. try it "on a snowy night" when the "fireplace is roaring."

Jun i Ⓩ *Japanese*   26 | 22 | 22 | E

Mile End | 156, ave. Laurier Ouest (rue St-Urbain) | 514-276-5864 | www.juni.ca

Juniphiles "go often" to this "real find" in Mile End where an "innovative" chef whips up "impeccable" sushi as well as some "truly creative" European-inflected Japanese mains, all offered in "gorgeous presentations"; expect upper-end pricing, "knowledgeable" service and a "serene" space made more "lively" by the "hip" clientele.

La Chronique *Eclectic/Québécois*   28 | 23 | 26 | VE

Mile End | 99, ave. Laurier Ouest (rue St-Urbain) | 514-271-3095 | www.lachronique.qc.ca

"Still one of the standard-bearers of Montréal haute cuisine", this "memorable" Mile End boîte continues to "dazzle" with Marc de Canck's "top-notch" Québécois-Eclectic fare offered à la carte or in a "world-class" seven-course tasting menu with "bold" wine pairings; in spite of an "understated" ambiance, prices are "sky-high", though "frugal" sorts sing the praises of the $28 prix fixe lunch on weekdays – *"bon appétit!"*

La Colombe ⓈM *French*   25 | 19 | 22 | E

Plateau Mont-Royal | 554, ave. Duluth Est (rue St-Hubert) | 514-849-8844

Loyalists "love" this Plateau "gem" showcasing "impeccable" Classic French cuisine in a "phenomenal" prix fixe menu that's "affordable" too thanks to a BYO policy with no corkage fee; the decor is "simple" but "cozy" and the staff "charming", so in all it "never fails to impress" for "dates" or other "special occasions"; P.S. "reservations essential."

	FOOD	DECOR	SERVICE	COST

Laloux *French*

27 | 25 | 27 | E

Plateau Mont-Royal | 250, ave. des Pins Est (ave. Laval) | 514-287-9127 |
www.laloux.com

"Prepare to be wowed" assert acolytes of this longtime Plateau "favor-ite" where "superb" French bistro standards are set down by "knowl-edgeable", "engaging" servers (voted No. 1 in the Montréal Survey); add in an "elegant", "faintly belle epoque" atmosphere, and you have a "lovely" choice for a "special" meal; P.S. cheeses and savory bites are offered in the adjoining wine bar, Pop!.

L'Atelier Ⓜ *Québécois*

24 | 22 | 23 | E

Mile End | 5308, boul. St-Laurent (rue Maguire) | 514-273-7442 |
www.restaurantlatelier.ca

This "solid Québécois" in Mile End pleases with "hearty" dishes like bison ribs and rabbit cassoulet; service is affable and the decor has a warm, "woodsy" feel, but most appealing is the BYO policy with no corkage fee, keeping costs reasonable and making it truly "worth the trip."

laurie raphaël *French/Québécois*

26 | 25 | 26 | VE

Downtown | Hôtel Le Germain | 2050, rue Mansfield
(bet. boul. de Maisonneueve O. & rue Sherbrooke O.) |
514-985-6072 | www.laurieraphael.com

"Star chef" Daniel Vézina's high-end dining room in Downtown's swanky Hôtel Le Germain lives up to the "Québéc City original" with "formidable" French-Québécois cuisine that's "daring" enough, yet "won't scare off the client" at a business meeting; "charming" touches in the muted interior include tableware designed with "flair" by Montréal artists, which is also for sale in the adjacent boutique along with kitchen utensils, vinegars and other *produits du terroir*.

Le Club
Chasse et Pêche Ⓧ *Eclectic/Québécois*

27 | 24 | 25 | VE

Old Montréal | 423, rue St-Claude (bet. rues Notre-Dame & St-Paul) |
514-861-1112 | www.leclubchasseetpeche.com

Its name translates to the hunting and fishing club, but "there's no need for a rod or rifle" at this Old Montréal enclave laying out chef Claude Pelletier's "hearty yet elegant" Eclectic-Québécois cuisine ("heavenly!") and "excellent" wines in an "enchanting" locale full of "old-world charm"; it's "costly", but factor in a staff that treats you like "royalty", and there's a reason that locals love it and visitors vow they "may just go back to Canada" for another taste; P.S. summer lunch on their terrace atop the historic Château Ramezay Museum "is as civi-lized as it gets."

Le Jolifou Ⓜ *French/Mexican*

27 | 20 | 25 | E

Little Italy/Petite-Patrie | 1840, rue Beaubien Est (rue Cartier) |
514-722-2175 | www.jolifou.com

"French food with a twist" is the draw at this "off-the-beaten-path" charmer in Petite-Patrie where Mexican flavors spice up classic Gallic grub (yes, it "sounds weird" but it's "delicious"); a "husband-and-wife team" oversees "personalized" service in the simply decorated space that's enlivened by little tin "trinkets" and toys from the 1920s, mak-ing it "a delight" all around.

	FOOD	DECOR	SERVICE	COST

Le Locale ❂ *French*
26 | 26 | 23 | E

Old Montréal | 740, rue William (bet. rues Prince & Queen) |
514-397-7737 | www.resto-lelocal.com

It's "definitely a scene" at this Old Montréal bistro where "young and beautiful" types turn out for "adventurous" French cooking courtesy of chef Charles-Emmanuel Pariseau and owner/local TV star Louis-François Marcotte; it's housed in a "modern", industrial-"chic" space with high ceilings, a "long open kitchen" and a lively lounge giving it a "funky" feel.

Leméac ❂ *French*
25 | 23 | 23 | E

Outremont | 1045, ave. Laurier Ouest (ave. Durocher) | 514-270-0999 |
www.restaurantlemeac.com

"Celebs, politicians" and "locals in the know" fill up this Outremont French, a "favorite" for "well-executed", "honest" bistro "classics" like duck confit and short ribs accompanied by "reasonably priced" wines; it's often "crowded" and "noisy", especially at brunch and after 10 PM when "fashionable" types file in for the $25 prix fixe special.

L'Express ❂ *French*
24 | 22 | 22 | M

Plateau Mont-Royal | 3927, rue St-Denis (bet. ave. Duluth & rue Roy) |
514-845-5333 | www.restaurantlexpress.ca

"Like Paris without the attitude", this "quintessential" bistro in the Plateau delivers "not-too-expensive" takes on the "classics" (like bone marrow and "killer frites") in a "chic", "typically French" setting with checkered floors and a zinc bar; after over 30 years on the scene, a few find it's "showing its age", though it remains a "favorite" for many, "particularly late at night"; P.S. "reserve well in advance."

Milos ❂ *Greek/Seafood*
28 | 24 | 25 | VE

Mile End | 5357, ave. du Parc (bet. ave. Fairmount & rue St-Viateur) |
514-272-3522 | www.milos.ca

"Sublime" "fresh" seafood "flown in daily" reels them in to Costas Spiliadis' Mile End Greek – rated No. 1 for Food in the Montréal Survey – where the flavors are so "authentic", some swear you can feel a "sea breeze flowing through" the rustic, "whitewashed" setting; a "gracious", "attentive" staff that "cuts fresh oregano tableside" completes the experience, and though all this comes at "stratospheric" prices, the $20 prix fixe lunch is "an amazing deal."

Moishe's Steak House *Steak*
25 | 18 | 23 | VE

Plateau Mont-Royal | 3961, boul. St-Laurent (bet. ave. Duluth &
rue Napoléon) | 514-845-3509 | www.moishes.ca

"Bring your appetite (and your platinum card)" to this Main "temple to meat", a "tradition" for "expertly grilled" steaks served alongside "Jewish-style sides" like latkes and chopped liver; opened in 1938, it strikes the majority as "still great after all these years", though a few kvetch about the "noise", "the lines, the service – oy vey."

Queue de Cheval
24 | 24 | 23 | VE

Steak House & Bar *Seafood/Steak*

Downtown | 1221, boul. René-Lévesque Ouest (rue Drummond) |
514-390-0090 | www.queuedecheval.com

A "monster of a steakhouse", this "big and ballsy" Downtown surf 'n' turfer across from the Bell Centre trades in "top-shelf" "well-aged"

FOOD DECOR SERVICE COST

meats, "fine" seafood and "traditional" à la carte accompaniments like loaded baked potatoes; it goes over well with the "expense-account" crowd that appreciates the "old-school fine-dining" feel complete with "pampering" service and a "power scene" centered around the cigar bar ("Cubans", anyone?).

Tasso Bar à Mezze ☒ *Greek*   - | - | - | M

Plateau Mont-Royal | 3829, rue St-Denis (rue Roy) | 514-842-0867 | www.tassobaramezze.com

Chef-owner Nicolas Mentzas (ex Toqué!) gives his midpriced Plateau Greek *psaro-taverna* (fish taverna) a shot of innovation, resulting in modern Mediterranean meze and seafood entrees plus a serious wine program; the minimalist decor with touches of cerulean blue evokes a sleek island villa, and the terrace situated on trendy St-Denis is ideal for people-watching.

Toqué! ☒Ⓜ *Québécois*   28 | 25 | 26 | VE

Old Montréal | 900, pl. Jean-Paul-Riopelle (rue St-Antoine O.) | 514-499-2084 | www.restaurant-toque.com

One of "the finest tables in Montréal", this "temple to dining" in the city's old quarter showcases chef-owner Normand Laprise's brand of "cutting-edge", "Québécois fusion cuisine", presented à la carte or in a "superb" menu degustation ("three hours of pure enjoyment"); it's a "top-of-the-line experience, and priced accordingly", following through with "sleek", "contemporary" design and "polite" servers who "take good care of you"; P.S. lunch is now served, and the chef has also opened midpriced Brasserie T!.

XO, Le Restaurant *Eclectic/French*   25 | 28 | 25 | VE

Old Montréal | St-James Hotel | 355, rue St-Jacques (rue St-Pierre) | 514-841-5000 | www.xolerestaurant.com

"Superb" swoon fans of this "expensive" enclave in the "ultrachic" St-James Hotel in Old Montréal, a veritable "playground for the rich and famous" that's rated No. 1 for Decor in our Survey thanks to its "spectacular old-world setting" in a historic Merchants Bank building; chef Michele Mercuri sends out "exquisite" French-Eclectic cuisine, while "wonderful desserts" and "attentive" service top off a near-"perfect" experience.

Toronto

TOP FOOD RANKING

Restaurant	Cuisine
29 Sushi Kaji	Japanese
27 Chiado/Senhor Antonio	Portuguese/Seafood
Terra	Eclectic
Scaramouche	French
Scaramouche Pasta Bar & Grill	French
26 North 44°	Continental
Auberge du Pommier	French/Mediterranean
Lai Wah Heen	Chinese
Canoe	Canadian
Harbour Sixty	Steak
Il Mulino	Italian
Nota Bene	American
Mistura	Italian
Bymark	Continental
25 Colborne Lane	Eclectic
Black Hoof	Eclectic
Célestin	French
Cava	Spanish
Hiro Sushi	Japanese
Pizzeria Libretto*	Italian
Starfish Oyster Bed & Grill*	Seafood
Lucien	Eclectic
Oro	Mediterranean

Ame 🗷Ⓜ *Japanese*   – | – | – | E
(aka Rain)

Entertainment District | 19 Mercer St. (John St.) | 416-599-7246 |
www.amecuisine.com

The Rubino brothers (of Food Network fame) teamed up with nightlife impresario Charles Khabouth for this reworking of their Entertainment District hub, Rain; now transformed into a modern Japanese restaurant, it purveys a multitude of specialties at the expected prices against the backdrop of a sexy, backlit bar bustling with beautiful people.

Auberge du Pommier 🗷 *French/Mediterranean*   26 | 25 | 25 | VE
York Mills | Yonge Corporate Ctr. | 4150 Yonge St. (bet. Hwy. 401 & York Mills Rd.) | 416-222-2220 | www.oliverbonacini.com

"Hogtown meets the French countryside" at this York Mills charmer, a "perennial favorite" for "romantic" feasts of "superb" Gallic-Med cuisine presented by a "first-class" staff; it's set in a "quaint" stone cottage from the 1860s, so while pricing is "steep", in all it makes for a "memorable evening."

Black Hoof ⊄ *Eclectic*   25 | 16 | 20 | E
Dundas West | 928 Dundas St. W. (bet. Bellwoods Ave. & Grace St.) | 416-551-8854 | www.theblackhoof.com

Toronto hipsters "hoof it on down" to this Dundas West Eclectic for a meat-centric menu featuring "divine" housemade charcuterie and

---

* Indicates a tie with restaurant above

other "decadent" dishes served with handcrafted cocktails and "interesting wines"; the "barlike" space has a "casual" vibe with close-set tables and Eames stools, and it's open till 1 AM Thursdays–Saturdays, making it well suited both for dinner and "late-night snacks."

Bymark 🗷 Continental
26 | 23 | 23 | VE

Financial District | TD Centre, Concourse Level | 66 Wellington St. W. (bet. Bay & York Sts.) | 416-777-1144 | www.bymark.ca

"A haven for business types flashing their platinum cards", this Financial District fallback located in the TD Centre delivers an "excellent" Continental menu from Mark McEwan starring a "famous" (if "ridiculously expensive") burger; "tireless attention to detail" includes "noattitude" service and an extensive wine list, so in spite of somewhat "gloomy" subterranean digs, most find it "never disappoints."

Canoe 🗷 Canadian
26 | 26 | 25 | VE

Financial District | Toronto Dominion Bank Tower | 66 Wellington St. W., 54th fl. (bet. Bay & York Sts.) | 416-364-0054 | www.oliverbonacini.com

Surveyors throw "three paddles up" for this Financial District "icon" – Toronto's Most Popular restaurant and rated No. 1 for Decor – that impresses guests with "spectacular views" of the city from its "romantic" 54th-floor perch atop the Toronto Dominion Bank Tower and equally "breathtaking" "classic Canadian" cuisine; add in near-"impeccable" service, and the consensus is "you really can't go wrong" here – just "save your pennies (you'll need lots!)"; Saturday and Sunday it's closed to the public, and open only for private events; P.S. an extensive renovation including walnut tabletops, a beaten-copper wall and a soapstone bar is not reflected in the Decor score.

Cava Spanish
25 | 17 | 23 | E

Midtown | 1560 Yonge St. (bet. Delisle Ave. & Heath St.) | 416-979-9918 | www.cavarestaurant.ca

Let your "taste buds travel" at this Midtown tapas stop transporting guests with Chris McDonald's "delectable" Spanish bites, entrees such as paella and "amazing wines" (many "reasonably priced" too); a "knowledgeable" staff eases the way with ordering, so the only downside is the somewhat "noisy" courtyard setting; P.S. don't miss the housemade ice cream at next door's sweet shop, Xococava.

Célestin 🅼 French
25 | 22 | 23 | VE

Midtown | 623 Mt. Pleasant Rd. (Manor Rd. E.) | 416-544-9035 | www.celestinrestaurant.com

"As close to Paris" as it gets in Midtown, this "elegant" retreat "dazzles" diners with "top-notch" French fare set down in "tasteful" converted-bank digs from the 1920s with an adjacent bakery vending "fantastic goodies"; foes find it "rather expensive", but it pays off with "unhurried" service that makes for a "lovely" experience all around; P.S. the Food score may not fully reflect a summer 2009 chef change.

Chiado/Senhor Antonio Portuguese/Seafood
27 | 22 | 25 | VE

Little Italy | 864 College St. (Concord Ave.) | 416-538-1910 | www.chiadorestaurant.com

"Outstanding" seafood is the hook at this "charming" Little Italy Portuguese, a "star" on the Toronto dining scene that offers "perfectly

FOOD | DECOR | SERVICE | COST

prepared" "modern interpretations of classic dishes" matched with "spectacular" regional vintages; the "understated" setting with wooden floors and white linen gains a lift from colorful artwork and a "knowledgeable" staff that "aims to please"; P.S. Senhor Antonio is the adjacent bar focusing on tapas and wines.

Colborne Lane ●⊠ *Eclectic*   25 | 24 | 22 | VE

Downtown Core | 45 Colborne St. (Leader Ln.) | 416-368-9009 | www.colbornelane.com

"Every mouthful is a discovery" at chef-owner Claudio Aprile's highly "experimental" Downtown Eclectic showcasing "sublime" creations that make use of "ingenious" ingredients and techniques ("try the nitrogen ice cream made right at your table"); despite some quibbles about "too-expensive" tabs for too-"small portions", many find it all worth it for such "a unique dining experience"; P.S. 10-course and 15-course tastings are also offered, in the dining room and private kitchen table room, respectively.

Harbour Sixty Steakhouse ● *Steak*   26 | 23 | 24 | VE

Harbourfront | Toronto Harbour Commission Bldg. | 60 Harbour St. (Bay St.) | 416-777-2111 | www.harboursixty.com

This "red-meat haven" on the Harbourfront pulls Leafs fans, "bankers and brokers" for "gargantuan" steaks and towering plates of seafood served in "grand" environs that have the feel of dining in "a rich uncle's home"; a "smooth" staff treats you "like a king", though many find it all "a little too over the top", especially the prices.

Hiro Sushi ⊠Ⓜ *Japanese*   25 | 15 | 21 | E

St. Lawrence | 171 King St. E. (Jarvis St.) | 416-304-0550

"Ten tables, one sushi master, zero fanfare" sums up this St. Lawrence Japanese, a go-to for "true foodies" thanks to chef-owner Hiro's "exceptional" raw fare featuring delicacies you've likely "never had before" (i.e. "don't expect California rolls"); perhaps the "tired" decor could use an "update", but it's really "all about the food" anyhow; P.S. frugal sorts say the "lunch prices are a deal."

Il Mulino *Italian*   26 | 21 | 24 | VE

Forest Hill | 1060 Eglinton Ave. W. (bet Camberwell & Glen Cedar Rds.) | 416-780-1173 | www.ilmulinorestaurant.com

"So Italian you could be in Florence" declare devotees of this "long-established" Forest Hill ristorante where "fantastic" "traditional" dishes and "spectacular" wines arrive via "professional, old-school waiters"; its elegant setting with vaulted ceilings and fine linens cements its status as "one of the top" in the city, with elevated prices to match.

Lai Wah Heen *Chinese*   26 | 22 | 24 | E

Downtown Core | Metropolitan Hotel | 108 Chestnut St. (bet. Bay St. & University Ave.) | 416-977-9899 | www.laiwahheen.com

For dim sum that "rivals Hong Kong or China", Toronto buffs beeline to this Downtown "fine-dining" destination in the Metropolitan Hotel known for its "extravagant" Chinese feasts of "delectable" morsels and Peking duck; the "upscale" dining room exudes "quiet elegance" and service is "unrushed", making this an "all-around outstanding" experience that's "in a class by itself."

	FOOD	DECOR	SERVICE	COST

Lucien *Eclectic*

| 25 | 22 | 23 | VE |

St. Lawrence | 36 Wellington St. E. (bet. Church & Yonge Sts.) | 416-504-9990 | www.lucienrestaurant.com

A "deliciously unique menu" courtesy of chef Scot Woods "dazzles" diners at this posh St. Lawrence storefront spotlighting "beautifully presented" contemporary Eclectic fare with "unusual" touches; "aside from the excess use of foam", many find it "among the best in the city", enhanced by "intelligent", "unobtrusive" service and a "beautiful" setting decked out with ironwork and chandeliers

Mistura ⑤ *Italian*

| 26 | 23 | 23 | VE |

Annex | 265 Davenport Rd. (bet. Avenue & Bedford Rds.) | 416-515-0009 | www.mistura.ca

A "tony crowd of who's who in the city" crams into this Annex Italian "hot spot" where "ebullient" chef Massimo Capra turns out "wonderful" "homemade" pastas and mains in a "dark, atmospheric" room; despite some complaints that it's "overpriced" and "overrated", it remains a fixture for "business dinners" and other "special occasions."

North 44° ⑤ *Continental*

| 26 | 24 | 25 | VE |

North Toronto | 2537 Yonge St. (bet. Keewatin & Sherwood Aves.) | 416-487-4897 | www.north44restaurant.com

Practically a "national treasure", Mark McEwan's longtime Continental "classic" in North Toronto still delivers "superlative" cuisine and wines backed by "first-class" service in "minimalist" surroundings; though a few fret it's not as "exciting" as it once was, most find it among the city's "finest" and no surprise – it's even better on an "expense account."

Nota Bene ⑤ *American*

| 26 | 24 | 25 | VE |

Queen West | 180 Queen St. W. (University Ave.) | 416-977-6400 | www.notabenerestaurant.com

A "boisterous crowd" fills up this "hugely popular" Queen West yearling doling out "excellent" New American fare (think steak tartare and pulled suckling pig) in a "slick" space decorated with abstract impressionist paintings; stellar "people-watching" fuels the "hip", "Manhattan-like" vibe, while "polished" service and relatively "reasonable" prices complete the package; P.S. "reservations are a must."

Oro ⑤ *Mediterranean*

| 25 | 23 | 25 | VE |

Downtown Core | 45 Elm St. (bet. Bay & Yonge Sts.) | 416-597-0155 | www.ororestaurant.com

"Enjoyable" Mediterranean cooking pleases the masses at this Downtown mainstay that's an all-around "consistent" bet for handmade pastas and hearty mains in an "attractive" brick- and wood-trimmed dining room; despite "high" prices, most maintain they "always look forward to a meal" here; "bravo!"

Pizzeria Libretto *Italian*

| 25 | 19 | 19 | M |

West Queen West | 221 Ossington Ave. (bet. Dundas & Rolyat Sts.) | 416-532-8000 | www.pizzerialibretto.com

Purists praise the "authentic Neapolitan" pizzas from the wood-burning oven at this West Queen West Italian also pumping out salads and antipasti based on local ingredients; prices are low, and the mood's "warm" and "upbeat" in spite of the no-reservations policy and "huge lines" outside.

	FOOD	DECOR	SERVICE	COST

Ruth's Chris Steak House *Steak*

| 23 | 19 | 23 | VE |

Downtown Core | Hilton Toronto | 145 Richmond St. W. (University Ave.) | 416-955-1455
Mississauga | 77 City Centre Dr. (Kariya Dr.) | 905-897-8555
www.ruthschris.ca

"Sizzling" steaks "slathered in butter" lie in store at these Toronto links in the U.S. steakhouse chain set in "typical" wood and leather–decked surroundings in Mississauga and in the basement of the Downtown Core's Hilton; in spite of "professional" service, foes find it all a bit "formulaic" and too "expensive" as well.

Scaramouche 🗺 *French*

| 27 | 25 | 27 | VE |

Forest Hill | 1 Benvenuto Pl. (Edmund Ave.) | 416-961-8011 | www.scaramoucherestaurant.com

A "classic", this "elegant" Forest Hill veteran "keeps getting better" with "superb" New French fare bested only by the "spectacular views" of the city and "flawless" service that's rated No. 1 in our Toronto Survey; though the bill is "expensive", it's a "can't miss" for a "special" night.

Scaramouche Pasta Bar & Grill 🗺 *French*

| 27 | 24 | 26 | VE |

Forest Hill | 1 Benvenuto Pl. (Edmund Ave.) | 416-961-8011 | www.scaramoucherestaurant.com

"All of the benefits" of the venerable Scaramouche at a "lower price point" can be found at this Forest Hill sib delivering similarly "outstanding", "creative" contemporary French cuisine (and pastas, natch) plus "wonderful" service in a polished, bistro-like setting boasting "terrific views" of Downtown; all said, "what else could you ask for?"

Starfish Oyster Bed & Grill *Seafood*

| 25 | 19 | 22 | E |

St. Lawrence | 100 Adelaide St. E. (bet. Church & Jarvis Sts.) | 416-366-7827 | www.starfishoysterbed.com

"The world is your oyster" at this "tiny" St. Lawrence seafood "gem" pairing "wonderfully fresh" fin fare with "local brews" and "crisp white wines" in a "simple" wood-lined setting; it thrives on a "casual", "not-too-fussy" vibe, from the "welcoming" staff down to the moderate tabs; P.S. "sit at the bar if you can."

Sushi Kaji Ⓜ *Japanese*

| 29 | 16 | 26 | VE |

Etobicoke | 860 The Queensway (Islington Ave.) | 416-252-2166 | www.sushikaji.com

Diners are "transported straight to Tokyo" at this "omakase-only" Etobicoke Japanese where "master" chef Mitsuhiro Kaji presides over an "epic sushi experience" – ranked No. 1 for Food in the Toronto Survey – featuring "phenomenal" dishes that are "divine" in their "simplicity"; "hole-in-the-wall" digs and "extraordinary" prices hardly deter the faithful.

Terra *Eclectic*

| 27 | 25 | 26 | VE |

Thornhill | 8199 Yonge St. (Kirk Dr.) | 905-731-6161 | www.terrarestaurant.ca

A "go-to" for "special occasions", this "romantic" Thornhill Eclectic woos suburbanites with "wonderful" cooking and "lovely" wines presented by a "gracious" staff; indeed, "your wallet will take a hit", but insiders insist this one "ranks up there" with the "best" in the city; P.S. live jazz Tuesday to Saturday.

Vancouver

TOP FOOD RANKING

	Restaurant	Cuisine
28	La Belle Auberge	French
	Vij's	Indian
	Cioppino's	Mediterranean
27	Le Crocodile	French
	Tojo's	Japanese
	Bishop's	Pacific NW
	West	Pacific NW
	Shiro	Japanese
26	Il Giardino di Umberto	Italian
	Blue Water	Seafood
	Vij's Rangoli	Indian
	Kitanoya Guu	Japanese
	Maenam	Thai
	Market by Jean-Georges	French
	La Régalade	French
	Au Petit Chavignol	French
	Refuel	Pacific NW
	Kingyo	Japanese
	La Buca	Italian
	Chambar	Belgian
	Diva at the Met	Pacific NW
25	Pear Tree	Continental
	La Quercia	Italian
	La Terrazza	Italian
	Bin 941 Tapas	Eclectic

Au Petit Chavignol *French*   26 | 22 | 26 | M

East Side | 845 E. Hastings St. (bet. Campbell & Hawks Aves.) |
604-255-4218 | www.aupetitchavignol.com

"Hello cheese heaven!" say fans of this "off-the-beaten-track" East
Side French bistro where the offerings include "amazing charcuterie",
"proper" fondues and raclette, "expertly matched" with "a magical
wine list" and served by "people who care"; yes, the neighborhood's
"dodgy", but there's a "cozy" vibe and the herd insists "everyone must
eat here" – or at least visit the adjacent shop, Les Amis du Fromage.

Bin 941 Tapas Parlour ◐ *Eclectic*   25 | 19 | 21 | M

West End | 941 Davie St. (bet. Burrard & Howe Sts.) | 604-683-1246 |
www.bin941.com

All that's "small" "rules" at this "busy" West End spot where chef Gord
Martin's midpriced Eclectic "bites" deliver "robust" flavors; "informative
service" and a "funky" vibe help make it a "find, especially for late-
night" noshers who don't mind "close quarters" and "earsplitting" music.

Bishop's *Pacific NW*   27 | 23 | 27 | VE

West Side | 2183 W. Fourth Ave. (bet. Arbutus & Yew Sts.) | 604-738-2025 |
www.bishopsonline.com

Diners "feel loved, not just well fed" at John Bishop's Pacific
Northwest "classic" on the West Side that again ranks No. 1 for

	FOOD	DECOR	SERVICE	COST

Service in the Vancouver Survey, courtesy of the "charming, thoughtful host"-owner and his "gracious", "flawless" staff; the "local, organic movement" plays out in "exceptional cuisine" that's served in a "simple yet elegant room", adding up to a "consistently pure and classy", if "pricey", evening that partisans praise as "impeccable in every sense."

Blue Water Cafe & Raw Bar ❶ *Seafood*

26	25	24	VE

Yaletown | 1095 Hamilton St. (Helmcken St.) | 604-688-8078 | www.bluewatercafe.net

"In a city with a school of competition", fin fans hie to chef Frank Pabst's "posh" converted warehouse in Yaletown, where "flawless", "sumptuous seafood" is served in "innovative", "eye-popping presentations" by an "outstanding" staff; an "elegant" raw bar for sushi and "oysters that are pure bliss", plus "extensive wine" offerings help fuel a "bustling" "see-and-be-seen" scene – just be sure to "bring the expense-account card."

Campagnolo *Italian*

-	-	-	M

East Side | 1020 Main St. (bet. Millross & National Aves.) | 604-484-6018 | www.campagnolorestaurant.ca

The focused style at this polished, vibrant salute to rustic Northern Italian cuisine from sommelier Tom Doughty and chef Robert Belcham has drawn crowds since day one to a rapidly revitalized, if still slightly gritty corner of the East Side; beyond the earth tones and exposed beams, diners find an affordable menu that includes housemade meats from The Cure Salumi, located upstairs, matched with wines from a regional list stocked in a cozy rear bar.

Chambar Belgian Restaurant ❶ *Belgian*

26	24	24	E

Downtown | 562 Beatty St. (bet. Dunsmuir & Pender Sts.) | 604-879-7119 | www.chambar.com

"If you can't be in Brussels", this "cool" Downtown Belgian "does a good take" with "top-drawer moules frites", "inventive cocktails" and an "incredible selection" of ales; "even if it's a bit loud", there's "everything to like" about this "not-too-pricey" pre-theater and "party scene", from the industrial decor featuring the works of local artists to an improved Service score for a "fantastic" staff that "treats you like family."

Cioppino's Mediterranean Grill & Enoteca 🗷 *Mediterranean*

28	23	25	VE

Yaletown | 1133 Hamilton St. (bet. Davie & Helmcken Sts.) | 604-688-7466 | www.cioppinosyaletown.com

Pino Posteraro is a "true celebrity chef" assure fans who promise a "profound" "culinary adventure" at this Yaletown Med where "amazing" "modern and traditional fare" is delivered with "extraordinary service" from a "beautiful open kitchen" in the "elegant", earth-hued space; though the "price tag matches his lofty talent" and you might "bring an extra credit card" for the "extensive wine list", it's a "can't-miss dining experience"; P.S. the more rustic-looking Enoteca is next door.

Diva at the Met *Pacific NW*

26	23	25	VE

Downtown | Metropolitan Hotel | 645 Howe St. (bet. Dunsmuir & W. Georgia Sts.) | 604-602-7788 | www.metropolitan.com

From "exquisitely prepared, beautifully plated" contemporary Pacific Northwest apps and entrees to "desserts to die for" to an "impeccable" staff that's "just friendly enough", this Downtown "dream" in the Metropolitan Hotel "has it all"; the contemporary setting of warm woods and marble is "elegant and comfortable", and cognoscenti conclude that yes, it's "expensive, but worth every penny."

Il Giardino di Umberto 🔡 *Italian* 26 | 25 | 25 | E

Downtown | 1382 Hornby St. (Pacific St.) | 604-669-2422 | www.umberto.com

"Legendary" Umberto "never ceases to amaze" *amici* of this Downtown "old-school Italian" "culinary anchor" where the "sumptuous" fare, "impressive, professional service" and "romantic setting" transport patrons to a "Tuscan villa"; sure, it's a wallet-lightener, but between the "movers and shakers" and "movie stars", there's "always a scene", especially on the "pretty patio" populated with even "prettier people."

Keg Steakhouse & Bar *Steak* 20 | 17 | 19 | M

Burnaby | 4510 Stillcreek Ave. (Willingdon Ave.) | 604-294-4626 ●
Downtown | 742 Thurlow St. (bet. Alberni & Robson Sts.) | 604-685-4388
Granville Island | 1499 Anderson St. (bet. Duranleau & Johnston Sts.) | 604-685-4735 ●
Richmond | 11151 No. 5 Rd. (bet. Horseshoe Way & Steveston Hwy.) | 604-272-1399
Surrey | 15146 100th Ave. (152nd St.) | 604-583-6700 ●
Surrey | 15180 32nd Ave. (152nd St.) | 604-542-9733
Surrey | 7948 120th St. (76th Ave.) | 604-591-6161
West Vancouver | Park Royal South Mall | 800 Marine Dr. (Taylor Way) | 604-925-9126 ●
Yaletown | 1011 Mainland St. (Nelson St.) | 604-633-2534
www.kegsteakhouse.com

Meat mavens "craving" a steak maintain this "Canadian success story" chophouse chain "never gets it wrong" with its *Flintstones*-size servings" at "reasonable prices"; fans praise the "quality" fare, and while "atmosphere and crowds vary widely by location" (Yaletown is "hot"), most return for "friendly service" and "good value."

Kingyo ● *Japanese* 26 | 23 | 24 | M

West End | 871 Denman St. (bet. Barclay & Haro Sts.) | 604-608-1677 | www.kingyo-izakaya.com

"Inventive", "eclectic" plates of "hip, well-prepared Japanese tapas" lure partyers to this "highly entertaining" (like to be shouted at?) mid-priced izakaya "tucked away in" the West End; "exotic drinks" from a bar resembling a temple are served by a "perky", "sweet" staff that "explains every dish in detail" while "having a blast", all contributing to the "upbeat" "Tokyo vibe."

Kitanoya Guu *Japanese* 26 | 17 | 20 | M

Downtown | 105-375 Water St. (W. Cordova St.) | 604-685-8682 ●
Downtown | 1698 Robson St. (Bidwell St.) | 604-685-8678 ●
Downtown | 838 Thurlow St. (bet. Robson & Smithe Sts.) | 604-685-8817 ●
Richmond | Aberdeen Center | 4151 Hazelbridge Way (bet. Browngate & Cambie Rds.) | 604-295-6612

Guu Garden ● *Japanese*

Downtown | 888 Nelson St. (Hornby St.) | 604-899-0855
www.guu-izakaya.com

"More adventurous eaters" revel in the "innovative" small-plates "Japanese pub fare" at these "rowdy izakayas", where the "delectable bites" and "whimsical, cheap cocktails" are presented by a "staff that hollers out greetings and orders" while seeming "genuinely happy to serve you"; despite having "to wait for a seat" and decor that's "not pretty", the experience "never disappoints."

La Belle Auberge ⑤Ⓜ *French* | 28 | 23 | 26 | E |

Ladner | 4856 48th Ave. (49th St.) | 604-946-7717 | www.labelleauberge.com

One of Vancouver's "best-kept secrets" and rated No. 1 for Food in the Vancouver Survey, this "world-class" French from "legendary chef" Bruno Marti delivers "divine", "deep flavors" via "exquisite", "seasonal menus" served in a "beautiful", "romantic" 1905 Victorian heritage house tucked away in the Ladner "countryside"; "charming", "impeccable" service completes a "delightful" if pricey dining experience that leaves surveyors who "could rhapsodize endlessly" sighing "I only wish I lived in the neighborhood."

La Buca *Italian* | 26 | 17 | 22 | M |

West Side | 4025 Macdonald St. (bet. 24th & 25th Aves.) | 604-730-6988 | www.labuca.ca

"Go early and often" for chef Andrey Durbach's "muscular" Italian dishes "that aren't afraid to go bold" with "simple, elegant, amazing flavors" root regulars of this "shoebox-sized" trattoria "secreted away" on the West Side; a "most excellent wine list" and "gracious, attentive service" contribute to the "heartwarming" atmosphere and "value", but the "handful" of seats dictate "you must have a reservation."

La Quercia Ⓜ *Italian* | 25 | 19 | 24 | E |

West Side | 3689 W. Fourth Ave. (Alma St.) | 604-676-1007 | www.laquercia.ca

Sandwiched "between a bank and a flower shop", this West Side "gem" of a "small room with a big heart" offers "deceptively simple yet simply delicious" Italian dishes from an "inspired", "hugely talented kitchen" that are delivered by a "knowledgeable, patient staff"; it may be "difficult to get in", but diners sitting "cheek-by-jowl" attest it "deserves the rave reviews."

La Régalade ⑤Ⓜ *French* | 26 | 20 | 23 | M |

West Vancouver | 102-2232 Marine Dr. (bet. 22nd & 23rd Sts.) | 604-921-2228 | www.laregalade.com

"Wonderful, rustic" "traditional French favorites" of "top quality" reign at this "homey", "comforting" West Vancouver bistro where "meat dishes are king" and the "friendly, helpful staff" contributes to the "authentic" ambiance; "portions are enormous" ("and you will try to finish every last bite"), still, those "not counting calories" advise "try to save room" for the "beautiful desserts."

La Terrazza *Italian* | 25 | 25 | 26 | E |

Yaletown | 1088 Cambie St. (Pacific Blvd.) | 604-899-4449 | www.laterrazza.ca

"Long-established" as a "favorite", this "stylish" Yaletown Italian with improved scores in all areas offers "flawless service", "elegant cuisine" and a "serious wine list" say devotees declaring "every detail is looked after"; the "beautiful" quarters with 30-ft. ceilings and a seasonal patio breathe a "wonderful ambiance" and befit "bringing your loved one."

Le Crocodile ☒ French

`27` `23` `27` `VE`

Downtown | 100-909 Burrard St. (Smithe St.) | 604-669-4298 | www.lecrocodilerestaurant.com

Everyone "wants to be a regular" at Michel Jacob's "refined" Downtown French where "phenomenal" "classic cuisine" "with flair" combines with "impeccable service" for an experience that's "pure class"; acolytes aver the "high-end", "extensive, alluring menu" and "excellent wine list" are "the utmost" and "draw you like a magnet" to the "warm", "upscale" bistro setting complete with banquettes and mirrors.

Maenam ● Thai

`26` `21` `24` `M`

West Side | 1938 W. Fourth Ave. (bet. Cypress & Maple Sts.) | 604-730-5579 | www.maenam.ca

"Throw out your preconceptions and try this" "upmarket" West Side Thai, a "bright spot" in Kitsilano offering "authentic, flavorful" plates "expertly executed" by chef-owner Angus An along with "elegant service" in a "modern", warm room with dark bamboo walls; even if some say "portions are small", most deem "prices reasonable" and find that the "flair" of the fare "complements a cool cocktail list."

Market by Jean-Georges French

`26` `25` `24` `E`

Downtown | Shangri-La Hotel | 1128 W. Georgia St. (bet. Bute & Thurlow Sts.) | 604-689-1120 | www.shangri-la.com

Jean-Georges Vongerichten's "hip and happening" outpost for "modern French cuisine in the Shangri-La Hotel has become a "home-run" "hot spot Downtown", offering local seafood and other fare that "lives up to the hype" in "gorgeous surroundings" – including an "impressive dining room", cafe with fireplace and "wonderful outdoor patio"; disciples declare that "servers know their menu", and though it's generally "not inexpensive", the "lunchtime prix fixe is a bargain."

Pear Tree, The ☒Ⓜ Continental

`25` `23` `25` `E`

Burnaby | 4120 E. Hastings St. (bet. Carleton & Gilmore Aves.) | 604-299-2772 | www.peartreerestaurant.net

It may be "a bit off the beaten path", but this "small, inviting" "gem in the heart of North Burnaby" is a "must-visit" for its "fresh", "seasonal" Continental cuisine; "minimalist decor is inviting enough" say locavores hailing chef-owner Scott Jaeger as one who "never ceases to amaze" with "flawless execution", and praising a staff that delivers "rock-steady", "personal" service."

Refuel Pacific NW

`26` `20` `24` `M`

West Side | 1944 W. Fourth Ave. (bet. Cypress & Maple Sts.) | 604-288-7905 | www.refuelrestaurant.com

"Fast for a few days" before dining at this West Side "mainstay locavore" suggest the "dazzled" denizens who vie for the "most coveted seats" across from chef Robert Belcham's "open kitchen" to watch the "obsessively sourced" Pacific Nortwest menus take shape; sommelier Tom Doughty oversees an "impressive cellar", and the "service can be amazing" in the "chic" but "understated" room; a post-Survey change from a white-linen experience to a more informal, less-pricey style including whole-hog suppers is not reflected in the Food score.

	FOOD	DECOR	SERVICE	COST

Shiro Japanese *Japanese*
27 | 14 | 21 | M

West Side | 3096 Cambie St. (W. 15th Ave.) | 604-874-0027

Raw fish fanciers "sit at the bar" and "watch the chef move gracefully" preparing "impeccably fresh", "authentic sushi" at this "tiny", "no-nonsense" West Side Japanese; so what if it's "cramped" say regulars who appreciate the "friendly staff" and insist that "at its cost", "it just doesn't get any better."

Tojo's ⊠ *Japanese*
27 | 21 | 24 | VE

West Side | 1133 W. Broadway (bet. Alder & Spruce Sts.) | 604-872-8050 | www.tojos.com

"Bring along your adventuresome persona", "sit at the bar" and "throw yourself at the mercy" of "passionate artist"/chef-owner Hidekazu Tojo "to fully experience" the "individual service" and "sublime", "exceptionally fresh" "fruits of the ocean" in "imaginative" presentations at this Japanese "pinnacle of sushi" located on the West Side; in the "almost cavernous" setting, surveyors say you're likely to "rub shoulders with movie stars, millionaires and artists" – just make sure to "have a rock star's wallet."

Vij's *Indian*
28 | 22 | 25 | E

West Side | 1480 W. 11th Ave. (bet. Granville & Hemlock Sts.) | 604-736-6664 | www.vijsrestaurant.ca

Those who "dream about lamb popsicles on a regular basis" have "champion of hospitality" Vikram Vij to thank, and they've voted his "hip, vibrant" West Sider Vancouver's Most Popular for its "unequivocal", "unforgettable" "Indian fusion" "experience"; regulars revel in "inspirational", "skillful preparations" incorporating "old-world spices" and delivered with "service like a ballet", and though "no reservations" are accepted, even "waiting for a table is an art form" with "complimentary appetizers in the bar."

Vij's Rangoli *Indian*
26 | 19 | 23 | M

West Side | 1488 W. 11th Ave. (bet. Granville & Hemlock Sts.) | 604-736-5711 | www.vijsrangoli.ca

Vijionaries who "don't have time" for the "eternal wait" next door score the "same delicious tastes" in the Indian "fast food with flair" ("but less formality") at this West Side "poor man's hit of heaven"; even though you might have to "elbow aside the ladies who lunch for a table", "attentive service" adds to the "cheerful" "cafeteria" atmosphere, and home cooks "love the option" of "fresh and frozen takeout."

West *Pacific NW*
27 | 24 | 26 | VE

West Side | 2881 Granville St. (W. 13th Ave.) | 604-738-8938 | www.westrestaurant.com

"Those who love exciting" cuisine "can't wait to go back" for the "imaginative", "perfectly prepared and artfully presented" seasonal Pacific Northwest plates at this "lively, congenial and sophisticated" West Sider that's a "tour de force" serving "heaven in every bite"; delivering a "full package" of "impeccable service", "incredible tasting menus" and "superb" vintages from a "must-see wall of wine", it's naturally "not inexpensive", but is "worth it" for a "truly fabulous" "night to remember."

EUROPE
RESTAURANT
DIRECTORY

Amsterdam

TOP FOOD RANKING

	Restaurant	Cuisine
28	Ron Blaauw	French/International
27	Yamazato	Japanese
	Van Vlaanderen	French/Mediterranean
	La Rive	French/Mediterranean
26	Bordewijk	French/Mediterranean
	Christophe'	French
	Blaauw aan de Wal	French/Mediterranean
	Visaandeschelde	International/Seafood
24	Chez Georges	Belgian/French
	Vermeer	French/International
	De Silveren Spiegel	Dutch
	Dylan	French
	Beddington's	French/Asian
23	Tempo Doeloe	Indonesian
	De Kas	Dutch/Mediterranean
	Vinkeles	French
	Aan de Poel	International
	Blue Pepper	Indonesian

Aan de Poel ⓈⓂ *International*   23 | 21 | 21 | E

Amstelveen | Handweg 1 | (31-20) 345-1763 | www.restaurantaandepoel.nl
"Ready-to-eat works of art" are the specialty of this "delicious"
International on the outskirts of Amsterdam in Amstelveen, where the
"passion for food" is quite evident; while the "modern" interior is "lovely"
in a "minimalist" way and the service "enthusiastic", it's the "beautiful
terrace" overlooking a "small lake" that draws the most applause.

NEW Anna Ⓢ *International*   - | - | - | E

Centrum | Warmoesstraat III | (31-20) 428-1111 | www.restaurntanna.nl
Located near the red light district in one of the most historic parts of
Amsterdam, this Centrum venue offers International dishes (tuna tartare, sauteed scallops a la plancha, veal entrecôte) in both prix fixe and
à la carte options plus 20 wines by the glass; wood floors and an earth-
tone color scheme give the interior a relaxed vibe, and diners can sit in an
outdoor terrace overlooking a medieval church square in nice weather.

Beddington's ⓈⓂ *French/Asian*   24 | 18 | 18 | E

Frederiksplein | Utrechtsedwarsstraat 141 | (31-20) 620-7393 |
www.beddington.nl
"Run by female chef" Jean Beddington, this "nice place" in Frederiksplein
offers a "hot menu" of "inventive" French-Asian dishes; still, some find
the "small", "sober" space with "only a few tables" somewhat "cold"
and suggest the "informal (but correct) service" "could use work."

Blaauw aan de Wal ⓈⓂ *French/Mediterranean*   26 | 22 | 23 | E

Centrum | Oudezijds Achterburgwal 99 | (31-20) 330-2257 |
www.blaauwaandewal.com
"Hidden away" at the end of an alley in the Centrum, this "small", "serene" spot with its own "private dining terrace" offers a "great respite

from the Red Light District" around the corner; its "cozy, peaceful" setting is home to "enthusiastic" staffers serving "terrific" French-Med fare "made from the best ingredients" and accompanied by a "well-selected" wine list; no wonder so many consider this "special place" to be "absolutely wonderful."

Blue Pepper *Indonesian* | 23 | 20 | 22 | M |
Centrum | Nassaukade 366 | (31-20) 489-7039 | www.restaurantbluepepper.com
Those seeking something beyond the "standard rijsttafel" head for this "top-notch" Centrum "treat" where a "creative" kitchen delivers "delicious" nouveau Indonesian dishes that are "full of flavor"; the "friendly staff" provides equally "sizzling service" and will happily "inform you about the details of the menu", though insiders insist that the "tasting menu is a must."

NEW Bolenius ⊠ *Dutch* | – | – | – | E |
Oud-Zuid | George Gershwinlaan 30 | (31-20) 404-4411 | www.bolenius-restaurant.nl
Vegetables come right from the kitchen garden at this Oud-Zuid Dutch offering artfully presented contemporary fare (including a number of prix fixe options) backed by a diverse wine list, including many by the glass; the stylish interior features an open kitchen, glass wine cabinets and wood-topped tables, and alfresco fans will enjoy terrace seating.

Bordewijk ⓜ *French/Mediterranean* | 26 | 18 | 23 | E |
Jordaan | Noordermarkt 7 | (31-20) 624-3899 | www.bordewijk.nl
The chef visits your table and "takes your order" at this "terrific place" in Jordaan, a "favorite" for its "incredible" French-Med "haute cuisine", "comprehensive wine list" and "fantastic" service; still, some sigh it's "too bad" the "noisy room" distracts, adding that it's also "less inviting" to tourists since the staff is not as welcoming "if you're not a native."

Chez Georges ⊠ⓜ *Belgian/French* | 24 | 21 | 23 | E |
Jordaan | Herenstraat 3 | (31-20) 626-3332
"It's always full" at this tiny Jordaan venue in the nicest part of Amsterdam, because the "beautifully classic" Belgian-French cuisine is "superb", particularly the "great-value" five-course tasting menu; a "staff that takes such pride in what it serves" and a "charming", "civilized" interior are other pluses; P.S. open Thursday–Saturday only.

Christophe' ⊠ⓜ *French* | 26 | 22 | 24 | VE |
Jordaan | Leliegracht 46 | (31-20) 625-0807 | www.restaurantchristophe.nl
"Brilliantly inventive", "beautifully presented" dishes that combine "upscale French cuisine" with "Mediterranean ingredients" and "African influences" "delight the eye and palate" at this canal-side Jordaan "jewel" manned by an "eager-to-please staff"; most report "a special night out", though a few think the atmosphere is "rather dull" – it's "as quiet and peaceful as the floral arrangements, and about as lively."

De Culinaire Werkplaats ⊠⊄ *International* | – | – | – | M |
Oud-West | Fannius Scholtenstraat 10 Huis | (31-20) 654-646-576 | www.deculinairewerkplaats.nl
The multicourse menu focused on vegetables, fruits and grains changes monthly (and is based around a theme) at this part design

studio, part International restaurant in Oud-West featuring a fully open kitchen; owners Marjolein Wintjes (designer) and Eric Meursing (chef) take their unique concept even further with regard to the bill – cocktails have a price but otherwise diners pay what they think is fair.

De Kas 🅕 *Dutch/Mediterranean*   23 | 26 | 21 | E

Oost | Frankendael Park | Kamerlingh Onneslaan 3 | (31-20) 462-4562 | www.restaurantdekas.nl

Set in an "impressively large" greenhouse situated in Frankendael Park in Oost, this "sparkling glass temple to food" takes the use of local, mostly organic ingredients to a "whole new level", creating a daily prix fixe menu of "stellar" Dutch-Med fare "based upon the day's harvest"; whether seated in the "stunning dining room" or on the "lovely terrace", expect an "absolutely enchanting" experience as you "inhale the heady fragrances" of "fresh vegetables and herbs" growing all around you.

De Silveren Spiegel 🅕 *Dutch*   24 | 22 | 22 | VE

Centrum | Kattengat 4-6 | (31-20) 624-6589 | www.desilverenspiegel.com

This "beautiful historic" Centrum treat "tucked away" near Centraal Station may be so "old" (circa 1614) that it "looks as though it's falling over", but its kitchen still "impresses" with an "interesting" array of "well-executed" "nouvelle Dutch" dishes; the "quaint" setting with "candles and lead-glass windows" exudes a "warm", "intimate" vibe abetted by a "great wine list" and "gracious" service.

D'Vijff Vlieghen *Dutch*   21 | 23 | 20 | E

Centrum | Spuistraat 294-302 | (31-20) 530-4060 | www.thefiveflies.com

"Small rooms connected by narrow winding corridors" spanning "five charming old houses" form a "marvelous" backdrop for this "Amsterdam institution" (voted the city's Most Popular restaurant) that's "still going strong" in the Centrum, serving "flavorful" Dutch dishes that are more "contemporary" than you'd expect; still, some say it's "living on its reputation" and complain that it's "chronically overfilled" with "tons of tourists" and "complacent", "slow" servers – so be prepared for a "long (though memorable) evening."

Dylan, The 🅕 *French*   24 | 26 | 23 | VE

Centrum | Dylan Hotel | Keizersgracht 384 | (31-20) 530-2010 | www.dylanamsterdam.com

This "don't-miss place" within the "hip" Dylan Hotel in the Centrum may be "trendy" because of its "sleek, cool" design, but it also "wows" foodies with its "beautifully presented" French brasserie-style cuisine; indeed, it's "tremendous across the board", save for the "stuck-up", "take-themselves-too-seriously" staff.

La Rive 🅕 *French/Mediterranean*   27 | 26 | 26 | VE

Oost | InterContinental Amstel | Professor Tulpplein 1 | (31-20) 520-3264 | www.restaurantlarive.nl

"You know you've a-Rived" when you dine at this "breathtaking waterfront" venue right on the river in the city's "premier hotel", the InterContinental Amstel in Oost; the "fabulous views" are abetted by "phenomenal" French-Med food, a "grand" setting and "wonderful" staffers willing to "wait on you hand and foot"; P.S. in the summer, "dine waterside" on the "beautiful terrace."

	FOOD	DECOR	SERVICE	COST

Le Restaurant 🅱️Ⓜ️🔄 *French/International* | - | - | - | VE |

Oud-Zuid | Tweede Jan-Steenstraat 3 | (31-20) 379-2207 | www.le-restaurant.nl

Foodies flock to this dinner-only French-International in Oud-Zuid serving chef-owner Jan de Wit's pricey tasting menu of classic dishes with a modern twist (and no vegetarian options); the intimate, white-tablecloth dining room features an open kitchen, and with only 22 seats, reservations are strongly recommended; P.S. cash-only.

Ron Blaauw | 28 | - | 24 | VE |

Amsterdam 🅱️Ⓜ️ *French/International*

Oud-Zuid | Sophialaan 55 | (31-20) 305-2760 | www.ronblaauw.nl

This "wonderful" French-International relocated from Ouderkerk aan de Amstel to new digs in Oud-Zuid, but the same "consistently high-quality" cuisine featuring "creative, tapaslike dishes" made with local products (including vegetables from its own garden) remains, making it No. 1 for Food in Amsterdam; servers who ensure "you're really pampered" plus a comfortable white-tablecloth dining room, complete with an open kitchen and marble bar, add to the experience; P.S. there's terrace seating in season.

🆕 Ron's Vis Van de Dag Ⓜ️ *Seafood* | - | - | - | M |

Ouderkerk aan de Amstel | Kerkstraat 56 | (31-20) 496-5848 | www.ronsvisvandedag.nl

Located in the former Ron Blaauw space in Ouderkerk aan de Amstel, this lower-priced sibling offers seafood galore (its name means fish of the day), plus tapas and a few meat dishes for the fin phobic; the ocean-centric theme carries over to the decor, with black-and-white fish enlivening the walls of the contemporary dining room; P.S. there's terrace seating.

Tempo Doeloe *Indonesian* | 23 | 15 | 19 | M |

Rembrandtplein | Utrechtsestraat 75 | (31-20) 625-6718 | www.tempodoeloerestaurant.nl

"Fantastic fare" keeps the trade brisk at this "classic" Indonesian *rijsttafel* purveyor, a "moderately priced" (and "crowded") Amsterdam "favorite" in "beautiful" Rembrandtplein, where the "patient servers will explain the menu"; a few say the "stuffy atmosphere" and "tight quarters" detract, but "foodies would travel far for cooking this authentic."

Van Vlaanderen 🅱️Ⓜ️ *French/Mediterranean* | 27 | 20 | 24 | E |

Leidseplein | Weteringschans 175 | (31-20) 622-8292 | www.restaurant-vanvlaanderen.nl

An "antidote to trendy places", this "lovely, low-key" spot in the Leidseplein purveys "fantastic" French-Med fare that "pleasantly surprises"; perhaps the "small", "informal" setting doesn't do justice to the "caliber of cuisine" (there's "not much space between the tables"), but nevertheless it's a "quiet" refuge from the "heart of the action", and the "capable waiters do their utmost to make your dinner a success."

Vermeer 🅱️ *French/International* | 24 | 23 | 24 | VE |

Centrum | NH Barbizon Palace Hotel | Prins Hendrikkade 59-72 | (31-20) 556-4885 | www.restaurantvermeer.nl

"Outstanding cuisine" is the hallmark of this "top-class" "favorite" in the Centrum's NH Barbizon Palace Hotel, where the French-

| | FOOD | DECOR | SERVICE | COST |

International food is "amazing" and the wine list "elaborate"; some find the dining room "elegant", others "a bit stiff", but all agree the "friendly staff" provides "impeccable service" at this overall "enjoyable" experience.

Vinkeles *French*

| 23 | 24 | 23 | VE |

Jordaan | The Dylan | Keizersgracht 384 | (31-20) 530-2010 | www.vinkeles.com

Set in an "atmospheric old bakery", this "posh" dining room in Jordaan's "hip" Dylan hotel offers an "exemplary" modern French menu in a "quiet yet sophisticated" milieu; yes, it's "quite expensive, even for Amsterdam", but in return you get "knowledgeable" service and an overall "impeccable attention to detail"; P.S. patrons can now make reservations to dine onboard a renovated wooden boat as it tours the canals.

Visaandeschelde *International/Seafood*

| 26 | 20 | 21 | E |

Rivierenbuurt | Scheldeplein 4 | (31-20) 675-1583 | www.visaandeschelde.nl

Fans seeking "wonderful" International cuisine with a "focus on seafood" head for this "very hip place" that's "a little out of the way" in the Rivierenbuurt; look for "really great fish" dishes (incorporating Japanese, French and Mediterranean influences) that are "nicely served" at "well-situated tables" by a "stellar" crew; P.S. "don't forget the excellent wines."

NEW Wilde Zwijnen Ⓜ *Dutch/International*

| - | - | - | M |

Amsterdam | Javaplein 3 | (31-20) 463-3043 | www.wildezwijnen.com

There might not be wild boar (its name's English translation) on the menu at this affordable Dutch venue, but diners will find seasonal dishes accented by French and Italian flavors (roasted pork chops, baked duck, fava ravioli) plus a compact wine list; a concrete floor, exposed light bulbs and scrap-wood furniture give it an industrial yet chic look popular with young professionals.

Yamazato *Japanese*

| 27 | 19 | 25 | VE |

Pijp | Hotel Okura | Ferdinand Bolstraat 333 | (31-20) 678-8351 | www.yamazato.nl

For "real Japanese food", this "absolute treat" in the Pijp's Hotel Okura serves "fresh", "fabulous presentations" of "some of the best sushi in Europe" along with other "outstanding" offerings, accompanied by an "extensive sake list"; given the "costly" tabs, it's too bad the "decor doesn't quite reach the same level", but "excellent service" from a "tri-lingual staff" more than compensates.

Athens

TOP FOOD RANKING

	Restaurant	Cuisine
29	Spondi	French/Mediterranean
27	Varoulko	Mediterranean/Seafood
26	Matsuhisa Athens	Japanese
	Milos	Greek/Seafood
	Papadakis	Greek/Seafood
25	GB Corner	Mediterranean
24	Ithaki	Mediterranean/Seafood
	7 Thalasses	Greek/Seafood
23	Hytra	Greek
	Il Buco*	Italian
	Ta Kioupia	Greek/Mediterranean
	Sale e Pepe	Italian
22	Alatsi	Greek
	Daphne's	Greek/Mediterranean
	Balthazar	Mediterranean
	Baraonda	Mediterranean
	Dionysos Zonar's	Greek/Mediterranean
21	Mamacas	Greek
20	Electra Roof Garden	Greek/Mediterranean
	Kafeneio*	Greek

Alatsi ●⊠ *Greek*   22 | 16 | 19 | E

Pangrati | Vrasida 13 | (30-210) 721-0501 | www.alatsi.gr

It "doesn't get any better if you're looking" for hearty "tastes from Crete" attest admirers of this Pangrati Greek; the flower-filled patio and prix fixe menus make it a "good choice for lunch" or dinner – just make sure you have time to linger as service can be a "little slow."

Balthazar ● *Mediterranean*   22 | 22 | 20 | E

Ampelokipi | Tsoha 27 & Bournazou | (30-210) 641-2300 | www.balthazar.gr

"The perfect venue for an Athenian night out", this "trendy" "see-and-be-seen" spot set in the "middle of Ampelokipi" serves up "tasty" Med fare that's "better than expected" "albeit expensive"; opt for the "beautiful garden" that's "especially nice in the summer" or settle inside the "dramatic" 100-plus-year-old mansion and soak up the scene ("after 12 AM, it's more like a club") – just "don't expect to be served" pronto.

Baraonda ● *Mediterranean*   22 | 24 | 20 | E

Ampelokipi | Tsoha 43-45 | (30-210) 644-4308 | www.baraonda.gr

Past the doorman and heavy black doors lies this "fine-dining" Mediterranean in Ampelokipi, a trendy lair serving "tasty", "consistent" fare in a "club"-like atmosphere; the "nice bar scene" gets "lively after hours", when media people, celebrities and hip twentysomethings slip into the lounge that's hung with red-velvet curtains and chandeliers to sip specialty cocktails and dance the night away.

---

* Indicates a tie with restaurant above

	FOOD	DECOR	SERVICE	COST

Daphne's *Greek/Mediterranean*
22 | 20 | 21 | E

Plaka | Lysikratous 4 | (30-210) 322-7971 | www.daphnesrestaurant.gr
"Pleasant" and "intimate" with "plenty of pure" Greek-Med fare on offer, this "well-sited" destination in a renovated neoclassical home "epitomizes the energy of the Plaka"; "traditional" decor enhanced by "garden tables" and a mural painted by the owner, plus a staff that "treats you like they know you", adds up to a "great Athens experience."

Dionysos Zonar's ⓜ *Greek/Mediterranean*
22 | 26 | 22 | E

Athens | 43 Robertou Galli | (30-210) 923-3282 | www.dionysoszonars.gr
It's all about "location, location, location" at this bi-level Greek-Med featuring floor-to-ceiling windows that afford diners an "incomparable view of the Acropolis", making it "one of the most romantic" retreats around; while the food is "tasty" and prices are "fair", it's the "magnificent" "vistas" that stand out in this "memorable" experience.

Electra Roof Garden *Greek/Mediterranean*
20 | 25 | 21 | E

Plaka | Electra Palace Hotel Athens | Nikodimou 18-20 |
(30-210) 337-0000 | www.electrahotels.gr
Greek-Med fare and "inspired" cocktails draw a mixed crowd to this dinner-only perch atop the Plaka's Electra Palace Hotel, a standout "not to be missed at night" for its "breathtaking, unobstructed view of the illuminated Acropolis" ("bring your camera"); though it might be a little "pricey", fans say it's "worth every euro", particularly when you can dine alfresco on a "summer night."

GB Corner *Mediterranean*
25 | 25 | 24 | VE

Syntagma | Hotel Grande Bretagne | Syntagma Sq. | (30-210) 333-0750 |
www.grandebretagne.gr
"Go at least once" to this "traditional" titan set in the lobby of the "truly grand", "historic Grande Bretagne" Hotel near Syntagma Square, where "wonderful Mediterranean cuisine", "attentive" service and an "excellent ambiance" prompts devotees to declare "you haven't done Athens properly" without a visit here (despite the "high" prices); the separately operated GB Roof Garden upstairs bewitches "day and night" with its "breathtaking", "romantic views of the Acropolis and the Parliament."

Hytra ⬤ⓜ *Greek*
23 | 20 | 23 | E

Psiri | Navarhou Apostoli 7 | (30-210) 331-6767 or 707-1118 |
www.hytra.gr

Galazia Hytra ⬤ⓜ *Greek*

Vouliagmeni | Astir Palace Hotel | 40 Apollonos St. | (30-210) 890-1556
This "cozy" Psiri Greek and its Vouliagmeni offshoot in a "magnificent location" inside the Astir Palace Hotel win favor for dishes filled with "wonderful flavors" and delivered with "lovely service"; while not a "trendy" choice, most concede "they try very hard and largely get it right"; P.S. Hytra is open October–May and Galazia Hytra is open mid-April–September.

NEW Il Buco ⬤ⓜ *Italian*
23 | 23 | 23 | E

Psiri | Sachtouri 2 | (30-210) 321-9388 | www.ilbuco.gr
"Pleasantly surprised" first-timers are "happy" to return to this eatery in trendy Psiri proffering Roman fare "based on what's available" sea-

sonally, including "outstanding house charcuterie" and "fresh" pasta; the century-old neoclassical building entices with its minimalist design plus views of the Acropolis.

Ithaki ● *Mediterranean/Seafood*   24 | 23 | 23 | VE

Vouliagmeni | 28 Apollonos | (30-210) 896-3747 | www.ithakirestaurantbar.gr

"Beg, borrow or steal, but get thee" to this "seductive" Vouliagmeni "seaside" "treasure" specializing in "simply excellent" Mediterranean seafood urge its "devout" fans; diners also drink in the "most beautiful scenery", including "unbeatable" views of the Saronic Gulf, so while prices are "astronomical", all chorus it's "worth the money."

Kafeneio Ⓩ *Greek*   20 | 14 | 20 | M

Kolonaki | Loukianou 26 | (30-210) 723-7757

"Watch the crowds" from your sidewalk perch at this "solid" Greek in the "central shopping area" of trendy Kolonaki where patrons sample "simple but very tasty" "well-made classics" for the "right" price; those in the know warn it's "not a place for intimate conversation", so instead just sit back and enjoy the "see-and-be-seen" "scene."

Matsuhisa Athens ● *Japanese*   26 | 24 | 24 | VE

Vouliagmeni | Astir Palace Hotel | 40 Apollonos | (30-210) 896-0510 | www.matsuhisaathens.com

"Famed" chef Nobu Matsuhisa lures the "beautiful" people to Athens' Most Popular restaurant with his "internationally tested" Japanese–South American creations including an "amazing" omakase menu, all proffered in an "unbeatable location" in Vouliagmeni's Astir Palace Hotel complex; yes, it's "pricey", but the "gorgeous" wood-and-marble setting plus sunset views of the Aegean prompt patrons to proclaim it "worth every euro."

Milos ● *Greek/Seafood*   26 | 21 | 24 | VE

Kolonaki | Hilton Athens | Vassilissis Sofias Ave. 46 | (30-210) 724-4400 | www.milos.ca

"Whether you're in NYC, Montréal" or this "jet-set location" in the landmark Hilton Athens, chef-owner Costas Spiliades makes "you feel like you're coming home" with his "tantalizing" Greek dishes made with "top-notch" ingredients; the "contemporary" decor is "white, crisp and relaxing", but be warned that it all comes with tabs priced for the "expense-account set."

Papadakis ●Ⓩ *Greek/Seafood*   26 | 19 | 22 | E

Kolonaki | Voukourestiou 47 & Fokilidou 15 | (30-210) 360-8621

Chef/cookbook author/TV host Argiro Barbarigou operates this sea-fooder on a citrus-tree-lined street in Kolonaki, offering "varied choices" of "excellent" "Greek food with a twist" that's "innovative yet true to traditional tastes"; though the minimalist interior may be a bit "plain", it's "comfortable."

Sale e Pepe ●Ⓩ *Italian*   23 | 17 | 20 | E

Kolonaki | Aristippou 34 | (30-210) 723-4102

"Simply great" say well-heeled oenophiles who settle into this cozy, rustic trattoria in Kolonaki near Lycabettus Hill to "enjoy" classic Italian dishes like risotto, langoustine salad and grilled polenta; fans proclaim it to have the "best wine list in Athens" made up of 500 inter-national choices from its vast cellar; P.S. check out the tasting events.

7 Thalasses ◐🗷 *Greek/Seafood*

| 24 | 21 | 23 | E |

Kolonaki | Omirou 11 & Vissarionos | (30-210) 362-4825

"Sea-foodies delight" in this stylish, nautically themed Kolonaki "gem", a "lively" Greek spot where an excellent staff serves a "choice of fresh fish that's just incredible"; regulars suggest checking out the "daily offerings", adding that while some dishes may be a bit "pricey", they're "well worth" the few extra clams.

Spondi ◐ *French/Mediterranean*

| 29 | 25 | 27 | VE |

Pangrati | Varnavas Sq. | Pyrronos 5 | (30-210) 756-4021 | www.spondi.gr

"Innovative" chef Arnaud Bignon "delights" "foodies" with "superb", "creative" cuisine, capped with desserts that "take you to the stars" plus a humongous wine list that "never fails to please", at this "little bit of" French-Mediterranean "heaven", rated No. 1 for Food in Athens and "in a class of its own"; the city's only Relais & Châteaux restaurant, it's set in a tri-level Pangrati villa covered in flowering plants, and patrons can "dine on the patio in warm weather" before bracing for the "astronomical" bill.

Ta Kioupia ◐ *Greek/Mediterranean*

| 23 | 22 | 24 | E |

Kolonaki | Dinokratous & An. Polemou 22 | (30-210) 740-0150 | www.takioupia.gr

Though the family that owns it has been in the business for decades, this eatery still manages to be "one of the best-kept secrets" in Kolonaki, serving "simply enjoyable" Greek-Med fare including veal steaks and clay-pot dishes; the two-floor, high-ceilinged digs boast classic white linens and a petite terrace overlooking Lycabettus Hill, prompting patrons to sigh isn't it "romantic"?

Varoulko ◐�💡🗷 *Mediterranean/Seafood*

| 27 | 20 | 24 | VE |

Kerameikos | Pireos 80 | (30-210) 522-8400 | www.varoulko.gr

There's "no menu" – instead, a server "asks your limitations" and chef-owner Lefteris Lazarou "cooks accordingly" at this dinner-only Med seafood mecca in historic Kerameikos where the "unique, delicious" fare is backed by "the best Greek wines"; critics call the interior "a bit dated", but if you "request outdoor terrace dining", the rooftop offers "breathtaking nighttime views of the Acropolis."

Barcelona

TOP FOOD RANKING

	Restaurant	Cuisine
28	Cinc Sentits	Catalan
27	Passadis del Pep	Mediterranean/Seafood
	Hofmann	Mediterranean
	Cal Pep	Mediterranean/Seafood
	Neichel	Mediterranean
	Gaig	Catalan
26	Yashima	Japanese
	ÀBaC	Catalan
	Arola	Catalan
	Jaume de Provença	Catalan
	Els Pescadors	International/Seafood
	Ca l'Isidre	Catalan/Mediterranean
	Botafumeiro	Galician/Seafood
	Drolma	Catalan
	Casa Leopoldo	Mediterranean/Seafood
	Tapas 24	Catalan
25	Bilbao	Catalan
	Comerç 24	International
	Alkimia	Catalan

ÀBaC ⚅Ⓜ *Catalan*   26 | 24 | 25 | VE

Sarrià-Sant Gervasi | Avda. Tibidabo1 | (34) 93-319-6600 |
www.abacbarcelona.com
"Exceptional", "imaginative" food by chef Jordi Cruz dazzles diners
at this "unique" upper Sant Gervasi Catalan with a "chic", "tranquil" hotel setting; "top-notch" treatment completes the
"unforgettable" experience, so fans say "forget the cost" and have a
"once-in-a-lifetime" meal.

Alkimia ⚅ *Catalan*   25 | 22 | 24 | E

Gràcia | Indústria 79 | (34) 93-207-6115 | www.alkimia.cat
"Playful and whimsical" yet "dead serious about flavor profiles",
this "superb" Gràcia Catalan by chef Jordi Vilà beckons with "inventive" dishes served by a "knowledgeable", "professional" staff
in a "minimalist" setting; though "not cheap", it offers real "value
for the money", and fans of the "delicious" tasting menus advise "go
big or go home."

Arola *Catalan*   26 | 24 | 24 | VE

Port Olímpic | Hotel Arts | Marina 19-21 | (34) 93-483-8090 |
www.arola-arts.com
"Epicures" enthuse over the "sophisticated tapas" and other "outstanding" dishes matched by "exciting Spanish wines" at this "modern" Catalan by Sergi Arola, a disciple of Ferran Adrià, in the Hotel
Arts; "superb" service and "lots of atmosphere", complete with "magnificent views" of Olympic Harbor plus live music and DJs on the
weekends, mean it's "excellent" all around – just "be prepared to
pay the price."

	FOOD	DECOR	SERVICE	COST

Bilbao ⌗ *Catalan* — 25 | 19 | 21 | E

Gràcia | Perill 33 | (34) 93-458-9624

"You'll eat extremely well" at this Gràcia longtimer serving "terrific typical Catalan" food and wine in a traditional setting occupying two floors of a 19th-century townhouse; though it may not be "luxurious", it's just right for sampling some "unparalleled" specialties without an exorbitant bill.

Botafumeiro ● *Galician/Seafood* — 26 | 21 | 24 | VE

Gràcia | Gran de Gràcia 81 | (34) 93-218-4230 | www.botafumeiro.es

"Exquisite" seafood is the "strong point" of this "classic", high-end Galician in Gràcia with a "busy" yet "elegant" vibe where "old-guard businesspeople" and other "locals and tourists" mix; the staff "goes out of its way" to ensure an "enjoyable" meal, and insiders advise "try to get a seat at the bar" for the liveliest (and most economical) time.

Ca l'Isidre ⌗ *Catalan/Mediterranean* — 26 | 21 | 25 | VE

Raval | Les Flors 12 | (34) 93-441-1139 | www.calisidre.com

"On a little side street" in the Raval, this "welcoming", "family-owned" place excels in "quality and freshness" with its seasonally attuned Catalan-Med cuisine and "sublime" desserts by chef Núria Gironés, daughter of owner Isidre; though pricey and perhaps "no longer in fashion" (and "thus easy to get a table"), it's still "very popular with the locals" thanks to a "gentle, caring attitude" among the staff and an "old-world", "less-is-more" dining room decorated with original Picassos and Mirós.

Cal Pep ⌗ *Mediterranean/Seafood* — 27 | 17 | 22 | E

Born-Ribera | Plaça de les Olles 8 | (34) 93-310-7961 | www.calpep.com

"Put yourself in the hands of the chefs and see what they bring you" at "spirited" owner Pep Manubens' "imitated but never equaled" tapas bar in El Born, known for "impeccable" Mediterranean seafood "cooked in a simple manner retaining all its flavor"; be prepared to "line up" for a seat at the "extremely long counter", but the "highly rewarding", "unbelievable" meal is "worth the wait" and the "splurge"; P.S. "if you're lucky" you'll be "sharing dishes" with your neighbors.

Casa Leopoldo Ⓜ *Mediterranean/Seafood* — 26 | 20 | 23 | E

Raval | Sant Rafael 24 | (34) 93-441-3014 | www.casaleopoldo.com

Simply "enchanting", this "well-preserved, traditional" Raval seafooder dating back to 1929 serves "excellent" Mediterranean "market food" that's a "favorite of gastronomes" in a "narrow", tiled dining room; though "somewhat expensive", it's "always full" and "noisy" with folks who appreciate its "consistent" quality.

Cinc Sentits ⌗ *Catalan* — 28 | 22 | 26 | VE

Eixample | Aribau 58 | (34) 93-323-9490 | www.cincsentits.com

"Simply sublime", this "completely original" Eixample Catalan (rated No. 1 for Food in Barcelona) takes you on a "roller coaster ride to bliss", "delighting at every turn" with its "imaginative, delicious" tasting menus by chef Jordi Artal; the "simple" room offers an understated backdrop as an "impeccable" staff provides "perfect" service and "premium" wine pairings, so go ahead and "treat yourself" – it more than "lives up to expectations."

	FOOD	DECOR	SERVICE	COST

Comerç 24 ☒Ⓜ *International*
25 | 22 | 24 | E

Born-Ribera | Comerç 24 | (34) 93-319-2102 | www.comerc24.com
"Every bite's a spectacular celebration of flavor" at this "daring", "popular" International tapas bar in El Born showcasing "surprising" "molecular preparations" by chef-owner Carles Abellán, a former "pupil" of Ferran Adrià; the "modern" space, "sublime" wines and "knowledgeable" service enhance the "awesome (but not cheap)" experience, so "even at the bar you feel like a king"; P.S. reserve ahead and "be prepared to dine for a few hours."

Drolma ☒ *Catalan*
26 | 25 | 26 | VE

Eixample | Hotel Majestic | Passeig de Gràcia 68 | (34) 93-496-7710 | www.drolmarestaurant.cat
"Old-world elegance and service" set the stage for "creative haute" Catalan cuisine, "beautifully prepared" by chef Fermí Puig at this "graceful" Eixample destination in the Hotel Majestic; while an "expensive" price tag is part of the package, it remains a "top" choice to "make an impression" and indulge among power players in an "expense-account" treat.

El Asador de Aranda ☒ *Castilian*
24 | 22 | 22 | E

Eixample | Londres 90 | (34) 93-414-6790
Eixample | Pau Claris 70 | (34) 93-342-5577
Tibidabo | Avda. del Tibidabo 31 | (34) 93-417-0115 ◑
www.asadordearanda.com
"You always eat well" at this Tibidabo destination in a Castilian chain (with two Eixample branches), where "fantastic" roast lamb is the star of a "limited" but "stupendous" menu; its "clean, well-decorated" dining room in a Modernista mansion partway up "a mountain overlooking Barcelona" makes it ideal for big "banquets" and other "special occasions", though a few admit "it hurts when the check comes."

Els Pescadors ◑ *International/Seafood*
26 | 19 | 22 | E

Poblenou | Plaça Prim 1 | (34) 93-225-2018 | www.elspescadors.com
"They really know how to cook fish" at this "first-class" Poblenou seafooder providing "perfect" preparations with International "variety" in a "quiet place outside of the tourist trail"; while both the service and interior are "adequate", the summer terrace is "just a miracle", and though a "little expensive", the overall quality makes prices seem "modest."

Gaig *Catalan*
27 | 24 | 25 | VE

Eixample | Cram Hotel | Aragó 214 | (34) 93-429-1017 | www.restaurantgaig.com
"Tradition and modernity" meet at this "refined rustic" Eixample classic dating back to 1869, where "genius" chef Carles Gaig crafts "excellent" "modern Catalan" cuisine that some call "El Bulli light"; with a "hotel setting" boasting "top-notch" service and fine "people-watching", it's a pricey place, but "one of the big ones" to hit.

Hofmann ☒ *Mediterranean*
27 | 24 | 26 | E

Gràcia | La Granada del Penedès 14-16 | (34) 93-218-7165 | www.hofmann-bcn.com
"Right up there" on the top tier, this "busy" restaurant/culinary school by chef/owner/teacher Mey Hofmann delivers "incredible"

Mediterranean dishes and pastries "beyond words" amid sleek, multi-room surroundings in an "old" building just off Gràcia; sure, it's "expensive", but it's more "affordable" than some, and a "lovely treat for a romantic evening"; P.S. closed Saturday–Sunday.

Jaume de Provença ☒ Catalan
26 | 21 | 23 | E

Eixample | Provença 88 | (34) 93-430-0029 | www.jaumeprovenca.com
The modern "classics" by pioneering chef Jaume Bargués rise "above expectations" at this longtime Eixample Catalan with a "stylish" flair; though "expensive", many consider it "reasonable" for some of the "best" food in town.

Neichel ☒☒ Mediterranean
27 | 24 | 26 | VE

Pedralbes | Beltrán i Rózpide 1-5 | (34) 93-203-8408 | www.neichel.es
"Masterfully prepared", "artistic" cuisine by chef-owner Jean-Louis Neichel enamors guests at this "splendid" Mediterranean overlooking a garden in residential Pedralbes; diners applaud the "unbeatable" staff's "discretion" ("you could go one night with your mistress and the next with your wife and never get caught"), and insist that while it "doesn't accommodate all budgets", "you must pay for quality."

Passadis del Pep ☒ Mediterranean/Seafood
27 | 21 | 25 | VE

Born-Ribera | Pla del Palau 2 | (34) 93-310-1021 | www.passadis.com
"You never see a menu and never have to make a decision" at this "cozy" unmarked Born-Ribera "gem" where the staff "keeps bringing more and more" "simply sublime", "authentic" Mediterranean seafood by chef-owner Joan Manubens; sure, it's a costly outing, but since a bottle of cava comes with every meal, it's easy to "walk out just wrecked and love every minute of it."

7 Portes ● Catalan
23 | 21 | 22 | E

Ciutat Vella | Passeig Isabel II 14 | (34) 93-319-3033 | www.7portes.com
A "legendary" "institution" (founded in 1836), this "expensive" Ciutat Vella Catalan, voted Most Popular in Barcelona, "still delivers" "traditional, well-prepared" classics including "delicious" paella in a setting "decorated to evoke nostalgia"; "professional" service "matches" the price, so though it's always "full of tourists", even those who find the food "average" say it's a "pleasure to visit."

Tapas 24 ●☒ Catalan
26 | 18 | 19 | M

Eixample | Diputació 269 | (34) 93-488-0977 | www.tapas24.net
"Outsmart the locals" by going at an off-hour, and you might beat the "queue out the door" to savor a "tapas-tasting fantasy" at this "tiny", "casual" Catalan "sister to Comerç 24" in the Eixample; even if service is "so-so", the crowd is "congenial" and the breakfast-to-midnight dishes always "a hit", so plenty of customers "could happily eat here every day."

Yashima Japanese
26 | 21 | 23 | E

Les Corts | Josep Tarradellas 145 | (34) 93-419-0697 |
www.yamashitagroup.com
"Impeccable" sashimi and "creative" sushi lead diners to dub this Les Corts spot one of the "best Japanese" restaurants in Barcelona; with barstools overlooking the kitchen, as well as private tatami rooms, it suits for business and dates, and can become extravagant – "your final check will depend on your appetite and resistance to temptation."

Berlin

TOP FOOD RANKING

	Restaurant	Cuisine
26	VAU	International
24	Lorenz Adlon	French
	Maxwell	French/International
	Gabriele	Italian/Mediterranean
23	Alt Luxemburg	French/Mediterranean
	Die Quadriga*	International/Scandinavian
	44	International
	Vox	International
	Ana e Bruno	Italian/Mediterranean
22	Hartmanns	German/Mediterranean
	Reinstoff	International
	Margaux	International
21	Aigner	Viennese
	Balthazar	International
	Grill Royal	Seafood/Steak
	Altes Zollhaus	German
	Borchardt	French/German
	Bocca/Bacco	Tuscan
	Diekmann	German/International

Aigner *Viennese*   21 | 19 | 19 | E
Mitte | Französische Str. 25 | (49-30) 203-751-850 |
www.aigner-gendarmenmarkt.de
"Pretty people" flock to this "popular" place in Mitte, on the
Gendarmenmarkt, where you'll "want to order seconds" of the "excellent", German-accented Viennese fare (the signature roast "duck is
spectacular") served by a "friendly, fast" staff; though located within
a typical GDR-style *'Plattenbau'* (concrete slab building), its "wonderful" 19th-century bistro setting was assembled from the former
Café Aigner in Vienna.

Altes Zollhaus ⊠Ⓜ *German*   21 | 17 | 20 | E
Kreuzberg | Carl-Herz-Ufer 30 | (49-30) 692-3300 |
www.altes-zollhaus-berlin.de
Located within an "old customs office" in a "picturesque setting" beside the Landwehrkanal in Kreuzberg, this "standby" boasts "rustic"
yet "dignified" decor that complements its "extensive menu" of "excellent" traditional *Deutsch* dishes, served by an "accommodating"
staff; some say it's "a bit touristic", but more maintain it "successfully
straddles the line between historical kitsch and authentic old-style
German eating"; P.S. its Smugglers Barn space is perfect for parties.

Alt Luxemburg ⊠ *French/Mediterranean*   23 | 21 | 25 | E
Charlottenburg | Windscheidstr. 31 | (49-30) 323-8730 |
www.altluxemburg.de
"One expects the old Kaiser to walk in" to this "wonderful place", a
"Berlin standard" not far from the Charlottenburg Castle, where the

---

* Indicates a tie with restaurant above

"fast service" is a match for the "comprehensive menu" of "delicious" New French–Med cuisine ("no schnitzel here") offered in a "quiet" room; no wonder so many regulars are "happy" to call it a "favorite."

Ana e Bruno ● *Italian/Mediterranean*   23 | 17 | 22 | E

Charlottenburg | Sophie-Charlotten-Str. 101 | (49-30) 325-7110 | www.ana-e-bruno.de

"Made for a lovely, quiet evening", this "cozy" Charlottenburg spot is home to an "ambitious" menu offering a taste of *"bella Italia"* via "inventive" Italian-Med cuisine at prices that may be "high" but are "appropriate for the quality of the food"; some call the decor "less than striking" – though a post-Survey overhaul may help – but at least "you know you're in good hands" with the "polite staff"; P.S. "tables are limited" so "be sure to make reservations."

Balthazar *International*   21 | 20 | 20 | E

Wilmersdorf | Kurfürstendamm 160 | (49-30) 8940-8477 | www.restaurant-balthazar.de

Tucked into a classical Berlin townhouse in Wilmersdorf (at the "less-fashionable end of Kurfürstendamm") is this urbane-looking International with Mediterranean and German accents that offers "high-class" cooking, a "great wine list" and "warm staff"; better yet, "you can walk away without emptying your wallet."

Bocca *Tuscan*   21 | 19 | 19 | E

Charlottenburg | Marburger Str. 5 | (49-30) 211-8687 | www.bacco.de

Bocca di Bacco ● *Tuscan*

Mitte | Friedrichstr. 167/168 | (49-30) 2067-2828 | www.boccadibacco.de

The Mannozzi family oversees this Tuscan pair, the original an old-fashioned trattoria (owned by father Massimo) that's been serving "good, traditional cuisine with no surprises" in Charlottenburg since the late-'60s; its 'mouth of Bacchus' offshoot in Mitte (owned by son Francesco) is more "sophisticated" and "upmarket", offering "nouvelle" fare and a "good selection of wines" in a "modern, stylish" setting; both are often "star-studded" and boast "fresh ingredients" and "attentive" staffers, making either one "worth a try."

Borchardt ● *French/German*   21 | 20 | 19 | E

Mitte | Französische Str. 47 | (49-30) 8188-6262 | www.borchardt-restaurant.de

"Popular" with "politicians, movie stars" and other "celebrity" types, this Mitte "classic" is known for its "wonderful" French-German fare – including "delicious fish" and some of the "best Wiener schnitzel in Berlin" – "hospitably" presented in a "beautiful" brasserie setting with "pre-war flair"; still, critics say "one pays for the stargazing" and "glam" scene, adding that certain "snooty" staffers are "less accommodating when serving Mr. and Ms. Average."

Diekmann *German/International*   21 | 18 | 21 | M

Charlottenburg | Meinekestr. 7 | (49-30) 883-3321
Dahlem | Châlet Suisse | Clayallee 99 | (49-30) 832-6362
Mitte | Hauptbahnhof | Europlatz 1 | (49-30) 2091-1929
www.j-diekmann.de

Of this "fantastic" trio serving "German food with a nouveau twist", the original, a brasserie on the ground floor of a townhouse in a "beautiful Charlottenburg spot", offers a "genteel experience"; the other branches offer various International accents (including an oyster bar at the Mitte outpost), but each is a "safe bet" for a "good selection" of "tasty", "well-prepared food" served by "friendly people."

Die Quadriga 🛇Ⓜ️ *International/Scandinavian*   23 | 25 | 23 | E

Charlottenburg | Brandenburger Hof | Eislebener Str. 14 | (49-30) 2140-5650 | www.brandenburger-hof.com

"A memorable meal" awaits at this "nice hotel dining" venue whose two rooms flank a "beautiful" Japanese garden in Charlottenburg's Brandenburger Hof; the "varied menu" features "exquisite" New Nordic fare with International touches, with an extensive all-German wine list and "incredible service"; sure, it's "somewhat expensive", but it's a "first-class" experience; P.S. there's occasional live jazz.

44 🛇 *International*   23 | 18 | 21 | VE

Charlottenburg | Swissôtel | Augsburger Str. 44 | (49-30) 220-100 | www.restaurant44.de

"Excellent", "inventive" International cooking that "never fails to excite" draws fans to this "quiet, romantic" venue in Charlottenburg's Swissôtel; critics, however, claim the menu "tries very hard to be interesting" but "overwhelms the taste buds with competing flavors"; N.B. ask for a table on the small terrace overlooking the famous Kurfürstendamm.

Gabriele Ⓜ️ *Italian/Mediterranean*   24 | 23 | 24 | E

Mitte | Hotel Adlon Kempinski | Behrenstr. 72 | (49-30) 2062-8610 | www.gabriele-restaurant.de

This "wonderful" dinner-only Italian-Med enjoys a prime location near both the Brandenburg Gate and U.S. Embassy, where a "charming" staff presides over an eclectic setting adorned with cushy leather chairs and banquettes, brass chandeliers and contemporary art.

Grill Royal ◐ *Seafood/Steak*   21 | 20 | 20 | E

Mitte | Friedrichstr. 105B | (49-30) 2887-9288 | www.grillroyal.com

"Great" steakhouse-seafooder in trendy Mitte (the "best location in Berlin") that plies "delicious" food and is "often packed" with a chic crowd that doesn't mind the "expensive" tabs; the spacious wood-and-marble setting includes a vintage motor boat, a "spectacular" terrace and a view of the Spree River.

Hartmanns ◐🛇 *German/Mediterranean*   22 | 20 | 19 | E

Kreuzberg | Fichtestr. 31 | (49-30) 6120-1003 | www.hartmanns-restaurant.de

Chef-owner Stefan Hartmann's intimate, "enjoyable" spot combines German and Mediterranean ingredients with "delicious", "very creative" results; set in the basement of a classical turn-of-the-century Kreuzberg townhouse, the minimalist space gets a kick of color from modern art and strikingly spare floral arrangements; P.S. recently added terrace seating has become very popular.

Lorenz Adlon 🛇Ⓜ️ *French*   24 | 24 | 22 | VE

Mitte | Hotel Adlon Kempinski | Unter den Linden 77 | (49-30) 2261-1960 | www.hotel-adlon.de

"Indulge yourself" at this "romantic" retreat in Mitte's Hotel Adlon Kempinski, just "steps from the Brandenburg Gate"; it features classic

FOOD DECOR SERVICE COST

French cuisine, a "comprehensive list" of "exquisite wines", a "stylish" setting and "refined staff" that gives one a "feeling of being pampered"; yes, it's "very expensive", but most agree they're prepared to "pay a little more" for such a "luxe" experience – after all, "you have to spoil yourself sometime."

Margaux ☒ *International*   22 | 23 | 20 | VE

Mitte | Unter den Linden 78 | (49-30) 2265-2611 | www.margaux-berlin.de
With its "impressive decor" and tasting menus (including a daily vegetarian option), this "fine-dining" venue in Mitte is a "chic", "cosmopolitan" showcase for the "world-class" creations of chef-owner Michael Hoffmann, whose "high-end" International fare is prepared with "amazing care" (and some avant-garde touches); "excellent" service, an "extraordinary wine list" and "unbelievable" desserts ice the cake; P.S. closed Mondays in July and August.

Maxwell *French/International*   24 | 21 | 16 | E

Mitte | Bergstr. 22 | (49-30) 280-7121 | www.restaurant-maxwell.de
For "some of the coolest dining" around, hipsters head to this "trendy" spot set in a "former brewery" in Mitte, where "inventive" French-International dishes (incorporating Asian, Italian and German influences) are offered in a "beautiful, high-ceilinged" space with "modern but not chilly furnishings"; sure, "service could be more efficient", but at least the "staff is friendly."

Reinstoff ●☒Ⓜ *International*   22 | 21 | 21 | E

Mitte | Schlegelstr. 26C | (49-30) 3088-1214 | www.reinstoff.eu
A remodeled "old warehouse" in Mitte is the site of this avant-garde restaurant where chef Daniel Achilles prepares a "tasty" International menu featuring regional products and influences from around the world; the modernist, all-black room is just as daring as the menu, though a few sniff it's "too cool for school."

VAU ☒ *International*   26 | 23 | 25 | VE

Mitte | Jägerstr. 54-55 | (49-30) 202-9730 | www.vau-berlin.de
This "exquisite-in-every-way" Mitte "oasis" next to the famous Gendarmenmarkt is rated Most Popular and No. 1 in Berlin for Food thanks to chef/TV personality Kolja Kleeberg's "heavenly menu" of "excellent", "extremely creative" International cuisine; a "quality wine list", "wonderful service" from a "thoughtful, unintrusive" staff and "crisp, modern" decor also enhance the "superb dining experience", but be aware that your "wallet will hurt" long after; P.S. the "lunch prices are more reasonable."

Vox ● *International*   23 | 23 | 24 | E

Tiergarten | Grand Hyatt | Marlene-Dietrich-Platz 2 | (49-30) 2553-1507 | www.vox-restaurant.de
"Everything's top-notch" at this hotel restaurant overlooking the Potsdamer Platz shopping area in Tiergarten's Grand Hyatt, where the service is "attentive", the "unconventional decor" is "stylish" and the "fantastic" food – ranging from "excellent sushi" to "interesting" International dishes – is a "pleasure for the palate"; no wonder some say they "would fly to Berlin just to have dinner here again."

Brussels

TOP FOOD RANKING

	Restaurant	Cuisine
28	Comme Chez Soi	French
	Bruneau	French
27	La Truffe Noire	French/Italian
	Sea Grill	International/Seafood
26	Le Passage	French
	La Maison du Cygne	French
25	Chez Marie	French
24	L'Ecailler du Palais Royal	Seafood
	Villa Lorraine*	Belgian/French
	L'Ogenblik	French
	Le Chalet de la Forêt	French
	San Daniele*	Italian
	Café des Spores	European
	Bon-Bon	Belgian/French
23	Blue Elephant	Thai
	Le Fourneau	French
	Scheltema	French
	L'Idiot du Village	French
	La Manufacture	French

Aux Armes
de Bruxelles *Belgian*   21 | 19 | 19 | E

Ilôt Sacré | Rue des Bouchers 13 | (32-2) 511-5550 |
www.armesdebruxelles.be
A "jewel" in the otherwise tourist-trap-laden Rue des Bouchers, this
Belgian "favorite" is a "popular", "prototypical brasserie" for "eating
like the locals"; "few things are better than mussels in Brussels" so the
ones here are a "must", along with "wonderful *waterzooi.*"

Belga Queen ● *Belgian*   18 | 27 | 17 | E

Lower Town | Rue du Fossé aux Loups 32 | (32-2) 217-2187 |
www.belgaqueen.be
"Sexy" describes the "fab" setting – an "ornate" stained-glass ceiling,
moody lighting and cool loos – of this Belgian brasserie housed in a
former belle epoque bank in the Lower Town; some gourmands gripe
that the "food is nothing to write home about" and say "stick to the
seafood platter" and raw bar, but scenesters are more intent scoping
out the "beautiful people" in attendance.

Blue Elephant *Thai*   23 | 22 | 21 | E

Uccle | Chaussée de Waterloo 1120 | (32-2) 374-4962 |
www.blueelephant.com
For more than 30 years, this Thai in Uccle (with other outposts from
London to Dubai) has been taking loyalists on a "wonderful culinary
journey" with its "fine", "wonderfully spiced" fare; a "beautiful" setting "complete with coconuts and flowers" leads to thoughts of "lush"
lands and away from the realities of "Belgian weather."

---

* Indicates a tie with restaurant above

	FOOD	DECOR	SERVICE	COST

Bon-Bon 🅈🅼 *Belgian/French* — 24 | - | 19 | E

Uccle | Rue des Carmélites 93 | (32-2) 346-6615 |
www.bon-bon.be

Chef Christophe Hardiquest's market-driven "modern" Belgian-French cuisine is "excellent" and earns him "rising star" status at this intimate bistro in Uccle; post-Survey it relocated to new digs with a modern, minimalist dining room done up in black and white.

NEW Bouchéry 🅈 *French* — - | - | - | E

Uccle | Chaussée d'Alsemberg 812A | (32-2) 332-3774 |
www.bouchery-restaurant.be

Chef Damien Bouchery has taken over the former Le Pain et le Vin space in Uccle where he whips up imaginative French dishes using unusual ingredients; turquoise globe lights brighten the white, minimalist interior, and if it's too pricey for some, there's also a bargain prix fixe lunch; P.S. there's garden seating in season.

Bruneau *French* — 28 | 25 | 28 | VE

Ganshoren | Ave. Broustin 73-75 | (32-2) 421-7070 |
www.bruneau.be

"Exquisite" is the word on this more than 30-year-old Classic French set in an elegant double townhouse in residential Ganshoren, about a 15-minute taxi ride from the City Center; chef-owner Jean-Pierre Bruneau's "outstanding" cuisine is complemented by equally "excellent service", a "tremendous" wine list, handsome dining rooms and a summer garden terrace; in sum, it's a very "costly" but "outstanding" experience; N.B. closed Tuesdays–Wednesdays.

Café des Spores 🅈 *European* — 24 | 20 | 23 | E

Saint-Gilles | Chaussée D'Alsemberg 103-108 | (32-2) 534-1303 |
www.cafedesspores.be

Fungi fans sprout up at this small, simple European cafe in Saint-Gilles for the namesake spores – "delicious" and "varied fresh mushroom dishes" that are market-driven; oenophiles can also be accommodated since there is a "fine array of wines" to complement the earthy ingredients.

Chez Marie 🅈🅼 *French* — 25 | 21 | 22 | E

Ixelles | Rue Alphonse de Witte 40 | (32-2) 644-3031

A firm favorite with EU professionals, this Classic French in Ixelles features chef Lilian Devaux's "delicious" cuisine, including a great "value" prix fixe lunch; "tiny", "warm" and "cozy", it's quite "romantic" thanks to "low lights" and an abundance of mirrors and candles; P.S. it has a wine cellar with 400+ labels.

Comme Chez Soi 🅈🅼 *French* — 28 | 24 | 27 | VE

Lower Town | Place Rouppe 23 | (32-2) 512-2921 |
www.commechezsoi.be

Pierre Wynants has retired, leaving his son-in-law, Lionel Rigolet, to present "sublime" French cooking at this Lower Town venue that's Voted No. 1 for Food and rated Most Popular in Brussels; an "attentive but unobtrusive" staff presides over the "fantastic" art nouveau setting (although the chef's table in the kitchen is an equally coveted spot), and even if this "gem" is "extremely expensive", it's such a "joy to visit" that many dub it "one of the world's great restaurants."

	FOOD	DECOR	SERVICE	COST

La Maison du Cygne ☒ *French*   26 | 27 | 24 | VE

Grand' Place | Rue Charles Buls 2 | (32-2) 511-8244 |
www.lamaisonducygne.be

A "stunning location" in a former 17th-century guildhall "overlooking
the historic Grand' Place" is the setting for this long-standing Classic
French, where velvet banquettes and paintings by Belgian masters are
a "magnificent" backdrop for the "excellent" cuisine, "exceptional service" and "extensive wine list"; given the stratospheric prices, it's
ironic that Karl Marx once worked on his Communist Manifesto here.

La Manufacture ☒ *French*   23 | 24 | 20 | E

Ste-Cathérine | Rue Notre Dame du Sommeil 12-20 | (32-2) 502-2525 |
www.manufacture.be

Set in a "famous old" former handbag factory - hence the name - this
"innovative", fashionable French in the up-and-coming Ste-Cathérine
district is "not expensive if you compare the price with the quality of the
meals"; the "great atmosphere" includes "sexy" staffers and a dramatic
industrial space outfitted with leather banquettes and stone tables.

La Truffe Noire ☒ *French/Italian*   27 | 22 | 25 | VE

Uccle | Boulevard de la Cambre 12 | (32-2) 640-4422 | www.truffenoire.com

A "must for truffle lovers", this "excellent" French-Italian in Uccle features the unearthed fungus from start (with carpaccio) to finish (sub-
stituting its sweet chocolate namesake at dessert); "perfect service"
and a "sophisticated" room with modern paintings round out the extravagant experience; of course, you'll be digging deep when it comes
time to pay the big bill.

L'Ecailler du Palais Royal ☒ *Seafood*   24 | 21 | 22 | VE

Grand Sablon | Rue Bodenbroek 18 | (32-2) 512-8751 |
www.lecaillerdupalaisroyal.be

Since 1967, not a morsel of meat has passed through the portals of
this "top-quality" Grand Sablon seafooder featuring "fish, just fish,
but the best" of the catch; "excellent service" and a "wonderful" duplex setting (one room with soothing traditional plaid decor, the other
a scarlet salon) make it "great for business lunches", but the exuber-
ant bar with "turquoise fish-scale tiles" is "good for single diners too."

Le Chalet de la Forêt ☒ *French*   24 | 23 | 22 | VE

Uccle | Drève de Lorraine 43 | (32-2) 374-5416 | www.lechaletdelaforet.be

A "beautiful, middle-of-the-woods" location sets the rustic tone at
this "charming" French venue in Uccle known for its "excellent" cooking and "extensive wine list"; though the "modern" interior plays second fiddle to the "terrific" alfresco terrace, either way it's a "special
experience" - and one that "you'll pay for."

Le Fourneau ☒Ⓜ *French*   23 | 20 | 21 | E

Ste-Cathérine | Place Sainte-Catherine 8 | (32-2) 513-1002 |
www.evanrestaurants.be

A "must-visit", this "excellent" French small-plates specialist is a
"place to return to whenever the season changes" given its "sophisticated" handling of ingredients on the "continuously changing menu" ;
you'll "love the location" on medieval Sainte Cathérine square, and inside, a handful of tables, a long bar and an open kitchen are arranged
in a spare but stylish black-and-white room.

	FOOD	DECOR	SERVICE	COST

Le Passage ⓩ *French* | 26 | 19 | 22 | E |

Uccle | Avenue Jean et Pierre Carsoel 13 | (32-2) 374-6694 |
www.lepassage.be
Set in a wealthy residential area in Uccle, this "exceptional" Belgian-
French offers "innovative", "simply delicious" cooking from a "fantastic chef", Rocky Renaud; though aesthetes find the minimalist decor
"fairly dull", what's on the plate more than distracts.

L'Idiot du Village ⓩ *French* | 23 | 21 | 21 | E |

Grand Sablon | Rue Notre-Seigneur 19 | (32-2) 502-5582
You'd be the idiot if you didn't book way ahead at this popular tiny
boîte tucked away in a 17th-century house in Grand Sablon; "inventive" French cuisine that "soars with flavor" and a "quirky" "bohemian-
chic" atmosphere with "whimsical" flea-market decor attract
"Eurocrats wanting to get in touch with their inner hippie."

L'Ogenblik ⓞⓩ *French* | 24 | 18 | 20 | E |

Ilôt Sacré | Galerie des Princes 1 | (32-2) 511-6151 | www.ogenblik.be
"What a bistro should be", this French stalwart is set in the "beautiful"
glassed-in Galeries Royales Saint-Hubert, the "oldest shopping arcade
in Europe"; there's "delicious food", an "excellent wine list", "attentive
service" and a homey atmosphere, and even though it's been a "favorite Brussels haunt" since 1969, it still attracts a cosmopolitan crowd.

San Daniele ⓩⓜ *Italian* | 24 | 20 | 21 | E |

Ganshoren | Ave. Charles-Quint 6 | (32-2) 426-7923 | www.san-daniele.be
"Family"-owned and -operated, this Ganshoren Italian offers such
"special" dining that the "expensive" tabs come as "no surprise"; the
food's "terrific", the service "pleasant" and the sleek, "chic" atmosphere is just the ticket for a "romantic" repast.

Scheltema ⓩ *French* | 23 | 19 | 19 | E |

Ilôt Sacré | Rue des Dominicains 7 | (32-2) 512-2084 | www.scheltema.be
Named after a Dutch poet, this "bustling" Classic French brasserie in
the Ilôt Sacré features "excellent seafood and desserts" served in a
big, burnished-wood setting; "friendly waiters" and an "Old Europe"
vibe "without the stiff upper lip" add to the "wonderful experience."

Sea Grill ⓩ *International/Seafood* | 27 | 23 | 27 | VE |

Lower Town | Radisson SAS Royal Hotel | Rue du Fossé aux Loups 47 |
(32-2) 212-0800 | www.seagrill.be
"Embedded in the Radisson SAS Royal Hotel" in the Lower Town is this
"top-class" international seafooder with "superb" cuisine, an "excellent wine list" and "incomparable service"; still, some carp about the
corporate atmosphere and sky-high prices – it's so "expensive" that
even "expense accounts will get strained here."

Villa Lorraine ⓩ *Belgian/French* | 24 | 25 | 25 | VE |

Uccle | Chaussée de la Hulpe 28 | (32-2) 374-3163 | www.villalorraine.be
Nestled on the fringes of the "beautiful" Bois de la Cambre in Uccle
(about a 20-minute taxi ride from the City Center) is this "landmark"
"temple of Belgian-French haute cuisine" set in a "posh" 19th-century
villa; "fine food", sterling service and a "stellar wine cellar" make for
lovely long lunches or "romantic evenings", particularly out on the
summer garden terrace.

Budapest

TOP FOOD RANKING

	Restaurant	Cuisine
28	Baraka	Asian/Mediterranean
	Vadrózsa	Hungarian/International
25	Kacsa	Hungarian/International
24	Gundel	Hungarian/International
	Fausto's	Italian
	Onyx	Hungarian/International
23	Café Kör	Hungarian/International
	Philippe le Belge	Belgian/Bistro
	Rézkakas	Hungarian/International
	Bistro Jardin	Hungarian/International
	Déryné Bistro	Hungarian/International
	Kisbuda Gyöngye	Hungarian/International
22	Csalogány 26	International
	Arcade Bistro	Hungarian/International
21	Pampas Argentine	Argentinean/Steak
	Cyrano	Hungarian/International
	Kárpátia*	Hungarian
	Chez Daniel	French

Arcade Bistro *Hungarian/International*   22 | 19 | 20 | M

Városmajor | Kiss János altábornagy utca 38 | (36-1) 225-1969 |
www.arcadebistro.hu

Hip young professionals flock to this "comfortable" yet "classy" venue
hidden behind foliage off a "quiet" square in residential Városmajor;
while it's "hard to find traditional dishes" on the "diverse" Hungarian-
International menu, the "simple, modern" offerings are prepared with
"high-quality" ingredients and served by an "attentive" crew; P.S. the
"lovely terrace" is a favorite weekend lunch destination.

Baraka *Asian/Mediterranean*   28 | - | 27 | E

Andrássy út | MaMaison Andrássy Hotel | Andrássy út 111 |
(36-1) 462-2189 | www.andrassyhotel.com

"Truly one of Budapest's great finds", this "outstanding" Asian-
Mediterranean (ranked No. 1 for Food in the city) moved uptown from
Belváros to a glam, silver-and-black deco space in the MaMaison
Andrássy Hotel; "running the show" are David and Leora Seboek, the
"husband-and-wife team" who oversee a "regularly changing menu"
of "inventive" dishes complemented by an "expensive wine list" and
"excellent service"; P.S. people-watchers note a number of "local
celebrities" in attendance.

Bistro Jardin *Hungarian/International*   23 | 22 | 21 | E

Belváros | Kempinski Hotel Corvinus | Erzsébet tér 7-8 | (36-1) 429-3777 |
www.kempinski-budapest.com

You "can always rely on" the "high standards" set at this Belváros "favorite" in the Kempinski Hotel Corvinus known for its "delicious"
Hungarian-International fare; "pleasant" atmospherics, an "elegant"

---

* Indicates a tie with restaurant above

setting (including a "nice" outdoor terrace) and "first-class" service help to justify the "expense"; P.S. adding to the "grand experience", there's live jazz on Sundays.

Café Kör 🍴🚭 *Hungarian/International*   23 | 18 | 23 | M

Lipótváros | Sas utca 17 | (36-1) 311-0053 | www.cafekor.com
Everyone from "intellectuals" to "tourists" to "expats" turns up at this "charming" place near St. Stephen's Basilica in Lipótváros, where a "wide choice" of "excellent", reasonably priced traditional Hungarian fare (plus some International dishes) is offered in "generous portions" by an "upbeat" crew; P.S. "don't skip dessert" – "you won't believe the variety of cakes and pastries!"

Centrál Kávéház *Hungarian*   17 | 19 | 16 | M

Belváros | Károlyi Mihály utca 9 | (36-1) 266-2110 | www.centralkavehaz.hu
There's always an "interesting crowd" in attendance at this Belváros coffeehouse that boasts an "authentic" 19th-century air that's particularly "welcoming"; true, "there may be better choices" for Hungarian food, and service verges on "perfunctory", but at least the staff "doesn't rush you", so it's a "great place to hang out and chat with friends."

Chez Daniel *French*   21 | 16 | 16 | E

Andrássy út | Szív utca 32 | (36-1) 302-4039 | www.chezdaniel.hu
"Good-sized portions" of "fine French food" are served at this "pleasant spot" in Andrássy út, where regulars "ask the chef to choose" for them to ensure a "memorable meal"; still, some are "stung" by the price tags, considering the "nothing-special decor" and service that's "acceptable but could be better"; P.S. wags wager it's fortunate that "Daniel's dog", who has the run of the restaurant, "is very well behaved."

Csalogány 26 🍴Ⓜ *International*   22 | 18 | 22 | E

Viziváros | Csalogány utca 26 | (36-1) 201-7892 | www.csalogany26.hu
In-the-know locals head for this small, unassuming International in Viziváros, where the "delicious", frequently changing menu includes organic vegetables from the retaurant's own garden; the simple bistro setting is enlivened by enormous arched windows and a closed-circuit flat-screen monitor that allows curious customers sneak-peeks into the chefs' doings in the kitchen.

Cyrano ● *Hungarian/International*   21 | 22 | 19 | E

Terézváros | Kristóf tér 6 | (36-1) 266-3096 | www.cyrano.hu
"Trendy and posh", this Hungarian-International boasts an "elegant" yet "relaxing ambiance" (and an unusual chandelier shaped like an inverted Christmas tree); the "consistently creative" kitchen is "always experimenting" with the "very good" menu, and the "attentive" staff is "well trained" – in short, it's "one of the better places for a stylish lunch or dinner near Váci utca", especially on the "outside terrace."

Déryné Bistro *Hungarian/International*   23 | 22 | 21 | E

Várnegyed | Krisztina tér 3 | (36-1) 225-1407 | www.cafederyne.hu
This circa-1914 Várnegyed coffeehouse has restyled itself into a "relaxed" yet hip hangout where "delectable" Hungarian-International

dishes are served in a space decked out with "comfortable" leather armchairs, a working fireplace and lots of polished wood; it's somewhat of a "people-watching" paradise, and just the ticket for chilling out, smoking a cigar and checking your e-mail.

Fausto's ⊠ *Italian* — 24 | 18 | 24 | E

Erzsébetvaros | Székely Mihály utca 2 | (36-1) 877-6210 | www.fausto.hu
A "great evening" of "chic eating" awaits at this "excellent Italian" "in the old Jewish quarter" in Erzsébetvaros, where the "top-notch service" is matched by chef Fausto Di Vora's "outstanding" Tuscan fare; perhaps the food's "expensive", but fans insist there's "value" for the money – you'll "pay more for less in many other restaurants on either side of the river."

Gundel *Hungarian/International* — 24 | 26 | 25 | VE

Városliget | Állatkerti út 2 | (36-1) 468-4040 | www.gundel.hu
"Memories are made" at this "venerable" Hungarian-International "legend" (rated Most Popular in the city) "near Hero's Square", a "palatial", "elaborately decorated", ultra-expensive salon with "turn-of-the-century grandeur" and "beautiful views" of Városliget; within its "elegant setting", a "cultured" staff indulges "lucky" patrons with "quality service" and a "delicious menu"; factor in "marvelous strolling musicians" playing "wonderful" live gypsy music and you can expect a "magical evening in a magical city"; P.S. jacket required.

Kacsa *Hungarian/International* — 25 | 19 | 23 | E

Viziváros | Fö utca 75 | (36-1) 201-9992 | www.kacsavendeglo.hu
Its "name means 'duck'", and naturally you'll find "excellent" renditions of that fowl on the "delicious, wide-ranging menu" at this "stellar" Hungarian-International in Viziváros, where the "amazing meals" are enhanced by "wonderful service" from a "lovely staff"; it's "pricey but not outrageous", and though the "decor could be improved", at least the "atmosphere is romantic", making it "a must when you're in Budapest."

Kárpátia *Hungarian* — 21 | 23 | 19 | E

Belváros | Ferenciek tere 7-8 | (36-1) 317-3596 | www.karpatia.hu
The "historic past makes its mark" on the present at this "fairly pricey" venue set in a circa-1877 Belváros building in which there's "not an unadorned inch" in the "over-the-top" yet mostly "tasteful" interior; the "varied" menu of "excellent" cuisine – including a "great Sunday smorgasbord" in winter – is "authentically Hungarian", the service a "pleasure" (even if a few fault certain "indifferent" staffers) and a "nice gypsy violin ensemble" helps cement its status as a true "taste of Budapest."

Kisbuda Gyöngye ⊠ Ⓜ *Hungarian/International* — 23 | 19 | 23 | E

Óbuda | Kenyeres utca 34 | (36-1) 368-9246 | www.remiz.hu
A 'pearl' in Óbuda, this Hungarian-International "favorite" is staffed by an "observant" crew with "high standards" serving "exceptionally well-prepared" fare with "all the good flavors of home cooking"; a few find the flea-market ambiance "a little contrived", but most are won over by its "intimate", old-world atmosphere and live piano – "what else do you need?"

	FOOD	DECOR	SERVICE	COST

Onyx ⧉ Ⓜ *Hungarian/International* | 24 | 22 | 23 | E |
Belváros | Vörösmarty tér 7-8 | (36-30) 503-0622 | www.onyxrestaurant.hu
Located in Belváros' historic Gerbeaud Patisserie, this "breath of fresh air" effortlessly blends traditional Hungarian dishes with "modern" International fare for "splurge"-worthy sums; most find it "highly creative", a few shrug "style over substance", but all agree that the elegant, neo-baroque setting – a mix of crystal chandeliers and plastic Philippe Starck furniture – mirrors the menu's merger of the conventional and the innovative.

Pampas Argentine | 21 | 19 | 20 | E |
Steakhouse *Argentinean/Steak*
Belváros | Vámház körút 6 | (36-1) 411-1750 | www.steak.hu
Carnivores "satisfy their red-meat cravings" at this Argentinean steakhouse in Belváros specializing in cuts of "quality" grilled meats that are "not easy to find" in Hungary; "plentiful", "bring-your-appetite" portions and a "rich selection of wine" trump the "high prices", "show-off" decor and service that "still has a way to go."

Philippe le Belge ⧉ Ⓜ *Belgian/Bistro* | 23 | 19 | 21 | E |
Lipótváros | Balzac utca 35 | (36-1) 350-0411 | www.philippe.hu
This "exceptionally good" Lipótváros Belgian offers regional dishes like "wonderful mussels" that are "artfully prepared" with a "bit of Hungarian flair"; the "lively, upscale" setting features a warm palette that feels somewhat Mediterranean, and if the pricing seems "high for Budapest", the payoff is "delicious" dining.

Rézkakas ❶ *Hungarian/International* | 23 | 22 | 25 | E |
Belváros | Veres Pálné utca 3 | (36-1) 318-0038 |
www.rezkakasrestaurant.com
An "excellent attitude toward customers" makes for "top-notch service" at this "truly captivating" Belváros venue set in a "romantic" wood-paneled room where the "terrific" Hungarian-International cuisine is complemented by "wonderful live music"; for such a "magical" (albeit "somewhat touristy") experience, most say "never mind the cost – what's important is that you enjoy yourself."

Spoon Café & Lounge *International* | 17 | 22 | 18 | E |
Belváros | Vigadó tér 3 Kikötö | (36-1) 411-0934 | www.spooncafe.hu
Set on a boat docked on the Danube by Belváros' Chain Bridge, this "stylish" tri-level "floating restaurant"/"fashionable lounge" attracts a "cooler-than-thou crowd" with its "novel" setting; some find the "wide-ranging" International menu "not particularly enticing", but most are content to "sit back and enjoy" the "spectacular view of Castle Hill across the river"; P.S. visiting the restrooms is "a must."

Vadrózsa ❶ *Hungarian/International* | 28 | 24 | 24 | E |
Rózsadomb | Pentelei Molnár utca 15 | (36-1) 326-5817 | www.vadrozsa.hu
"Come hungry" to this "outstanding" "off-the-beaten-path" Rózsadomb 'Wild Rose' where the "fresh" Hungarian-International food is "lovingly prepared" from the "finest ingredients"; its "elegant" setting (with a "charming private garden") is "a little magical" thanks to a pianist and a "polite" staff that provides "wonderful old-world service" – so "if you can't live in a mansion", at least "you can dine in one."

Copenhagen

TOP FOOD RANKING

	Restaurant	Cuisine
28	Noma	Scandinavian
27	Era Ora	Italian
	Restaurationen	Danish/French
26	Søllerød Kro	French
	Kong Hans Kælder	French/Danish
25	Krogs Fiskerestaurant	French/Seafood
	Alberto K	Scandinavian
24	Pierre André	French
23	Slotskælderen hos Gitte Kik	Danish
	Kanalen	French/Danish
	Le Sommelier	French
	Acquamarina	Italian/Seafood
22	MASH	American/Steak
	Ricemarket	Thai
	Royal Cafe	Danish
	Fifty Fifty	Japanese
21	Kiin Kiin	Thai
	Herman	Danish/International
	Salt	Scandinavian

Acquamarina *Italian/Seafood* | 23 | 21 | 23 | E |

Indre By | Borgergade 17 A | (45-33) 11-17-21 | www.acquamarina.dk
Simple Italian fare with an emphasis on seafood is the thing at this "very good" venue in Indre By, described by its owners as 'the feminine side of Era Ora'; the "bright" modern design includes light-blue flooring with a wavelike design that suggests dining on the Mediterranean shore.

Alberto K ☒ *Scandinavian* | 25 | 24 | 23 | E |

Vesterbro | Radisson Blu Royal | Hammerichsgade 1, 20th fl. | (45-33) 42-61-61 | www.alberto-k.dk
The "superb" modern Scandinavian cuisine "melts in your mouth" at this "fantastic" place with "to-die-for views" on the 20th floor of the Radisson Blu Royal in Vesterbro; its "so-cool interior" is overseen by a staff that "treats you like a dignitary", so even if the cost is as "high" as the altitude, most maintain it's "worth the krone."

Café Victor *Danish/French* | 17 | 17 | 14 | E |

Kongens Nytorv | Ny Østergade 8 | (45-33) 13-36-13 | www.cafevictor.dk
Brace yourself for "pretty people" at this "classic but hip" Kongens Nytorv "fixture" that's "still hot" with the "well-heeled" set; the space has a cafe with a "limited menu" as well as a full-fledged restaurant serving "good French" fare (at lunch, they serve Danish dishes); though critics report "snobbish" service, few fault the "fun atmosphere."

Era Ora ☒ *Italian* | 27 | 21 | 24 | VE |

Christianshavn | Overgaden Neden Vandet 33B | (45-32) 54-06-93 | www.era-ora.dk
This "always-crowded" Northern Italian set on the canal in Christianshavn plies "authentic" Tuscan and Umbrian fare "bursting

with natural flavors" (and "accompanied by delicious wines"); fans call it "excellent in every way", given the "warm, efficient" service and a "gorgeous atmosphere" that "matches the gorgeous food"; "bring a really fat wallet", though – it's "wildly expensive."

Fifty Fifty *Japanese*   22 | 20 | 21 | E

Vesterbro | Vesterbrogade 42 | (45-33) 22-47-57 | www.fiftyfiftyfood.dk
There's more than a 50/50 chance both carnivores and finatics will "love" this "cool" Japanese in Vesterbro since it offers both grilled meats and raw fish; "good value and high standards" have made it a "fast favorite" of the "beautiful people."

Herman 🗷 *Danish/International*   21 | 22 | 19 | VE

Vesterbro | Nimb Hotel | Bernstorffsgade 5 | (45-88) 70-00-00 | www.nimb.dk
Fans (including the country's current queen) dub top chef Thomas Herman's small Danish-International "excellent", and it's also got "location, location, location" going for it as it's housed in a "magnificent" Moorish-inspired setting in the luxury Nimb Hotel overlooking Tivoli Gardens; sure, it's "expensive", but less-pricey on-premises options include a brasserie, steakhouse, wine bar, dairy, über-bakery and a very stylish cocktail bar.

Kanalen 🗷 *French/Danish*   23 | 20 | 22 | E

Christianshavn | Wilders Plads 2 | (45-32) 95-13-30 | www.restaurant-kanalen.dk
"Good-size portions" of "delicious" French-Danish fare are paired with an "excellent wine list" at this "charming", "upmarket" spot in "beautiful" Christianshavn with a "lovely canal view"; the "simple" space may be "a bit tight", but most find its "intimate" atmosphere to be "cozy" and "romantic."

Kiin Kiin *Thai*   21 | 21 | 20 | E

Nørrebro | Guldbergsgade 21 | (45-35) 35-75-55 | www.kiin.dk
"Hip" and "ambitious" entry that "takes Thai to another level" via the chef-owner's "modern interpretation" of Siamese cuisine; throw in a "spacious seating", futuristic decor (i.e. big golden Buddhas) and a "trendy" bohemian locale in Nørrebro, and no wonder fans feel it "deserves praise."

Kong Hans Kælder 🗷 *French/Danish*   26 | 25 | 24 | VE

Kongens Nytorv | Vingaardsstræde 6 | (45-33) 11-68-68 | www.konghans.dk
"One of the best culinary experiences" in Kongens Nytorv can be found at this "historic" wine cellar set in King Hans' royal mint (the city's "oldest" building), where "out-of-this-world" French-Danish cuisine – with an emphasis on "top-notch" fish – is served in a "lovely" setting with "nicely spaced tables" by a "personable" staff; yes, you'll "pay through the nose", but "you should visit at least once in your lifetime."

Krogs Fiskerestaurant 🗷 *French/Seafood* 25 | 20 | 22 | VE

Indre By | Gammel Strand 38 | (45-33) 15-89-15 | www.krogs.dk
The "fabulous" "fresh" fish is "fit for a king" at this "old-fashioned" French seafooder in Indre By, voted the Most Popular restaurant in Copenhagen; though the "sublime food" is certainly the "center of at-

FOOD | DECOR | SERVICE | COST

tention", everything about this "high-class" place is "elegant", from the "superb service" to the "lovely setting" and "wonderful wine pairings" – which helps explain the "ferociously expensive" tabs.

Le Sommelier *French*   23 | 18 | 23 | E

Kongens Nytorv | Bredgade 63-65 | (45-33) 11-45-15 | www.lesommelier.dk

"As the name indicates", the "fantastic wine list" at this Kongens Nytorv venue is "in a class of its own", but rest assured that the French cuisine is equally "outstanding", ditto the "warm welcome" from the "professional" staff; a few feel the decor of its "large, open" and "very white" interior "could be better", but others praise the "relaxed", "well-laid-out" space.

MASH *American/Steak*   22 | 18 | 20 | E

(aka Modern American Steak House)

Copenhagen | Strandvejen 235 | (45-33) 13-93-00
Indre By | Bredgade 20 | (45-33) 13-93-00
www.mashsteak.com

The "name says it all" (it's short for 'Modern American Steak House') at this "carnivore's dream" in Indre By that strives to bring a taste of Manhattan to Copenhagen; surveyors split on the result: "homesick" fans like the "good quality" beef "served with panache" in a white-tiled room, but foes counter it's merely "ordinary", adding "you might need a medic when you see the bill"; P.S. there's another outpost in Hellerup.

Noma ⏁Ⓜ *Scandinavian*   28 | 25 | 26 | VE

Christianshavn | Strandgade 93 | (45-32) 96-32-97 | www.noma.dk
Rated No. 1 for Food in Copenhagen and probably the city's toughest reservation, this "breathtaking" Scandinavian is set in a "rustic-chic" waterfront warehouse in Christianshavn; foodies rave about "magician" chef René Redzepi's "experimental" cooking, employing ancient Nordic cooking techniques (i.e. smoking, salting, pickling) that eschew olive oil, foie gras and truffles in favor of "overlooked ingredients" like berries and seaweed, making for a "whole new way of eating"; as for the pricing, start applying for that "second mortgage."

Pierre André ⏁Ⓜ *French*   24 | 18 | 23 | E

Indre By | Ny Østergade 21 | (45-33) 16-17-19 | www.pierreandre.dk
Named for the proprietors' two sons, this French brasserie in Indre By features chef-owner Philippe Houdet's "exciting", "elegant" cooking, served by an "observant" team overseen by his wife, Sussie; some see a "romantic edge" to the "traditional" decor, others sigh it's "not the most exciting in the city", but all agree it adds up to "great value for the money."

Restaurationen ⏁Ⓜ *Danish/French*   27 | 21 | 27 | VE

Indre By | Møntergade 19 | (45-33) 14-94-95 | www.restaurationen.dk
"Run by people who truly love good food", this "amazing" Danish-French in Indre By offers a "well-rounded" five-course prix fixe menu nightly – "no à la carte!" – of "innovative, gorgeous dishes" accompanied by an "excellent wine" list; a few find "nothing to cheer about" in the "nice-but-nothing-special" decor, but most maintain the overall experience is "absolutely superb."

	FOOD	DECOR	SERVICE	COST

Ricemarket *Thai*   22 | 19 | 16 | M

Indre By | Kultorvet 38 | (45-35) 35-75-30 | www.ricemarket.dk
Set in Kultorvet, the inner city square in Indre By, this "great little Thai"
lures crowds with "tasty" cooking and one of the best value-for-money
wine lists in town; it's too bad about the "inexperienced" service and
rather hectic atmosphere, but ultimately the "cheap" pricing
keeps regulars regular.

Royal Cafe, The *Danish*   22 | 21 | 20 | E

Indre By | Strøget | Amagertorv 6 | (45-38) 12-11-22 | www.theroyalcafe.dk
"Delicious" Danish 'smushies' – sushi-inspired riffs on *smørrebrød*,
traditional open-faced sandwiches – and "superb pastries" are the order of the day at this "conveniently located" spot in the middle of the
Strøget designer shopping district; it's geared toward "on-the-run"
types, but loyalists linger in the funky baroque interior with its glittering chandeliers, Georg Jensen cutlery and royal portraits.

Salt *Scandinavian*   21 | 21 | 18 | E

Indre By | Copenhagen Admiral Hotel | Toldbodgade 24-28 |
(45-33) 74-14-44 | www.saltrestaurant.dk
Sir Terence Conran's "stylish adaptation of a waterfront warehouse" is
the "well-designed setting" of this "thoroughly enjoyable" venue in
Indre By's Copenhagen Admiral Hotel; the "innovative" menu of
"delicious" modern Scandinavian cuisine is backed up by an "unex-
pectedly good wine list", but some say the "competent" staff "could be
warmer"; N.B. the inspiration for the restaurant name comes in part
from having each table topped with three kinds of sea salt.

Slotskælderen hos Gitte Kik 🖼🅼 *Danish*   23 | 21 | 21 | E

Indre By | Fortunstræde 4 | (45-33) 11-15-37
An "outstanding purveyor" of "good, old-fashioned Danish open sandwiches", this lunch-only "classic" *smørrebrød* specialist has been on
the scene in Indre By since 1910; choose from the likes of herring or
tiny shrimp, beer or schnapps and join the crowd of MPs from the
nearby parliament building that frequents this popular place.

Søllerød Kro 🅼 *French*   26 | 24 | 25 | VE

Holte | Søllerødvej 35 | (45-45) 80-25-05 | www.soelleroed-kro.dk
For French food "at its best", a "to-die-for wine list" and an "evening to
remember", check out this 1677 "charmer" in Holte, about a 20-
minute cab ride from the city center; housed in an "authentic Danish
cottage" surrounded by a garden and pond, it comes with an "impossibly romantic atmosphere" and a very "expensive" price tag.

Dublin

Ananda _Indian_ | 24 | 21 | 22 | E |

Dundrum | Dundrum Town Ctr. | 2-4 Sandyford Rd. | (353-1) 296-0099 |
www.anandarestaurant.ie

A "notch above the rest", this "impressive" Indian in Dundrum takes "typical fare to a contemporary level" via creative spicing and thoughtful presentation; the muted, stylish setting is "lovely" and the service "charming", making for a "fantastic all-around experience" – save for the somewhat "expensive" tabs; P.S.the same owners run less pricey Jaipur outposts located throughout the city

Bon Appetit Ⓜ _French_ | 22 | 20 | 21 | E |

Malahide | 9 James Terr. | (353-1) 845-0314 | www.bonappetit.ie

Located in the "lovely" seaside town of Malahide, north of Dublin, this "great dining experience" showcases the "excellent" French cooking of chef Oliver Dunne, served in a muted, cream-colored setting; sure, it's pricey, but insiders report that the tasting menu is "good value for the money"; N.B. there's also a more casual brasserie downstairs.

Chapter One Ⓢ Ⓜ _International_ | 23 | 23 | 24 | E |

Parnell Square | Dublin Writers Museum | 18-19 Parnell Sq. |
(353-1) 873-2266 | www.chapteronerestaurant.com

"You can almost hear Joyce and Yeats reading their work while you're dining on delicious food" at this International in the Dublin Writers Museum; considered one of the city's "finest", with a "good value pre-theater menu" from Tuesday–Saturday, it's a "must" for libation-lovers who salute the "inspirational" setting with its infamous Irish Coffee.

---

* Indicates a tie with restaurant above

	FOOD	DECOR	SERVICE	COST

China Sichuan *Chinese*
21 | 18 | 19 | M

Dundrum | The Forum | Ballymoss Rd., Sandyford Industrial Estate | (353-1) 293-5100 | www.china-sichuan.ie

This "authentic" Sichuan in an industrial park in Dundrum is back with a menu full of the same inventive, "better than expected" Chinese cooking showcasing top-quality Irish seafood; despite "haphazard service" and not much decor, "affordable" pricing carries the day.

Dax 🖂 Ⓜ *French*
22 | 20 | 21 | E

City Center | 23 Upper Pembroke St. | (353-1) 676-1494 | www.dax.ie

The "limited menu changes often so there is usually something new" at this French brasserie in the City Center that fans say is "not overpriced" given the "great ingredients"; the basement setting in a Georgina townhouse is "subdued" but "suave" and comfortable, making it a pleasant place to "while away an evening."

Eden *Irish*
22 | 21 | 22 | E

Temple Bar | Meeting House Sq. | (353-1) 670-5372 | www.edenrestaurant.ie

"Located in throbbing Temple Bar", this "buzzy" Irish "staple" boasts "sophisticated food", a "modern" setting and "friendly" service; "lots of locals" descend to dine on the legendary 'smokies' (smoked haddock with crème fraîche and cheddar cheese), and in summer the candlelit terrace is a "great scene" and place to watch films and shows.

Fallon & Byrne 🖂 *French*
22 | 21 | 20 | E

City Center | 11-17 Exchequer St. | (353-1) 472-1010 | www.fallonandbyrne.com

"Keep it up" order admirers of this French brasserie that's "conveniently located" in the City Center and "consistently good", with a particularly "excellent-value lunch menu"; a "polished staff" presides over a high-ceilinged, New York-like setting, and there's also a "very good" wine bar in the cellar as well as a "lovely grocer on the ground floor."

Jaipur *Indian*
22 | 15 | 17 | M

City Center | 41 S. Great George's St. | (353-1) 677-0999 | www.jaipur.ie

One of the "best Indians in Dublin" (and sibling to Ananda), this "authentic" subcontinental in a trendy part of the bustling City Center features low-key decor – light wood, chrome and floor-to-ceiling windows – that makes for a "nice environment"; prices are moderate to begin with, but there's a "great early-bird special" too; P.S. there are a number of other outposts throughout the city.

La Maison 🖂 *French Bistro*
25 | 22 | 22 | E

City Center | 15 Castle Market St. | (353-1) 672-7258 | www.lamaisonrestaurant.ie

"Very much a French restaurant", this small, big-windowed bistro in the City Center plies an "excellent" menu of "delicious" food and wine in an atmospheric "old-Europe" setting; "priceless" staffers "make the meal an event" and help distract from the "expensive" tabs.

L'Ecrivain 🖂 *Irish/French*
25 | 23 | 24 | VE

City Center | 109A Lower Baggot St. | (353-1) 661-1919 | www.lecrivain.com

"High-end" Irish-New French that's one of the city's "top picks" thanks to "loquacious" chef-owner Derry Clarke's "excellent, imaginative" fare; "staffers that make you feel like a guest in their home" preside over a quietly luxurious duplex setting that's "full of suits" during the week, while a pianist on Thursdays–Saturdays attracts the "special-occasion" crowd.

Lobster Pot 🖫 *Seafood*

| 22 | 17 | 21 | E |

Ballsbridge | 9 Ballsbridge Terrace | (353-1) 668-0025 | www.thelobsterpot.ie

A local favorite, this long-standing, "old-school" seafooder (Mornay sauce, anyone?) offers "frolicking fresh fish" in Ballsbridge, the embassy district, just south of the City Center; a "veteran staff" presides over a warm, "walking-back-into-a-time-machine" setting that includes an open fireplace, maritime memorabilia and a dessert cart.

Marco Pierre White Steakhouse & Grill *Steak*

| 23 | 21 | 21 | VE |

City Center | 51 Dawson St. | (353-1) 677-1155 | www.fitzers.ie

"Enjoyable" City Center steakhouse from "star chef" Marco Pierre White offering a menu wider than the name suggests along with "dapper" service; though surveyors split on the end result – "top class" vs. "another case of style over substance" – there's agreement on the "expensive" cost.

Mermaid Café *Irish*

| 21 | 18 | 22 | E |

Temple Bar | 69-70 Dame St. | (353-1) 670-8236 | www.mermaid.ie

This "lively" stalwart, on the edge of Temple Bar, is still going strong with "exceptionally well-prepared" modern Irish fare served by a "professional staff"; the high-ceilinged, open-kitchen setting may be simple but that doesn't keep it from being "one of the city's best loved eateries"; N.B. the daily changing lunch menu is one of Dublin's biggest bargains.

One Pico *French/Irish*

| 25 | 23 | 23 | VE |

City Center | 5-6 Molesworth Pl., Schoolhouse Ln. | (353-1) 676-0300 | www.onepico.com

Set in an 18th-century coach house "tucked away" in a lane off St. Stephen's Green is this French-Irish "gem" from chef-owner Eamonn O'Reilly; a "subtly elegant setting" is the backdrop for "wonderful", "top-quality" food, "accommodating service" and "amazing wines"; of course, dining at "one of Dublin's better restaurants" comes at a price.

Patrick Guilbaud 🖫 *French*

| 27 | 25 | 26 | VE |

City Center | 21 Upper Merrion St. | (353-1) 676-4192 | www.restaurantpatrickguilbaud.ie

"Every city has its famous restaurant and this is Dublin's" say fans of Patrick Guilbaud's "excellent all-round" French in City Center (voted Most Popular in the city), featuring Guillaume Lebrun's "revelatory" cuisine, 500 "world-class wines", "outstanding service" and "amazing", "luxe surroundings" adorned with 20th-century Irish art; the "blow-the-budget" tabs don't sting so much since "Bono may be at the next table."

Seasons *Irish/European*

| 26 | 25 | 27 | VE |

Ballsbridge | Four Seasons Hotel | Simmonscourt Rd. | (353-1) 665-4000 | www.fourseasons.com/dublin

"Exactly what you'd expect from the Four Seasons", this Irish-European in Ballsbridge offers "outstanding service", "excellent cuisine" and a

FOOD | DECOR | SERVICE | COST

"posh" setting with a fireplace, conservatory windows and an abundance of flowers; it all adds up to a "top-tier", "high-priced" experience, and some swear that the "Sunday brunch is the best in the world."

Shanahan's on the Green *Steak/Seafood*

| 25 | 24 | 26 | VE |

St. Stephen's Green | 119 St. Stephen's Green | (353-1) 407-0939 | www.shanahans.ie

"Great steaks – but gosh do you pay for them" – turn up at this opulent chophouse "conveniently located" on St. Stephen's Green, where the "portions are mammoth" ("I hope they have a defibrillator on the premises"), and the glamorous Georgian setting is far from typical of the genre; it's "loved by locals" for its seafood selection, "amazing wine list", celeb clientele and service that exudes "Irish charm"; P.S. "check out JFK's rocker in the Oval Office bar."

Tea Room *Irish/International*

| 24 | 23 | 20 | E |

Temple Bar | The Clarence | 6-8 Wellington Quay | (353-1) 407-0826 | www.theclarence.ie

A "cathedral to fine food" in the "über-hip", U2-owned Clarence hotel, this "chic", "spacious" Irish-International features "soaring ceilings", "tall windows", "acres of blond wood" and "heavenly" cuisine; it's "perfect for romance, business" or "people-watching", so if you're big on "buzz" and "only in town for a short time", this is the place.

Thornton's 🅂 Ⓜ *Irish/French*

| 27 | 19 | 25 | VE |

St. Stephen's Green | Fitzwilliam Hotel | 128 St. Stephen's Green | (353-1) 478-7008 | www.thorntonsrestaurant.com

Voted No. 1 for Food in the city, chef Kevin Thornton's "poetic, highly personal" Irish-French venue in St. Stephen's Green is "unsurpassed", with dishes made from the "highest quality fresh local ingredients" and served by a "perfect yet friendly" staff; sure, it's "very expensive", but most maintain it's a "great way to start or finish a trip to Dublin"; N.B. a refurb may outdate the above Decor score.

Winding Stair *Irish*

| 21 | 20 | 22 | M |

City Center | 40 Ormond Quay | (353-1) 872-7320 | www.winding-stair.com

This former City Center landmark with a bookstore downstairs and an Irish eatery above has changed owners again, but it still offers "reasonably priced", "wholesome fresh" food made from "quality ingredients" (many of them organic) and an extensive wine list; the "bright, airy" setting is simple, but big windows provide "lovely" views of the river Liffey.

Florence

TOP FOOD RANKING

	Restaurant	Cuisine
27	Enoteca Pinchiorri	Italian
26	Fuor d'Acqua	Seafood
	La Giostra	Tuscan
	Taverna del Bronzino	Italian
	Cibrèo	Italian
24	Cammillo Trattoria	Italian
	L'Osteria Di Giovanni	Tuscan
	Cantinetta Antinori	Italian
	Buca dell'Orafo	Tuscan
	Buca Lapi	Tuscan
	Il Latini	Tuscan
	Baccarossa	Mediterranean/Seafood
23	Sabatini	Tuscan
	Zibibbo	Italian/Mediterranean
	Enoteca Pane E Vino	Tuscan
	Trattoria Garga	Tuscan
	La Beppa Fioraia	Italian/Tuscan
	Cavolo Nero	Tuscan/International

Alle Murate ☑ *Italian* 22 | 21 | 21 | E

Duomo | Via del Proconsolo, 16R | (39-055) 240-618 | www.allemurate.it
"Modern Zen meets old-world history" at this "romantic" Italian near the
Duomo known for "comforting" fare bursting with "innovative" flavors
plus a "surprise behind the doors" – frescoes dating back to the 14th
century; whether "with your lover" or mate, you're in for a "delightful
evening", replete with a "unique atmosphere" and "charming service."

Baccarossa *Mediterranean/Seafood* 24 | 22 | 22 | M

Santa Croce | Via Ghibellina, 46/R | (39-055) 240-620 | www.baccarossa.it
"Not to be missed", this Med-seafooder off the tourist track is "worth
the walk" to Santa Croce for its "consistently good" fresh fish, meat
and pastas; the "excellent" wine list (including a large by-the-glass selection) and warm room, tastefully decorated with wood furnishings
and antiques, add to the reasons it's "recommended to friends."

Buca dell'Orafo ☒☑ *Tuscan* 24 | 19 | 20 | M

Ponte Vecchio | Via dei Girolami 28/R | (39-055) 213-619 |
www.bucadellorafo.com
Set in the cantina of a palace from the 1200s on a "small street near
the Ponte Vecchio", the Monni family's "elegant", "old-style" standby
is renowned for its "zesty", "unpretentious" "Tuscan specialties"
made with "fresh, seasonal ingredients" and backed by "excellent"
wine; it's frequented by "many locals" (further "testament" to its
"great cuisine"), and the staff "treats you like long-lost" relations.

Buca Lapi ☒ *Tuscan* 24 | 20 | 21 | E

City Center | Via del Trebbio, 1R | (39-055) 213-768 | www.bucalapi.com
"Go with a healthy appetite" and join the "locals and tourists" who reserve tables at this circa-1880 "temple to beef" in the basement of an

FOOD | DECOR | SERVICE | COST

11th-century palazzo off ritzy Tornabuoni where "saber-tooth–sized" *bistecca alla fiorentina* ("always done rare") "rules" and "hearty" "Tuscan classics abound"; the "old-school" room "strewn" with travel posters is "cozy", making it a "favorite" that's definitely "worth the pilgrimage"; P.S. dinner only.

Cammillo Trattoria *Italian*

24 | 19 | 22 | M

Oltrarno | Borgo Sant Jacopo, 57/R | (39-055) 212-427

"Still favored by Florentines even though tourists long ago invaded it", this "genuine" "old-timer" (circa 1945) in a "terrific location" in the Oltrarno district remains a "real" Italian "treat", offering "homestyle Tuscan food" that devotees declare "habit-forming"; "attentive service" plus a "comfy" feel are additional reasons diners keep "coming back"; P.S. closed Tuesday–Wednesday.

Cantinetta Antinori ☒ *Italian*

24 | 24 | 24 | E

Duomo | Piazza Antinori, 3 | (39-055) 292-234 | www.cantinetta-antinori.com

"Impeccably prepared" creations "designed to please every palate" served alongside a "sensational" "wine list worthy of the family pedigree" (the famous Antinori "vintners of Tuscany") make this "refined" Italian, set in a 15th-century Renaissance palazzo near the Piazza Duomo, "one of the most attractive gastronomic spots in Firenze"; the "lovely" rustic "room itself is a masterpiece" and the service is "warm and friendly", so it's little wonder admirers agree it's "absolutely not to be missed"; P.S. closed Saturday–Sunday.

Cavolo Nero ☒ *Tuscan/International*

23 | 20 | 20 | E

San Frediano | Via dell' Ardiglione, 22/R | (39-055) 294-744 | www.cavolonero.it

Join "lots of local residents" for a "delightful meal" at this chef-owned spot behind the Carmine church in the San Frediano district serving contemporary Tuscan-International cuisine (including vegetarian and gluten-free offerings) in an "intimate" room or seasonal garden; the "young ambiance" and "nice, informal" service with "no pretenses" further heighten its allure.

Cibrèo ☒ *Italian*

26 | 22 | 23 | E

St. Ambrogio | Via Andrea del Verrocchio, 8R | (39-055) 234-1100 | www.fabiopicchi.it

"Attentive" chef-owner Fabio Picchi sometimes "sits down" with diners himself and "recites the menu", upping the "wow" factor at this "romantic" St. Ambrogio Italian, voted Florence's Most Popular restaurant, where "unpredictable" offerings like "cock's comb and tripe" (but "beware", "no pasta") can lead to a "crazy, delightful, delicious experience"; the dishes arrive "like a perfect ballet" in this "exquisite feast" for those "willing to pay the freight"; P.S. check out Picchi's "more rustic", "affordable" Trattoria Cibrèo on the corner (same kitchen) along with a cafe, Il Teatro del Sale.

Enoteca Pane E Vino ☒ *Tuscan*

23 | 21 | 22 | M

Oltrarno | Piazza di Cestello, 3R | (39-055) 247-6956 | www.ristorantepaneevino.it

"Bustling with locals and tourists alike", this two-level Tuscan "gem" with a barnlike interior in the Oltrarno district boasts "well-prepared" fare that's not only "satisfying" but full of "fanciful flavors" and ele-

	FOOD	DECOR	SERVICE	COST

vated by a 300-bottle wine list including "excellent" options by the glass; the vibe is "fun and lively" and the service "amiable", making it "just what you would expect" at a "comfortable" enoteca.

Enoteca Pinchiorri 🗷Ⓜ *Italian*   27 | 26 | 26 | VE

Santa Croce | Via Ghibellina, 87 | (39-055) 242-757 | www.enotecapinchiorri.com

"Mortgage your house" if you must to dine at Annie Féolde's "stunning" Renaissance "beauty" "at least once in your life" assert acolytes of this "luxurious" Croce Italian, voted No. 1 for Food in Florence for its "fantastic" cuisine and "divine" wine list (ask for a tour of partner Giorgio Pinchiorri's "out-of-this-world" cellar) matched by "equally superb service"; prices are "wickedly high", but it's a "very rare case" when the tabs equal the "truly elegant fine-dining experience."

Fuor d'Acqua 🗷 *Seafood*   26 | 23 | 24 | VE

San Frediano | Via Pisana, 37/R | (39-055) 222-299

"Enjoy" the "wonderfully fresh fish" sourced daily from the coast plus other "incredible seafood" dishes with "flair" at this "very chic" San Frediano venue popular with the fashion and entertainment set; the "sharp and simple, minimalist decor" featuring a vaulted brick ceiling and the "impeccable service" also win favor – just "prepare to pay" as it's "really expensive."

Il Latini Ⓜ *Tuscan*   24 | 18 | 21 | M

City Center | Via dei Palchetti, 6R | (39-055) 210-916 | www.illatini.com

"Get there early" and "be willing to wait your turn among the throngs" at this "rustic", "feel-good" Tuscan in City Center, where "friendly, generous" servers deliver a "true groaning board" of "dynamite" "regional cooking" for a "fair price"; "superb" wine plus the experience of eating "with strangers" at communal tables completes the very appealing picture.

La Beppa Fioraia *Italian/Tuscan*   23 | 21 | 18 | M

Oltrarno | Via Erta Canina 6/R | (39-055) 234-7681 | www.labeppafioraia.it

Tailored to the "young" crowd, this "fashionable" Tuscan-Italian in the Oltrarno area has a "pleasant" colorful setting and plans to open a must-reserve garden space; the price is "certainly right" and the staff is "extremely welcoming" – two more reasons why it's well "suited for dinners among friends."

La Giostra ☻ *Tuscan*   26 | 21 | 24 | E

Duomo | Via Borgo Pinti, 12/R | (39-055) 241-341 | www.ristorantelagiostra.com

"Hospitable" owners – twin sons from a "noble family" – generate a "warm and welcoming" vibe at this "memorable" Duomo Tuscan where the "generous portions" of "refined", "well-prepared" plates add to the "overall" "great experience"; the lack of signage outside can be a bit "deceiving", but the "unique interior" enhanced by "twinkling lights" is quite "lovely" and "cozy."

L'Osteria Di Giovanni *Tuscan*   24 | 21 | 24 | M

Duomo | Via del Moro, 18/R | (39-55) 284-897 | www.osteriadigiovanni.it

"The finest Tuscan ingredients are prepared and served with infinite care and charm" at Giovanni Latini's "delightful" midpriced dining room near the Duomo, a "sublime alternative to the bustle" of his family's Il Latini restaurant nearby; the staff "couldn't be more welcoming", serving "extras not ordered" and making the "dinner very special."

Sabatini 🗷Ⓜ *Tuscan*   23 | 22 | 23 | E

Duomo | Via Panzani, 9/A | (39-055) 282-802 | www.ristorantesabatini.it
"Grand" in an "old-fashioned way", this "elegant" Tuscan near the Duomo is especially "pleasurable" "on a beautiful Roman night" when you can sit in the garden and dine on "classic" dishes off the "vast menu"; the "efficient staff" "makes you feel truly important and pampered", and though a few snipe "you must enjoy the tourists with it", others counter it's a "solid choice."

Taverna del Bronzino 🗷 *Italian*   26 | 23 | 25 | E

Piazza Indipendenza | Via delle Ruote, 25/R | (39-055) 495-220
The staff "makes you feel as though" they exist "to make you happy" remark admirers of this "commendable establishment" "off the beaten path" in the Piazza Indipendenza that's known for "phenomenal" Italian cuisine plus a "wide selection of wine"; the setting, a Renaissance palazzo with velvet chairs, a vaulted ceiling and "terracotta floors", is "charming", one more reason it's deemed a "must whenever in Florence."

Trattoria Garga *Tuscan*   23 | 21 | 22 | E

Duomo | Via del Moro 48/R | (39-055) 239-8898 | www.garga.it
"Delicious and dreamy", this "arty" "backstreet eatery" near the Duomo serves a "well-considered" menu of *"fantastico"*, "flavorful" Tuscan dishes, including the "citrus pasta that you've heard about" ("can't wait to return for more"); "from the flamboyantly painted walls" and "unique" sculptures to the "hospitable" staff, it's an impressive experience and "one to seek out."

Zibibbo *Italian/Mediterranean*   23 | 20 | 21 | E

Careggi | Via di Terzollina, 3A | (39-055) 433-383 |
www.trattoriazibibbo.it
"Wonderful" chef-owner Benedetta Vitali (ex Cibrèo) and her "cordial staff" always deliver "something exciting" at this Italian-Med "mecca for foodies" that's "worth the short trip" "from the city proper" to the Careggi hills; enhancing the experience are the "large selection of wines" and modern setting with a glass skylight, red accents and views of the Medici tower.

Frankfurt

TOP FOOD RANKING

	Restaurant	Cuisine
25	Gargantua	French/Mediterranean
	Villa Rothschild	German
	Osteria Enoteca	Italian
24	Restaurant Français	French
	Goldman	German
	Silk	International
23	Aubergine	Italian/French
	Ivory Club	Indian/Steak
	Sushimoto	Japanese
	Emma Metzler	French/German
	Heimat Essen & Weine	German

Apfelwein Wagner ● *German*   16 | 14 | 14 | M

Sachsenhausen | Schweizer Str. 71 | (49-69) 612-565 |
www.apfelwein-wagner.com

For a taste of "typical Frankfurt", try this "apple-wine pub" in
Sachsenhausen, rated Most Popular in the city; the "down-to-earth"
digs may be "bleak", the "simple" German fare "unexceptional"
("pork, pork and more pork") and the "rough", "gruff" staffers "un-
couth" (typical for this type of establishment), but "fast service",
"moderate prices" and the city's "signature beverage" make it "popular among locals and tourists alike."

Aubergine ⊠ *Italian/French*   23 | 22 | 23 | E

City Center | Alte Gasse 14 | (49-69) 920-0780 | www.aubergine-frankfurt.de
There's a small red awning marking this "superb" City Center spot
where one can expect "extravagant, freshly prepared" Italian-French
fare as well as "attentive service" from a "nice, young" staff; owner
and native Sardinian Paolo Vargiu's "incredible attention to detail" extends from the "excellent" wine list and "tasteful decor" "right down
to the Versace plates" that grace the few tables.

Edelweiss ● *Austrian*   20 | 15 | 21 | M

Sachsenhausen | Schweizer Str. 96 | (49-69) 619-696 |
www.edelweiss-ffm.de

"Friendly service" combined with a "relaxed atmosphere" lends a "holiday" feel to this "comfortable" Sachsenhausen pseudo–ski lodge
where the "authentic" Austrian food (including some "wonderful"
Wiener schnitzel) is accompanied by a selection of "super brews to wash
everything down"; P.S. don't miss the large heated smokers' terrace.

Emma Metzler Ⓜ *French/German*   23 | 21 | 22 | E

Sachsenhausen | Museum of Applied Art | Schaumainkai 17 |
(49-69) 6199-5906 | www.emma-metzler.com

"Hidden" in Sachsenhausen's Museum of Applied Art, this "tricky-to-
find" venue offers a "modern" regional French-German menu backed
up by an excellent wine list; the "tasteful but spartan" setting (in a
Richard Meier building) includes an "open kitchen", white furniture
and glass walls overlooking a "lovely garden."

	FOOD	DECOR	SERVICE	COST

Gargantua ☒ *French/Mediterranean*
25 | 19 | 20 | VE

Westend | Park Gallery | An der Welle 3 | (49-69) 720-718 |
www.gargantua.de

Monika Winterstein-Trebes, the widow of late chef-owner Klaus
Trebes, has kept intact the "creative, well-executed menu" of "incredible" New French–Med fare that makes this "exceptional bistro" in
Westend justifiably "famous" (and No. 1 for Food in Frankfurt); "good
service" and a winning wine list are other reasons it's "well worth" a
visit; yes, it's quite expensive, but such an "excellent" experience offers "good value for the money"; P.S. a post-Survey move to a modern
setting in an office complex behind the old Opera House (complete
with a terrace) is not reflected in the Decor score.

Goldman Restaurant ☒ *German*
24 | 21 | 23 | E

Ostend | Goldman 25hours Hotel | Hanauer Landstr. 127 |
(49-69) 40586-89806 | www.goldman-restaurant.de

"Casual" sums up the scene at this Ostend hotel venue that plies a
"fantastic" Nouvelle German menu where the "pride in preparation" is
plainly evident; a "friendly" mood and "knowledgeable" service make for
"good value for the money" – no wonder it enjoys such a "hip" reputation.

Heimat Essen & Weine *German*
23 | 20 | 23 | E

City Center | Berliner Str. 70 | (49-69) 2972-5994 |
www.heimat-frankfurt.com

"Comfort food, German-style" turns up at this "outstanding" dinner-only venue in City Center where the "delicious" contemporary offerings and "excellent wine cellar" speak to "refined palates"; the striking
oval space – reminiscent of Edward Hopper's iconic painting,
Nighthawks – doesn't have many seats, so be sure to reserve in advance; P.S. there's also terrace seating.

Holbein's *German/International*
19 | 21 | 16 | E

Sachsenhausen | Städel Kunstmuseum | Holbeinstr. 1 |
(49-69) 6605-6666 | www.holbeins.de

"Beautiful, stylish decor" is the point at this "posh joint" that's "nicely
located in the Städel museum" in Sachsenhausen, a "wonderful setting" ("in summer, sit on the terrace" overlooking the gardens) "for a
great meal" of "tasty" German-International fare made from "particularly fresh ingredients"; still, some complain about "long waits" and
suggest that the generally "well-trained staff" is "not accommodating"
when "stressed"; P.S. Monday is dinner-only.

Ivory Club *Indian/Steak*
23 | 23 | 21 | VE

City Center | Taunusanlage 15 | (49-69) 7706-7767 | www.ivory-club.de

"Quite different from anything else" in Frankfurt, this "league-of-its-own" City Center venue offers "delicious" Indian fare though it's also
"well known for its steaks"; the "clubby, colonial" decor in the "dark"
room includes "library shelves" and lots of "rich mahogany", making
the "watch-your-wallet" tabs easier to bear; P.S. it offers valet parking.

Osteria Enoteca ☒ *Italian*
25 | 18 | 23 | E

Rödelheim | Arnoldshainer Str. 2 | (49-69) 789-2216 |
www.osteria-enoteca.de

"Fresh", "delicious Italian food" (including "great antipasti") draws urbanites to this bi-level venue in the somewhat "remote suburb" of

FOOD DECOR SERVICE COST

Rödelheim, where guests must ring a bell to gain access to the romantically lit, off-white dining room; add in a "good wine list" and an "accommodating" staff and you'll see why many label it a "special-occasion place" that's "worth the trip"; P.S. a post-Survey chef change may outdate the Food score.

Restaurant Français ⊠ *French* · · · · · · · · 24 | 22 | 24 | VE

City Center | Steigenberger Frankfurter Hof | Am Kaiserplatz | (49-69) 215-118 | www.frankfurter-hof.steigenberger.de
Set in "Frankfurt's dowager hotel", City Center's Steigenberger Frankfurter Hof, this "formal special-occasion restaurant" has been "nicely upgraded" in recent years, and now attracts a "less-stuffy clientele" with its "gourmet New French selections", "excellent service", "extremely civilized" decor and lovely terrace; "make sure you have plenty of room on your credit card", though, because though "you'll feel like royalty", you'll need access to the state treasury to settle the bill"; P.S. closed Saturday and Sunday.

Silk ⊠Ⓜ *International* · · · · · · · · · · · · · · 24 | 25 | 22 | VE

Ostend | Cocoon Club | Carl-Benz-Str. 21 | (49-69) 900-200 | www.schmecken.net
"Not your everyday dining experience", this dinner-only "bed restaurant" in Ostend set "inside the famous Cocoon Club" is appropriately "cool and modern", though some find it "hard to eat" in a reclining position; the "amazing", "all-white" setting and "excellent" multicourse tasting menu of Eclectic fare make for "unique", albeit very expensive, dining; P.S. dinner service for all patrons starts at 8 PM sharp.

Sushimoto Ⓜ *Japanese* · · · · · · · · · · · · · 23 | 16 | 18 | E

City Center | Westin Grand Hotel | Konrad Adenauer Str. 7 | (49-69) 131-0057 | www.sushimoto.eu
Guests "wonder if you can eat as well" in Tokyo as at this "unexpected" Japanese in City Center's Westin Grand; despite decor that "isn't world-shaking" and a staff that could use "a better knowledge of German" and English, it's a "must for fans" seeking "fantastic, fresh meals" featuring "excellent sushi" and teppanyaki selections; P.S. those who find the tabs "too high" should check out the more "moderately priced set menu" at lunch.

Villa Rothschild *German* · · · · · · · · · · · · 25 | 24 | 24 | VE

Königstein im Taunus | Hotel Villa Rothschild Kempinski | Im Rothschildpark 1 | (49-61) 742-9080 | www.kempinski.com
"Splurge" diners tout this "astoundingly expensive" eatery set on the grounds of the Hotel Villa Rothschild Kempinksi, the former summer residence of the Rothschild family in Königstein im Taunus; an "exquisite" contemporary German menu prepared in the 'classic French style' is buttressed by "extraordinary service" and a tastefully "magnificent ambiance", so despite the high tabs, many find it to be "quite good value for the money"; P.S. more relaxed dining can be found in Tizian's Brasserie, also attached to the hotel.

Geneva

TOP FOOD RANKING

	Restaurant	Cuisine
29	Domaine de Châteauvieux	French
26	Auberge du Lion d'Or	French
25	Patara	Thai
	Le Tsé-Fung	Chinese
24	Le Floris	French/Mediterranean
	Rasoi by Vineet	Indian
	Chez Jacky	French
	La Favola	Italian
	Miyako	Japanese
	L'Auberge d'Hermance	French
23	L'Entrecôte Couronnée	French
	Vertig'O*	French/Mediterranean
	Relais de Chambésy	French
	Il Lago	Italian
	Le Grill	International
	Le Relais de l'Entrecôte	Steak
	Le Chat-Botté	French

Auberge du Lion d'Or *French*   `26` `24` `25` `VE`
Cologny | 5 Place Pierre-Gautier | (41-22) 736-4432 |
www.liondor.ch
Worth the trip "outside of town", this "excellent, old-school" inn in
Cologny, deemed the Most Popular eatery in Geneva, boasts a "contemporary" gastronomic restaurant and a "pretty", more casual bistro, "both of which serve fabulous French food"; the setting
"overlooking the lake" is "magnificent" and the service "impeccable"
at this "not-to-be-missed experience."

Brasserie Lipp ● *French*   `18` `17` `15` `E`
Left Bank | Confédération Centre | 8 Rue de la Confédération |
(41-22) 318-8030 | www.brasserie-lipp.com
"Modeled on its Paris namesake", this "busy", "buzzy" Left Bank boîte
has "everything you'd expect" in a "typical French brasserie" – a
"noisy", art nouveau setting "packed" with patrons at "too-small tables"
enjoying "consistently good" traditional fare served by sometimes-
abrupt staffers; it also offers "salvation for those who don't eat on a
strict Swiss timetable", as it's "seemingly always open."

Chez Jacky 🅱 *French*   `24` `15` `21` `E`
Right Bank | 9-11 Rue Necker | (41-22) 732-8680 |
www.chezjacky.ch
For "distinguished dining", try this "great little restaurant" with a
"slightly off-the-beaten-track" Right Bank address that only "adds to
its cachet"; the "imaginative" French cooking is a good "value" (regulars recommend you "stick to the excellent, affordable set menu"),
and a "friendly staff" further enhances the "pleasant" atmosphere;
P.S. "dining on the patio is just wonderful."

---

* Indicates a tie with restaurant above

	FOOD	DECOR	SERVICE	COST

Domaine de Châteauvieux ⏱Ⓜ *French* — 29 | 25 | 27 | VE

Satigny | Domaine de Châteauvieux | 16 Chemin de Châteauvieux, Peney-Dessus | (41-22) 753-1511 | www.chateauvieux.ch
Ranked No. 1 for Food in greater Geneva, this "deluxe" venue in a "marvelous" Satigny setting overlooking the Rhône offers some of "the best" dining in town; "creative" chef Philippe Chevrier produces "superb" New French fare paired with a "fantastic wine list" and "impeccably served" by an "attentive, efficient" crew in a "lovely room" with "panoramic countryside views"; for best results, you'll need a "well-filled billfold", but everyone should experience this "true gastronomic delight" at least "once."

Il Lago *Italian* — 23 | 26 | 23 | VE

Right Bank | Four Seasons Hôtel des Bergues | 33 Quai des Bergues | (41-22) 908-7110 | www.fourseasons.com/geneva
Set in the Four Seasons Hôtel des Bergues on the Right Bank, this "elite" Northern Italian offers "excellent" cuisine and a "great wine list" that showcases bottles from France, Switzerland and Italy, proffered in a "beautiful" "formal setting" complete with extravagant floral displays and views of the Rhône; "off-the-charts" pricing comes with the territory.

La Favola ⏱ *Italian* — 24 | 22 | 19 | E

Old Town | 15 Rue Jean Calvin | (41-22) 311-7437 | www.lafavola.com
It's no fairy tale: a "most memorable meal" can be found at this "tiny gem" in the heart of Old Town, a "wonderful retreat" where "fabulous" Italian dishes and wines (with a few Ticino selections) are served with "personalized attention" in a "cute" duplex "jewel box"; though both floors are "sweet", regulars navigate the "tight staircase" for a "table upstairs"; P.S. don't miss some of the "best tiramisu ever."

L'Auberge d'Hermance *French* — 24 | 23 | 24 | E

Hermance | L'Auberge d'Hermance | 12 Rue du Midi | (41-22) 751-1368 | www.hotel-hermance.ch
Peripatetic patrons willing to drive "15 minutes outside of the city" will be rewarded with an undeniably "great meal" at this "idyllic" French inn set in the medieval village of Hermance, where a "professional" staff will seat you either in an "intimate" "antique" dining room, a "delightful" glass-walled winter garden or on the "beautiful terrace"; wherever you wind up, however, expect "attractively presented dishes" from a "superb kitchen."

Le Chat-Botté ⏱ *French* — 23 | 22 | 23 | VE

Right Bank | Hôtel Beau-Rivage | 13 Quai du Mont-Blanc | (41-22) 716-6666 | www.beau-rivage.ch
A "favorite for many years", this "elegant" French venue in the Right Bank's Hôtel Beau-Rivage features "enchanting" cuisine and a "very nice wine list", all "effortlessly served" in a "refined setting" resembling a "grand palace"; yes, "it'll cost you", but most feel the "quality equals the price."

Le Floris ⏱Ⓜ *French/Mediterranean* — 24 | 23 | 22 | E

Anières | 287 Route d'Hermance | (41-22) 751-2020 | www.lefloris.com
"Magnificent" views of Lake Geneva echo the "high standards" of this French-Med "treat" nestled in the posh suburb of Anières; sure, the

"fancy" menu (including vegetarian options) is "expensive", but the service is so "pampering" and the outdoor terrace so "fabulous" that most agree it's "worth the cost"; N.B. an attached bistro, Café de Floris, offers "more moderate prices."

Le Grill International

23 | 22 | 23 | VE

Right Bank | Grand Hotel Kempinski | 19 Quai du Mont-Blanc | (41-22) 908-9220 | www.kempinski-geneva.com

At this expensive but "enjoyable" International in the Grand Hotel Kempinski, patrons select their own status steak (e.g. Swiss Simmental, French Charolais) or seafood (Scottish salmon, Brittany blue lobster) from two glassed-in refrigerators, then watch their preparation in the open kitchen; floor-to-ceiling windows offer "beautiful" views of Lake Geneva, its iconic Jet d'Eau and snow-capped Mont Blanc.

L'Entrecôte Couronnée French

23 | 18 | 19 | E

Right Bank | 5 Rue des Pâquis | (41-22) 732-8445 | www.restaurants-geneve.ch/entrecote-couronnee

This "lively" little Right Bank French place features an "excellent" namesake steak along with "endless frites", but other "quality" dishes – based on local ingredients – have many "coming back for more"; wooden furnishings and ceiling fans lend a bistro ambiance.

Le Relais de l'Entrecôte ⧆ Steak

23 | 18 | 17 | M

Left Bank | 49 Rue du Rhône | (41-22) 310-6004 | www.relaisentrecote.fr

"Choice is not the strong suit" of this "single-dish" steakhouse on the Left Bank, but fans tout its "classic frites" and "addictive" steak sauce ("guaranteed to have you licking the plate"); the "only disadvantage" is that it's "difficult to get a table" in the "noisy", "cramped" space, but most "don't mind standing in line" when the prices are so "fair."

Les Armures French/Swiss

19 | 19 | 17 | E

Old Town | Hôtel Les Armures | 1 Rue Puits-St-Pierre | (41-22) 310-3442 | www.hotel-les-armures.ch

Just "steps from all the points of interest in Old Town", this "longtime favorite" in the "lovely" Hôtel Les Armures is "crowded" with "conventioneers and tourists" seeking "stereotypical" Swiss food from a "traditional menu" (think "great fondue and raclette") along with classic French dishes; be warned, though, that the "overpowering smell" of melted cheese may stay with you for a "long time."

Le Tsé-Fung Chinese

25 | 22 | 22 | VE

Bellevue | La Réserve Genève | 301 Route de Lausanne | (41-22) 959-5888 | www.lareserve.ch

Bellevue's "über-stylish" La Réserve Genève hotel is home to this "exclusive getaway" that brings "China to Switzerland" via an "incredible" Chinese menu notable for its lack of any traces of Asian fusion; ok, the pricing is "over-the-top", but compensations include a silky, red-lacquer-and-gold-leaf setting and a "beautiful" summer terrace overlooking the lake and Mont Blanc.

Miyako ⧆ Japanese

24 | 18 | 22 | VE

Right Bank | 11 Rue de Chantepoulet | (41-22) 738-0120 | www.miyako.ch

"One of the best Japanese restaurants in Geneva", this Right Bank spot serves up "fresh" sushi and sashimi, plus "wonderful teppanyaki", to "business" types in a "traditional" (some say "stuffy") room; though the "excellent" staffers are "all very willing to help" ensure that guests "enjoy a nice evening", some still wonder whether the experience "justifies the excessive prices."

Patara *Thai*

25 | 19 | 19 | E

Right Bank | Hôtel Beau-Rivage | 13 Quai du Mont-Blanc | (41-22) 731-5566 | www.patara-geneve.ch

"Part of a high-class chain" with additional locations in Singapore, Taipei and London, this "deluxe" Thai in a "great" Right Bank location offers "excellent" (albeit "high-priced") Siamese cuisine delivered by "attentive" staffers in a "pretty setting" replete with ceiling fans, wooden blinds and fresh flowers; still, some purists pout that the fare's "not authentic enough", while others opine that service suffers when it's "overcrowded."

Rasoi by Vineet 🗷 🅼 *Indian*

24 | 24 | 24 | VE

Right Bank | Mandarin Oriental | 1 Quai Turrettini | (41-22) 909-0006 | www.rasoi.ch

There's "real depth and subtlety" to be found on the menu of this haute Indian in the Right Bank's Mandarin Oriental hotel, where the "thrilling flavors" make for a "classy take" on subcontinental cuisine; the "stylish" setting, lavishly adorned with mother of pearl and silver foil (and including an all-weather terrace), hints at the "very expensive" tabs to come.

Relais de Chambésy 🗷 *French*

23 | 22 | 22 | E

Chambésy | 8 Place de Chambésy | (41-22) 758-1105 | www.relaisdechambesy.ch

"Genius chef" Philippe Chevrier is the mind behind this "charming" outpost in the posh Right Bank suburb of Chambésy, where "classic" French dishes are served in three rustic, fireplace-equipped dining rooms; though prices are relatively modest by Geneva standards, diners who order wine by the bottle are advised "make sure to hit the bank" first – lest the tabs "blow your expense account" out of the water.

Vertig'O 🗷 🅼 *French/Mediterranean*

23 | 22 | 24 | VE

Right Bank | Hôtel de la Paix | 11 Quai du Mont-Blanc | (41-22) 909-6073 | www.hoteldelapaix.ch

"Pleasing" cuisine, "excellent" service, "stunning" contemporary decor and a "beautiful location on the lake shore" make for a "winning" experience at this French-Med that replaced the former Café de la Paix in the venerable, same-named Right Bank hotel; however, you may well get vertigo when the "exorbitant" bill arrives.

Hamburg

TOP FOOD RANKING

	Restaurant	Cuisine
25	Haerlin	French/Mediterranean
	Seven Seas*	French
	Henssler & Henssler	Japanese
24	Atlantic	International
23	Jacobs	French/Mediterranean
	Landhaus Scherrer	German
	Le Canard Nouveau	Mediterranean
	Doc Cheng's	Eurasian
	Fischereihafen	Seafood
22	Stock's Fischrestaurant	German/Seafood
	Cox	French/Mediterranean
21	IndoChine	French/Vietnamese
	Engel	German

Atlantic Restaurant 🗷 *International*　　24 | 22 | 25 | VE

St. Georg | Hotel Atlantic Kempinski Hamburg | An der Alster 72-79 | (49-40) 288-8860 | www.kempinski.atlantic.de

"Although you can't go wrong with anything" on the menu, the seafood is particularly "amazing" at this "echt" International in the "beautiful old-world" Hotel Atlantic Kempinski; indeed, everything at this jacket-required spot is "top-drawer" – from the "perfect service" to the "classic" setting with its view of Lake Alster; just remember that "excellence comes at a price"; P.S. the arrival of new chef Peter Könemann may outdate the above Food score.

Cox *French/Mediterranean*　　22 | 15 | 18 | E

St. Georg | Lange Reihe 68 | (49-40) 249-422 | www.restaurant-cox.de

"Satisfied" surveyors are "surprised" by the "creativity" of the "excellent" New French–Med as well as modern German cooking by long-time kitchen crew Tilo Moldt and Holger Dankenbring at this St. Georg venue; its "restrained" decor elicits "contradictory opinions" with some terming it "tasteful", while others yawn "boring"; still, most agree that the staff offers "good advice" on what to order from the "short", "innovative" menu.

Doc Cheng's 🗷 *Eurasian*　　23 | 22 | 23 | E

Neustadt | Fairmont Hotel Vier Jahreszeiten | Neuer Jungfernstieg 9-14 | (49-40) 349-4333 | www.hvj.de

An "all-round" winner, this "high-class establishment" in the Fairmont Hotel Vier Jahreszeiten boasts a "nice team" (new chef Philip Troppenhagen arrived in 2010, possibly outdating the Decor score), both in its "show kitchen" (where chefs prepare their "great Eurasian fusion fare" in front of you) and on the floor, where "accommodating" staffers "make every effort" to ensure guests "feel well cared for"; rounding out the "top-notch dining" experience is the "stylish Shanghai Express decor", which somehow makes the "elevated prices" seem almost "appropriate."

---

* Indicates a tie with restaurant above

	FOOD	DECOR	SERVICE	COST

Engel *German*   — 21 | 19 | 19 | E

Flottbek | Landeanlage Teufelsbrück | (49-40) 824-187 |
www.restaurant-engel.de

Parked on the deck of a landing pier in Flottbek, this small, "laid-back"
place is known for the "unbeatable views" of the Elbe and its "busy
shipping traffic"; the German cuisine is equally "enjoyable", though a
few say the service is "typically cold for Germany"; try the snack bar
downstairs at the ferry pier for a more casual snack.

Fischereihafen *Seafood*   — 23 | 14 | 19 | E

Altona | Grosse Elbstr. 143 | (49-40) 381-816 |
www.fischereihafenrestaurant.de

"Excellent quality and outstanding selection" are hallmarks of this
"traditional" ("not trendy") fish house offering "skillfully prepared",
"classic seafood" that's "as fresh as it comes", served by a "friendly"
crew that really "knows the menu"; some say the "dignified" decor is
getting "a bit dowdy", but all appreciate its "great" dockside location
in Altona, complete with a "wonderful view."

Haerlin 🅈 🅼 *French/Mediterranean*   — 25 | 21 | 25 | VE

Neustadt | Fairmont Hotel Vier Jahreszeiten | Neuer Jungfernstieg 9-14 |
(49-40) 3494-3310 | www.hvj.de

Tied for No. 1 for Food in Hamburg, this "top spot" in the Fairmont
Hotel Vier Jahreszeiten is "distinguished" by chef Christoph Rüffer's
"superb" French-Med cuisine, "gracious service" (the staffers are "so
attentive they know what you want before you do") and an "excellent
location" affording "lovely views of the Alstersee"; in short, this
"dream" of a place makes you "feel special", even if you're not one of
its "famous guests from radio, television and politics."

Henssler & Henssler 🅈 *Japanese*   — 25 | 21 | 22 | E

Altona | Grosse Elbstr. 160 | (49-40) 3869-9000 | www.hensslerhenssler.de

"TV chef" Steffen Henssler and his father run this "hip" Japanese in
Altona, featuring a 13-ft.-long sushi bar stocked with fish that "can't
get much fresher"; the "modern" room is "stylish" and the service
"friendly", though its "trendy" following can make for "noisy" dining;
Henssler's second restaurant, Ono, is located at Lehmweg 17.

IndoChine *French/Vietnamese*   — 21 | 21 | 19 | E

Altona | Neumühlen 11 | (49-40) 3980-7880 | www.indochine.de

The "people-watching is as important as the cuisine-eating" at this
"creative" French-Vietnamese in Altona with an "unbeatable" waterfront location featuring "nice views of Hamburg's harbor"; brace yourself for a "trendy" scene – think giant Buddha statues and a downstairs
"bar made of ice" – that's just the ticket for "hosting clients."

Jacobs *French/Mediterranean*   — 23 | - | 22 | VE

Nienstedten | Hotel Louis C. Jacob | Elbchaussee 401-403 |
(49-40) 8225-5407 | www.hotel-jacob.de

"Exquisite" French-Med fare, an "excellent" wine list, "confident"
staffers and "classic decor" combine at this "elegant" establishment in
Nienstedten's Hotel Louis C. Jacob, voted Most Popular in Hamburg;
whether you enjoy "top chef" Thomas Martin's "imaginative" cooking
in a room newly renovated and adorned with "wonderful oil paintings"
or out on the "magnificent tree-shaded terrace overlooking the Elbe

	FOOD	DECOR	SERVICE	COST

River", the experience will "remain in your memory a long time" – but be sure to bring a "fat wallet"; P.S. closed Tuesdays.

Landhaus Scherrer 🗹 *German*   23 | 16 | 20 | VE

Ottensen | Elbchaussee 130 | (49-40) 880-1325 | www.landhausscherrer.de

"Old-world charm abounds" at this pricey German in Ottensen, close to the Elbe River, where an "obliging" staff provides guests with "super recommendations" from the "creative menu" of "first-class" modern cookery; some feel the "decor could be better", but more insist that its "homelike atmosphere" helps to make it "ideal for a cozy get-together"; there's also a "less-expensive" adjoining bistro, Ö1, with terrace dining in summer; P.S. the Decor score may be outdated by an upcoming interior redecoration.

Le Canard Nouveau 🗹Ⓜ *Mediterranean*   23 | 20 | 20 | VE

Ottensen | Elbchaussee 139 | (49-40) 8812-9531 | www.lecanard-hamburg.de

This "excellent" Mediterranean in Ottensen is "one of the best restaurants in town" and also comes with perhaps the "most stunning view of the Elbe River"; true, it's "very expensive" but "always worth it", particularly if you get a seat on the terrace or the table in the private-feeling chef's corner, with windows looking into the kitchen.

Rive ◑ *Mediterranean/Seafood*   17 | 19 | 17 | E

Altona | Van-der-Smissen-Str. 1 | (49-40) 380-5919 | www.rive.de

Romantics suggest a "table by the window" or on the "sunny terrace" of this "posh" Med seafooder also blessed with a "fantastic" Altona location boasting an "exceptional view of the Elbe"; the "something-for-everyone" menu includes many "imaginative" creations, though foes cite "nothing-special decor", just "ok service" and "high costs", saying it's "better for a light snack and drinks than an evening out."

Seven Seas Ⓜ *French*   25 | 21 | 22 | E

Blankenese | Süllberg Hotel | Süllbergstr. 12 | (49-40) 866-2520 | www.suellberg-hamburg.de

Located in the Süllberg Hotel in Blankenese, one of Hamburg's most prestigious residential areas, this "unique dining experience" offers "exquisitely prepared" haute French cuisine (tied for No. 1 for Food in the city) served in a glowing, modern setting by "excellent" staffers; but what makes it a "romantic" destination is its "priceless view" of the river Elbe; P.S. closed Mondays and Tuesdays.

Stock's Fischrestaurant Ⓜ *German/Seafood*   22 | 15 | 21 | M

Poppenbüttel | An der Alsterschleife 3 | (49-40) 602-0043 | www.stocks.de

German seafooder set in a replica of an 18th-century thatched house "pleasantly located near Treudelberg Park" in residential Poppenbüttel; fans imagine the "excellent" fish "jumped directly out of the water onto the plate with a brief stopover in the frying pan" and ignore the "meager" decor, given the moderate tabs.

Istanbul

Balikci Sabahattin *Seafood*   25 | 17 | 20 | E

Sultanahmet | Cankurtaran Seyit Hasan Kuyu Sokak 1 |
(90-212) 458-1824 | www.balikcisabahattin.com
"Authentic", "freshly made mezes" and "excellent fish" lure loyalists
to this Sultanahmet seafooder "near the Blue Mosque" set in a restored mansion behind the Armada Hotel; for the best atmosphere
"sit at an outside table", then relax and enjoy a "classic Turkish experience"; P.S. the formerly fixed-price menu is now à la carte, resulting
in somewhat higher tabs.

Borsa *Turkish*   26 | 16 | 25 | E

Harbiye | Istanbul Lutfi Kirdar Convention & Exhibition Ctr. |
(90-212) 232-4201
Sariyer | Istinye Park Shopping Mall | Istinye Bayiri Caddesi 73 |
(90-212) 345 5333
Uskudar | Adile Sultan Palace | Siraevler Sokak 12 | (90-216) 460 0304
www.borsarestaurants.com
Voted Istanbul's No. 1 for Food, the Harbiye original of this culinary institution is renowned for "excellent traditional" Turkish cuisine ("best
doner kebab in town") ably presented by a courteous crew; a "handy
address" in the Lutfi Kirdar convention center ("five minutes from major hotels") makes it a natural for a "businesslike" "older crowd" that
also appreciates the "lovely" glassed-in terrace "overlooking the sea
and the city"; there are additional locations in Istinye and Uskudar.

Del Mare *Seafood*   23 | 18 | 20 | E

Cengelkoy | Kuleli Caddesi 53/4 | (90-216) 422-5762 | www.del-mare.com
The menu is extensive, the food "delicious" and the service "kind" at
this Cengelkoy seafooder set in a historic former distillery building;
still, its "biggest asset" of "dining alfresco in the moonlight" on the ex-

	FOOD	DECOR	SERVICE	COST

pansive terrace with a "fantastic view of the Bosphorus is what leaves most "breathless"; boat service is available from Kurucesme on the European side with a phone call in advance.

Develi *Turkish*   25 | 13 | 21 | M

Ataxehir | Vedat Gunyol Caddesi 9 | (90-212) 575-6868
Etiler | Tepecik Yolu 22 | (90-212) 263-2571
Kalamis | Kalamis Marina | Munir Nurettin Selcuk Caddesi | (90-216) 418-9400
Samatya | Gumusyuzuk Sokak 7 | (90-212) 529-0833
www.develikebap.com

"Fun, frantic and fabulous", these "outstanding kebab houses" specializing in spicy Southeastern Turkish–style fare are "where the locals go" to fill up for relative "pennies" – though it's also "friendly to business travelers" who "can't go wrong" with any of the "multitude of meat selections"; maybe the "decor isn't great", but the Samatya original's "pleasant open-air rooftop" provides a panoramic "view of the harbor"; Develi Marin in the Kalamis Marina expands the chain's offerings to seafood.

Feriye Lokantasi ◑ *Turkish/Ottoman*   23 | 24 | 22 | E

Ortakoy | Ciragan Caddesi 40 | (90-212) 227-2216 | www.feriye.com

"Summer is the best time" to dine at this "beautiful" converted police station in Ortakoy known for its "lovely terrace" and "one of Istanbul's most spectacular views" of the Bosphorus Bridge ("unforgettable at sunset"); indeed, the location is so "breathtaking" that it's "almost difficult to focus" on the "succulent" Turkish-Ottoman cuisine, comparatively extensive wine list and service that's "as good as it gets."

Istanbul Culinary Institute ✆ *Turkish*   25 | 19 | 22 | M

Tepebasi | Mesrutiyet Cadessi 59 | (90-212) 251-2214 | www.istanbulculinary.com

As "interesting diversions" go, it's hard to top this "great experience" in a Tepebasi cooking school where culinary students concoct "experimental menus" that bring a "fresh perspective" to "old-world" Turkish-International fare; the "casual" setting, located at street level with some sidewalk seats and on an airy mezzanine with floor-to-ceiling windows, is as "pleasant" as the pricing.

Konyali *Turkish/Ottoman*   24 | 19 | 22 | E

Levent | Kanyon Shopping Mall | Buyukdere Caddesi 185 | (90-212) 353-0450
Sultanahmet | Topkapi Palace | Divan Yolu Caddesi | (90-212) 513-9696
www.konyalilokantasi.com

For those "coming to Istanbul for the first time", this "memorable" venue in Sultanahmet is a "must-try", having served "authentic" Turkish-Ottoman dishes to everyone from kings and queens to tourists for half a century; while the Levent spin-off in the Kanyon Shopping Mall is "reliable" enough (and serves alcohol), insiders say the flagship location in Topkapi Palace (lunch only, closed Tuesdays) is far superior, given the "sublime views" from its terrace.

Kosebasi *Turkish*   23 | 16 | 20 | M

Beylikduzu | Hurriyet Bulvari, Skyport Residence 1/22 | (90-212) 876-8824
Fenerbahce | Fuatpasa Caddesi, Kurukahveciler Sokak | (90-216) 363-5856
Levent | Camlik Sokak 15/3 | (90-212) 270-2433

(continued)

Kosebasi

Nisantasi | Bronz Sokak 5A | (90-212) 230-3868 ◐
www.kosebasi.com.tr

"You can't miss" at this modern, "upscale" Turkish chain, a "local fa-vorite" with a "wide array" of "tantalizing", "sizzling" kebabs, "plenti-ful" meze and large, affordable wine lists; execs from the nearby business districts often entertain foreign clients here, although a few fear they've "opened too many branches" to sustain the high quality.

Laledan *Seafood*   24 | 27 | 26 | VE

Besiktas | Ciragan Palace Kempinski | Ciragan Caddesi 32 |
(90-212) 326-4646 | www.kempinski-istanbul.com

This "stunning" seafooder in the Ciragan Palace Kempinski has fans rhapsodizing over its "spectacular" Bosphorus views and elegant interi-ors ("like dining in a museum"); staffers provide near "perfect service" along with "world-class food and wine" to a well-heeled clientele, leaving a dazed few to sigh that with surroundings "so pretty" they "can't remember how the meal was."

Paper Moon ◑ *Italian*   22 | 22 | 21 | VE

Etiler | Akmerkez Residence | Ahmet Adnan Saygun Caddesi |
(90-212) 282-1616 | www.papermoon.com.tr

"Playboys, models" and other "beautiful" specimens make up the "scene" at this upscale Italian in Etiler's Akmerkez Residence hotel, and though many "go for the people-watching", they wind up "staying for the food"; "good" pastas, risottos and wood-fired pizzas are served in the Milano-"chic" dining room or the garden, but because the experience can be "über-expensive", it's best for those with "expense accounts."

Poseidon *Seafood*   25 | 20 | 22 | E

Bebek | Cevdetpasa Caddesi 58/1 | (90-212) 287-9531 |
www.poseidonbebek.com

It's not surprising that a place named after the Greek god of the sea specializes in seafood, but this one in posh Bebek may be the "best" in town, offering a "wonderful variety of well-prepared dishes" served by an "attentive staff"; the aquatic emphasis expands to their "unforget-table dining terrace" and its "fantastic view of the Bosphorus."

Seasons Restaurant *Turkish/Mediterranean* 25 | 26 | 27 | VE

Sultanahmet | Four Seasons Hotel | Tevkifhane Sokak 1 |
(90-212) 402-3150 | www.fourseasons.com/istanbul

At the center of what was a "former prison" in Sultanahmet lies this "intimate" glass-walled restaurant, Istanbul's Most Popular and a place to "mingle with the upper crust" over "marvelous" Turkish-Med meals and "excellent local wines" ("order with abandon – it's all good"); icing the cake is "extraordinary", "typical-Four-Seasons-quality" ser-vice from an "attentive" staff; an outdoor terrace is open in summer, while the lavish Sunday brunch is popular year round.

Sunset Grill & Bar *International*   23 | 26 | 25 | VE

Ulus Park | Adnan Saygun Caddesi Yol Sokak 2 | (90-212) 287-0357 |
www.sunsetgrillbar.com

"Out of the City Center" but nevertheless a "must-go", this Ulus Park spot with "terrace tables overlooking the city and the Bosphorus" is "one of Istanbul's best options for summer dining", plus the "magnificent" vistas are visible from the open interior; "great" International eats (e.g. "unbeatable" but "expensive" sushi and steaks) come courtesy of a "wonderful" staff, so in all ways "it's worth the trip."

Tike *Turkish* | 25 | 18 | 20 | E |

Florya | Germeyan Sokak | (90-212) 574-0505
Gunesli | Kocman Caddesi Ziyal Plaza 38, C Blok | (90-212) 630-5930 ⊠
Kadikoy | Kazim Ozalp Caddesi 58 | (90-216) 467-5914
Kemerburgaz | Arcadium Shopping Mall | (90-212) 322-3255
Levent | Karanfil Sokak 5 | (90-212) 281-8871
www.tike.com.tr

"Everyone knows" about this burgeoning chain of "upscale kebab houses" famed for its "delicious", "perfectly seasoned" grilled meat skewers and "tasty" meze and salads; the "modern", "trendy" settings and ample alfresco seating appeal to "crowds" of affluent types, as do the indoor/outdoor bars featured at the original Levent location.

Topaz *Turkish/Mediterranean* | 22 | 22 | 22 | E |

Gumussuyu | Inonu Caddesi 50 | (90-212) 249-1001 |
www.topazistanbul.com

A "stunning view of the Bosphorus" that verges on the "heavenly" greets visitors to this "mandatory stop" in Gumussuyu that offers both "traditional Turkish" and Ottoman cuisine as well as "modern Mediterranean" dishes; sure, the pricing is "high-end" and yes, there are lots of "tourists" in evidence, but most feel this "lovely place" is destined to be "a classic for years to come."

Tugra ◐ *Turkish/Ottoman* | 25 | 28 | 27 | VE |

Besiktas | Ciragan Palace Kempinski | Ciragan Caddesi 32 |
(90-212) 326-4646 | www.kempinski-istanbul.com

"Mind-blowingly beautiful", this "fabulous" jewel box "overlooking the glittering Bosphorus" makes it clear you're "dining in the palace" of a sultan (now the Ciragan Palace Kempinski in Besiktas); expect "wonderful" Turkish and Ottoman fare, a wine list that's among the best, "excellent" live music by a kanun (zither)-playing singer and tabs that may necessitate dipping into the royal treasury; P.S. the menu offers half Ottoman/Turkish dishes from the 1910s and half modern fare.

Ulus 29 *Turkish/International* | 24 | 26 | 22 | VE |

Ulus Park | Ahmet Adnan Saygun Caddesi Yol Sokak 1 |
(90-212) 358-2929 | www.club29.com

Perched on a hilltop inside Ulus Park, this "always 'in'" eatery offers "drop-dead" vistas – not only a "famous" panoramic Bosphorus view of both bridges but also glimpses of the "beautiful people" – from an "elegant" mod-minimalist space that serves up "top-level", premium-priced Turkish-International cuisine.

Zuma ◐ *Japanese* | 24 | 22 | 20 | VE |

Ortakoy | Salhane Sok 7 | (90-212) 236-2296 | www.zumarestaurant.com
"Even if you are already stuffed, you can't resist" the "fantastic fare" at this Ortakoy Japanese that's a spin-off of its buzzy sibs in London and Hong Kong; ultra-expensive sushi and robata are served in a "memorable" glass-and-bamboo setting with a "lovely dining terrace" (summer only) and enhanced by "great views of the Bosphorus."

Lisbon

TOP FOOD RANKING

	Restaurant	Cuisine
26	Varanda	French
25	O Mercado do Peixe	Seafood
	Gambrinus	Portuguese
	Restaurante 100 Maneiras	Portuguese
	Bocca	Portuguese
24	Casa da Comida	Portuguese
	Tavares Rico	Portuguese/International
	Solar dos Presuntos	Portuguese
23	Adega Tia Matilde	Portuguese
	A Casa do Bacalhau	Portuguese/Seafood
	Mezzaluna	Italian
	A Travessa	International
22	Pap'Açorda	Portuguese
	Eleven	Mediterranean
	Alma	Portuguese
21	XL	Portuguese/International
	Panorama	International
19	Bica do Sapato	Portuguese/Japanese
	Olivier Restaurante	Mediterranean

A Casa do Bacalhau ⊠ *Portuguese/Seafood*   23 | 19 | 20 | E

Beato | Rua do Grilo 54 | (351-21) 862-0000 |
www.acasadobacalhau.com

Voted Most Popular in Lisbon, this "tradition" that's set in a botanic
garden near the Beato convent dishes its signature Portuguese cod
prepared "in as many ways as you can think of"; architecturally intact
with modern touches and a domed ceiling, the 18th-century building
makes you "feel like you're eating at home – in a good way."

Adega Tia Matilde ⊠ *Portuguese*   23 | 12 | 18 | M

Praça de Espanha | Rua da Beneficencia 77 | (351-21) 797-2172 |
www.adegatiamatilde.com

Diners who "used to go" with their grandparents now "take their family" to this midpriced Portuguese standby that's been serving "truly
classic", "simple" fare in Praça de Espanha since 1937; sure, the traditional tiled decor "needs an improvement" and servers friendly "to
usual customers" may "give a different attention to first-time visitors", but it's still "a good option", especially for those looking "to go
where the locals eat"; P.S. closed for dinner on Saturday and
lunch on Sunday.

Alma *Portuguese*   22 | 17 | 18 | E

Santos | Calçada Marquês de Abrantes 92/94 | (351-21) 396-3527 |
www.alma.co.pt

Go to this "small" Santos spot "for the experience" urge gastronomes
who delight in the "interesting tastes" of chef-owner Henrique Sá
Pessoa's "original" Asian-influenced Portuguese menu backed by a
"simple but agreeable wine list"; the toque also has a TV show, which
helps explain why the place is "always full", so reserve in advance.

	FOOD	DECOR	SERVICE	COST

A Travessa ☒ International   23 | 24 | 21 | E

Madragoa | Travessa do Convento das Bernardas 12 |
(351-21) 390-2034 | www.atravessa.com

What a "wonderful experience" exclaim fans of this "beautiful but casual" International spot in the 17th-century Convento das Bernardas in the historical quarter of Madragoa; the cuisine, a "mixture" of Belgian and Portuguese flavors, is "very good" indeed, offering "value for the money", with regional wine selections and beer from Belgium to boot.

Bica do Sapato Portuguese/Japanese   19 | 23 | 17 | E

Santa Apolónia | Avenida Infante D. Henrique, Armazém B, Cais da Pedra |
(351-21) 881-0320 | www.bicadosapato.com

"Traditional" Portuguese dishes with a "modern twist", plus the opportunity to "see and be seen" while scoping out "local celebs galore", attract a "trendy" crowd to this "well-known" waterfront warehouse near Santa Apolónia co-owned by actors Catherine Deneuve and John Malkovich; "although it's expensive" and the service leaves something to be desired, the "nice view of the Tagus River" and a "super atmosphere" still make it "worthwhile"; P.S. there's a separate sushi bar upstairs.

Bocca ☒ Portuguese   25 | 23 | 25 | E

Marquês de Pombal | Rua Rodrigo da Fonseca 87D | (351-21) 380-8383 |
www.bocca.pt

"One of the best places to enjoy a top meal", this Marquês de Pombal "foodie paradise" helmed by chef Alexandre Silva "fully satisfies all senses" with its "creative", "beautifully presented" Portuguese dishes backed by "some of the best wines from any region in Portugal"; add in "cool, casual and cosmopolitan" decor plus "outstanding service" and there's no wonder "it's hard to find better for the price."

Casa da Comida ☒ Portuguese   24 | 22 | 23 | E

Jardim das Amoreiras | Travessa das Amoreiras 1 | (351-21) 386-0889 |
www.casadacomida.pt

An "oasis in Lisbon" is how admirers describe this "lovely" 18th-century townhouse in Jardim das Amoreiras where the "inspired Portuguese" menu features "creative and interesting" dishes delivered with "friendly, courteous" service; to enhance the "unique" dining experience, some start an "intimate, leisurely evening" with cocktails in the wood-paneled lounge before moving to the interior walled garden.

Eleven ☒ Mediterranean   22 | 25 | 22 | VE

São Sebastião da Pedreira | Jardim Amália Rodrigues |
Rua Marquês de Fronteira | (351-21) 386-2211 | www.restauranteleven.com

For "creative", contemporary Mediterranean cooking, "strong wine pairings" and "wonderful views", head to chef Joachim Koerper's "elegant, modern" eatery, set on a hill above Parque Eduardo Sentimo; numbers-crunchers carp that the "food, though wonderful" doesn't "achieve the heights" expected for a "restaurant of this caliber", while the "cost, on the other hand, exceeds all bounds."

Gambrinus ● Portuguese   25 | 18 | 24 | VE

Baixa | Rua das Portas de Santo Antão 23 | (351-21) 342-1466 |
www.gambrinuslisboa.com

Offering a "touch of the old world" in the Baixa, this "traditional" Portuguese is renowned for its "excellent" seafood and service – and "sobering" prices; though its "old-fashioned" decor featuring dark-wood paneling, leather chairs and stained glass prompts some to quip to might be time "to renovate", it still feels "magical" to most.

Mezzaluna ☒ *Italian* | 23 | 18 | 20 | M |

Rato | Rua Artilharia UM 16 | (351-21) 387-9944 | www.mezzalunalisboa.com

An "interesting group of patrons" adds to the appeal of this Rato Italian that dishes out "excellent" *cucina* in a simply decorated setting with dark wood and cream walls; "pleasant" service and moderate prices make it a natural choice for "kids and families."

Olivier Restaurante ●☒ *Mediterranean* | 19 | 20 | 16 | E |

Chiado | Rua de Alecrim 23 | (351-21) 342-2916 | www.restaurante-olivier.com

Olivier da Costa's "buzzy", "trendy" eatery in Chiado remains "popular with the locals" and travelers who come to dine on his "tasty" Mediterranean fare; "people-watching at the bar", "unpretentious service" and a "stylishly casual" vibe are additional incentives to "certainly go again."

O Mercado do Peixe *Seafood* | 25 | 15 | 19 | E |

Monsanto | Estrada Pedro Teixeira, Vila Simão, Caramão da Ajuda | (351-21) 361-6070 | www.mercadodopeixe.web.pt

Enthusiasts who "love" this Monsanto standby agree that while the understated decor may not be a highlight, the "really fresh" seafood makes it "worth the trip"; make your selection from the large array displayed at the traditional Portuguese market near the entrance, then watch it being prepared on the big grill in the middle of the dining room before enjoying the "excellent" results.

Panorama *International* | 21 | 22 | 19 | E |

São Sebastião da Pedreira | Sheraton Lisboa Hotel & Spa | Rua Latino Coelho 1, 25th fl. | (351-21) 312-0000 | www.sheratonlisboa.com

The panoramic "view is spectacular" at this lofty dining room in the "classy" Sheraton Lisboa Hotel & Spa say admirers who gaze out at the sights below while "enjoying" International cuisine made with market-fresh ingredients; add in "prompt, courteous" service and "it's one of the best places" in town "for a romantic dinner", though wallet-watchers note the "cost is rather high."

Pap'Açorda ☒Ⓜ *Portuguese* | 22 | 19 | 20 | E |

Bairro Alto | Rua da Atalaia 57-59 | (351-21) 346-4811

Serving "old-school food in a new-school environment", this "Lisbon institution" in the narrow streets of the Bairro Alto specializes in "traditional Portuguese" fare, including its namesake açorda (a bread stew of shellfish, garlic and coriander), with a somewhat "modern twist"; "tourists", professionals and "local celebrities" often mix at the lively marble-topped bar.

Restaurante 100 Maneiras ●☒ *Portuguese* | 25 | 19 | 24 | E |

Bairro Alto | Rua do Teixeira 35 | (351-21) 099-0475 | www.restaurante100maneiras.com

Buckle up for a "palatable adventure" at this "small" Portuguese "find" in Bairro Alto where a "friendly staff" starts the meal off right and chef

Ljubomir Stanisic wows diners with "innovative", "delicious" tasting menus highlighting "interesting ingredients" in "funky combinations"; not only is the experience "unforgettable", it also provides "good value for the money", so it's no wonder patrons deem it "definitely worth the visit"; P.S. Bistro 100 Maneiras opened in Chiado in 2010.

Solar dos Presuntos ☒ *Portuguese*   24 | 14 | 21 | M

Baixa | Rua das Portas de Santo Antão 150 | (351-21) 342-4253 | www.solardospresuntos.com

"Food lovers" craving "traditional Portuguese fare done with care" "return" to this "affordable" Restaurant Row standby in the Baixa for "simple", "delicious" dishes including regional specialties from Minho and "excellent seafood"; the modest, warm-hued space attracts a mixed crowd, and regulars insist "the service is great to anyone" who stops by.

Tavares Rico ☒ *Portuguese/International*   24 | 27 | 25 | VE

Chiado | Rua da Misericórdia 35-37 | (351-21) 342-1112 | www.tavaresrico.pt

"The gilded, mirrored dining room" and "perfect service" "provide authentic old-world charm" at this "romantic", "elegant" legend in Chiado, the city's oldest restaurant, dating back to 1784; "delicious" Portuguese-International cuisine bursting with "beautifully refined flavors" matches the "gorgeous setting", making for a "special" meal.

Varanda *French*   26 | 24 | 26 | VE

São Sebastião da Pedreira | Four Seasons Hotel Ritz | Rua Rodrigo da Fonseca 88 | (351-21) 381-1400 | www.fourseasons.com/lisbon

"Everything about it is outstanding" declare devotees of this "lovely" French affair in the Four Seasons, voted No. 1 for Food in Lisbon for its "great variety" of "classic and modern dishes" that are "simply perfect"; yes, it's quite "expensive", but "immaculate" service and a "beautiful atmosphere" befit the costly bill; P.S. the lunch buffet is "the best value" you'll find "anywhere."

XL ●☒ *Portuguese/International*   21 | 18 | 17 | E

Lapa | Calçada da Estrela 57-63 | (351-21) 395-6118

In the Lapa district "near the Assembleia de Republica" you'll find this fashionable chef-owned Portuguese-International spot turning out "unusual" dishes accompanied by a wine list that's "just sensational"; the "little room" done up in warm colors with rustic and sophisticated touches is "very pleasant" and the "views of the pretty people are not too bad, either."

London

TOP FOOD RANKING

	FOOD	DECOR	SERVICE	COST

	Restaurant	Cuisine
29	Ledbury	French
28	Pied à Terre	French
	Dinings	Japanese
	Le Gavroche	French
	Hunan	Chinese
	Gordon Ramsay/68 Royal	French
27	Square	French
	Dinner/Heston Blumenthal	British
	Chez Bruce	British
	Marcus Wareing	French
	Café Japan	Japanese
	L'Oranger*	French
	Nobu London	Japanese
	River Café	Italian
	Scott's	Seafood
	Murano	European
	Alain Ducasse/Dorchester	French
	L'Atelier de Joël Robuchon	French
	Wilton's	British/Seafood
	Harwood Arms	British
	La Petite Maison	Mediterranean
	Kiku	Japanese
26	Umu	Japanese
	Zuma	Japanese

Alain Ducasse at The Dorchester 🅢🅜 French
27 | 26 | 26 | VE

Mayfair | The Dorchester | 53 Park Ln., W1 (Hyde Park Corner/Marble Arch) | (44-20) 7629-8866 | www.alainducasse-dorchester.com

"The food and service are the stars" of chef Alain Ducasse's "nirvana" in The Dorchester, where an "impeccable" staff "guides diners" through the the New French menu; the set-price lunch is "fantastic value", though everything else is "expensive", "you only live once!"

Café Japan 🅜 Japanese
27 | 10 | 21 | M

Golders Green | 626 Finchley Rd., NW11 (Golders Green) | (44-20) 8455-6854

"Luxuriant" sushi and sashimi sold in "large slices" for "cheap" prices make this Golders Green Japanese "popular", and sometimes "chaotic", so "booking is advisable"; the "neon-lit" decor in the "noisy" room may be "old ", but "efficient", "caring service" compensates.

Chez Bruce British
27 | 21 | 26 | VE

Wandsworth | 2 Bellevue Rd., SW17 (Balham/Wandsworth Common Rail) | (44-20) 8672-0114 | www.chezbruce.co.uk

"Understated elegance" still sums up the decor of this "pride of Wandsworth Common", but a recent expansion has imbued it with

---

* Indicates a tie with restaurant above

"new vim and vigour", while chef-owner Bruce Poole's "inventive" Modern British menu is as "superb" as ever (and "pricey" too, but ultimately "phenomenal value"); it's a bit "out of town", but with an "adventurous wine list", "not-to-be-missed cheese board" and "attentive", "charming service" as part of the package, it's "well worth the trek."

Dinings ☒ *Japanese*
28 | 15 | 21 | E

Marylebone | 22 Harcourt St., W1 (Edgware Rd.) | (44-20) 7723-0666 | www.dinings.co.uk

Epicures estimate that "90% of the dishes can't be found anywhere else" than at this "innovative" Marylebone Japanese, serving up "smashing" small plates, "outstanding sushi" and "fantastic" cooked dishes in "spartan" basement digs "no larger than a shoebox" and an equally tiny ground-floor sushi bar; no surprise, it's "expensive", but most are "happy to pay the price" – hence, "getting a table is super hard."

NEW Dinner by Heston Blumenthal *British*
27 | 26 | 25 | VE

Knightsbridge | Mandarin Oriental Hyde Park | 66 Knightsbridge, SW1 (Knightsbridge) | (44-20) 7201 3833 | www.dinnerbyheston.com

Possibly the "hottest restaurant" opening of the past year, this Mandarin Oriental newcomer presents chef Heston Blumenthal's "sublime, unique", "exciting" Modern British menu "inspired by historic recipes" and rife with "baffling juxtapositions", such as the "work-of-art" 'meat fruit' starter (the overall concept is "far different than the Fat Duck", but just as "outstanding"); an "attentive" staff and a "stylish, grand" setting with "nice views" of Hyde Park and into the "fish-bowl kitchen" add to its appeal, with "expense-account" prices the "only drawback."

Gordon Ramsay at 68 Royal Hospital Rd. ☒ *French*
28 | 25 | 28 | VE

Chelsea | 68 Royal Hospital Rd., SW3 (Sloane Sq.) | (44-20) 7352-4441 | www.gordonramsay.com

"Despite spreading himself thin as a pancake", Gordon Ramsay makes sure the "standards don't slip" at his "temple of haute cuisine" in Chelsea, where chef Clare Smyth's "sublime" New French menu is a "delight from start to finish" and "full of surprises"; in the "sedate", "intimate, luxurious setting", a "wonderful sommelier" (part of the "professional", "gracious" staff) proves "extremely helpful" with the "to-die-for wine list", and while everything is "ultraexpensive", it's "worth every penny" for an "unforgettable" experience.

Harwood Arms *British*
27 | 19 | 21 | E

Fulham | 27 Walham Grove, SW6 (Fulham Broadway) | (44-20) 7386-1847 | www.harwoodarms.com

"Brilliance and sheer audaciousness" are the hallmarks of the "addictive" Modern British menu (featuring "exceptional" Scotch eggs and plenty of game) at this "casual", "lively" Fulham gastropub that most find "affordable"; the "wide range of ales and wines" and "charming country" setting add to the "stellar" experience, but "the limited number of tables makes getting a reservation difficult", so plan ahead or try to squeeze in at the bar.

	FOOD	DECOR	SERVICE	COST

Hunan ☒ *Chinese* | 28 | 13 | 22 | E |

Pimlico | 51 Pimlico Rd., SW1 (Sloane Sq.) | (44-20) 7730-5712 |
www.hunanlondon.com

At this "characterful Chinese" on Pimlico Green, the father-son chef-owner team ask "what you don't like, then serve course after course" of "amazing" Hunan small plates with "vibrant flavors", some "hot as a pistol", "until you can't take any more"; additionally, the "outstanding", "affordable" wine list is "a great fit with the food", plus it dulls the pain of the "cramped, tired" setting and "pricey" fare (it's "worth it").

Ivy, The ◐ *British/European* | 22 | 22 | 23 | E |

Covent Garden | 1-5 West St., WC2 (Leicester Sq.) | (44-20) 7836-4751 |
www.the-ivy.co.uk

The "X factor" is palpable at this "energetic" Covent Garden "class act" that attracts "a famous face or four" for its "high-standard", "delish" Modern British–Euro "comfort food"; but "everyone is a star" in the eyes of the "stellar" staff, whose "professionalism" mitigates the "trauma of getting a reservation" and paying the "expensive" bill.

J. Sheekey ◐ *Seafood* | 26 | 22 | 24 | VE |

Covent Garden | 28-32 St. Martin's Ct., WC2 (Leicester Sq.) |
(44-20) 7240-2565 | www.j-sheekey.co.uk

Though it attracts a "glamorous", "celeb"-dotted crowd, the "real star is the impeccable fish" offered at this "memorable" Covent Garden "institution" with a "clubby", "dark-paneled" "labyrinth" of "nooks and crannies", some "romantic", others with "too many people sitting too close together"; "warm", "swift service" and a "delightful wine list" help make the "expense-account" prices seem "worth it", but remember that it's "always crowded", so a "reservation is a must."

Kiku *Japanese* | 27 | 20 | 24 | E |

Mayfair | 17 Half Moon St., W1 (Green Park) | (44-20) 7499-4208 |
www.kikurestaurant.co.uk

"Expensive and worth it" exclaim dinner diners of this "smart", "brightly lit" Mayfair "gem" where "excellent sushi and sashimi" is offered alongside "wonderful" "tempura, shabu-shabu" and other Japanese dishes; lunchtime can be a "bargain" thanks to the set menus, while service is "attentive and friendly" at all times.

La Petite Maison *Mediterranean* | 27 | 21 | 21 | VE |

Mayfair | 54 Brooks Mews, W1 (Bond St.) | (44-20) 7495-4774 |
www.lpmlondon.co.uk

Go with "a group" to "share" and "graze" among "exquisite combinations" of "outstanding", "full-of-flavor" Mediterranean small and large plates at this "big", "inviting" Mayfair "hot spot"; sure, it's "expensive", "hectic", "noisy" and there's "room for improvement" in the service department, but those are quibbles – "to call it anything but incredible would be a disservice."

L'Atelier de Joël Robuchon *French* | 27 | 24 | 24 | VE |

Covent Garden | 13-15 West St., WC2 (Leicester Sq.) |
(44-20) 7010-8600 | www.joel-robuchon.com

"A sublime experience from a sublime chef", this "hip" Theatrelander stars Joël Robuchon's "artfully presented", "mind-blowing" New French menu flush with small plates (some find them "too small") sold at "huge

FOOD DECOR SERVICE COST

prices" (though "worth it"); "smiley, attentive service" holds sway throughout the tri-tiered space, comprising the "vibrant" red L'Atelier ("sit at the counter" for a "full view" of the "amazing" cooks), the "sleek, quiet", dinner-only La Cuisine and the "even swankier cocktail lounge."

Ledbury, The *French* | 29 | 25 | 28 | VE |

Notting Hill | 127 Ledbury Rd., W11 (Notting Hill Gate/Westbourne Park) | (44-20) 7792-9090 | www.theledbury.com

The "exhilarating tastes and textures" of "challenging chef" Brett Graham's New French dishes make for "ethereal" meals, which once again earn London's No. 1 Food rating at this Notting Hill destination whose setting is an "attractive, modern" "combination of haute and "neighborhood"; "exemplary service" includes a "friendly, passionate" sommelier who "recommends perfect matches" from the "outstanding wine list", and while the sum total is "very expensive", it's "worth every penny" (bargain-hunters find the set lunch an "excellent value").

Le Gavroche ⚅ *French* | 28 | 24 | 27 | VE |

Mayfair | 43 Upper Brook St., W1 (Marble Arch) | (44-20) 7408-0881 | www.le-gavroche.co.uk

The imagined "patron saint of fantastic dining" blesses this "magical experience" from Michel Roux, Jr. in a "plush" Mayfair cellar boasting "old-world charm", "old-fashioned luxury" and "intensely flavored", "technically spot-on" Classic French cuisine; the "phenomenal service" features a "helpful sommelier" who runs a "deep wine list", and while it is "very expensive", most find it ultimately "worth every *centime*", especially the "amazing-value" set lunch.

L'Oranger ⚅ *French* | 27 | 25 | 27 | VE |

St. James's | 5 St. James's St., SW1 (Green Park) | (44-20) 7839-3774 | www.loranger.co.uk

For "special nights out" and "relaxing" lunches, this "elegant", "charming" St. James's "standard" "stays on top" with "wonderful" Classic French cuisine and "formal", "gracious service"; just know that such "mature dining" comes at a grown-up price; P.S. in clement weather, try for the "lovely private courtyard in the back."

Marcus Wareing at The Berkeley ⚅ *French* | 27 | 26 | 26 | VE |

Belgravia | The Berkeley | Wilton Pl., SW1 (Hyde Park Corner/Knightsbridge) | (44-20) 7235-1200 | www.marcus-wareing.com

Advocates aver it's "difficult to imagine a more satisfying dining experience" than that offered at this "sumptuous" setting within Belgravia's Berkeley Hotel, where the "unobtrusive, knowledgeable" staff convey Marcus Wareing's "stylishly presented", "breathtaking" New French fare, and "a sommelier worth listening to" offers advice on the "extensive" wine list; unsurprisingly, this brand of "out-of-this-world" "excellence" is "expensive", which is why the "faint of credit card" opt instead for the "fantastic-value" set lunch.

Murano ⚅ *European* | 27 | 22 | 26 | VE |

Mayfair | 20 Queen St., W1 (Green Park) | (44-20) 7495-1127 | www.angela-hartnett.com

From "wonderful" amuse-bouches to "mind-blowing" desserts, with seemingly "endless" "extras" throughout, everything at chef Angela Hartnett's "Italian-inspired" Modern European in Mayfair is "divine" (foodies "highly recommend treating yourself to the tasting menu"); the "intimate", "graceful" white room is "a little too formal" for some, but the "exemplary" staff conveys "warmth", and while prices are "very expensive", "you get what you pay for."

Nobu London *Japanese* 27 | 21 | 23 | VE

Mayfair | Metropolitan Hotel | 19 Old Park Ln., W1 (Hyde Park Corner) | (44-20) 7447-4747 | www.noburestaurants.com

Despite a "rather simple" Old Park Lane setting and competition from "brash, younger rivals", Nobu Matsuhisa's "distinguished" "dining experience" is still pretty much "unbeatable" thanks to its "fabulous" "fresh-from-the-sea" sushi and "phenomenal" Japanese-Peruvian plates; though the generally "pleasant", staff tends to be strict about the "table limits", so best to come with a "menu plan" – not to mention "a lot" of money.

Pied à Terre ⊠ *French* 28 | 22 | 27 | VE

Bloomsbury | 34 Charlotte St., W1 (Goodge St.) | (44-20) 7636-1178 | www.pied-a-terre.co.uk

An absolute "must" declare devotees of this Charlotte Street "favorite" where "exquisite", "conversation-stopping" New French cuisine comes "beautifully presented", and the infamous "bacon-brioche rolls alone are worth a transatlantic flight"; perhaps the Bloomsbury setting's "nothing to write home about", but it's "comfortable and discreet", while a "responsive", "engaged" crew "make you feel [so] special" that you "never regret" the not-inconsiderable expense.

River Café *Italian* 27 | 24 | 25 | VE

Hammersmith | Thames Wharf | Rainville Rd., W6 (Hammersmith) | (44-20) 7386-4200 | www.rivercafe.co.uk

From "simple pastas" to "wood-grilled specialities" and everything in between, "exquisite" flavors infuse each "divine" daily changing dish at this "vibrant" "bastion" of "cutting-edge-creative" Italian cuisine, which is "worth the trek" all the way to Hammersmith and the "eye-watering" prices; though the "modern" dining room offers "no view of the river", there are "fascinating" sights to behold in the open kitchen, home to an "efficient" staff that toils "with style and a smile"; P.S. in summer, book a terrace table ("well in advance").

Scott's *Seafood* 27 | 24 | 25 | VE

Mayfair | 20 Mount St., W1 (Bond St./Green Park) | (44-20) 7495-7309 | www.scotts-restaurant.com

"Flawless shellfish" plucked from an "iced display" behind the "convivial bar" and "divine seafood" preparations are snapped up by "chic", "upper-crust" clientele at this "posh", "contemporary" Mayfair "piscatorial palace" known for its "major buzz factor" and "nosebleed prices"; though a few folks say they were "made to feel like commoners" because they're not on the "A-list", the vast majority recall "feeling special and appreciated" by an "impeccable" staff.

Square, The *French* 27 | 24 | 27 | VE

Mayfair | 6-10 Bruton St., W1 (Bond St./Green Park) | (44-20) 7495-7100 | www.squarerestaurant.com

"Magnificent from start to finish", this Mayfair "jewel" with "elegant, refined decor" stars chef Philip Howard's "creative, colorful, divine"

FOOD DECOR SERVICE COST

New French cuisine, which is "served with exacting precision" by "flawless" staffers who "anticipate your needs"; the food is "seriously expensive", as is the "encyclopaedic wine list", but for a "special occasion", it's "guaranteed sophisticated."

Umu ☒ *Japanese*

26 | 26 | 25 | VE

Mayfair | 14-16 Bruton Pl., W1 (Bond St./Green Park) | (44-20) 7499-8881 | www.umurestaurant.com

"Bring a yen for exquisite Japanese food and plenty of yen to pay" at this "sexy", "intriguing" Mayfair purveyor of "masterfully prepared", "modern and traditional" Kyoto-influenced kaiseki and à la carte menus (including sushi), plus an "extraordinary wine and sake list", which the "well-informed" staff delivers to a "hushed, reverential" crowd; meanwhile, the budget-minded note that the set lunches can be "good value."

Wilton's ☒ *British/Seafood*

27 | 24 | 27 | VE

St. James's | 55 Jermyn St., SW1 (Green Park/Piccadilly Circus) | (44-20) 7629-9955 | www.wiltons.co.uk

It's "not the cheapest or the hippest" – in fact, it's "wallet-busting" and "unapologetically old school" – but for "peerless" seafood, "perfect game" and additional "superior" Traditional British "treats", this "clubby" 1740s "national treasure" in St. James's is "not to be missed"; "waiters as old as the cobblestones outside" and "waitresses in nursery-room frocks" "coddle" their clientele, including "the Tory party at play" and other "gentlemen" who wouldn't dare "take their jackets off."

Wolseley, The ❶ *European*

22 | 26 | 22 | E

Piccadilly | 160 Piccadilly, W1 (Green Park) | (44-20) 7499-6996 | www.thewolseley.com

"You don't have to be famous to be treated famously" at London's Most Popular restaurant, a "gorgeous" Piccadilly "grand cafe" where "enthusiastic", "choreographed service" shuttles "varied" Modern Euro fare that's "sensational" "for breakfast, lunch, dinner or whenever" to "boisterous", "attractive clientele" ("hedgies, celebs, ladies who lunch", "tourists"); "it's not cheap", but "you do get what you pay for", and though reservations are "vital at virtually any time", "there are a few tables saved for walk-ins – how "refreshing!"

Zuma *Japanese*

26 | 24 | 21 | VE

Knightsbridge | 5 Raphael St., SW7 (Knightsbridge) | (44-20) 7584-1010 | www.zumarestaurant.com

"Avant-garde sushi" is as much of a "knockout" as the rest of the "Japanese creations" at this "hip and happening, loud and lovely" Knightsbridge "zoo" that's invariably "cruelly overbooked", though walk-ins might try the robata grill or the "mosh pit" of "models, actors, sports stars, rich Europeans and old men with pretty young girls" at the "glamorous" bar; wherever you "squash" in, you won't escape the sometimes "snooty" staff and their "manic table-turning", which can sting given the "high-end" prices; P.S. "if you can say 'fresh fish' three times fast, you haven't drunk enough from the excellent sake list."

Madrid

TOP FOOD RANKING

	Restaurant	Cuisine
27	DiverXO	International
	Santceloni	Mediterranean
	Zalacaín	International
	La Terraza del Casino	Spanish
	Viridiana	International
26	El Pescador	Seafood
	Goizeko Kabi/Wellington	Basque
	O'Pazo	Galician/Seafood
25	Astrid y Gastón	Peruvian
	Horcher	International
	Sergi Arola Gastro	Mediterranean
	Príncipe de Viana	Basque/Navarraise
	Combarro	Galician/Seafood
	La Bola	Madrilian
	Asador Frontón	Basque/Navarraise
	Asiana Next Door	Asian/Peruvian
	Ramón Freixa Madrid	Catalan
24	Casa Lucio	Castilian
	José Luis	Basque
	La Máquina	Seafood
	Goya	International/Spanish
	Entre Suspiro y Suspiro	Mexican
	Sudestada*	Asian
	Taberna Gaztelupe*	Basque

Asador Frontón ●⊠ *Basque/Navarraise*　　25 | 19 | 22 | E
Salamanca | Velázquez 54 | (34-91) 576-5741
Asador Frontón II ●⊠ *Basque/Navarraise*
Chamartín | Pedro Muguruza 8 | (34-91) 345-3696
www.asadorfronton.es
"Excellent", "classical" Basque-Navarraise fare – including some of
the "best meat in Madrid" – earns praise for this pair in Chamartin and
Salamanca; those in the know warn they can be "crowded", but they're
still "good places to take a visiting friend."

Asiana Next Door Ⓜ *Asian/Peruvian*　　25 | 23 | 21 | E
Centro | Travesía de San Mateo 4 | (34-91) 310-4020
"Before going out" and sampling the "good nightlife", Centro "locals"
head to chef-owner Jaime Renodo's "Peruvian-Asian hybrid" for "delicious" dishes bursting with an "overwhelming" "explosion of flavors";
fans also praise the "excellent pisco sours" and "fantastic" ambiance.

Astrid y Gastón ⊠ *Peruvian*　　25 | 23 | 24 | VE
Chamberí | Paseo de la Castellana 13 | (34-91) 702-6262 |
www.astridygastonmadrid.com
"Fantastic" ceviches and other "excellent, modern Peruvian" plates
are complemented by "smooth" pisco sours at this "stylish" Chamberí

---

* Indicates a tie with restaurant above

import by global impresario Gastón Acurio; "excellent" service enhances the "hot" scene, so "high prices" don't deter the crowds.

Botín Restaurante ● *Castilian* — 23 | 22 | 20 | E

Centro | Cuchilleros 17 | (34-91) 366-4217 | www.botin.es

"Go for" the "succulent" roast pig and other "phenomenal", "traditional" dishes at this "authentic" Castilian "classic" off Plaza Mayor, where "Hemingway ate" and rumor has it "Goya was a busboy"; often considered the "oldest restaurant in the world", it features "old-fashioned, friendly service" and "rustic" surroundings that make you "really feel the history", so while it's "touristy", "hectic" and "pricey", it's still "a must" for a "fun experience."

Café de Oriente ● *Basque* — 21 | 23 | 20 | E

Centro | Plaza de Oriente 2 | (34-91) 547-1564 |
www.cafedeoriente.es

A "breathtaking" location "in front of the Royal Palace" distinguishes this Basque cafe where you can "sit outside on a sunny day", dine on "delicious" tapas and "watch Madrid pass by"; some feel the food and service are "lackluster" for the cost, but it's "comfortable" and "full of tradition", so many don't mind paying for the "privileged" "perch".

Casa Lucio ● *Castilian* — 24 | 18 | 22 | E

La Latina | Cava Baja 35 | (34-91) 365-3252 | www.casalucio.es

"You may encounter a famous matador" or even a "film star" at this "see-and-be-seen" "landmark" (voted Most Popular in Madrid) serving "legendary" *huevos rotos* (broken eggs) among other "stupendous" Castilian plates that are a "real representation of the flavors of Spain"; though the atmosphere is "nothing fancy", a "professional" staff and "lively" ambiance – plus "accessible" tabs – make reservations "a must"; P.S. closed August–September.

Combarro ● *Galician/Seafood* — 25 | 20 | 23 | VE

Tetuán | Reina Mercedes 12 | (34-91) 554-7784 | www.combarro.com

"Fresh seafood of the highest quality" stands out at this high-end Tetuán Galician with a "classical" three-floor setting tended by an "extremely attentive" team; it's "a little pricey", but "perfect for a special occasion" or just an "everyday indulgence."

DiverXO 🖩🅜 *International* — 27 | 20 | 23 | VE

Tetuán | Calle Pensamiento 28 | (34-91) 570-0766 |
www.diverxo.com

Chef-owner David Muñoz is a "young, promising artist", crafting "the most creative", "perfectly executed" tasting menus from "first-class ingredients" at this "incredible" International in Tetuán voted No. 1 for Food in Madrid; "extremely polite service" elevates the meal, and though "your wallet may suffer", it's worth it for the "unforgettable experience"; P.S. you might need to reserve "a month in advance."

El Pescador ●🖻 *Seafood* — 26 | 20 | 22 | E

Salamanca | José Ortega y Gasset 75 | (34-91) 402-1290

"A temple of pristine seafood", this Salamanca mainstay sources from its own fish farm to provide "wonderful" meals in an "elegant", nautical-style setting; attracting young professionals, tourists and even the Royal Family, it's "simple but impressive."

	FOOD	DECOR	SERVICE	COST

Entre Suspiro y Suspiro ◧ *Mexican*   24 | 22 | 20 | E

Centro | Caños del Peral 3 | (34-91) 542-0644 |
www.entresuspiroysuspiro.com

This "modern" Centro Mexican facing Opera square "eschews anything resembling a cliché" with its "original", "exquisite" food complemented by "good Spanish wines" and "excellent" tequila; everything is "attentively served" in a "beautiful" space, so while a touch "pricey", it's still "worth the visit."

Goizeko Kabi ◐◧ *Basque*   26 | 21 | 23 | VE

Tetuán | Comandante Zorita 37 | (34-91) 533-0214

Goizeko Wellington ◐◧ *Basque*

Salamanca | Wellington Hotel | Villanueva 34 | (34-91) 577-0138
www.goizekogaztelupe.com

"Expect to find high-society people" hobnobbing at this Salamanca and Tetuán duo serving "thoughtful", "delectable" Basque cooking in rooms "simply" decorated in warm tones; service is "respectful without being overwhelming", and while a few dissenters dub it "pretentious", the "small portions and big checks" hardly deter its followers.

Goya *International/Spanish*   24 | 25 | 24 | VE

Retiro | Hotel Ritz | Plaza de la Lealtad 5 | (34-91) 701-6767 |
www.ritzmadrid.com

"From breakfast to dinner", "you're treated like royalty by the white-glove staff" at this "delightful" Spanish-International, the "epitome of elegance" at the Ritz; the "exquisite" food is served against a "beautiful" deco-accented backdrop, complete with a "grand piano" and summer garden, so luxe lovers say "don't miss it" despite the mighty tabs.

Horcher ◧ *International*   25 | 23 | 27 | VE

Retiro | Alfonso XII 6 | (34-91) 522-0731 | www.restaurantehorcher.com

"Grand as ever", this "venerable" "oasis of civility" near Retiro Park acts as a "conservatory of the great German and Austrian traditions" in the preparation of its "fabulous" International fare, capped off by "costly wines" and "excellent" desserts; "impeccable" service enhances the experience, leaving patrons impressed that this "type of restaurant still exists"; P.S. jacket and tie required.

José Luis ◐ *Basque*   24 | 18 | 22 | E

Chamartín | Rafael Salgado 11 | (34-91) 457-5036 | www.joseluis.es

"Go crazy and try a bit of everything" at this circa-1960 "classic" across from Bernabeu Stadium, where the "creative, succulent" Basque tapas and entrees come with consistently "good" service; though the decor's not exactly "up to date", most agree it's "ideal" for small plates – "you may find them cheaper elsewhere, but not better."

La Bola ◧⇄ *Madrilian*   25 | 19 | 20 | M

Centro | Bola 5 | (34-91) 547-6930 | www.labola.es

Guests say the "impressive" *cocido* ("stew cooked in a clay pot") "is almost better than grandmother's" at this Madrilian "must" in Centro, a "small", "homey" 1870 tavern "famous" for its singular specialty; "quick" service and moderate prices are additional pluses, yet even with its "down-to-earth" demeanor it's still "frequented by football players and celebrities" hankering for some home cooking.

	FOOD	DECOR	SERVICE	COST

La Máquina ❶ *Seafood* 24 | 18 | 22 | E

Tetuán | Sor Ángela de la Cruz 22 | (34-91) 572-3318 |
www.grupolamaquina.es

"Quality" seafood and other "fresh seasonal" specialties are matched
by a well-selected Spanish wine list at this "epicurean" Tetuán eatery
that's "comfortable" and "warm"; "perfect" for business dining, it's "a
little pricey" but "reasonable" for its robust offerings.

La Terraza del Casino 🖺 *Spanish* 27 | 27 | 27 | VE

Puerta del Sol | Casino de Madrid | Alcalá 15 | (34-91) 532-1275 |
www.casinodemadrid.es

Now that El Bulli has closed, this "outstanding" Spaniard "atop the
classical Casino de Madrid" social club is the place to go for "extraordinary", "lighthearted" cuisine (including "lots of spherifications and
emulsions") "inspired" by consulting chef Ferran Adrià and crafted by
former pupil Paco Roncero; a "glamorous", "belle epoque" setting and
"off-the-charts" service complete the pricey picture, so "if you're going
to really step it up one night on your trip, this is the experience" to have.

O'Pazo ❶🖺 *Galician/Seafood* 26 | 20 | 23 | E

Azca | Reina Mercedes 20 | (34-91) 553-2333

"See and be seen" eating some of the "best seafood in Europe" at this
Azca Galician that's the "ideal restaurant to indulge" in "to-die-for"
delicacies, many from the owner's private fisheries; an Isabelline-style
room with a "modern look" and "pleasant" service complete the picture that's "extraordinary" all around.

Príncipe de Viana ❶🖺 *Basque/Navarraise* 25 | 21 | 26 | VE

Chamartín | Manuel de Falla 5 | (34-91) 457-1549

A mature "who's who of Madrid" relishes the "amazing" seasonal
Basque-Navarraise cuisine at this "elegant" Chamartín "favorite" with
"outstanding, haute bourgeois service in the old style"; with a ground-
floor bar and more formal, jacket-required dining upstairs, it's a "pricey"
place, "but you can always be sure you'll get what you're paying for."

Ramón Freixa Madrid 🖺Ⓜ *Catalan* 25 | 23 | 24 | VE

Salamanca | Hotel Unico Madrid | Claudio Coello 67 | (34-91) 781-8262 |
www.ramonfreixamadrid.com

"*Muy bien*" exclaim fans of the "creative, modern" dishes at this
"pitch-perfect", high-end Salamanca Catalan holding just a handful of
tables, with crisp black-and-white decor and a peaceful garden view;
chef-owner Ramón Freixa lends a "personal touch" to the "amazing
service", and the tasting menu and à la carte options keep the experience tailored to guests' preferences.

Santceloni *Mediterranean* 27 | 25 | 26 | VE

Chamberí | Hotel Hesperia | Paseo de la Castellana 57 | (34-91) 210-8840 |
www.restaurantesantceloni.com

"Stunning" dishes "attuned to the seasons", along with "incredible"
cheeses, are "off the charts" at this "near-perfect" Med in the Hotel
Hesperia, originally opened by late Catalan culinary "giant" Santi
Santamaría, and now overseen by Can Fabes alum Óscar Velasco; with
"beautiful" skylit surroundings and "attention to personal service", it
attracts a "high-class clientele" – so "keep your wallet strapped in, it's
going to be a bumpy ride!"

	FOOD	DECOR	SERVICE	COST

Sergi Arola Gastro ☒ *Mediterranean* — 25 | 22 | 22 | VE

Chamberí | Calle Zurbano 31 | (34-91) 310-2169 | www.sergiarola.es
"A full-evening food extravaganza" that's decidedly "different from your normal grub" awaits at this "incredibly good" Chamberí Mediterranean from owner Sergi Arola and chef Manuel Berganza; the minimalist interior is fittingly "modern", though a few would like to see "better service" and note that since the cost "leaves your credit card shaking", it's a "once-in-a-lifetime experience for us mere mortals."

Sudestada ☒ *Asian* — 24 | 17 | 22 | M

Chamberí | Calle Ponzano 85 | (34-91) 533-4154 | www.sudestava.es
An Argentine-Vietnamese partnership produces some of the "purest, freshest, least Westernized Southeast Asian cuisine around", matched by a "charismatic" wine and drink list, at this "amazing" destination in Chamberí; despite a rather simple, "underwhelming" space, the "excellent" staff provides everything you need for an "incredible meal", so it impresses for "special occasions."

Taberna Gaztelupe ◑ *Basque* — 24 | 17 | 23 | E

Tetuán | Comandante Zorita 32 | (34-91) 534-9116 | www.goizekogaztelupe.com
For a "phenomenal array of Basque food", including "good meats" and seafood among other "refined" iterations, head to this upscale Tetuán tavern resembling a "rustic" country house; it attracts a professional crowd during the day and friends and families at night; P.S. closed Sundays in July and August.

Teatriz ◑ *International* — 19 | 24 | 18 | E

Salamanca | Hermosilla 15 | (34-91) 577-5379 | www.grupovips.com
An "old theater" in Salamanca "made over by designer Philippe Starck" offers a "fresh ambiance for a "young", "fashionable" crowd at this "high-priced" International with a tapas bar occupying the former stage; surveyors are split on the food, with some commending "care in the preparation and presentation" and others calling it an "overpriced" "afterthought", but many agree that with the right crowd it "can be fun."

Viridiana ◑☒ *International* — 27 | 21 | 25 | VE

Retiro | Juan de Mena 14 | (34-91) 523-4478 | www.restauranteviridiana.com
Chef-owner Abraham García, the "dean" of "inspired" International cooking for over 20 years, is "still going strong" with his "ingenious" cuisine at this "piece of history" near Retiro Park; with "phenomenal" service, a "whimsical setting decorated with Buñuel film posters" and other touches reflecting the chef's "sense of humor", it's "loads of fun" and easy to forget the "high" tabs, so faithful fans "love, love, love" it.

Zalacaín *International* — 27 | 23 | 27 | VE

Salamanca | Álvarez de Baena 4 | (34-91) 561-4840 | www.restaurantezalacain.com
"Tradition and quality" are "well guarded" at this gastronomic "gold standard" in Salamanca that "lives up to its reputation" with "the best" International fare and "fabulous" wine presented by a "world-class" staff that tends to "all details"; the "sumptuous" setting has an "understated elegance" that's perfect for "VIP" dining, and given the premium price, many save it "only for very special occasions"; P.S. closed in August.

Milan

TOP FOOD RANKING

	Restaurant	Cuisine
28	Il Luogo di Aimo e Nadia	Italian
27	Sadler	Italian
	Joia	Vegetarian
26	D'O	Italian
	Il Teatro	Italian/Mediterranean
25	Da Giacomo	Seafood/Tuscan
	Cracco	Italian
	Dongio'	Calabrian
24	Dal Bolognese	Emilian
	Armani/Nobu	Japanese
	Al Porto	Seafood
23	Alfredo Gran San Bernardo	Milanese
	Don Carlos	Italian
	Al Girarrosto	Italian
	Acanto	International/Italian
	Il Sambuco	Seafood
	Antica Trattoria della Pesa	Milanese

Acanto *International/Italian*   23 | 23 | 24 | E

Repubblica | Hotel Principe di Savoia | Piazza della Repubblica 17 |
(39-02) 6230-2026 | www.hotelprincipedisavoia.com
Diners "can't wait to return" to this "consistently good" Italian-
International in Repubblica's Hotel Principe di Savoia to savor "fresh",
"traditional" dishes delivered by "old-school waiters in jackets"; fans
"love the atmosphere" whether they're sitting in the "beautiful"
"bling-bling" dining room or the "romantic" "little garden", either of
which make for an "enjoyable" meal.

Alfredo Gran San Bernardo Ⓢ *Milanese*   23 | 20 | 23 | E

Garibaldi | Via Borgese 14 | (39-02) 331-9000 |
www.alfredogransanbernardo.com
"Milanese tradition" reigns supreme at this "old-style" Garibaldi
standby on the Via Borgese serving "classic" fare including risotto in a
relaxed yet "refined atmosphere"; insiders confide that it's "one of the
city's less-appreciated restaurants" and praise the "excellent" service.

Al Girarrosto *Italian*   23 | 20 | 21 | M

San Babila | Corso Venezia 31 | (39-02) 7600-0481 | www.algirarrosto.com
Owned by the Michi family since 1943, this "lovely" "little gem" near
Piazza San Babila is a "favorite with journalists and the media set" who
come for the "authentic" Italian fare and "complete and reasonable"
wine list; "classical" decor, "friendly" service and "acceptable" prices
enhance a "wonderful" experience; P.S. closed Saturdays.

Al Porto Ⓢ *Seafood*   24 | 21 | 23 | E

Porta Genova | Piazzale Generale Cantore | (39-02) 8940-7425 |
www.ristorantealportomilano.it
The "food is always excellent in every season" at this "refined" seafooder that dishes out "some of the freshest fish in town" and "superb

homemade pasta" in a setting that was formerly a Porta Genova customs house; with "friendly" service and a "pleasant" ambiance, "the tables are always full" and patrons leave "happy."

Antica Trattoria della Pesa *Milanese*   23 | 21 | 22 | M

Garibaldi | Viale Pasubio 10 | (39-02) 655-5741

Though "tourists have found" this "cozy", "family dining establishment" "tucked away" in a 19th-century weigh station in Garibaldi, "locals still predominate" say diners who go for the "extra special Milanese *cucina*"; the staff is "welcoming" and "those who love tradition" praise the "authentic" vibe and "lovely atmosphere", while beancounters declare the "price is definitely affordable."

Armani/Nobu *Japanese*   24 | 24 | 22 | VE

Montenapoleone | Via Pisoni 1 | (39-02) 6231-2645 | www.armaninobu.it

"When you need a sushi and fashion fix", follow the "beautiful people" to this "trendy" minimalist Japanese with a Peruvian accent housed above Giorgio Armani's boutique in the shopping district of Montenapoleone; the "sleek digs", "delicious dishes" and club downstairs make it the "place to be" for the "see-and-be-seen" set, though "considering all the hype", some "expected more."

Cracco 🅱 *Italian*   25 | 23 | 25 | VE

Duomo | Via Victor Hugo 4 | (39-02) 876-774 | www.ristorantecracco.it

Chef-owner Carlo Cracco "scores big" with this "seductive" Italian a "few steps away from the Duomo" offering "innovative cuisine" that's "everything it's cracco'd up to be, and then some"; aficionados advise you to forget about your "wallet", and instead focus on the "wonderful wine list", "tasteful, contemporary" decor and "world-class service" that all deliver a "divine dining experience."

Da Giacomo 🅱🅼 *Seafood/Tuscan*   25 | 20 | 23 | E

Porta Vittoria | Via Pasquale Sotto Corno 6 | (39-02) 7602-3313 | www.giacomomilano.com

Fans "love the crowd, love the room" as they join "fashionistas" and publishing types at this Tuscan "king of seafood" known for its "creatively prepared" dishes, including "fish of exceptional quality" delivered by "professional, polite" servers; though the "always hopping" space can often be "noisy", that's a small price to pay for an otherwise "top-class" meal.

Dal Bolognese 🅱 *Emilian*   24 | 21 | 23 | E

Repubblica | Piazza della Repubblica 13 | (39-02) 6269-4843

"Comfort food" such as Bolognese sauces that "as you'd expect, are fantastic", plus a "wide selection of wines" are served in a "prime location for viewing beautiful people", luring "locals" to this "excellent" Emilian – a sibling of the Rome original – next door to the stylish Hotel Principe di Savoia; the "trendy" "scene" sometimes resembles a "catwalk", but the garden is "spectacular" and the atmosphere "elegant", so "what else do you need?"

D'O - La Tradizione in Cucina 🅱🅼🢩 *Italian*   26 | 20 | 24 | M

Cornaredo | Via Magenta 18 | (39-02) 936-2209

The "creativity and simplicity" of dishes made with "fresh, seasonal ingredients" results in a "superlative" meal declare devotees who endure a "long waiting list" ("at least two months in advance" for dinner) to squeeze into the "small" rustic dining room at this Cornaredo Italian; the "cordiality of the staff" coupled with "affordable" tabs make the package all the more "pleasant."

Don Carlos *Italian*   23 | 22 | 23 | E

Montenapoleone | Grand Hotel et de Milan | Via Manzoni 29 | (39-02) 7231-4640 | www.ristorantedoncarlos.it

Surveyors are captivated by the "allure" of this Italian in Montenapoleone's Grand Hotel et de Milan that delivers a "super" experience via its creative dishes and 250-bottle-strong wine list; opera music plays in the background (it's named after Verdi's composition) and theatrical paintings and sketches decorate the walls; P.S. it's one of the few area restaurants sometimes open after La Scala lets out.

Dongio' ☒ *Calabrian*   25 | 18 | 21 | M

Porta Romana | Via B. Corio 3 | (39-02) 551-1372

"Pleasant and bright" with a "friendly staff and cool atmosphere", this "little" Calabrian "jewel" in Porta Romana dishes out "incredible home-made pasta" and other "delicious" plates; "extremely competitive prices" and a "wonderful ambiance" make it "great for a night out with friends", just "remember to book in advance" as it gets a "bit crowded."

Il Luogo di Aimo e Nadia ☒ *Italian*   28 | 21 | 27 | VE

Bande Nere | Via Montecuccoli 6 | (39-02) 416-886 | www.aimoenadia.com

Surveyors agree "one of the best" dining experiences "you'll ever have" is at Aimo and Nadia Moroni's "outstanding" Italian gem, voted No. 1 for Food in Milan; sure, "you need to have money" to indulge, and the Bande Nere locale may be "out of the way", but an "astonishing" wine list and an "exemplary" staff that delivers "personal service with style" make for a "fabulous" meal that's decidedly "worth the trip."

Il Sambuco ☒ *Seafood*   23 | 20 | 21 | E

Corso Sempione | Hotel Hermitage | Via Messina 10 | (39-02) 3361-0333 | www.ilsambuco.it

"You are in very good hands" at this "real surprise" of a seafooder tucked in Corso Sempione's Hotel Hermitage say fans of its "superb" "fish-based dishes" and "impressive wine list"; "attentive (but not invasive)" service and alfresco seating in the garden are additional pluses; P.S. closed for lunch on Saturday and all day Sunday.

Il Teatro ☒ *Italian/Mediterranean*   26 | 26 | 26 | VE

Montenapoleone | Four Seasons Hotel | Via Gesù 6/8 | (39-02) 7708-1435 | www.fourseasons.com/milan

"Visit for the thrill of your life", or at least of your vacation, urge admirers who find it a "true delight" to dine on chef Sergio Mei's "delicious", "splurge"-worthy fare at this "upscale" Italian-Med in Montenapoleone's Four Seasons Hotel, located just "a few steps from the main shopping area"; the "service is outstanding" plus there's a "great bar for drinks", all making for a "perfect evening."

Joia ☒ *Vegetarian*   27 | 21 | 23 | VE

Porta Venezia | Via Panfilo Castaldi 18 | (39-02) 2952-2124 | www.joia.it

Herbivores say an "amazing vegetarian experience" comes via chef-owner Pietro Leemann's "unique", "artfully presented" dishes spotlighting "interesting culinary combinations" at this "contemporary" wood-and-stone destination in Porta Venezia; it may not be "for everyone", especially those looking for "big Italian portions" or small tabs, but the "pleasant atmosphere" and "excellent" service help to win over fans who urge "go and enjoy."

Sadler 🛎 *Italian* | 27 | 24 | 26 | VE |

Navigli | Via Ascanio Sforza 77 | (39-02) 5810-4451 | www.sadler.it

"Fantastic", "beautiful dishes" are "full of originality" and look "like Miró paintings" at chef-owner Claude Sadler's Italian "gourmet treat" located "far from the center of Milan" in Navigli; an "inviting room" manned by "attentive" servers also helps make it a "winner", and if you balk at the prices, regulars remind "you'll forget the cost" but "you won't forget the dining experience."

10 Corso Como Cafè ☽ *Italian/International* | 19 | 23 | 20 | E |

Garibaldi | Corso Como 10 | (39-02) 2901-3581 | www.10corsocomo.com

"*Chicissimo!*" cry shoppers who duck into this "glam", "super-trendy" Italian-International cafe (voted Milan's Most Popular) that's part of Carla Sozzani's "hip" "concept store" in Garibaldi; it may not be "for serious eating" but is still "worth a visit" to watch the "fashion world pass" while enjoying "cocktails and nibbles" or lunch "with the beautiful people" and other "fashion-addicted" patrons.

Trattoria Milanese 🛎 *Milanese* | 23 | 19 | 20 | M |

Duomo | Via Santa Marta 11 | (39-02) 8645-1991

"Eat meatballs with confidence" at this "classic" trattoria, set in a brick-arched, stone-columned 14th-century building near the Duomo, where diners "instantly" "feel welcome" and the "traditional Milanese cuisine" includes the likes of "mouthwatering pasta" and "perfect, creamy risotto"; with a vibe that feels like "grandma's kitchen" and "reasonable prices", it's no wonder that admirers say it should be "the first place to head to" in Milan.

Moscow

TOP FOOD RANKING

	Restaurant	Cuisine
25	Mario	Italian
24	Palazzo Ducale	Italian
23	Café Pushkin	French/Russian
	Cantinetta Antinori	Tuscan
22	Vogue Café	International
21	Bistrot	Italian
	Cheese	Italian
	Uzbekistan	Uzbeki/Chinese/Arabic
20	Galereya	International
	Shinok	Ukrainian
	Vanil	French
19	White Sun of the Desert	Uzbeki/Chinese/Arabic
	Scandinavia	Scandinavian
18	Café des Artistes	Italian

Bistrot ● *Italian*   21 | 21 | 17 | VE

Savvinskaya naberezhnaya | 12/2 Bolshoi Savvinskiy pereulok |
(7-499) 248-4045 | www.restsindikat.com
The setting and menu of the award-winning Bistrot Italy's Forte dei
Marmi inspired this collaboration in Savvinskaya naberezhnaya; the
result is a "great looking" white-and-cream villa equipped with a
courtyard, a fountain and several working fireplaces that serve as a
backdrop for some "very good" Italian food; still, wallet-watchers note
"as always, Moscow restaurants are overpriced."

Café des Artistes ● *Italian*   18 | 19 | 18 | E

Tverskaya | 5/6 Bolshaya Dmitrovsky | (7-495) 692-4042
A "great location" close to Tverskaya and opposite the Moscow Art
Theater makes this Italian eatery ideal for a pre- or post-play dinner; the
"food is good – not great" – but it's a "reliable" spot with an art nouveau
interior, and in summer its "relaxing" sidewalk cafe (on a pedestrian-
only street) is a prime perch for "people-watching" and "taking in the
local scene"; P.S. the actual entrance is on Kamergersky pereulok.

Café Pushkin ● *French/Russian*   23 | 27 | 23 | E

Tverskaya | 26A Tverskoy bulvar | (7-495) 739-0033 | www.cafe-pushkin.ru
This "classic" Russian-French "must" set in a "richly decorated mansion" off Tverskaya boasts a "magical", multilevel setting consisting of
a first floor decorated like a "beautiful" 19th-century chemist's shop
(open 24/7) as well as a "more expensive" "upstairs Imperial library"
where jackets are required; either way, it's "high-priced and touristy",
but it's Moscow's Most Popular and worth a visit to hang with an "il-
lustrious" clientele of "movers, shakers and mafia."

Cantinetta Antinori ● *Tuscan*   23 | 23 | 20 | VE

Arbat | 20 Denezhny pereulok | (7-499) 241-3771 |
www.cantinetta-antinori.com
The "latest hangout for oligarchs" is this "fashionable" Novikov-
owned Tuscan below the Old Arbat, where Antinori family wines (100

by the bottle and 30 by the glass) are paired with "superb" "authentic" dishes served in a two-story rustic-chic setting in a historical mansion; some say it's "hard to justify the price", but "when you're sick of sour cream and borscht, this is the place" to go.

Cheese *Italian*

| 21 | 20 | 17 | VE |

Tsvetnoy Boulevard | 16/2 Sadovaya-Samotechnaya ulitsa | (7-495) 650-7770 | www.cheese-restaurant.ru

An open kitchen turns out expensive, "high-quality" dishes like octopus carpaccio and "great pasta" at this Italian near Tsvetnoy Boulevard; the ground floor resembles a block of Swiss cheese, while the upstairs room is a more conventionally decorated burgundy-colored space.

Galereya ◐ *International*

| 20 | 21 | 18 | E |

Boulevard Ring | 27 Petrovka ulitsa | (7-495) 790-1596 | www.cafegallery.ru

Owned by Russian restaurant czar Arkady Novikov, this "trendy" venue in Boulevard Ring is frequented by "beautiful women taller than you are" who "would give Claudia and Giselle inferiority complexes"; maybe the "crowd's better" than the International food that "costs an arm and a leg", but it's open 24/7 and the "people-watching" is prime.

Mario ◐ *Italian*

| 25 | 15 | 19 | VE |

1905 Year/Krasnaya Presnya | 17 Klimashkina ulitsa

Voted No. 1 for Food in Moscow and judged by many to be the "best Italian" in town, this split-level spot in Krasnaya Presnya offers "excellent" pasta and fish dishes; glam owner Tatiana Kurbatskaya oversees the clubby room that attracts rich young Russians and the business elite who all seem to know each other, and despite "outrageous" prices and service that's "like the weather", the "kitchen is Gibraltar" here.

Palazzo Ducale ◐ *Italian*

| 24 | 22 | 21 | VE |

Tverskaya | 3 Tverskoy bulvar | (7-495) 789-6404 | www.palazzoducale.ru

"Great pasta for the price of caviar" can be found at this "authentic", über-expensive Italian in Tverskaya run by the owner of Mario; while a few call it a "poseur paradise", most praise the "top-notch service", "strong wine list" and "rich decor" evocative of a Venetian palace featuring paintings, mirrors, chandeliers and a gilded, gondola-shaped bar.

Scandinavia *Scandinavian*

| 19 | 16 | 18 | E |

Tverskaya | 7 Malye Palashevsky pereulok | www.scandinavia.ru

A "popular expat place" in Tverskaya, this "consistently good" Scandinavian offers a "varied menu" that includes everything from herring to halibut; a "friendly" staff presides over the "chic" Swedish country house setting, and in summer its "famous garden" (with a less-expensive menu) is "one of the best outdoor hangouts in Moscow."

Shinok ◐ *Ukrainian*

| 20 | 23 | 18 | E |

1905 Year/Krasnaya Presnya | 2 1905 Goda ulitsa | (7-495) 651-8101 | www.shinok.ru

To say this 24-hour Ukrainian in Krasnaya Presnya has the most "unique decor of any restaurant in the world" may be an understatement given its "faux farmhouse" setting stocked with "live domestic animals" (cows, hens and rabbits) and overseen by a lady who sits and knits when not otherwise occupied with her charges; the rustic grub is "filling" and "satisfying", but it clearly plays second fiddle to the scenery.

	FOOD	DECOR	SERVICE	COST

Uzbekistan ☽ *Uzbeki/Chinese/Arabic*

| 21 | 25 | 20 | E |

Tsvetnoy Boulevard | 29 Neglinnaya ulitsa | (7-495) 623-0585 | www.uzbek-rest.ru

This Uzbeki-Chinese-Arabic near Tsvetnoy Boulevard shares space and the same menu with its sister restaurant, The White Sun of the Desert; a "cavernous" palatial setting stocked with sofas, pillows and carpets makes guests "feel like a sultan" and encourages lingering over "tasty" dishes, while a summer garden and belly dancing add to the indolent atmosphere.

Vanil *French*

| 20 | 19 | 18 | VE |

Kropotkinskaya | 1/9 Ostozhenka ulitsa | (7-495) 637-1082 | www.novikovgroup.ru

Admirers enamored of this "trendy" French in posh Kropotkinskaya assert "if you bring your better half here for a date, all your sins will be forgotten" – thanks to pricey but "very good" food and a candlelit modern setting with brick walls, banquettes and views of the reconstructed 19th-century Christ the Savior Cathedral; owned by Novikov and two Russian-film-world luminaries, it's one of the older posh eateries in Moscow.

Vogue Café ☽ *International*

| 22 | 19 | 19 | E |

Lubyanka | 7/9 Kuznetsky Most ulitsa | (7-495) 623-1701 | www.novikovgroup.ru

Not surprisingly, given its moniker and affiliation with the Russian magazine of the same name, this "trendy" International across from TSUM, from Moscow restaurant magnate Arkady Novikov, draws a "fashionable" following; some say it's more for "meeting than eating", but proponents praise the "stylish" setting and "very good food" that's fairly priced for "such quality."

White Sun
of the Desert ☽ *Uzbeki/Chinese/Arabic*

| 19 | 23 | 18 | E |

Tsvetnoy Boulevard | 29 Neglinnaya ulitsa | (7-495) 625-2596 | www.bsp-rest.ru

Named after and inspired by a cult Soviet film, this Uzbeki-Chinese-Arabic theme restaurant near Tsvetnoy Boulevard shares space and the same menu with its sibling, Uzbekistan; a kitschy setting – stocked with a tree trunk, life-size papier-mâché soldiers and wizened hookah smokers – is the bizarre backdrop for "fresh and authentic" dishes that feature some "startling options" like an "entire roast lamb on a spit" that you can pre-order.

Munich

TOP FOOD RANKING

	Restaurant	Cuisine
27	Tantris	French/International
25	Vue Maximilian	Bavarian/International
	Schuhbeck's	Bavarian/Mediterranean
	Boettner's	International
24	Königshof	French/International
	Mark's	French/International
	Dallmayr	French/Mediterranean
	Osteria Italiana	Italian
23	Sushibar	Japanese
	Retter's	German/International
	Acquarello	Italian
22	Alpentraum	Austrian/Bavarian
	Paulaner am Nockherberg	German
	Käfer-Schänke	Italian/International
	Hippocampus	Italian
	Austernkeller	French/Seafood
	Einstein	International
21	Dukatz	French
	Mangostin Asia	Pan-Asian

Acquarello *Italian*   23 | 15 | 21 | VE

Bogenhausen | Mühlbaurstr. 36 | (49-89) 470-4848 | www.acquarello.com
Touted by some as the "best Italian in town", this small spot in residential Bogenhausen draws diners with "excellent" fare that "reflects the creativity of the chef", an expansive wine list and a "knowledgeable" staff; despite its "good reputation", however, some cite "kitschy decor" and "too-expensive" tabs.

Alpentraum ⊠ *Austrian/Bavarian*   22 | 22 | 21 | E

Maxvorstadt | Karlstr. 10 | (49-89) 200-030-730 | www.alpenraum.net
Located on the ground floor of an office building in Maxvorstadt, this subtly "stylish" Austro-German gives "classic Alpine" cooking and interior design some "modern", up-to-date tweaks; some find it "excellent", some "just eclectic", but there's agreement that "eating and drinking is an art" here.

Austernkeller *French/Seafood*   22 | 19 | 21 | E

Innenstadt | Stollbergstr. 11 | (49-89) 298-787 | www.austernkeller.de
This "favorite" in the Altstadt section of Innenstadt has been serving "quality" French cuisine for more than 30 years; its cellar setting is "romantic" and service reliably "friendly", but regulars say the "highlight" of the menu is its "fantastic seafood", including "excellent lobster Thermidor" and (as the name indicates) some of "the best" oysters in town.

Boettner's ●⊠ *International*   25 | 22 | 26 | VE

Innenstadt | Pfisterstr. 9 | (49-89) 221-210 | www.boettners.de
For a "terrific slice of old Munich", locals head to this elegant Innenstadt International (in a "great location" in historic Altstadt)

that's been run by the same family for more than a century; its "inno-vative chef" thrills German palates with his "grand selection of spe-cialties", while an "attentive" staff and "beautiful" decor enhance its reputation as the "perfect place for a really good meal."

Dallmayr ⊠Ⓜ *French/Mediterranean*   24 20 21   E

Innenstadt | Dienerstr. 14-15 | (49-89) 213-5100 | www.dallmayr.de
An Innenstadt "institution", this "upmarket" venue features a "gourmet emporium" downstairs that's "akin to a food museum", featuring a "tremendous selection of delicacies", from oysters to some of the "finest coffee" in town; upstairs, a "top-notch restaurant" offers "delicious" French-Med cuisine enhanced by a "posh" setting and "smart" service – just "don't expect to get a table without a reservation, even for lunch."

Dukatz ⊠ *French*   21 20 21   M

Innenstadt | Schäfflerhof | Maffeistr. 3A | (49-89) 710-407-373 |
www.dukatz.de
Recently relocated to a new Innenstadt address, this "buzzy" bi-level bistro offers "good" "contemporary takes" on French cuisine, though some say the "fun" atmosphere trumps all ("go to be seen rather than for the food"); the "bright" setting includes a ground-floor bar/cafe topped by a more "elegant" dining room, but no matter where you sit, "reasonable" pricing makes it a "nice" choice for a "casual" meal.

Einstein *International*   22 20 22   E

Innenstadt | St.-Jakobs-Platz 18 | (49-89) 202-400-333 |
www.einstein-restaurant.de
Though the owner and name have changed, the menu and chef remain the same at this International in the Innenstadt Jewish community center that bills itself as the only glatt kosher restaurant in Bavaria; the "tasty traditional" offerings are so "excellent" that wags say "the chef cooks with a high IQ"; N.B. closed for Friday dinner and all day Saturday.

Hippocampus *Italian*   22 21 21   E

Bogenhausen | Mühlbaurstr. 5 | (49-89) 475-855 |
www.hippocampus-restaurant.de
"Always fresh" and "absolutely delicious" Italian cuisine keeps the crowds returning to this "quite popular" Bogenhausen destination; its "exquisite" setting includes dark-walnut paneling, marble floors and bronze art nouveau lamps, as well as a torch-lit terrace in summer.

Käfer-Schänke *Italian/International*   22 20 19   E

Bogenhausen | Prinzregentenstr. 73 | (49-89) 416-8247 |
www.feinkost-kaefer.de
"Excellent Italian food" along with "out-of-the-ordinary" International dishes are served in an "old-world" setting at this "classic" in suburban Bogenhausen; service is "friendly" (even when things get "hectic"), but "great people-watching" helps pass the time; P.S. "don't miss their downstairs gourmet store", the "ultimate German delicatessen."

Königshof *French/International*   24 21 24   E

Innenstadt | Hotel Königshof | Karlsplatz 25 | (49-89) 551-360 |
www.koenigshof-hotel.de
With "superior" New French–International creations courtesy of chef Martin Fauster and "accommodating" service from a "discreet" staff,

	FOOD	DECOR	SERVICE	COST

this "fine-dining" venue in the Hotel Königshof offers an "elegant experience" befitting a "king's court"; the "exclusive ambiance" is enhanced by "plush" design details and a dramatic view of Innenstadt's Karlsplatz; P.S. the prix fixe "gourmet dinner, including wines with each course, is spectacular."

Lenbach ●🗷Ⓜ International | 18 | 20 | 18 | E |

Innenstadt | Ottostr. 6 | (49-89) 549-1300 | www.lenbach.de

"Hip comes to Munich" in the form of this 19th-century Innenstadt palace–turned–"modern" urban ode to the Seven Deadly Sins thanks to the "über-trendy" design of Sir Terence Conran; a "fast", "pretty" staff serves International dishes (including "great sushi") that are "varied" and "fanciful", though "you may need to view them with a magnifying glass"; late-night hours and a "catwalk atmosphere" keep it "in vogue."

Mangostin Asia Pan-Asian | 21 | 19 | 16 | E |

Thalkirchen | Maria-Einsiedel-Str. 2 | (49-89) 723-2031 | www.mangostin.de

An "unusual atmosphere" and "unusually delicious" Pan-Asian fare make it "easy to think you're in a different country" at this Thalkirchen "jewel" near the zoo, where "authentic" dishes are served in a trio of Japanese-, Thai- and colonial-style dining rooms (or outside in the beer garden); some cynics say it's "past its prime" and find the service "lacking", but most maintain it's a "real joy", especially for its "great" dinner and Sunday brunch buffets.

Mark's French/International | 24 | 21 | 24 | VE |

Innenstadt | Mandarin Oriental | Neuturmstr. 1 | (49-89) 2909-8875 | www.mandarinoriental.com

"Inspired" Med-International cuisine is "perfectly executed" and delivered by "well-trained" staffers at this "awesome place" in Innenstadt's Mandarin Oriental hotel; a few find the "quiet" dining room a "little boring" and say the "surreal prices" verge on "excessive", but the monthly changing, six-course menu (including wine) and the special summertime late-night, three-course dinner are especially "worth a try."

Osteria Italiana 🗷 Italian | 24 | 21 | 21 | E |

Maxvorstadt | Schellingstr. 62 | (49-89) 272-0717 | www.osteria.de

"Historically interesting", this "well-preserved", circa-1890 Italian in Maxvorstadt is one of the oldest restaurants in town and offers a "nice break from heavy German food" via "outstanding" dishes accompanied by wines from a "fantastic list"; the "intimate" interior (decorated with original 19th-century murals) is "not too formal", the mood similarly "relaxed" and the crowd mainly "locals", among them a few incognito celebs.

Paulaner am Nockherberg German | 22 | 20 | 18 | M |

Giesing | Hochstr. 77 | (49-89) 459-9130 | www.nockherberg.com

The Paulaner brewery folks supply the "authentic Bavarian feel" at this "typical beer garden" in Giesing that hosts one of the largest Oktoberfest tents each year (it's as "enormous" as the "liter brews everyone's drinking"); suds aside, though, the moderately priced, "good German" fare - such as "well-made" Weißwurst and roast pork - is itself "worth stopping" for.

	FOOD	DECOR	SERVICE	COST

Retter's 🚫Ⓜ *German/International*   23 | 18 | 22 | E

Innenstadt | Frauenstr. 10 | (49-89) 2323-7923 | www.retters.de
Oenophile Nicole Retter is the mind behind this German-International restaurant/wine shop in Innenstadt, and while the "creative" cuisine is "inspired" (often by the ingredients from the adjacent Viktualienmarkt), it's the potential "great pairings" with any of 300 "excellent" selections by the bottle and 25 by the glass that's generating the buzz; the setting is a handsome, wood-paneled townhouse with ample garden seating in summer.

Schuhbeck's Restaurant in den   25 | 20 | 25 | VE
Südtiroler Stuben 🚫 *Bavarian/Mediterranean*

Innenstadt | Platzl 6-8 | (49-89) 216-6900 | www.schuhbeck.de
"Traditional Bavarian cuisine" gets a "contemporary Mediterranean" spin (read: "not so heavy") at this gourmet spot next to the Hofbräuhaus in Innenstadt that's owned by "famous" TV-chef Alfons Schuhbeck; "clever" food combinations, "exceedingly attentive" service, a "superb" wine list and "beyond-expense-account" pricing are all part of an experience that many say is one of the "best restaurants in Munich" for truly "adult dining."

Sushibar *Japanese*   23 | 19 | 21 | E

Innenstadt | Maximilianstr. 34 | (49-89) 2554-0645 🚫
Schwabing | Marschallstr. 2 | (49-89) 3889-9606
www.sushibar-muc.de
Like the name says, sushi is the specialty at this small place that some say serves the "freshest raw fish in town"; the setting is light, modern and urbane, and it's parked in one of the quieter quarters of tourist hot spot Schwabing; N.B. the Maximilian Strasse offshoot opened post-Survey.

Tantris 🚫Ⓜ *French/International*   27 | 23 | 26 | VE

Schwabing | Johann-Fichte-Str. 7 | (49-89) 361-9590 | www.tantris.de
Austrian chef Hans Haas incorporates regional influences and culinary trends at this "outstanding" French-International in Schwabing, and ranked No. 1 for Food and Most Popular in Munich; his "superb" daily changing prix fixe menus are paired with sommelier Paula Bosch's "inspired wines" and complemented by "remarkable", "feel-like-a-king" service, so though a few fault the "over-the-top" decor and "outrageous" prices, most insist "you get what you pay for."

Vue Maximilian *Bavarian/International*   25 | 23 | 25 | VE

Innenstadt | Hotel Vier Jahreszeiten Kempinski | Maximilianstr. 17 | (49-89) 2125-2125 | www.kempinski-vierjahreszeiten.com
This venue in the historic Hotel Vier Jahreszeiten Kempinski takes its name from the view of Maximilian Strasse, the city's most beautiful and exclusive boulevard; a redone interior that's less "stuffy" than before is the "lovely" backdrop for the "top-notch", top-priced Bavarian-International cuisine on offer, made from local and seasonal ingredients.

Paris

TOP FOOD RANKING

	Restaurant	Cuisine
28	Taillevent	Haute Cuisine
	Le Cinq	Haute Cuisine
	Guy Savoy	Haute Cuisine
	L'Astrance	New French
	Pierre Gagnaire	Haute Cuisine
	L'Ambroisie	Haute Cuisine
	Alain Ducasse	Haute Cuisine
	L'Atelier de Joël Robuchon	Haute Cuisine
	Le Grand Véfour	Haute Cuisine
	Les Ambassadeurs	Haute Cuisine
27	Lasserre	Haute Cuisine
	Michel Rostang	Classic French
	La Braisière	Gascony
	Le Bristol	Haute Cuisine
	Dominique Bouchet	Classic French
	Le Meurice*	Haute Cuisine
	Le Pré Catelan	Haute Cuisine
	Relais d'Auteuil	Haute Cuisine
26	Apicius	Haute Cuisine
	Au Trou Gascon	Southwest
	Hiramatsu	Haute Cuisine/New French
	Carré des Feuillants	Haute Cuisine
	L'Arpège	Haute Cuisine

Alain Ducasse
au Plaza Athénée 🗹 *Haute Cuisine*   28 | 27 | 27 | VE

8ᵉ | Plaza Athénée | 25, av Montaigne (Alma Marceau/Franklin D. Roosevelt) | (33-1) 53-67-65-00 | www.alain-ducasse.com

The legendary Alain Ducasse serves up "a meal of a lifetime" at his Paris flagship, an "*ancien régime* meets high-tech" destination in the Plaza Athénée; "from the amuse-bouches to the delightful candy cart" and tea made from "live herbs snipped by white-gloved waiters", the Haute Cuisine is "probably similar to what the angels are eating", while "exceptional" service "without the starch" makes each diner feel like "the most important client in the world"; it's all "divine" – and though the bill can shock, consider it "tuition toward [learning] the art of eating."

Apicius 🗹 *Haute Cuisine*   26 | 26 | 26 | VE

8ᵉ | 20, rue d'Artois (George V/St-Philippe-du-Roule) | (33-1) 43-80-19-66 | www.restaurant-apicius.com

It's easy to "fall in love" with "movie-star-handsome" chef-owner Jean-Pierre Vigato and his Haute Cuisine venue, a "stunning" mansion located in the 8th with "spectacular decor" and a "hidden garden", plus service that's "close to perfection"; "the food trumps all", "with the best of the French classics with creative influences"; fans swear it "outshines" the rest, though "alas, it's impossible to get a reservation."

---

* Indicates a tie with restaurant above

	FOOD	DECOR	SERVICE	COST

Au Trou Gascon ⧄ *Southwest* — 26 | 19 | 24 | E

12ᵉ | 40, rue Taine (Daumesnil) | (33-1) 43-44-34-26 | www.autrougascon.fr
"Let's hear it for the Southwest!" shout supporters of Alain Dutournier's original "off-the-beaten-track" eatery in the 12th that's "worth every travel minute"; "a mixture of classics and innovations", its Gascon cuisine includes "the best confit de canard I've ever had", "transcendent cassoulet" and other "superb heart-attack food" served in "spare but elegant surroundings"; though the wine list's "a little short" of by-the-glass offerings, that's "made up for by a huge selection of Armagnacs", so for most "the real trick is to get up from the table after a meal" here.

Carré des Feuillants ⧄ *Haute Cuisine* — 26 | 23 | 25 | VE

1ᵉʳ | 14, rue de Castiglione (Concorde/Tuileries) | (33-1) 42-86-82-82 | www.carredesfeuillants.fr
"One of the great ones", this Haute Cuisine table "adjacent to the Place Vendôme" "deserves more recognition" than it gets, since "inventive veteran" Alain Dutournier prepares "divine", "classical" food with Southwestern flavors, plus, in autumn, "the best game menu in Paris", accompanied by a "wine list that's tops" and service that's almost "at the level of the food"; while "elegant", "the decor reminds one of the Ice Queen's palace", but overall, the experience is "memorable", so "order with abandon if your wallet can afford it."

Dominique Bouchet ⧄ *Classic French* — 27 | 21 | 24 | VE

8ᵉ | 11, rue Treilhard (Miromesnil) | (33-1) 45-61-09-46 | www.dominique-bouchet.com
Although it's "hidden" in the upper 8th arrondissement, those who find this haven declare it "delivers 100% on the promise of greatness reflected in Bouchet's résumé", which includes Les Ambassadeurs; a "joy of a man", the chef-owner makes contemporary, "creative preparations" of French classics while steering clear of trendy "foams and froths"; converts also compliment the "modern but warm interior" and "polite, attentive service from English-speaking waiters"; so, travelers, take note: "this is the food that you went to Paris for."

Guy Savoy, Restaurant ⧄Ⓜ *Haute Cuisine* — 28 | 25 | 27 | VE

17ᵉ | 18, rue Troyon (Charles de Gaulle-Etoile) | (33-1) 43-80-40-61 | www.guysavoy.com
Clearly, his ventures in Las Vegas "haven't distracted" chef-owner Guy Savoy – his "modern", "elegantly understated" Rue Troyon flagship remains "consistently superior in every way"; the "innovative" cooking "brings Haute Cuisine as close to art as it can come", the "formal but friendly" service hits a "high watermark" ("the staff all but spoon-fed us") "and – unusual for a big-name chef – M. Savoy often is actually at the restaurant"; yes, they charge "ridiculous prices", but since "you can't take it with you, leave some of it here"; N.B. a move to the Hôtel de la Monnaie is planned for late 2011.

Hiramatsu ⧄ *Haute Cuisine/New French* — 26 | 25 | 26 | VE

16ᵉ | 52, rue de Longchamp (Boissière/Trocadéro) | (33-1) 56-81-08-80 | www.hiramatsu.co.jp
The "meticulous attention to detail, immaculate presentation, and delicate sauces and flavors" offer a "spectacular experience" at this

Haute Cuisine destination owned by chef Hiroyuki Hiramatsu in the 16th; though it's "becoming more Frenchified", the "inventive" fare still offers "an uncanny union of Gallic complexity and Japanese elegance", while waiters who are "responsive, helpful and elegant without being stuffy" warm the slightly "cold", if "refined", dining room; most are "just waiting to go back", even though it's "sooo expensive."

La Braisière ☒ Gascony

27 | 19 | 23 | E

17ᵉ | 54, rue Cardinet (Malesherbes) | (33-1) 47-63-40-37

The "quiet contented murmurings" attest to the "masterful" cuisine found in this "hidden gem" for "imaginative" Gascon gastronomy in the 17th arrondissement, with connoisseurs claiming it offers "more value for the money than the better-knowns"; despite "neutral"-toned decor, the ambiance is "cozy" and "down-to-earth", while the "relaxed service encourages you to linger over your meal and savor every bite."

L'Ambroisie ☒Ⓜ Haute Cuisine

28 | 27 | 26 | VE

4ᵉ | 9, pl des Vosges (Bastille/St-Paul) | (33-1) 42-78-51-45 | www.ambroisie-paris.com

It's like "dining in a nobleman's home" at this "smoothly run", "aptly named" Haute Cuisine haven "serving food of the gods" along with a "top flight wine list" that helps to "rationalize" the "damage the bill inflicts"; "the most intimate of Paris' grand restaurants" (only 40 seats), it's also possibly the "toughest table in town" – and beware of "being exiled to the back room" – but "who wouldn't want to be king of the Place des Vosges, even just for a few hours?"

L'Arpège ☒ Haute Cuisine

26 | 24 | 25 | VE

7ᵉ | 84, rue de Varenne (Varenne) | (33-1) 47-05-09-06 | www.alain-passard.com

It's like "tasting such fundamental products as tomatoes, lobster, potatoes for the first time" aver acolytes of the "astonishingly intense experience" provided by this Haute Cuisine temple in the 7th arrondissement, where chef-owner Alain Passard has a "genius" for turning even "simple vegetables" and seafood (no red meat) into a "religious experience"; the "elegant" Lalique-paneled setting may seem "spare" ("beware the downstairs dining room"), "the service stiffly correct" and the bill the "most expensive" you've ever seen (after all, "an onion is just an onion") – unless, as many do, you think of the "food as art."

Lasserre ☒ Haute Cuisine

27 | 28 | 28 | VE

8ᵉ | 17, av Franklin D. Roosevelt (Franklin D. Roosevelt) | (33-1) 43-59-02-13 | www.restaurant-lasserre.com

Experience "elegance personified" at this "old-world" "orchid-filled" establishment in the 8th; combining "great classics with innovations", the "brilliant" Haute Cuisine, now overseen by chef Christophe Moret (ex Alain Ducasse at the Plaza Athénée), bags bushels of compliments, as does the "flawless" staff, but the real raves are for the "fabulously '60s" technical touches, "from the James Bond entrance by the mini-lift" to the "unique open roof" (it's the "best topless place in town!"); "it all adds up to one magical evening for which you'll pay – but without the sense of being robbed."

L'Astrance 🏛Ⓜ️ *New French* | 28 | 22 | 27 | VE |

16ᵉ | 4, rue Beethoven (Passy) | (33-1) 40-50-84-40

He's been at it 10 years, but "young, passionate" chef/co-owner Pascal Barbot still "manages to wow the most blasé palates" with "inventive" New French cuisine that's "otherworldly", "intellectual" and always "surprising" (especially at dinner, when the "no-choice" tasting menu is the only option) at this "hard-to-get-into" table in the 16th, where a near-"flawless" staff with a "personal touch" services the small, "sophisticated" room; aesthetes argue "they could rethink the decor, but with bookings two months in advance, why – and when?"; N.B. open Tuesday–Friday only.

L'Atelier de Joël Robuchon ◑ *Haute Cuisine* | 28 | 24 | 24 | VE |

7ᵉ | Hôtel Pont Royal | 5, rue de Montalembert (Rue du Bac) | (33-1) 42-22-56-56 | www.joel-robuchon.net
NEW **8ᵉ** | Publicis Drugstore | 133, av des Champs-Elysées (Charles de Gaulle-Etoile/George V) | (33-1) 47-23-75-75 | www.joel-robuchon.com

In the tony 7th, the idolized chef's "Asian-sleek" "canteen for the rich" has them queuing at the door, then sitting "on a stool at a counter" ("singles welcomed") and watching the kitchen turn out "sublime", "cutting-edge" Haute Cuisine; tapas-size portions offer "a great way to sample the offerings" from the Robuchon repertoire, though the "hearty of appetite" must be "prepared to pay a fortune"; cynics snap that the staff, while "attentive", displays "typical French insouciance", but the only really "irksome" item is the no-reservations policy (except for very early and very late); N.B. the Publicis Drugstore branch opened post-Survey.

La Tour d'Argent 🏛Ⓜ️ *Haute Cuisine* | 25 | 28 | 26 | VE |

5ᵉ | 15-17, quai de la Tournelle (Cardinal Lemoine/Pont-Marie) | (33-1) 43-54-23-31 | www.latourdargent.com

Defiant (and dominant) devotees "don't care if it's considered uncool" – this Haute Cuisine table "is still one of the most magical of Parisian places", with its "spectacular views of Notre Dame"; "make sure you ask for a window table when you book, and for heaven's sake order the pressed duck" "with its numbered certificate" – though in recent years the menu has been "updated" with some other "excellent" options, served by an initially "haughty" but truly "outstanding staff"; so let the grouches grimace she's "a grande dame in decline" – this tower remains "a reason to sell off your worldly goods for one meal here before you die"; N.B. the post-Survey arrival of chef Laurent Delarbre may outdate the above Food score.

Le Bristol *Haute Cuisine* | 27 | 28 | 27 | VE |

8ᵉ | Hôtel Le Bristol | 112, rue du Faubourg St-Honoré (Miromesnil) | (33-1) 53-43-43-40 | www.lebristolparis.com

When an "extravagant experience" is in order, this "special-night-out kind of place" in the 8th is "close to perfect", with "two separate dining rooms, depending upon the season": an oak-paneled, "sumptuous circular room" in winter and an "exquisite" garden in summertime; chef Eric Frechon's "phenomenal", "cutting-edge" Haute Cuisine is worth the "ooh-la-la" prices, "particularly for those who like strong tastes in original combinations", while the "exceptional" service extends to "a

FOOD   DECOR   SERVICE   COST

silver tray of cleaning items" in case a customer should splash gravy on his recommended jacket.

Le Cinq   *Haute Cuisine*
28 | 29 | 28 | VE

8e | Four Seasons George V | 31, av George V (Alma Marceau/George V) | (33-1) 49-52-71-54 | www.fourseasons.com/paris

"Come here for the meal of your life" swoon sated surveyors who say this Haute Cuisine table in the 8th, voted Tops in Decor and Service, is "perfect in every way", from the "delectable", "adventurous" menu to the "exquisite" classic decor with "vases of flowers everywhere" to the "surprisingly friendly service", "as personal as it is professional" (even offering "a box of reading glasses" to farsighted diners); yes, this "splendid splurge" "will rob you of every last euro", but "the experience is so wonderful, somehow one doesn't mind"; N.B. the Food score doesn't reflect the arrival of Eric Briffard (ex Les Elysées).

Le Grand Véfour ☒ *Haute Cuisine*
28 | 29 | 28 | VE

1er | Palais Royal | 17, rue de Beaujolais (Palais Royal-Musée du Louvre) | (33-1) 42-96-56-27 | www.grand-vefour.com

Chef Guy Martin's "exquisite" Haute Cuisine offers a "glorious feast for the senses in the midst of old-world luxury" at this "mythic address" in the 1st; "dripping with atmosphere", the "exceptional setting" – a gilded box of a room with a painted ceiling and brass plaques engraved with the names of its celebrated clientele (Napoleon, Josephine, Colette, Maria Callas) - is animated by a staff that's "professional and welcoming"; true, such "royal treatment needs a royal treasury" when the bill comes – but "it meets every expectation"; N.B. closed weekends.

Le Meurice ☒ *Haute Cuisine*
27 | 28 | 27 | VE

1er | Hôtel Meurice | 228, rue de Rivoli (Concorde/Tuileries) | (33-1) 44-58-10-55 | www.meuricehotel.com

"One of the great French chefs in one of Paris' prettiest dining rooms" sums up "the Haute Cuisine experience" at the Hôtel Meurice; loaded with luxe items like truffles and caviar, "culinary wizard" Yannick Alléno's "food is just exquisite", and matched by the "balletlike" service "gliding" within the "grand, gorgeous" and "gilded" space done up with Philippe Starck's silver chairs and abstract glass sculpture; "yes, it's expensive" – but "the experience is magnificent."

Le Pré Catelan ☒Ⓜ *Haute Cuisine*
27 | 28 | 26 | VE

16e | Bois de Boulogne, Route de Suresnes (Pont-de-Neuilly/Porte Maillot) | (33-1) 44-14-41-14 | www.precatelanparis.com

"Haute Cuisine of the highest order", "impeccable" service and, of course, that "beautiful location" in the Bois de Boulogne – small wonder that a "phenomenal dining experience" awaits at this "elegant, enduring" classic; though redone in contemporary tones of beige, bronze and gray, the decor retains its "magical" imperial aura, and while the "prices are budget-busting", most declare "cost be damned" because "lunch in the garden on a summer afternoon is pure bliss."

Les Ambassadeurs   *Haute Cuisine*
28 | 29 | 28 | VE

8e | Hôtel de Crillon | 10, pl de la Concorde (Concorde) | (33-1) 44-71-16-16 | www.crillon.com

The "sumptuous" "gold and marble" surroundings of the Crillon Hôtel are "like being inside a jewel box", a "perfect showplace" for "inventive" Haute Cuisine and an 1,100-label wine list *"extraordinaire"*; the service is "choreographed to perfection" while remaining "refreshingly friendly", and though the experience may "relieve you of many euros", "you get a lot for the price"; P.S. the post-Survey arrival of chef Christopher Hache, most recently of La Grande Cascade, may outdate the above Food score.

Michel Rostang ⓈⒶ *Classic French* **27 | 24 | 27 | VE**

17ᵉ | 20, rue Rennequin (Péreire/Ternes) | (33-1) 47-63-40-77 | www.michelrostang.com

"Where charm and sophistication intersect", you find chef-owner Michel Rostang's "chic" table in the 17th, whose "every detail is perfect", from the "superb" cuisine ("rich, rich" "but delicious") to the "charming maitre d'" and "flawless staff" to the "wood-paneled beauty" of the decor; yes, it's "a bit too pricey" – but after 30-plus years, this is "still among the best of the Classic French" establishments; P.S. "in season, ask to be truffled for the entire meal."

Pierre Gagnaire ⓈⒶ *Haute Cuisine* **28 | 25 | 27 | VE**

8ᵉ | Hôtel Balzac | 6, rue Balzac (Charles de Gaulle-Etoile/George V) | (33-1) 58-36-12-50 | www.pierre-gagnaire.com

"Let your senses explore uncharted territory" during a "breathtaking meal" at this "brilliant", completely "unforgettable" Haute Cuisine haven in the 8th, serving what many describe as "the most innovative food" in Paris ("Pierre Gagnaire is to gastronomy what Picasso was to contemporary art"); yes, the master's "science experiment"–like creations, while "out of this world", are "too out there" for some; but the "exceptional service" in the discreet dove-gray and blond-wood dining room makes you "feel like royalty", and to the vast majority, it's "worth every euro (damn dollar!)."

Relais d'Auteuil **27 | 20 | 26 | VE**
"Patrick Pignol" ⓈⒶ *Haute Cuisine*

16ᵉ | 31, bd Murat (Michel-Ange-Molitor/Porte d'Auteuil) | (33-1) 46-51-09-54 | www.relaisdauteuil-pignol.com

"If you're adventuresome", join the "well-to-do neighborhood clientele" that congregates at this Haute Cuisine table out toward the Porte d'Auteuil, which, while "outrageously expensive", is considered "one of the best in Paris" for the eponymous chef-owner's traditional French food and "outstanding wine"; the "warm welcome of Madame Pignol" now comes in renovated (post-Survey) quarters done up in stainless steel – it's a "really lovely" experience, all 'round.

Taillevent ⓈⒶ *Haute Cuisine* **28 | 28 | 28 | VE**

8ᵉ | 15, rue Lamennais (Charles de Gaulle-Etoile/George V) | (33-1) 44-95-15-01 | www.taillevent.com

"You're at home the minute you enter" this "elegant", "spectacular modern art"–adorned townhouse in the 8th, which – though recently sold – shines on as Paris' No. 1 for Food and Popularity; guests would "gladly borrow from the kids' college fund" to sample "service that's not just an art form, but a religion" as it delivers chef Alain Solivérès' "classic", sometimes "inventive", but always "decadent and luscious" Haute Cuisine, backed by "a prodigious wine list"; in short, "why wait for heaven, when you can go to Taillevent?"

Prague

TOP FOOD RANKING

	Restaurant	Cuisine
26	Allegro	Italian/Mediterranean
25	Aquarius	International
	V Zátiší	Czech/International
	Essensia	Eurasian
24	U Zlaté Hrušky	Czech/International
	Rybí trh	International/Seafood
	U Modré Ruze	Czech/International
23	U Modré Kachnicky	Czech
	Kampa Park	International
	Mlýnec	International
	Imperial Cafe	Czech
	Oliva	Mediterranean
	Coda	International
	Bellevue	Czech/International
22	Hergetova Cihelna	Czech/International
	Pálffy Palác	French
21	Alcron	Seafood

Alcron, The ⓩ *Seafood*   `21` `19` `22` `E`

New Town | Radisson SAS Alcron Hotel | Stěpánská 40 | (420) 222-820-000 | www.radissonsas.com

Known as a "private" refuge for well-heeled travelers, businessmen and in-the-know locals, this "wonderful little seafood restaurant" in the Radisson SAS Alcron Hotel is "great with fish", as is evidenced by dishes like sea bass roasted in salt crust; the "art deco setting" is "lovely", but some surveyors who are "a bit jaded" judge the atmosphere "not very warm."

Allegro *Italian/Mediterranean*   `26` `24` `27` `VE`

Old Town | Four Seasons Hotel | Veleslavínova 2A | (420) 221-426-880 | www.fourseasons.com/prague

"Not your typical hotel dining" room, this "truly first-rate" venue located in Old Town "wows" with an "ultimate experience" that's just as "wonderful" as you'd expect from the Four Seasons; indeed, it's ranked No. 1 for Food in Prague thanks to "fantastic" Italian-Mediterranean cuisine "beautifully presented" in a "lavish" dining room by "charming" staffers; P.S. "come early to get a window seat" for a truly "spectacular view" of the Charles Bridge and the "fairy-tale" castle.

Aquarius *International*   `25` `23` `19` `E`

Little Quarter | Alchymist Grand Hotel & Spa | Trziště 19 | (420) 257-286-019 | www.alchymisthotel.com

This International is located in the Little Quarter's Alchymist Grand Hotel & Spa, four romantically refurbished 16th-century buildings; "great" cuisine and a "fantastic" setting – a vaulted, mirrored space that opens to a courtyard – make for an "enchanting experience", and the "price is very good [for the] value" to boot; N.B. there's also live music Thursday–Saturday.

Bellevue *Czech/International*
23 | 23 | 24 | VE

Old Town | Smetanovo nábrezí 18 | (420) 222-221-443 | www.zatisigroup.cz

An "incredible dining experience" lies ahead at this "grand" Old Town venue that boasts a "magnificent view of the river, Charles Bridge and Prague Castle"; "impeccable" staffers deliver "delicious", "up-to-date" Czech-International cuisine, and those who thought the decor somewhat "faded" will be pleased by the recent remodel resulting in a plush, "romantic" interior and a more open layout that highlights the panoramic vista.

Coda *International*
23 | 23 | 23 | E

Little Quarter | Hotel Aria | Trziste 9 | (420) 225-334-761 | www.codarestaurant.cz

The "beautiful" Hotel Aria is home to this Eclectic "hot spot" that offers "exceptional food" and "exceedingly friendly service"; the glass-topped atrium dining room is flooded with daylight, and there's a "great view" from the "gorgeous" terrace that includes St. Nicholas Church, Prague Castle and countless romantic terra-cotta rooftops.

Divinis Wine Bar *Italian*
- | - | - | M

Old Town | Týnská 21 | (420) 222-325-440 | www.divinis.cz

A well-known Czech celebrity chef runs this popular midpriced Italian eatery and personally oversees the quality and authenticity of the ingredients, resulting in tasty, regional dishes, accompanied by choice wines; closely set tables and a relaxed, rustic setting – bleached wood, brick walls, draped fabrics – create a charming and friendly atmosphere, which in turn attracts a loyal, well-to-do following; P.S. the winding, cobblestone streets in this Old Town neighborhood are prime for an after-dinner stroll.

Essensia *Eurasian*
25 | 25 | 25 | VE

Little Quarter | Mandarin Oriental Hotel | Nebovidská 459/1 | (420) 233-088-888 | www.mandarinoriental.com

A "cut above the competition" and "one of the best places to take business clients" is this Mandarin Oriental Hotel venue housed in a converted 14th-century monastery, where "brilliant" Eurasian cuisine is served in a series of five "beautiful" vaulted rooms by an "attentive staff"; it can be pricey, but pragmatists point out that "expensive eating in Prague would be considered cheap in London or Paris"; P.S. the garden terrace offers alfresco dining in warmer months.

Hergetova Cihelna *Czech/International*
22 | 25 | 21 | E

Little Quarter | Cihelná 2b | (420) 296-826-103 | www.cihelna.com

An "amazing location" on the riverbank provides a "fantastic view of the Charles Bridge" that's "alone worth a visit" to this "must stop" in the Little Quarter; even better, the "modern" menu offering International items as well as regional Czech dishes is "excellent", ditto the "very good" service.

Imperial Cafe *Czech*
23 | 25 | 25 | E

Prague 1 | Prague Imperial Hotel | Na Porící 15 | (420) 246-011-600 | www.hotel-imperial.cz

Located in the recently renovated art deco Prague Imperial Hotel, on the edge of Old Town, this "beautiful" Czech serves breakfast, lunch and dinner; the "glorious setting" – Moorish-inspired tiles, elaborate towering columns, marble tables, expansive windows and a high ceiling – is an over-the-top backdrop for "food that's very good."

Kampa Park *International*   23 | 24 | 22 | E

Little Quarter | Na Kampe 8B | (420) 296-826-102 | www.kampapark.com
Perennially "popular" (and voted Prague's Most Popular), this "renowned" "favorite" located on the Little Quarter's "historic Kampa Island" (right under the Charles Bridge) offers two terraces for "contemporary fine dining at the water's edge"; loyalists laud the "lovely" interior and "inventive", "top-quality" International menu, but surveyors split on the "efficient" staffers, with some swearing they "couldn't be more friendly" and others opining that they "need an attitude adjustment."

NEW La Gare Brasserie *French*   - | - | - | M

Prague 1 | V Celnici 3 | 222-313-712 | www.lagare.cz
This multifaceted establishment in a lively corner of Prague 1 near the Masaryk train station is a happy marriage of two concepts: French brasserie and 'Boutiques Gourmandes', offering fresh bread, pastries, pâté, cold cuts, cheese, wine and take-home meals; the multilevel seating, streetside terrace and colorful space create an informal but attractive atmosphere in which a friendly staff serves fairly priced, no-nonsense classics – foie gras, rabbit Provençale, mussels marinière – to a mix of locals and tourists at a price that makes guests want to come back again and again.

Mlýnec *International*   23 | 21 | 21 | E

Old Town | Novotného Lávka 9 | (420) 221-082-208 | www.zatisigroup.cz
With its "great location" on a pier at the foot of the Charles Bridge in Old Town, this "superb" spot offers "very nice views" along with "wonderful food" and "top-flight service"; the "interesting" International menu includes some local dishes, and the "good-quality wine list" features Moravian selections.

Oliva ⌧ *Mediterranean*   23 | 21 | 22 | M

New Town | Plavecká 4 | (420) 222-520-288 | www.olivarestaurant.cz
In-the-know locals have taken to this "stylish" Mediterranean in New Town that pays homage to the olive in some of its "delicious" dishes and also in the pale-green color of its walls; "fresh food", "friendly owners" and fair prices make many say they "wish this favorite were in their neighborhood."

Pálffy Palác *French*   22 | 24 | 19 | E

Little Quarter | Valdštejnská 14 | (420) 257-530-522 | www.palffy.cz
This "delightful" "favorite" features a "romantic", "candlelit" setting "in an old nobleman's palace close to the castle" in the Little Quarter, where "excellent" French food is served along with "good local wines" by an "able" staff; P.S. the "ancient building" also houses a "music conservatory", so sometimes "you dine to the sounds" of its students.

Rybí trh *International/Seafood*   24 | 19 | 23 | E

Old Town | Týnský Dvur 5 | (420) 224-895-447 | www.rybitrh.cz
You might not expect "simply divine" seafood in a "land-locked country", but you'll find it at this Old Town fish market/restaurant, where

the "excellent" International menu offers a "great choice" of "creatively prepared" fish; the savvy staff has a knack for "fulfilling unspoken wishes", the "understated" interior is appropriately decorated with "nice aquariums" and, as for the cost, "quality" has its price.

SaSaZu Asian   - | - | - | M
Prague 7 | Bubenské NábreÝæí 306 | (420) 284-097-455 | www.sasazu.com

At this chic and trendy venue located in Prague's former meat market, the original industrial shell has been kitted out with brightly colored walls, paper lanterns and loose arrangements of armchairs and sofas, all overlooked by watchful Buddha statues; the innovative Asian menu, grouped by primary ingredient and provenance, encourages diners to create their own well-priced culinary experience; it's all backed up by beats from the live DJ, and after dinner guests can move on to drinks at the bar or hit the club of the same name, next door.

U Modré Kachnicky Czech   23 | 23 | 21 | E
Little Quarter | Nebovidská 6 | (420) 257-320-308
U Modré Kachnicky II Czech
Old Town | Michalská 16 | (420) 224-213-418
www.umodrekachnicky.cz

The name translates as 'At the Blue Duckling', and this Little Quarter "stalwart" is a "must stop" for those wanting to taste the "true local flavor" of Prague; its "rustic rooms" are "quirky" but "comfortable", while the "well-done" homestyle Czech cooking with an "emphasis on game" and "regional specialties" is proffered by "gracious" staffers; N.B. there's a newer offshoot in Old Town.

U Modré Ruze Czech/International   24 | 21 | 22 | E
Old Town | Rytírská 16 | (420) 224-225-873 | www.umodreruze.cz
Boasting a "lovely subterranean setting", this "first-class establishment" (whose name means 'At the Blue Rose') is located in a "15th-century cellar" in Old Town with "charming", barrel-vaulted stone walls that lend a "medieval feel" to the proceedings; "authentic" Czech cuisine as well as International offerings are backed up by a "small but reliable wine list."

U Zlaté Hrušky Czech/International   24 | 23 | 21 | M
Castle Quarter | Nový svet 3 | (420) 220-941-244 | www.uzlatehrusky.cz
A "golden find", this "quaint" "sleeper" on a "picturesque cobbled street" in the Castle Quarter offers a traditional Czech menu (including "wonderful game and fish") as well as some International items; the "pleasantly furnished" interior "transports you to another century" and is frequented by "lots of locals", all enjoying the "authentic" cuisine and "gracious service."

V Zátiší Czech/International   25 | 20 | 23 | E
Old Town | Liliová 1 | (420) 222-221-155 | www.zatisigroup.cz
"Excellent" local Czech specialties are "exquisitely cooked" with a "modern" International accent at this "lovely" venue off Betlemska Square in Old Town; "creative" cuisine, "first-rate wines", "impeccable service" and an "intimate" setting make for "feasts fit for bohemian royalty", and though a few feel "there are equally good places" charging "much less money", most report a "wonderful dining experience" here.

Rome

TOP FOOD RANKING

	Restaurant	Cuisine
26	La Pergola	Italian/Mediterranean
	La Rosetta	Seafood
25	Felice a Testaccio	Roman
	Vivendo	Italian
	Antico Arco	Italian
	Trattoria Monti	Italian
	Agata e Romeo	Roman
	Al Vero Girarrosto Toscano	Tuscan
	Mirabelle	Italian
	Quinzi & Gabrieli	Seafood
24	La Terrazza	Italian/Mediterranean
	Sora Lella	Roman
	Colline Emiliane	Emilian
	Primo al Pigneto*	Italian
	Girarrosto Fiorentino	Tuscan
	Vecchia Roma	Roman
	Piperno	Roman/Jewish
	Il San Lorenzo	Mediterranean
	Pierluigi	Italian
	Checchino dal 1887	Roman
23	Al Moro	Roman
	Sabatini	Roman
	Giggetto al Portico d'Ottavia	Roman/Jewish
	Dal Bolognese	Emilian
	Imàgo	International/Italian

Agata e Romeo ☒ *Roman*   25 | 23 | 24 | E

Esquilino | Via Carlo Alberto, 45 | (39-06) 446-6115 | www.agataeromeo.it
"Innovative" "Roman-style" *cucina* that's "not your standard Italian" is "the main attraction" at this Esquilino family-run spot; though "a bit pricey", fans say "engaging" service, an "intimate" setting and "interesting wine list" make for a "memorable meal"; P.S. closed weekends.

Al Moro ☒ *Roman*   23 | 18 | 20 | E

Barberini | Vicolo delle Bollette, 13 | (39-06) 678-3495 | www.ristorantealmororoma.com
"Fellini loved" this circa-1929 Italian "close to the Trevi Fountain", and the "glitterati" plus "well-heeled regulars" still frequent it for "divine" "Roman cooking" in "wood-paneled" environs with "lots of character"; it's "expensive" and unknowns might encounter "steely-eyed" service, but it's worth it to experience a true "classic."

Al Vero Girarrosto Toscano ◑ *Tuscan*   25 | 21 | 23 | E

Via Veneto | Via Campania, 29 | (39-06) 482-1899 | www.alverogirarrostotoscano.com
"A corner of Tuscany in the heart of Rome" sums up this longtimer (since 1969) "tucked away near Villa Borghese" and pulling a crowd

---

* Indicates a tie with restaurant above

ranging from "tourists" to "business people"; "known for its Fiorentina T-bone steak" and "wonderful antipasti", it backs up its "excellent" cooking with "warm" service and a "cozy" "basement setting" – "you'll feel right at home when you walk in."

Ambasciata d'Abruzzo ● *Roman/Abruzzese*   23 | 20 | 21 | M

Parioli | Via Pietro Tacchini, 26 | (39-06) 807-8256 | www.ambasciatadiabruzzo.com

"You won't leave hungry" after digging into the "basket of salumi" starter, "very flavorful" pastas and other "traditional" Abruzzese-Roman "comfort food" at this fixture in the "posh" Parioli neighborhood; "chic yet informal decor", a "boisterous" atmosphere and "helpful, friendly" servers also help make it "worth the cab ride" – just "don't go if on a diet"; P.S. closed for three weeks in August.

Antico Arco ●☒ *Italian*   25 | 22 | 22 | E

Gianicolo | Piazzale Aurelio, 7 | (39-06) 581-5274 | www.anticoarco.it

Though "a little out of the way" (and thus "undiscovered by most tourists"), this "upscale" Italian's "innovative", "refined" fare and "magic location" on Gianicolo Hill make it "well worth" the trip, especially when you factor in the "amazing wine list", "simple" but "elegant" contemporary ambiance and "pleasant", "hip" servers; the wine bar is an option when you don't have a reservation.

Checchino dal 1887 ●☒Ⓜ *Roman*   24 | 19 | 20 | E

Testaccio | Via di Monte Testaccio, 30 | (39-06) 574-6318 | www.checchino-dal-1887.com

"If you are an adventurous eater", you'll appreciate this family-owned "institution" in Testaccio (the old slaughterhouse area) that's been turning "any part of an animal" into a "delicacy" since "the year of its name" – and the offal-averse will also find more mainstream Roman fare, including "excellent pasta"; an "exceptional wine list", "helpful staff" and "back in time" ambiance complete the picture; P.S. closed in August.

Colline Emiliane Ⓜ *Emilian*   24 | 14 | 21 | M

Barberini | Via degli Avignonesi, 22 | (39-06) 481-7538

"*Delicioso!*" proclaim fans of this "small", family-owned Emilian near the Trevi Fountain; there may be "no decor to speak of" ("like eating at your aunt's house"), but with "honest" food, "good service" and not-outrageous prices it's "popular", so you'd best "book and be on time."

Dal Bolognese Ⓜ *Emilian*   23 | 21 | 22 | E

Piazza del Popolo | Piazza del Popolo, 2 | (39-06) 361-1426

It's a prime "place to be seen" for "celebrities, politicians" and "wannabes", but this "buzzing" "institution" "wonderfully located in the Piazza del Popolo" is also a prime place to dine thanks to "luscious" Emilian fare, including a famed bollito misto trolley; it's "not for everyone's wallet" and some find it a bit "attitudinal", but overall it's "great fun", especially on the "always packed" terrace.

Felice a Testaccio *Roman*   25 | 18 | 21 | M

Testaccio | Via Mastro Giorgio, 29 | (39-06) 574-6800 | www.feliceatestaccio.com

The "*tonnarelli cacio e pepe*" is a "do not miss" at this long-standing (since 1936) Testaccio spot that's also a "good bet" for other "authen-

	FOOD	DECOR	SERVICE	COST

tic Roman pasta" and more; the brick-walled setting gets "busy", so don't even "think of going without first making a reservation."

Giggetto al
Portico d'Ottavia Ⓢ *Roman/Jewish* | 23 | 19 | 20 | M |

The Ghetto | Via del Portico d'Ottavia, 21A | (39-06) 686-1105 | www.giggettoalportico.it

The "wonderful fried artichokes" ("best in the world") are "definitely worth the trip" to this midpriced trattoria serving "Roman-Jewish staples" in a "charming part" of The Ghetto; inside is "noisy" and rather "average"-looking, so insiders try to "score an outdoor sidewalk table" with a view of the ruins of Ottavia's portico.

Girarrosto Fiorentino *Tuscan* | 24 | 19 | 22 | E |

Via Veneto | Via Sicilia, 46 | (39-06) 4288-0660 | www.girarrostofiorentino.it

"A meat lover's heaven" declare admirers who praise the "best *bistecca fiorentina*", "veal to die for" and other "home cooking" with "Tuscan flair" at this Via Veneto stalwart near "many of the best hotels"; an "excellent wine list", "attentive service" and a "setting you can dress up for" further justify the "moderately expensive" tabs.

Il San Lorenzo ● *Mediterranean* | 24 | 20 | 21 | E |

Campo dei Fiori | Via dei Chiavari, 4 | (39-06) 686-5097 | www.ilsanlorenzo.it

"Impeccable fish" and other "fresh", Neapolitan-accented "seafood specialties" star at this "upscale" Med near Campo dei Fiori; "housed in an ancient building" that's been "tastefully modernized", it boasts a bar adorned with oyster shells, all overseen by a "professional" staff.

Imàgo *International/Italian* | 23 | 25 | 25 | VE |
(fka Hassler Rooftop)

Trinitá dei Monti | Hotel Hassler | Piazza Trinità dei Monti, 6 | (39-06) 6993-4726 | www.imagorestaurant.com

"A stunning view over Rome from the top of the Spanish steps" serves as backdrop to the "interesting, creative dishes" at this "elegant" International-Italian in the "historic" Hotel Hassler; "very attentive" service and a "*molto* trendy" vibe are part of the package, but if you're not part of the "moneyed set", it helps to have "an expense account."

La Pergola ⓈⓂ *Italian/Mediterranean* | 26 | 25 | 26 | VE |

Monte Mario | Rome Cavalieri | Via Alberto Cadlolo, 101 | (39-06) 3509-2152 | www.romecavalieri.it

German chef Heinz Beck is the "magnificent" talent behind the "artfully presented" dishes at this "elegant" yet "warm" Italian-Med in Monte Mario's Rome Cavalieri Hotel, ranked the city's No. 1 for Food and Most Popular; an "impressive wine list", "fantastic" service and a rooftop with "a better view of Rome than the pope gets" make for an "outstanding" experience that's "worth every euro" ("and you need a lot of them"); P.S. dinner only; closed in February and two weeks in August.

La Rosetta Ⓢ *Seafood* | 26 | 20 | 22 | VE |

Campo Marzio | Via della Rosetta, 8 | (39-06) 686-1002 | www.larosetta.com

"A singular focus on serving the best the sea has to offer" distinguishes this "special-occasion" stalwart near the Pantheon; its "first-

FOOD | DECOR | SERVICE | COST

class" fare is dished out in an upscale "modern space" by a mostly "welcoming" crew, making the experience "well worth" the "crazy prices" for most.

La Terrazza *Italian/Mediterranean*   24 | 25 | 25 | VE

Trinitá dei Monti | Hotel Eden | Via Ludovisi, 49, 6th fl. | (39-06) 4781-2752 | www.edenroma.com/en/laterrazzadelleden

For a "phenomenal" view arrive early to this dining room on the "elegant" Hotel Eden's rooftop and "watch the sun set" over Rome while enjoying "superb" Italian-Mediterranean fare; "opulent" decor, a "very good wine list" and "excellent" service round out the "classy", if "expensive", experience; P.S. there's also a bar with piano music and an outdoor terrace with a separate bar.

Mirabelle *Italian*   25 | 25 | 25 | VE

Via Veneto | Hotel Splendide Royal | Via di Porta Pinciana, 14, 7th fl. | (39-06) 4216-8838 | www.mirabelle.it

Expect to be "treated like royalty" while enjoying "sublime" fare backed by an "outstanding" wine list at this "elegant" Italian off the Via Veneto; it also boasts "beautiful views" of Rome courtesy of its seventh-floor perch in the Hotel Splendide Royal, making it a "perfect spot to celebrate" – just be prepared to leave with a "lighter" wallet; P.S. a recent chef change may outdate the Food score.

Pierluigi ●Ⓜ *Italian*   24 | 20 | 23 | E

Campo dei Fiori | Piazza dé Ricci, 144 | (39-06) 686-1302 | www.pierluigi.it

"Excellent" Italian cuisine – "especially the seafood" – and "beautiful open-air" seating on the picturesque Piazza dé Ricci bring a mix of "locals" ("from toddlers to grandparents") and tourists to this "find" near the Campo dei Fiori; "customer-oriented" service is another reason why fans "hope it stays the same forever."

Piperno Ⓜ *Roman/Jewish*   24 | 18 | 21 | E

The Ghetto | Via Monte de' Cenci, 9 | (39-06) 6880-6629 | www.ristorantepiperno.it

"Worth it just for the *carciofi alla giudia*" say enthusiasts of this Roman "favorite" in The Ghetto known for its "excellent" if "expensive" "classic" Jewish specialties; service is "professional", and though there's debate about its "old-world feel" ("warm" vs. "stodgy"), most agree that eating outside on the "beautiful, quiet piazza" is a "special experience"; P.S. closed in August.

Primo al Pigneto Ⓜ *Italian*   24 | 22 | 21 | M

Pigneto | Via del Pigneto, 46 | (39-06) 701-3827 | www.primoalpigneto.it

"Hip, young and the 'in' place to be" say fans of this "real find" "a ways out" in Pigneto; with an "excellent" Italian menu that "changes often", a large wine list and "modern setting", it's a boon for locals and "well worth the journey" for visitors.

Quinzi & Gabrieli *Seafood*   25 | 19 | 20 | VE

Campo Marzio | Via delle Coppelle, 5 | (39-06) 687-9389 | www.quinziegabrieli.it

It's all about the "divine seafood" including "the freshest fish in all of Rome" at this "high-end" piscine paradise in a "buzzy area" near the

FOOD DECOR SERVICE COST

Pantheon; if the service and decor (featuring murals of three seaport cities) don't draw as much praise, the fact that it's "always packed" speaks for itself – just "be sure your credit card" can take the hit.

Sabatini *Roman*
23 | 20 | 22 | E

Trastevere | Piazza Santa Maria, 13 | (39-06) 581-2026 | www.ristorantisabatini.com

"Sit out on the Piazza [Santa Maria] and pretend you are in a Fellini movie" at this "charming" Trastevere fixture whose "traditional" Roman fare (including "beautifully prepared seafood") is "good enough to attract" locals despite its reputation as a "tourist destination"; a "romantic evening" can also be had in one of the three indoor dining rooms, though most concede it's "best" outside.

Sora Lella 🅢 *Roman*
24 | 20 | 21 | E

Isola Tiberina | Via di Ponte Quattro Capi, 16 | (39-06) 686-1601 | www.soralella.com

In a "wonderful location" on Isola Tiberina (an island in the Tiber River), this family-run Roman offers "well-executed" classics such as *tonnarelli alla cuccagna,* which has been on the menu since 1961; though a few warn it may be "living on [its] past reputation", more say it still delivers "very flavorful" meals in a "peaceful", "informal" setting.

Trattoria Monti *Italian*
25 | 20 | 24 | M

Trinitá dei Monti | Via di San Vito, 13A | (39-06) 446-6573

"Consistently good", "authentic" fare from the Le Marche region, including "delicious" "homemade pastas", makes this "small" trattoria "off the beaten track" in Trinitá dei Monti worth seeking out; assets also include a "friendly" staff ("take their advice on the best dishes of the day") and, better still, "bargain prices."

Vecchia Roma *Roman*
24 | 21 | 22 | E

The Ghetto | Piazza Campitelli, 18 | (39-06) 686-4604 | www.ristorantevecchiaroma.com

"Outstanding traditional Roman cuisine", including "grilled baby calamari to die for", is served by an "expert staff" at this longtimer in The Ghetto; views on the interior diverge ("lovely, intimate" vs. a little "cramped" and "stuffy"), but all agree that sitting outside in "one of the prettiest piazzas in Rome" is "wonderful"; P.S. closed Wednesdays; a recent chef change may outdate the Food score.

Vivendo 🅢 🅜 *Italian*
25 | 26 | 25 | VE

Piazza della Repubblica | St. Regis Grand Hotel | Via Vittorio Emanuele Orlando, 3 | (39-06) 4709-2736 | www.stregis.com/vivendo

"Superb" sums up this "luxurious", "special-occasion" Italian in the St. Regis Grand Hotel praised for its "outstanding" fare, "immaculate service" and "beautiful setting" with "well-spaced tables to enable relaxed conversation"; it's an "expensive but very worthwhile treat."

Stockholm

TOP FOOD RANKING

	Restaurant	Cuisine
28	Wedholms Fisk	Swedish/Seafood
27	Oaxen Skärgårdskrog	Swedish
	Mathias Dahlgren	Swedish
	F12	International
26	Lux Stockholm	International/Swedish
	Ulriksdals Wärdshus	Swedish/International
25	Eriks Bakficka	International/Swedish
24	Operakällaren	International
	Pontus!	International
23	Prinsen	Swedish/French
	Brasserie Le Rouge	French/Italian
22	Kungsholmen	International
	Aquavit	Swedish/American
	Den Gyldene Freden*	Swedish
	Eriks Gondolen	French/Swedish
	Smak på Restaurangen	Swedish/International
21	Clas på Hörnet	Swedish

Aquavit Grill
& Raw Bar *Swedish/American*

`22` `21` `20` `VE`

City Center | Clarion Hotel Sign | Östra Järnvägsgatan 35 |
(46-8) 676-9850 | www.aquavitgrillrawbar.se

Surveyors split on this Clarion Hotel Sign venue, an offshoot of Swedish-born chef Marcus Samuelsson's original Aquavit in NYC; enthusiasts praise the "excellent" Swedish–New American food and sleek "Scandinavian-chic" setting that attract "beautiful people" seeking a "perfect evening" out, but cynics nix "expensive" tabs, "noisy" acoustics and "service that needs to shape up."

Berns Asian *Asian*

`19` `24` `18` `E`

City Center | Berns Hotel | Berzelii Park | (46-8) 5663-2222 |
www.berns.se

"You have to love" the "fabulously over-the-top" interior of this "massive place" in City Center; its "trendy, aristocratic" crowd ensures there's always "excitement in the air", but even they admit you "go for the drinks" and the "scene" – service is only "adequate" and the "competent" Asian fare is almost "an afterthought."

Brasserie Le Rouge 🗷 *French/Italian*

`23` `24` `22` `E`

Gamla Stan | Brunnsgränd 2-4 | (46-8) 5052-4430 |
www.lerouge.se

A "very hip place" in Gamla Stan, this "stunning" venue from chef Melker Andersson offers a "delicious" French-Italian menu that more than "lives up to expectations"; but it's the over-the-top "can-can" decor – a cross between the Moulin Rouge and a crimson red "bordello" – that draws the most response, ranging from "romantic" to "so tacky it's fun."

---

* Indicates a tie with restaurant above

	FOOD	DECOR	SERVICE	COST

Clas på Hörnet 🖾 *Swedish* — 21 | 20 | 20 | E
Vasastan | Hotel Clas på Hörnet | Surbrunnsgatan 20 | (46-8) 165-136 | www.claspahornet.se
This "charming" Swede set in a "quaint", circa-1731 Vasastan inn serves "tasty" traditional fare, with an emphasis on fish; a "lovely" candlelit Gustavian-style setting overlooking a garden and "stellar service" lead loyalists to reserve it for an "adult evening."

Den Gyldene Freden 🖾 *Swedish* — 22 | 24 | 23 | E
Gamla Stan | Österlånggatan 51 | (46-8) 249-760 | www.gyldenefreden.se
"Beautiful old-world" 18th-century surroundings define this "charming" Gamla Stan "favorite"; nearly "everyone loves this place" for its combination of "cozy" ambiance, "efficient service" and traditional Swedish dishes (plus some International offerings), even if some say it's "too bad" it's "getting a little staid" and "touristy" of late.

Eriks Bakficka 🖾 *International/Swedish* — 25 | 17 | 24 | E
Östermalm | Fredrikshovsgatan 4 | (46-8) 660-1599 | www.eriks.se
Owned by Erik Lallerstedt, "one of Sweden's best chefs", this "charming bistro" in the "expensive residential quarter" of Östermalm is a "favorite haunt of locals" – indeed, the "well-heeled" guests all seem to "know each other" as they gather within its "formal dining room" or "cozier bar section" to enjoy "fine" Swedish-International cuisine; true, it's "a little pricey", but regulars report it offers "excellent value."

Eriks Gondolen 🖾 *French/Swedish* — 22 | 26 | 22 | VE
Södermalm | Stadsgården 6 | (46-8) 641-7090 | www.eriks.se
Though it's the "breathtaking view of Stockholm" (including vistas of the harbor and Old Town) that "really makes it stand out", fans report "fine" dining on "wonderful" Swedish-French cuisine and "excellent service" at this "great place to watch the sunset" suspended high above Södermalm; even those who feel the "very expensive" fare is "secondary" to the venue's visual delights declare do "come for a drink" and "mingle at the nice bar."

F12 🖾 *International* — 27 | 22 | 24 | VE
City Center | Rödbodtorget 2 | (46-8) 248-052 | www.f12.se
A "favorite" for many, this "consistently excellent" City Center venue is run by "people who care about food" – namely "talented" chef-owners Melker Andersson (a "god in Stockholm") and Danyel Couet, whose "flavorful", albeit expensive, International fare is served by a "helpful staff" in a "first-rate setting"; those intimidated by its "innovative" tasting menu can now choose a traditional one or order à la carte.

Kungsholmen *International* — 22 | 22 | 20 | E
Kungsholmen | Norr Mälarstrand Kajplats 464 | (46-8) 5052-4450 | www.kungsholmen.com
Swedish restaurant guru Melker Andersson of the highly rated F12 "has done it again" at this "trendy" waterfront International in Kungsholmen where patrons mix and match their meal from a variety of seven "upmarket" "gourmet food courts" serving everything from soups and salads to sushi; a "hip crowd congregates" in the "delightful setting" that includes a floating terrace offering "drinks by the sea where the sun never seems to set."

	FOOD	DECOR	SERVICE	COST

Lux Stockholm ☒Ⓜ *International/Swedish*   26 | 19 | 22 | E

Lilla Essingen | Primusgatan 116 | (46-8) 619-0190 |
www.luxstockholm.com

Set in Lilla Essingen Island's "tastefully redone" "old Electrolux building" (hence the name), this "amazing" venue popular with "hip" types may be "so trendy it hurts", but even the "cool atmosphere" plays second fiddle to the "first-class" Swedish-International fare and "attentive" service; its "spacious dining room" is "beautifully minimalist" to some, "austere" for others, but there's no debate about that "gorgeous view."

Mathias Dahlgren ☒Ⓜ *Swedish*   27 | 24 | 26 | VE

City Center | Grand Hôtel Stockholm | Södra Blasieholmshamnen 6 | (46-8) 679-3584 | www.mathiasdahlgren.com

This dual venue in the Grand Hôtel in City Center comes courtesy of "one of the top chefs in Sweden", Mathias Dahlgren (ex Bon Lloc); Matsalen, the dinner-only main dining room, offers "outstanding" "innovative" cuisine served by a "wonderful" crew in a "sophisticated" setting with views of the Royal Palace, and can cost "a little more than you paid for your first car"; the chef's "attention to detail" also applies to Matbaren, the "less-expensive" bistro that's an "excellent choice for a business lunch or casual dinner."

Oaxen Skärgårdskrog Ⓜ *Swedish*   27 | 25 | 27 | VE

Mörkö | Oaxen 34 | (46-8) 5515 3105 | www.oaxenkrog.se

There's something "magical" about this "very different experience", starting with its "enchanted" setting on Mörkö (part of the Stockholm Archipelago) that boasts a panoramic view of the bay of Himmerfjärden; look for a "modern" Swedish menu stressing "local produce" paired with a "seductive" wine list at this truly "unique" spot; P.S. new ownership as of August 2011 may usher in some changes.

Operakällaren ☒Ⓜ *International*   24 | 27 | 23 | VE

Kungsträdgården | Royal Opera House | Karl XII:S Torg | (46-8) 676-5801 | www.operakallaren.se

This "magnificent" "landmark" in Kungsträdgården's "lovely" Royal Opera House is "so popular it's almost a cliché" (indeed it's voted Stockholm's Most Popular) thanks to the hordes of "hip, see-and-be-seen" folks who "go for the scene" and to "check out the latest fashions"; the "opulent" interior, "formal" service and "delicious" International haute cuisine are similarly "superb", and "worth every penny" – once the shock of the "astronomical" tabs wears off.

Pontus! ☒ *International*   24 | - | 23 | VE
(fka Pontus in the Green House)

Norrmalm | Brunnsgatan 1 | (46-8) 5452-7300 | www.pontusfrithiof.com

Expect a "fantastic" experience at this bastion of "great dining" whose habitués praise owner Pontus Frithiof's "artful kitchen" for delivering a "delicious" International menu offering Swedish, French and Asian specialties; given the "friendly" service and "reasonably priced gems on the wine list", fans say "don't miss it" – "if you have the money to spare"; N.B. post-Survey, the restaurant moved from Gamla Stan to this new location in Norrmalm, and a recent expansion into a neighboring space allows for separate areas, including seafood and cocktail bars and a show kitchen/private dining room.

	FOOD	DECOR	SERVICE	COST

Prinsen   *Swedish/French* | 23 | 22 | 23 | E |

Norrmalm | Mäster Samuelsgatan 4 | (46-8) 611-1331 | www.restaurangprinsen.se

The "food is excellent and the service accommodating" at this Norrmalm "classic" that "never disappoints" with its "innovative" Swedish-French fare, whether enjoyed at one of the "outside tables" or in its "more formal" wood-paneled dining room; it's a "power-lunch" favorite for financial industry types as well as a nighttime "tourist" haunt, and though it's "a bit expensive", word is it "always gives you value for your money."

Smak på Restaurangen 🖾 *Swedish/International* | 22 | 21 | 18 | E |

City Center | Oxtorgsgatan 14 | (46-8) 220-952 | www.restaurangentm.com

"Sampling" mavens swear by the "Scandinavian-tapas concept" of this City Center Swedish-International (from the "owner of F12") where you "order by numbers" – choosing a variety of "tasty" small courses, each "well-paired" with "different wines"; it's a "fun way" to sample a lot of "great food", while the bustling room packed with "pretty people" adds to the experience.

Sturehof ❶ *Swedish/Seafood* | 20 | 18 | 18 | E |

Stureplan | Sturegallerian 42 | Stureplan 2 | (46-8) 440-5730 | www.sturehof.com

A "smart", "stylish crowd" of locals and "hip tourists" hails this "huge, fun place" conveniently located in the "hub of Stockholm's cool Stureplan district" for its "high-quality" traditional Swedish menu with a seafood emphasis; three "lively" bars and a generally "buzzing atmosphere" make it "too bustling" for fans of quiet dining, but "lively" sorts love the "great people-watching" – especially from the "wonderful terrace in summertime."

Ulriksdals Wärdshus Ⓜ *Swedish/International* | 26 | 23 | 26 | VE |

Solna | Ulriksdals Slottspark | (46-8) 850-815 | www.ulriksdalswardshus.se

"Well worth every minute of travel" to its "out-of-the-way" location – in the "peaceful park" of Ulriksdals Castle in Solna – this "gem" is a "rite of passage" when visiting Stockholm thanks to its "excellent" Swedish-International cuisine (including a "fine smörgåsbord" served at lunch, weekends and holidays); throw in a "superb wine cellar" and "formal" service from a "thoughtful staff", and no wonder enthusiasts insist this "favorite" is "perfect for festive occasions"; a veranda has recently been added for outdoor dining in summer.

Wedholms Fisk 🖾 *Swedish/Seafood* | 28 | 21 | 26 | VE |

City Center | Arsenalsgatan 1 | (46-8) 611-7874 | www.wedholmsfisk.se

"Old-school" Swedish seafooder in City Center rated No. 1 for Food in Stockholm, where a "first-rate" chef uses "fresh", "fantastic fish" as the basis for "superb, simply prepared" dishes that are "not too elaborate"; perhaps the decor is "rather plain" and the atmosphere "quiet", but the "efficient" staff provides "excellent service" – yet another reason to "book in advance."

Venice

Al Covo *Seafood*   25 21 24 E

Castello | Calle della Pescaria, 3968 | (39-041) 522-3812 |
www.ristorantealcovo.com

"Divine fish and seafood", "simply and elegantly prepared", comes
"highly recommended" at this "intimate" Castello "gem" run by a
Texan pastry chef and her Venetian chef-husband known for their
"wonderful hospitality"; the decor might be fairly "basic", but an "attentive" staff and "warm" atmosphere add to a "thoroughly enjoyable"
experience; P.S. closed Wednesday–Thursday.

Antiche   24 20 22 E
Carampane 🚫Ⓜ *Italian*

San Polo | Rio Terà delle Carampane, 1911 | (39-041) 524-0165 |
www.antichecarampane.com

It's worth the "trek" to San Polo to experience this little "treasure"
dishing out "seriously good" Italian cooking – "you won't have fresher
fish unless you pull it out of the Adriatic yourself"; factor in "friendly"
service in a cozy, kitschy, photo-adorned dining room, and it's a place
to return to "many, many times."

Antico Pignolo *Venetian/Seafood*   24 24 23 E

San Marco | Calle dei Specchieri, 451 | (39-041) 522-8123 |
www.anticopignolo.com

"Fresh seafood for all tastes" "never disappoints" at this "popular"
Venetian steps from "historic" Piazza San Marco; an "elegant atmosphere" inside, beautiful "garden surroundings" outside and a sizable
wine list add to the appeal, but just know that the bill can be as "memorable" as the meal.

---

* Indicates a tie with restaurant above

	FOOD	DECOR	SERVICE	COST

Cip's Club *Venetian*

| | 24 | 26 | 25 | VE |

Giudecca | Hotel Cipriani | Isola della Giudecca, 10 |
(39-041) 520-7744 | www.hotelcipriani.com

From the private speedboat ride to Giudecca island to the "delicious" *cucina,* "extravagant" wines and service that caters to "every whim", this dinner-only Venetian in the Cipriani hotel is a place to indulge your inner "billionaire"; it's best enjoyed on the "charming" terrace with "peerless" views of St. Mark's and the lagoon – all in all, a "memorable" "must" if you "can bankroll it"; P.S. open from the end of March to early November only.

Club del Doge *Venetian/Mediterranean*

| | 25 | 26 | 25 | VE |

San Marco | Hotel Gritti Palace | Campo Santa Maria del Giglio, 2467 |
(39-041) 794-611 | www.starwoodhotels.com

"You'll feel like a doge" indeed at this "civilized" Venetian-Med in the Hotel Gritti Palace where "superb, elegant and refined" applies equally to the food, setting and service; for best results, sit on the terrace and savor the "to-die-for" view of the Grand Canal – just be advised "you'll need a kingdom" if you want to make dining here "a regular habit."

Corte Sconta 🖫Ⓜ *Venetian/Seafood*

| | 25 | 20 | 22 | E |

Castello | Calle del Pestrin, 3886 | (39-041) 522-7024 |
www.veneziaristoranti.it

"Superb seafood" stars at this "out-of-the-way" Castello Venetian; the kitchen blends "originality" with "respect" for tradition, service is "personable" and the "peaceful" interior is augmented by a "charming" courtyard garden, so even those who find it "on the expensive side" believe their "extra euros were lost in a good cause."

Da Ivo 🖫 *Tuscan/Venetian*

| | 24 | 23 | 23 | E |

San Marco | Calle dei Fuseri, 1809 | (39-041) 528-5004 |
www.ristorantedaivo.com

Arrive "on foot or by water" to this "old favorite" "right on a canal" near St. Mark's Square; its "broad" menu of "classic" Tuscan-Venetian specialties, including what fans call "the best" steak *fiorentina,* is backed by a "comprehensive" wine list, "accommodating" service and a "romantic" vibe, though some say the "tiny", minimalist setting means you'd best "like the people at the next table."

Fiaschetteria Toscana *Venetian*

| | 24 | 21 | 22 | E |

Cannaregio | Salizada San Giovanni Grisostomo, 5719 |
(39-041) 528-5281 | www.fiaschetteriatoscana.it

"Despite the name", which reflects its Tuscan wine shop origins, this "warm" "haven" in Cannaregio deals in "sublime" Venetian cuisine fashioned from "local, fresh" ingredients, including "impeccably prepared seafood"; service is "gracious", the "comfortable" setting includes a "small terrace in summer", and while it's not cheap, fans find it "reasonable (for Venice)"; P.S. closed Tuesdays.

Fortuny *Italian*
(fka Cipriani)

| | 26 | 27 | 26 | VE |

Giudecca | Hotel Cipriani | Isola della Giudecca, 10 | (39-041) 520-7744 |
www.hotelcipriani.com

"A bit of paradise" sums up this ultra-"elegant" Italian in Giudecca's Hotel Cipriani; reached by a quick boat ride from St. Mark's Square, it's among the "tops in all categories", with "delicious" food, "impeccable" service and a "beautiful" setting "overlooking the water"; you need a fortune-y to dine here, but "you only live once" so settle in with some "cocktails on the terrace" and "enjoy the view."

Harry's Bar *International/Venetian* | 21 | 23 | 21 | VE |

San Marco | Calle Vallaresso, 1323 | (39-041) 528-5777 | www.cipriani.com

"History abounds" at this "legendary" circa-1931 San Marco bar/restaurant (voted Venice's Most Popular), famed as the birthplace of the Bellini and still "hopping" with "tourists" and others imagining they see "Hemingway at the next table"; views on the food range from "terrific" to "ok" and service may "depend on who you are", but if you can handle the "eye-popping" prices, it's a "must-do" at least once if only "to say you've been."

Harry's Dolci *International/Seafood* | 24 | 23 | 24 | VE |

Giudecca | Sestiere Giudecca, 773 | (39-041) 522-4844 | www.cipriani.com
In a "wonderful setting overlooking the Giudecca Canal", this Harry's Bar spin-off offers similar International-Venetian fare but earns a higher Food score as well as praise for its "less formal" vibe, "courteous" service and slightly lower prices; terrace tables are the best place to savor the "world-class" view; P.S. closed mid-October–Easter.

La Vecia Cavana Ⓜ *Venetian/Seafood* | 24 | 22 | 22 | E |

Cannaregio | Rio Terà SS Apostoli, 4624 | (39-041) 528-7106 | www.marsillifamiglia.it
Located in a renovated 16th-century *cavana* (boathouse) in Cannaregio, this family-owned Venetian seafooder is praised for its "great cuisine", "thorough" service and "very refined atmosphere"; two spacious rooms make it good for dining with large groups, and diners with food allergies will appreciate separate gluten-free and vegetarian menus.

La Zucca *Venetian* | 24 | 20 | 21 | M |

Santa Croce | Calle del Spezier, 1762, Santa Croce 1762, Ramo de Megio | (39-041) 524-1570 | www.lazucca.it
Expect "imaginative" contemporary Venetian cooking including "many vegetarian options" at this "charming" eatery in Santa Croce where "delicious dishes" at "very reasonable" prices lure locals and travelers alike; the "cozy" interior features renderings of the namesake (pumpkin), while outside offers "fabulous tables" along a "quiet canal"; P.S. reservations not accepted for large groups.

L'Osteria di Santa Marina Ⓢ *Venetian* | 25 | 20 | 22 | E |

Rialto | Campo Santa Marina, 5911 | (39-041) 528-5239
"A high-end dining experience without the stuffiness" can be had at this Rialto Venetian serving "authentic" "home cooking" with "creative" touches; "good local wines", a "comfortable" setting (with outdoor seating) and "friendly" service make it that much more "memorable."

Osteria alle Testiere ⒮Ⓜ *Seafood* | 26 | 18 | 22 | E |

San Marco | Calle del Mondo Novo, 5801 | (39-041) 522-7220 | www.osterialletestiere.it
"Book ahead" if you want to experience this "tiny" "true gem" off Campo Santa Maria Formosa, rated No. 1 for Food in Venice thanks to

its "exceptional", "extremely fresh and inventive" seafood dishes; expect "cheek by jowl" seating in a simple space with an "inviting", "laid-back" vibe – overall it's well "worth the effort" to hook a table.

Terrazza Danieli   *Italian/International*   23 | 26 | 25 | VE

Castello | Hotel Danieli | Riva degle Schiavoni, 4196, 5th fl. | (39-041) 522-6480 | www.danielihotelvenice.com

"Dazzling views" best enjoyed from a "terrace table" make this "glamorous" rooftop Italian-International in Castello's Hotel Danieli one of the most "gloriously romantic" places in Venice; the food is "better than it has to be" and service is "lovely", so while prices can be as stunning as the scenery, that's one more reason why "you will always remember" your visit.

Trattoria al Gatto Nero   24 | 21 | 22 | M
da Ruggero 🅼 *Venetian*

Burano | Via Giudecca, 88 | (39-041) 730-120 | www.gattonero.com

It's "worth a detour to Burano", some 40 minutes by boat from Venice, to sample the "terrific seafood and pasta" at this "charming" chef-owned Venetian; situated "away from the main street", it boasts a homey, "relaxed" vibe, dining rooms of varying sizes and outdoor seats with views of the brightly colored houses the island is known for.

Trattoria da Romano   *Venetian*   24 | 21 | 23 | M

Burano | Via Galuppi, 221 | (39-041) 730-030 | www.daromano.it

This family-run local favorite "on the main street of Burano" rewards those who make the roughly 40-minute boat trip from Venice with "excellent fish" and what fans call the "world's best risotto"; the big interior is adorned with artwork donated by patrons, while outside seats let you "view the crowds walking along the strip."

Vecio Fritolin   *Venetian/Seafood*   24 | 19 | 19 | M

Sestiere | Calle della Regina, 2262 | (39-041) 522-2881 | www.veciofritolin.it

Set in a "historic" building near the Rialto Bridge, this "rustic" seafooder comes "recommended" for its "very good" *fritolini* (deep-fried fish, which can also be wrapped in paper and taken to go) and other "typical" Venetian fare; "cozy" confines and "affordable" prices boost its appeal.

Vini da Gigio 🅼 *Venetian*   24 | 19 | 23 | E

Cannaregio | Fondamenta San Felice, 3628A | (39-041) 528-5140 | www.vinidagigio.com

"Go once" and you'll "always want to come back" to this "charming", "cozy" family-run trattoria "a bit off the beaten path" in Cannaregio offering "superior" Venetian cuisine backed by an "intriguing" wine list and "friendly" service; if a few feel it's "declined recently" and advise it's "better if you're a local", it's "still a favorite" for most; P.S. closed Monday–Tuesday.

FOOD | DECOR | SERVICE | COST

Vienna

TOP FOOD RANKING

Restaurant	Cuisine
28 Steirereck	Austrian/International
26 Imperial	Austrian/International
24 Demel	Austrian/International
Eisvogel	Austrian
Walter Bauer	Austrian/International
Mraz & Sohn	Austrian/International
Korso bei der Oper	International
Kim Kocht	Korean/International
Anna Sacher	Viennese
23 Artner Franziskanerplatz	Austrian/International
Zum weissen Rauchfangkehrer	Austrian
22 Österreicher im MAK	Viennese
DO & CO	Austrian/International
Plachutta	Austrian
Goldene Zeiten	Chinese
21 Fabios	Italian/Mediterranean
Indochine 21*	French/Vietnamese
Ella's	Mediterranean

Anna Sacher Ⓜ *Viennese*   24 | 25 | 23 | VE

Innere Stadt | Hotel Sacher Wien | Philharmonikerstr. 4 |
(43-1) 5145-6840 | www.sacher.com

"Vienna's original grande dame" in Innere Stadt is back after a refurb, and fans say it's just as "lavish and formal" as ever, now offering a traditional Viennese menu with a "lighter, contemporary touch"; "regal service", "over-the-top" green-velvet decor and "luxury" pricing come with the territory at this "tourist hot spot"; P.S. don't miss its "world-famous Sachertorte" for dessert.

Artner Franziskanerplatz *Austrian/International*   23 | 23 | 22 | E

Innere Stadt | Franziskanerplatz 5 | (43-1) 503-5034 |
www.artner.co.at

An "inviting respite" in Innere Stadt, this "stylish" eatery from restaurateur Markus Artner offers an "outstanding" Austrian-International menu served in "stylish" digs, including a not-to-be-missed "bar in the cellar"; "no-attitude" service, an "excellent wine list" ("they have their own vineyard") and "good value for the money" make it "one of the easiest restaurants in Vienna."

Café Landtmann ● *Austrian*   18 | 20 | 17 | E

Innere Stadt | Dr. Karl Lueger Ring 4 | (43-1) 241-000 | www.landtmann.at

You almost expect to "see Dr. Freud at the next table" at this "grand old coffeehouse" in Innere Stadt, where "authentic Viennese coffee" and "traditional" Austrian eats are served by "friendly" waiters in a "splendidly historical" space that offers "great people-watching" on its terrace; though not as pricey as psychoanalysis, it is on the "expensive" side.

---

* Indicates a tie with restaurant above

	FOOD	DECOR	SERVICE	COST

Demel *Austrian/International* | 24 | 22 | 18 | E |

Innere Stadt | Kohlmarkt 14 | (43-1) 5351-7170 | www.demel.at
"Expand your waistline and thin out your wallet" at this "posh" "pastry nirvana", rated Most Popular in Vienna for its "fantastic array" of "beautifully decorated" cakes and other desserts showcased in "world-famous window displays"on the Innere Stadt's tony Kohlmarkt; the Austrian-International menu, by contrast, is "unimpressive", and service can be "iffy", so many prefer to just sit back with some "fabulous" *kaffee und kuchen* and "watch the master bakers at work."

DO & CO Albertina ● *Austrian/International* | 22 | 21 | 20 | E |

Innere Stadt | The Albertina | Albertinaplatz 1 | (43-1) 532-9669

DO & CO Stephansplatz ● *Austrian/International*

Innere Stadt | Stephansplatz 12 | (43-1) 535-3969
www.doco.com
A "reliable mix" of Austrian and International cuisine (including some "superb Japanese" dishes) are "prepared in front of you" at this "see-and-be-seen" spot atop the contemporary glass Haas Haus building in Innere Stadtalong; the "modern, urban" interior has a "NY feel", there are "stunning views of St. Stephan's Cathedral" and the beautiful Stephansplatz, and service is "competent" and "friendly"; N.B. it has a younger sibling in the Albertina museum.

Eisvogel *Austrian* | 24 | 20 | 22 | E |

Leopoldstadt-Prater | Riesenradplatz 5 | (43-1) 908-1187 |
www.stadtgasthaus-eisvogel.at
Parked "near the famous Ferris wheel" in Leopoldstadt's Prater park, this circa-1805 venue burned down in 1945 and has been recently re-built in a more "Vegas-like" style; the "excellent" Viennese menu in-cludes both "classics" as well as more "inventive" dishes and service is "helpful", leaving only the "kitschy location" as a sticking point.

Ella's ⊠ *Mediterranean* | 21 | 21 | 19 | M |

Innere Stadt | Judenplatz 9-10 | (43-1) 535-1577 | www.ellas.at
This modern Med in Innere Stadt has surveyors salivating over its "ex-ceptional fare" and moderate prices; the "modern, minimalist" space features white tablecloths and black banquettes set against deep-red and orange walls, but in the summer "make a reservation for outside" on the "beautiful" terrace on Judenplatz.

Fabios *Italian/Mediterranean* | 21 | 21 | 20 | VE |

Innere Stadt | Tuchlauben 6 | (43-1) 532-2222 | www.fabios.at
"Meet the people who count" at this Innere Stadt "hot spot" where "authentic" Italian-Med cuisine is served by a "friendly" crew in "trendy, modern" digs furnished with lots of "dark wood" and leather; still, some find the "masculine" setting "oppressive" and the service "overbearing", saying you're really paying for the "good location."

Goldene Zeiten *Chinese* | 22 | 21 | 20 | E |

Innere Stadt | Dr. Karl Lueger-Platz 5 | (43-1) 513-4747 |
www.goldenezeiten.at
This Chinese may be the "best there is in Vienna" thanks to a chef-owner who peppers his "authentic" menu with elaborate Shanghainese and Sichuan dishes, complemented by an extensive wine list that includes

some rare Austrian vintages; relocated from the suburbs to Innere Stadt, the bright modern setting features butter-yellow walls and soaring ceilings that are punctuated by enormous red lamps.

Imperial *Austrian/International* | 26 | 26 | 27 | VE |

Innere Stadt | Hotel Imperial | Kärntner Ring 16 | (43-1) 5011-0356 | www.hotelimperialvienna.com

"You're treated like an emperor" at this "superlative" Austrian-International housed in Innere Stadt's "grand" Hotel Imperial that provides "outstanding" cuisine and "flawless" service in a "plush", wood-paneled Victorian room decorated with Hapsburg portraits; a "marvelous pianist" embellishes the "old-world" mood, making it a "slice of heaven on earth" for most – albeit at "hellish prices."

Indochine 21 ❶ *French/Vietnamese* | 21 | 19 | 19 | E |

Innere Stadt | Stubenring 18 | (43-1) 513-7660 | www.indochine.at

Across the street from the Museum für Angewandte Kunst (MAK) in Innere Stadt, this French-Vietnamese is a "nice change of pace" from typical Viennese cooking, offering "delectable" dishes with "unusual taste combinations" and "competent" service, all of which leaves diners with just one complaint – that it's "overpriced"; P.S. a post-Survey design revamp (which may outdate the Decor score) swapped out Asian elements for a modern, mainstream style.

Kim Kocht ❶☒Ⓜ *Korean/International* | 24 | 18 | 20 | E |

Alsergrund | Lustkandlgasse 4 | (43-1) 319-0242 | www.kimkocht.at

A "gourmet experience" awaits at this Alsergrund boîte, where chef-owner Sohyi Kim's "inventive" Korean-International cuisine emphasizing organic ingredients is "unbelievably tasty"; "even first-time visitors feel at home" thanks to the "courteous" staff, though it's "impossible to get a table" in the "mini", 24-seat room "unless you know the chef well."

Korso bei der Oper *International* | 24 | 25 | 25 | VE |

Innere Stadt | Hotel Bristol | Mahlerstr. 2 | (43-1) 5151-6546 | www.restaurantkorso.at

For the "best bet after the opera", try this "opulent" nearby venue in Innere Stadt's Hotel Bristol known for its "superb" International menu; service is "polished and professional", the wine list "excellent" and the "beautifully appointed" room evokes "old Vienna" in all its "elegance", so "don't look at the prices" and you'll have a truly "special evening"; P.S. a post-Survey chef change may outdate the Food score.

Mraz & Sohn ☒ *Austrian/International* | 24 | 21 | 19 | E |

Brigittenau | Wallensteinstr. 59 | (43-1) 330-4594 | www.mraz-sohn.at

This "excellent, high-quality" Austrian-International may be located in the downscale neighborhood of Brigittenau, but foodies flock here nevertheless to sample the creations of chef Markus Mraz, a molecular gastronomy pioneer in Vienna; the "casual" setting belies sophisticated touches like its legendary wine list and a choice selection of cheeses.

Österreicher im MAK *Viennese* | 22 | 23 | 21 | E |

Innere Stadt | Museum für Angewandte Kunst | Stubenring 5 | (43-1) 714-0121 | www.oesterreicherimmak.at

"One of the best chefs in Austria", Helmut Österreicher (ex Steirereck), brings his culinary art to the Museum for Applied Arts at this expansive venue, and the result is "well-done", "slightly modernized" Viennese food; the "wonderful location" is only exceeded by the "even greater interior design", which includes soaring ceilings and a chandelier made from 200 wine bottles.

Plachutta *Austrian*   22 | 14 | 19 | E

Hietzing | Auhofstr. 1 | (43-1) 877-7087
Innere Stadt | Wollzeile 38 | (43-1) 512-1577
Nussdorf | Heiligenstädterstr. 179 | (43-1) 370-4125
www.plachutta.at

"If you like *tafelspitz*, you can't go wrong" at this "dependable" trio of "authentic" Austrians where that signature Viennese dish and other "varieties of traditional boiled beef" are "unbeatable" if a bit "expensive"; a "charming" staff presides over the "simple", "bourgeois" digs that are "comfortable" even when they get "noisy and crowded."

Steirereck ⌧ *Austrian/International*   28 | 25 | 26 | VE

Landstrasse | Im Stadtpark | Am Heumarkt 2A | (43-1) 713-3168 |
www.steirereck.at

"By far the best" restaurant in Vienna and voted No. 1 for Food here, this Landstrasse landmark is a "fairy-tale" experience, featuring chef Heinz Reitbauer's "exquisite" Austrian-International cuisine, "cheese and bread carts that put others to shame", an "excellent" wine cellar and "first-class" service; the move to its current Stadtpark address has been a "fantastic success", thanks to the "exquisite" renovation of a century-old pavilion into a "knockout" setting with "no shortage of space."

Walter Bauer ⌧ *Austrian/International*   24 | 18 | 26 | E

Innere Stadt | Sonnenfelsgasse 17 | (43-1) 512-9871
Regulars have "never been disappointed" by this "hidden gem" in a small, circa-1505 medieval house parked "on a quiet street" in one of the oldest parts of Innere Stadt; a "wide-ranging" Austrian-International menu is complemented by a "superb wine list", "attentive staff" and "intimate" setting.

Zum weissen Rauchfangkehrer ⌧ *Austrian*   23 | 20 | 23 | E

Innere Stadt | Weihburggasse 4 | (43-1) 512-3471 |
www.weisser-rauchfangkehrer.at

For a "taste of Vienna", fans tout this "lovely old place" (circa 1844) near Stephansplatz offering "outstanding", mostly organic takes on "traditional Viennese fare"; "personable service" and a "classic setting" with lots of "country-style" charm make it "worth a return visit."

Warsaw

TOP FOOD RANKING

	Restaurant	Cuisine
25	Dom Polski	Polish
24	La Rotisserie	French
	Rózana	Polish
23	Rubikon	Italian
	U Kucharzy	Polish
	Parmizzano's	Italian
22	Likus	Italian
	Michel Moran	French/Mediterranean
	Belvedere	International/Polish
21	Qchnia Artystyczna	International
	Boathouse	Italian/Mediterranean
	Sushi Zushi*	Japanese
	Villa Nuova	Eclectic
	Oriental	Asian/Sushi

Belvedere *International/Polish*   22 | 26 | 23 | E

Srodmiescie | ul. Agrykola 1 | (48-22) 558-6700 | www.belvedere.com.pl
On top of its "stupendous location" – a 19th-century orangery in Lazienki Park with an open-air terrace overlooking "lush grounds" – this "classic" "fine-dining" venue in Srodmiescie, Warsaw's Most Popular restaurant, offers "well-executed" Polish-International fare to a mixed crowd including "trendy" types; it's an "excellent" place for a "special dinner", so long as "you have money to throw around."

Boathouse *Italian/Mediterranean*   21 | 17 | 17 | E

Saska Kepa | Wal Miedzeszynski 389A | (48-22) 616-3223 | www.boathouse.pl
"Ideal for larger groups", this spacious ground-floor "haven" right on the river in Saska Kepa is a "lovely place to dine" on "excellent" Italian-Med fare; it's especially "noteworthy" in the summer when you can opt for "charming outdoor seating" – just "beware the mosquitoes!"

Dom Polski *Polish*   25 | 21 | 21 | E

Saska Kepa | ul. Francuska 11 | (48-22) 616-2432 | www.restauracjadompolski.pl
"Traditional Polish" fare is yours at this "fabulous" venue in Saska Kepa, a residential area on the Vistula River; it's "still one of the best" (and Warsaw's No. 1 for Food), and a "great place to get to know" the cuisine thanks to a kitchen that excels at "tried-and-true recipes" – just "be hungry when you come, as the portions are big"; N.B. a recent expansion and the addition of a garden may outdate the Decor score.

La Rotisserie *French*   24 | 21 | 24 | E

Old Town | Mamaison Hotel Le Régina Warsaw | ul. Koscielna 12 | (48-22) 531-6070 | www.leregina.com
Set in an "elegantly appointed" room in the Mamaison Hotel Le Régina in the new part of Old Town, this "fine" French offers a "delicious"

---

* Indicates a tie with restaurant above

FOOD | DECOR | SERVICE | COST

menu – and an equally delicious view of the Vistula River; the staff "works hard to make sure you're happy", and there's a bonus "adjoining courtyard" for dining in warmer weather.

Likus Concept Store Restaurant 🖾 *Italian*

22 | 24 | 22 | VE

Srodmiescie | ul. Krakowskie Przedmiescie 16/18 | (48-22) 492-7409 | www.likusconceptstore.pl

Part of a restaurant/wine shop/clothing store complex in Srodmiescie, this "hard-to-find" Italian is set in a "splendidly restored" "old bathhouse" that's been jazzed up with ultramodern furniture; the cooking falls somewhere between "good" and "excellent", and though very "expensive", it's certainly "worth the price."

Michel Moran
Bistro de Paris 🖾 *French/Mediterranean*

22 | 16 | 19 | E

Srodmiescie | pl. Pilsudskiego 9 | (48-22) 826-0107 | www.restaurantbistrodeparis.com

French-Med in the rear of the National Theatre in Srodmiescie, where "talented" chef Michel Moran prepares "very good" cuisine that emphasizes seafood and relies on "excellent ingredients"; the "elegant", wood-paneled setting overlooks Norman Foster's Metropolitan building, and in season the impressive, columned terrace is a prestigious perch that comes with a "charming summer menu."

Oriental, The *Asian/Sushi*

21 | 19 | 22 | E

Srodmiescie | Sheraton Warsaw Hotel | ul. B. Prusa 2 | (48-22) 450-6705 | www.sheraton.pl

A "staff that couldn't be more helpful" makes for "exceptional" dining at this "good bet" situated in Srodmiescie's Sheraton Hotel; folks who "walk in to see what smells so delicious" stick around for the "authentic", "quality" Asian fare (as well as sushi) served in a "pleasant", "atmospheric" space.

Parmizzano's *Italian*

23 | 18 | 21 | E

Srodmiescie | The Marriott Warsaw | al. Jerozolimskie 65/79 | (48-22) 630-5096 | www.marriott.com/wawpl

"Forget the usual hotel-type places" – this Srodmiescie spot is a "true Italian gem" thanks to a "chef who's really passionate" about turning out "heavenly" dishes, "great service" and a setting that reminds some of a "quiet place in Sicily"; P.S. business sorts also say it's a "safe choice" for an "excellent light lunch."

Qchnia Artystyczna *International*

21 | 21 | 17 | E

Srodmiescie | al. Ujazdowskie 6 | (48-22) 625-7627 | www.qchnia.pl

Supporters of this "stylish" Srodmiescie venue set in Ujazdowskie Castle (home to the Center for Contemporary Art) tout its "imaginative" International cooking, "vibrant" setting and "great view of the park"; it's "popular with the hip and wealthy" for a "lovely lunch" or a "romantic dinner", though some say "service could be more professional."

Rózana ❶ *Polish*

24 | 22 | 24 | E

Mokotów | ul. Chocimska 7 | (48-22) 848-1225 | www.restauracjatradycja.pl

This "traditional" place in Mokotów offers an "authentic, upscale" Polish menu that's quite "exceptional", although "quite conservative, with little or no experimentation" in the kitchen; "helpful" service and "rooms full of flowers" keep it "popular" with "touristy" types.

Rubikon *Italian*

| 23 | 21 | 22 | M |

Mokotów | ul. Wróbla 3/5 | (48-22) 847-6655 | www.rubikon.waw.pl
"One of the best Italians in Warsaw", this bi-level Mokotów venue offers a moderately priced, seasonally changing menu ferried by a "very polite" staff; the ground floor is casual, the more elegant upstairs has an art deco feel and there's a "luscious patio" for summer dining.

Santorini *Greek*

| 18 | 18 | 19 | M |

Saska Kepa | ul. Egipska 7 | (48-22) 672-0525 | www.kregliccy.pl
For a "real taste of Greece", check out this "charming", "established" spot in Saska Kepa that offers a "good choice of meze"; insiders advise ignoring the facade of its "ugly communist-style building", as inside awaits a "nice" blue-and-white taverna that brings a "touch of the Mediterranean to Eastern Europe."

Sushi Zushi *Japanese*

| 21 | 19 | 21 | E |

Srodmiescie | ul. Zurawia 6/12 | (48-22) 420-3373 | www.sushizushi.pl
A circular sushi bar dominates the "elegant" room of this "recommended" Japanese in Srodmiescie where the "beautiful preparations" are sliced by Polish chefs; the atmosphere is "sleek" and the food is "served with style", though some killjoys grumble it's "too pricey for dead fish."

U Kucharzy ● *Polish*

| 23 | 20 | 21 | E |

Srodmiescie | Hotel Europejski | ul. Ossolinskich 7 | (48-22) 826-7936 | www.gessler.pl
At this Polish venue set in the Hotel Europejski, the chefs not only prepare "delicious" meals out in the open (using organic ingredients from the restaurant's own farm), but serve them in a series of white-tiled rooms as well; still, surveyors split on the overall experience: "unique" vs. "uneven."

Villa Nuova *Eclectic*

| 21 | 19 | 20 | E |

Wilanow | ul. Stanislawa Kostki-Potockiego 23 | (48-22) 885-1502 | www.villanuova.pl
A restored manor house in Wilanow surrounded by a luxuriant garden is the setting for this "very nice" Eclectic where the "extravagant", cream-colored decor is a match for the "equally extravagant menu"; though "a bit of a drive if you come from the center of the city", it's worth it for a more than "pleasant experience."

Zurich

TOP FOOD RANKING

	Restaurant	Cuisine
27	Rico's Kunststuben	French
26	Pavillon	Mediterranean
	Lindenhofkeller	Swiss/International
25	Wirtschaft	International
24	Restaurant	International
	Ginger	Japanese
	Casa Aurelio	Spanish
	Orsini	Italian
23	Casa Ferlin	Italian
	Sala of Tokyo*	Japanese
	Da Angela	Italian
	Asian Place	Asian
	Sein	International
	Accademia	Italian
	Emilio*	Spanish
	Il Giglio	Italian
22	Widder	International
	Rive Gauche	Mediterranean
	Zentraleck	International

Accademia el Gusto 🗷 *Italian* `23` `18` `23` `VE`
Kreis 4 | Rotwandstr. 48 | (41-44) 241-6243 | www.accademiadelgusto.ch
"One of Zurich's stalwarts", this "classic Italian" in Kreis 4 features "exceptional food" (including "extremely good pastas") served at an "exceptional price"; though service is equally "excellent", a few feel the "formal staff" may be "slightly supercilious if you don't arrive dressed in an Armani suit."

Asian Place 🗷 *Asian* `23` `17` `20` `E`
Glattbrugg | Renaissance Zurich Hotel | Thurgauerstr. 101 | (41-44) 874-5721 | www.asianplace.ch
The "name says it all" at this "delightful surprise" in the Renaissance Zurich Hotel, near the airport in the new Glattpark neighborhood, that makes "you feel you're in Asia" with its "wide selection" of "exciting", "exotic dishes" from Japan, China and Thailand, served by an "efficient" staff; some call the prices "inflated", but others say they're "justified by the quality of the food" and the "tranquil" location.

Brasserie Lipp *French* `18` `17` `16` `E`
Kreis 1 | Uraniastr. 9 | (41-43) 888-6666 | www.brasserie-lipp.ch
Like its famed Parisian namesake, this Kreis 1 spot is a "true French brasserie" in every respect – from its "authentic" decor and "high noise level" to its "nostalgic bar", "big wine list" and "dependable" (if "expected") menu featuring "specialties from *plateau de fruits de mer* to Alsatian choucroute"; most find it "enjoyable", even though the always "crowded" confines mean you may "have to wait and wait."

---

* Indicates a tie with restaurant above

	FOOD	DECOR	SERVICE	COST

Casa Aurelio 🗷 *Spanish*

24 | 17 | 18 | E

Kreis 5 | Langstr. 209 | (41-44) 272-7744 | www.casaaurelio.ch
There's "something special" about dining at this Spanish restaurant in Kreis 5, a perennially "popular" spot drawing an interesting mix of locals and celebs with its "outstanding food", "substantial portions", "nice wine list" and "obliging" service; some say it's "somewhat noisy" and "slightly worn out", yet sometimes "patrons are the best decor."

Casa Ferlin 🗷 *Italian*

23 | 16 | 21 | E

Kreis 6 | Stampfenbachstr. 38 | (41-44) 362-3509 | www.casaferlin.ch
"It's been around a long time but it holds up well" is the consensus on this family-owned Italian in Kreis 6, where "large portions" of "excellent traditional dishes" ("fresh pasta", the "best homemade ravioli") are served by an "attentive" team; some find the decor "dark and dated", but devotees declare "that's part of the charm."

Da Angela 🗷Ⓜ *Italian*

23 | 19 | 22 | E

Kreis 9 | Hohlstr. 449 | (41-44) 492-2931 | www.daangela.ch
An "unlikely" setting in Kreis 9, "not the fashionable part of Zurich", is home to this "top-notch" Italian serving "interesting" food accompanied by a "wine list to be remembered"; sure, it's "expensive" and the "decor could be improved", but a "perfect hostess" and a "simple garden terrace" compensate.

Emilio *Spanish*

23 | 9 | 18 | E

Kreis 4 | Zweierstr. 9 | (41-44) 241-8321 | www.restaurant-emilio.ch
A genuine "Spanish feel" pervades this Kreis 4 venue that delivers authentic, "good-quality" grub like "can't-be-beat paella" and some of the "best chicken in the world" (which is "nearly worth the obscene price"); still, the "not-so-attentive service" "could be better" – and as for the "rather poor" decor, "well . . ."

Ginger 🗷 *Japanese*

24 | 18 | 19 | VE

Kreis 8 | Seefeldstr. 62 | (41-44) 422-9509 | www.ginger-restaurant.ch
Some of the "freshest sushi in town" turns up at this "small", "cool" Japanese in Kreis 8, where "creative" chefs slice up some mighty "great" fish; sit at the H-shaped bar and choose dishes that "revolve before you" on a carousel or are "obligingly served" in one of the few booths; remember, though, that it all comes at a "premium price", and those "little plates add up quickly."

Il Giglio 🗷 *Italian*

23 | 16 | 19 | E

Kreis 4 | Weberstr. 14 | (41-44) 242-8597 | www.ilgiglio.ch
Locals love this "small, intimate" Italian in Kreis 4 for its "nice, clean" dishes, many of which are accented with tomatoes imported from Calabria; the decor may be "nothing special", but the "pleasant" staff always provides "polite service"; P.S. look for "excellent wines of the month at moderate prices."

Kronenhalle *Swiss/French*

22 | 24 | 22 | VE

Kreis 1 | Rämistr. 4 | (41-44) 262-9900 | www.kronenhalle.com
The former owner's "splendid collection" of "genuine" art treasures including "original works by Picasso, Chagall and Matisse" makes for a "wonderful atmosphere" at this "pricey" "perennial favorite", Zurich's Most Popular restaurant, centrally located in Kreis 1 – and

there are "masterpieces on the plate" too, in the form of "fabulous" Swiss-French dishes that are "elegantly served" by an "expert" staff; P.S. for the best celeb spotting, "get a seat on the main floor."

Lindenhofkeller Ⓢ Swiss/International
26 | 20 | 24 | E

Kreis 1 | Pfalzgasse 4 | (41-44) 211-7071 | www.lindenhofkeller.ch
"Outstanding meals" await at this "upmarket" venue in Kreis 1, where the wine list has "depth and breadth" and the "excellent" menu "changes with the seasons", but always features "sophisticated" Swiss-International fare; a "pleasant" staff that's "amenable to customers' wishes" and a "cozy" setting (plus a "beautiful garden") seal the deal.

Orsini Italian
24 | 19 | 25 | VE

Kreis 1 | Hotel Savoy Baur en Ville Paradeplatz | Am Münsterhof 25 | (41-44) 215-2727 | www.savoy-baurenville.ch
"Superb service" from an "attentive" staff draws visitors to this "reliable" "businessman-and-banker hangout" in the Savoy Baur en Ville hotel in Kreis 1; "cuisine purists" praise the kitchen for its "splendid", "no-nonsense" Italian fare abetted by a "good wine list" and a "formal" setting with "classic decor"; in sum, "you will not be disappointed" here.

Pavillon Mediterranean
26 | 23 | 26 | VE

Kreis 1 | Baur au Lac | Talstr. 1 | (41-44) 220-5020 | www.bauraulac.ch
"Top class all the way", this "exceptional" Kreis 1 venue, in "one of Europe's classiest hotels", offers "outstanding meals" of "grand" Mediterranean fare, along with an "excellent wine selection"; an "extremely attentive staff" presides over the "elegant" dining room with a "view of the garden and canal"; yes, it's very "expensive", but "you get what you pay for and then some."

Restaurant, The International
24 | 25 | 24 | VE

Kreis 7 | Dolder Grand Hotel | Kurhausstr. 65 | (41-44) 456-6000 | www.thedoldergrand.ch
"Zurich's top hotel", the Dolder Grand in Kreis 7, is the setting for this "simply outstanding" "high-end" International that's best known for its prix fixe lunch comprised of an "endless procession of tapas"; "impeccable service", "beautiful views of the city" and a "crème-de-la-crème" crowd make the "steep" tabs easier to digest.

Rico's Kunststuben Ⓢ Ⓜ French
27 | 24 | 26 | VE

Küsnacht | Seestr. 160 | (41-44) 910-0715 | www.kunststuben.com
"One of the finest restaurants in Switzerland", this "splendid" French "classic" is "first rate in every way", and voted No. 1 for Food in Zurich; "outstanding" chef Horst Petermann has passed the scepter to his protégé, Rico Zandonella, and together the two now maintain the "highest standards", producing "unbelievably good" culinary creations that are "almost too beautiful to eat", while Iris Petermann presides over the "special" staff and stylishly renovated decor; all told, it's an "unforgettable dining experience" that's "worth the short trip to Küsnacht" – just be warned that the "bill will also be unforgettable."

Rive Gauche Ⓢ Mediterranean
22 | 22 | 22 | VE

Kreis 1 | Baur au Lac | Talstr. 1 | (41-44) 220-5060 | www.agauche.ch
This "informal restaurant in the very formal Baur au Lac hotel" draws a mix of celebs, local professionals and affluent guests to its "central

location" in Kreis 1; an "excellent" selection of "inventive" Mediterranean cuisine emphasizing light seasonal dishes is "served with Swiss efficiency" in a "classic", clubby setting – no wonder many call it their "favorite place to dine in Zurich."

Sala of Tokyo ⊠ⓂⓂ Japanese

23 | 15 | 19 | VE

Kreis 5 | Limmatstr. 29 | (41-44) 271-5290 | www.sala-of-tokyo.ch
"Quality and presentation" make for a "great" dining experience at this "traditional" Japanese in Kreis 5; of course, there's "excellent sushi", but the "varied" menu also features specialties like shabu-shabu, sukiyaki, robatayaki and tempura; even those who deem the decor only "ok" agree that the "ever-so-charming presence" of chef/co-owner Sala Ruch-Fukuoka improves the ambiance.

Sein ⊠ International

23 | 20 | 21 | E

Kreis 1 | Schützengasse 5 | (41-44) 221-1065 | www.zuerichsein.ch
"Innovative" International fare, "luxurious" tapas at the bar and "real Swiss service" draw different crowds to this Kreis 1 venue: "suits and ties" at lunch vs. hip types at night; a "beautiful bright" vibe permeates this vibrant mirrored space, luring in all who just want to be "Sein."

Widder International

22 | 23 | 23 | VE

Kreis 1 | Widder Hotel | Rennweg 7 | (41-44) 224-2526 | www.widderhotel.ch
A "classy" hotel in Kreis 1 composed of a series of historic townhouses provides the "lovely setting" for this "upmarket" "fine-dining" venue where the International menu is "excellent" and the staff "takes pride in what they do"; with such "all-around quality", it's no wonder the place is "popular" – and a visit to the Widder Bar after dinner with its live piano music is the "cherry on the cake."

Wirtschaft zum Wiesengrund ⊠Ⓜ International

25 | 20 | 23 | E

Uetikon am See | Kleindorfstr. 61 | (41-44) 920-6360 | www.wiesengrund.ch
Although "somewhat challenging to find" in Uetikon am See, this "safe-bet" International is worth seeking out for its "conversation piece"-worthy food "impeccably served" in a "small" room that's either "cozy" or "cramped", depending on who's talking (though tables are set in the lush garden in summer); maybe the tabs are "steep", but "the Swiss are used to paying high prices for quality."

Zentraleck ⊠Ⓜ International

22 | 20 | 21 | E

Kreis 3 | Zentralstr. 161 | (41-44) 461-0800 | www.zentraleck.ch
The young chef/co-owner of this small Kreis 3 International concocts "creative" dishes that are matched with "excellent wines" and served by a "flawless" crew in a simple, "cozy" setting heavy on the polished wood; overall, most pronounce it a "delight."

UNITED STATES
RESTAURANT
DIRECTORY

Atlanta

TOP FOOD RANKING

Restaurant	Cuisine
29 Bacchanalia	American
28 Quinones Room	American
Aria	American
McKendrick's	Steak
Bone's	Steak
27 Kevin Rathbun	Steak
di Paolo	Italian
La Grotta	Italian
Chops Lobster Bar	Seafood/Steak
Hal's on Old Ivy	Steak
Rathbun's	American
MF Buckhead	Japanese
Nan Thai Fine Dining	Thai
Kyma	Greek/Seafood
26 MF Sushibar	Japanese
Pure Vida	Pan-Latin
Busy Bee Cafe	Soul Food
New York Prime	Steak

Aria ☒ *American* | 28 | 25 | 26 | E |

Buckhead | 490 E. Paces Ferry Rd. NE (Maple Dr.) | 404-233-7673 | www.aria-atl.com

"Bravo" bellow boosters who "can't get enough" of this "flawless" New American in Buckhead, offering "fantastic" fare, "glamorous cocktails" and selections from a "superior" wine list, as well as "impeccable" service complete with "smiles"; the "showstopper" space begins with a "cool, beaded [curtain] entry" into a "transporting" dining room, and includes a "romantic" wine cellar that's a "favorite" for "special occasions" or "intimate dinners"; it's "everything a fine restaurant should be."

Bacchanalia ☒ *American* | 29 | 25 | 27 | VE |

Westside | Westside Mktpl. | 1198 Howell Mill Rd. (bet. 14th St. & Huff Rd.) | 404-365-0410 | www.starprovisions.com

This "pantheon" of "perfection" "reigns supreme" as Atlanta's No. 1 for Food and Most Popular, thanks to the "gourmet firepower" of its "divine" New American "delectables" that'll "bring tears to your eyes", made better by "excellent" "wine pairings" and "impeccable" service; the "phenomenal" Westside "warehouse setting" has an "urban vibe" (though some find it "dreary"), and casual sorts can "sit at the bar" in "shorts and flip-flops" and order à la carte; wallet-watchers warn of "car payment"–size tabs, but for foodies it's a "fantasy come true."

Bone's Restaurant *Steak* | 28 | 23 | 27 | VE |

Buckhead | 3130 Piedmont Rd. NE (Peachtree Rd.) | 404-237-2663 | www.bonesrestaurant.com

"You can almost taste the prestige" at this "marvelous" "carnivore's castle" and "Buckhead boys' hangout" that for more than 30 years has been serving "beautifully prepared steaks" "like butta", "phenomenal martinis" and a "fantastic wine list" (now presented to diners on an iPad), delivered by "extraordinary" servers who "treat you like a regular even if you're not one"; "major deals are consummated" and "special" "parties go on" in the "clubby", "masculine" dining room and "semi-private rooms", so "expense-account" prices notwithstanding, most agree this "comfortable" "Atlanta classic" "never gets old."

Buckhead Diner ● ☒ *American*   23 | 21 | 23 | M

Buckhead | 3073 Piedmont Rd. NE (Paces Ferry Rd.) | 404-262-3336 | www.buckheadrestaurants.com

"Ball gowns, blazers and blue jeans" are "all welcome" at this "perennial favorite" from the Buckhead Life Group offering a "broad menu" of "wonderful" New American "comfort food" at "reasonable prices", served in a "retro-glam dining room" that's a "wonderful step back in time"; the "no-reservations policy" makes for "lengthy waits" (they do have a call-ahead system), but service is usually "quick and crisp", and though critics pan it as "loud", "expensive" and "totally overrated", most are "still crazy for this place after all these years."

Busy Bee Cafe *Soul Food*   26 | 13 | 22 | I

Downtown | 810 Martin Luther King Jr. Dr. SW (Paschal Ave.) | 404-525-9212 | www.busybeeatl.com

"One of a vanishing line of truly Southern restaurants", this "family-friendly" Downtown haunt has boosters buzzing over its "shockingly good fried chicken" and other "soulful" soul food "to die for", doled out by a "staff rich with character"; you can scope out some "great church hats" in the otherwise no-frills digs that are "always packed" with "native Atlantans" and tourists alike.

Canoe *American*   25 | 26 | 26 | E

Vinings | Vinings on the River | 4199 Paces Ferry Rd. NW (Woodland Brook Dr.) | 770-432-2663 | www.canoeatl.com

Making a "comeback" after "epic floods" shut it down in 2009, this Vinings New American helps fans "get away from it all" with its "fantastic" gardens and what some say is the "No. 1 patio in town", amid a "picturesque setting on the Chattahoochee River"; the "superb" staff "does a phenomenal job catering" to every whim of "regulars" and "out-of-town guests" while serving chef Carvel Grant Gould's "inventive, seasonal" cuisine, which includes "lots of game" and is backed by a "terrific wine list"; what's more, the "very reasonable prices" make it a "fantastic value."

Chops Lobster Bar *Seafood/Steak*   27 | 25 | 26 | E

Buckhead | Buckhead Plaza | 70 W. Paces Ferry Rd. (Peachtree Rd.) | 404-262-2675 | www.buckheadrestaurants.com

A "rock-solid" "classic" from the Buckhead Life Group, this "clubby beef and fish palace" attracts a "good mix of businesspeople and plain (rich!) folks" with "perfectly prepared beef" and some of the "best inland seafood in the Southeast", served by a staff that "knows what you need before you realize it"; downstairs is a "unique 'tiled cave'" setting, while upstairs is a "carnivore"-centric space that can get "loud", and while some find it "overpriced", most deem it "money well spent" for a "perfect power" meal or "romantic" "evening out."

di Paolo ⓂItalian   27 | 23 | 25 | M

Alpharetta | Rivermont Sq. | 8560 Holcomb Bridge Rd. (Nesbit Ferry Rd.) | 770-587-1051 | www.dipaolorestaurant.com

Though Atlanta's No. 1 Italian can be "expensive", some fanatics "would pay triple" for chef-owner Darin Hiebel's "seasonally changing" fare and "first-class wine pairings"; the "wonderful" servers "can't do enough" in the "comfortable" space with a "cozy" bar, and despite its "bizarre location" in an "ugly Alpharetta strip mall", it's an "unbeatable" experience that "never gets old", even for the "loyal base."

Hal's on Old Ivy ⓈSteak   27 | 19 | 25 | E

Buckhead | 30 Old Ivy Rd. NE (Piedmont Rd.) | 404-261-0025 | www.hals.net

There's "no denying the steaks are A+" at this Buckhead chophouse that's "retro in the right ways" with its *Mad Men*-era menu" of "outstanding" fare including "French Quarter classics" (e.g. "exquisite crawfish tails", "incredible bread pudding"); "perfect waiters" navigate the "intimate" (some say "cramped") dining room, while the "packed", smoker-friendly "piano bar" pulses with "preppy-but-aging" singles clutching "big drinks"; P.S. the post-Survey addition of a second-floor dining room and patio helps ease the squeeze.

Kevin Rathbun Steak ⓈSteak   27 | 25 | 25 | E

Inman Park | 154 Krog St. (Lake Ave.) | 404-524-5600 | www.kevinrathbunsteak.com

"Prime beef" "aged perfectly and cooked within an inch of amazing" is the star at this "cool" steakhouse "off the beaten track" in Inman Park from "congenial" "celebrity chef" Kevin Rathbun (Krog Bar, Rathbun's), with a supporting cast of "imaginative" apps, sides that "really shine", "superlative desserts" and service that "rocks"; even if some quip it's so "dark" you need a "head lamp" to see, there's "high energy" emanating from the "modern" "wood"-centric space and "Beltline patio", and sure, it's "expensive", but "what steakhouse isn't?"

Kyma Greek/Seafood   27 | 25 | 25 | E

Buckhead | 3085 Piedmont Rd. NE (Paces Ferry Rd.) | 404-262-0702 | www.buckheadrestaurants.com

This "chic" Greek from the Buckhead Life Group earns "rave reviews" for its "large selection" of "fabulous" fin fare and other "excellent" dishes so "authentic" "you'll likely overlook" the fact that it "seems to be priced in euros" quip some, who consider it "worth the splurge" for a "celebration" or that "special someone"; "hunky Mediterranean guys" provide "polished" service in the "stunning" space where "white-washed walls" and a "fresh seafood display" set the stage for a "lively" scene that makes people think they're by the "Aegean", "not Piedmont."

La Grotta ⓈItalian   27 | 22 | 27 | E

Buckhead | 2637 Peachtree Rd. NE (bet. Lindbergh Dr. & Wesley Rd.) | 404-231-1368

La Grotta Ravinia ⓈItalian

Dunwoody | Crowne Plaza Ravinia Hotel | 4355 Ashford Dunwoody Rd. (Hammond Dr.) | 770-395-9925
www.lagrottaatlanta.com

"Spectacular service" from "old-world-style waiters" coupled with "superb Italian cuisine" that "loyalists" laud as a "benchmark" in the city makes this "elegant" Buckhead "classic" and its Dunwoody "sister" a "Rome away from Rome" that's "highly recommended" for "special occasions"; the "inviting", "comfortable" settings are "like stepping back in time" – with "lovely patios" reminiscent of a "private garden in Italy" – so the "civilized crowd" "doesn't mind the prices."

McKendrick's
Steak House *Steak*

28 | 24 | 25 | E

Dunwoody | Park Place Shopping Ctr. | 4505 Ashford Dunwoody Rd. (Perimeter Ctr.) | 770-512-8888 | www.mckendricks.com

For a "business lunch" or a "special occasion", Dunwoody denizens are "blown away" by this "beltway" bastion of beef "near Perimeter Mall" that "hits the spot" (and has improved scores to show it) with "perfect steaks", seafood that "shines" and a "great wine selection", all delivered by a "first-rate" staff that "understands customer service"; even though the "old-time men's club" dining room can get "noisy", it's still "classy" and "worth the price."

MF Buckhead *Japanese*

27 | 26 | 24 | VE

Buckhead | 3280 Peachtree Rd. (Piedmont Rd.) | 404-841-1192 | www.mfbuckhead.com

"Mouths water just thinking about" the "transporting" experience at this "fancy-schmancy" Buckhead spot that unseated its sibling, MF Sushibar, as this Survey's top-rated Japanese and comes "highly recommended" for "world-class sushi" and other "deliciousness" from the "fantastic robata grill"; a "helpful" staff and "opulent" decor "impress" "business-lunchers" and other "high-maintenance" types (read: "not the place for flip-flops"), and while critics cry "overpriced", devotees declare it a "culinary destination well worth" the "sticker shock"; P.S. a late-night lounge opened post-Survey.

MF Sushibar *Japanese*

26 | 22 | 22 | E

Midtown | 265 Ponce de Leon Ave. (Penn Ave.) | 404-815-8844 | www.mfsushibar.com

"The 'M' is for 'magic'" remind regulars of this Midtown "decadent" "delight" from the Kinjo Brothers (of MF Buckhead fame) where "perfect sushi" crafted from the "freshest" fish exudes the "essence of sea"; the digs are "high on the hip factor", though the staff can be "aloof" (even as it "grates fresh wasabi" at your table), and while detractors decry the "dent in your wallet", waves of "enthusiasts" who don't mind "paying handsomely" shrug "why compromise with raw fish?"

Miller Union ⊠ *American*

- | - | - | E

Westside | 999 Brady Ave. (bet. 10th & 11th Sts.) | 678-733-8550 | www.millerunion.com

Named after the stockyards of its Railroad Historic District neighborhood, this collaboration of restaurant veterans Neal McCarthy (ex-manager of Sotto Sotto) and Steven Satterfield (ex-chef of Watershed) is the showcase for New American fare with a Southern bent and a seasonal farm-fresh focus; design group ai3 has turned the warehouse-space notion on its ear, with intimate dining rooms softened with cabinetry, windows and antique armoires – it's cozy, even when packed to the rafters (which it usually is).

	FOOD	DECOR	SERVICE	COST

Nan Thai Fine Dining *Thai*
27 | 27 | 26 | E

Midtown | 1350 Spring St. NW (17th St.) | 404-870-9933 |
www.nanfinedining.com

Rated Atlanta's top Thai and No. 1 for Decor, this "exotic trip for the
senses" is "both a culinary and visual delight" with "pricey", "artfully
prepared" fare so "exceptional" "you'll be tempted to lick the bowl",
served in a "gorgeous" Midtown setting with gold columns, a sunken bar
and "destination" "restrooms that feel like a spa"; a "beautiful", "gracious" staff blends in with the "sophisticated" scene, and while a few
regulars rally for "new specialties", most "wouldn't change a thing."

New York Prime *Steak*
26 | 22 | 24 | E

Buckhead | Monarch Tower | 3424 Peachtree Rd. NE (Lenox Rd.) |
404-846-0644 | www.newyorkprime.com

"Red meat, red wine and tobacco" equal "man-night defined" at this
"old-school steakhouse" in the heart of Buckhead where "excellent
steaks" are accompanied by "ridiculous-size side dishes" plus "lots of
smoke"; "friendly, service-oriented bartenders" who "pour a stiff
drink" add to the "noisy", rather "mature scene", and while critics carp
it's "pre-recession overpriced", others who "bring an expense account" deem it "worth every penny."

Pura Vida 🗷 *Pan-Latin*
26 | 20 | 23 | M

Poncey-Highland | 656 N. Highland Ave. NE (bet. North Ave. &
Ponce de Leon Blvd.) | 404-870-9797 | www.puravidatapas.com

At this "innovative" Poncey-Highland Pan-Latin, "celebrity chef" Hector
Santiago's "out-of-this-world" tapas will "get your taste buds going",
while "killer mojitos", "consistently attentive service" and "fabulous
tango-ing" (live dancers perform bi-weekly) make it a "kicky" choice to
"have a celebration" whether in "a group or a date"; it's a "wonderful"
scene that's "full of life" – but cognoscenti point out it's "not cheap."

Quinones Room at Bacchanalia 🗷 Ⓜ *American*
28 | 27 | 28 | VE

Westside | Courtyard of Bacchanalia | 1198 Howell Mill Rd. (bet. 14th St. &
Huff Rd.) | 404-365-0410 | www.starprovisions.com

"Your every need is anticipated" by the "stellar staff" of Bacchanalia's
"marvelous" sibling, voted Atlanta's No. 1 for Service by fans who are
"pampered and plied" with a "simply stunning" tasting menu of "off-the-
chart" New American fare exhibiting a "decidedly Southern influence",
plus "excellent wine pairings" that are "worth" the "splurge"; the
"beautiful room" resembles an "elegant home", setting the stage for an
"undeniably flawless" experience that is "unbeatable" "for the price."

Rathbun's 🗷 *American*
27 | 23 | 25 | E

Inman Park | Stove Works | 112 Krog St. NE (bet. Edgewood Ave. NE &
Irwin St. NE) | 404-524-8280 | www.rathbunsrestaurant.com

This "top-of-the-crop" New American in Inman Park is "deserving of
its ratings" declare devotees dazzled by its "devilishly delicious" offerings, from the "incredible" "small and large plates" to the "awesome"
desserts, backed by a "fab" wine list; "congenial celebrity chef" Kevin
Rathbun and his "skilled", "happy" staff "make you feel special" in a
"spirited", "electric" setting with a "jumping" "bar scene" as well as a
"quieter" "wine room" and "lovely outdoor patio"; sure, the "price is
high" but most conclude it's "well worth it."

Baltimore

TOP FOOD RANKING

	Restaurant	Cuisine
28	Charleston	American
	Volt	American
27	Prime Rib	Seafood/Steak
	Samos	Greek
	Di Pasquale's	Italian
	Tasting Room	American
	Thai Arroy	Thai
	Peter's Inn	American
	Linwoods	American
	Salt	American
	Thai Landing	Thai
	Chameleon Cafe	American
	Faidley's	Seafood
26	Helmand	Afghan
	Woodberry Kitchen	American
	Black Olive	Greek/Seafood
	Tersiguel's	French
	Milton Inn	American
	Sushi Sono	Japanese
	Jack's Bistro	Eclectic
	Koco's	Pub Food
	La Scala	Italian

Black Olive *Greek/Seafood*   26 | 22 | 24 | E

Fells Point | 814 S. Bond St. (Shakespeare St.) | 410-276-7141 | www.theblackolive.com

"Get up close and personal with your food" at this "Greek paradise" in Fells Point, where patrons choose from the "fresh fish on ice" then chill as it's "beautifully" "deboned and served tableside"; it may be the "closest you can get to the Mediterranean in Baltimore", though with "expense-account" pricing some say it's "best for a special occasion."

Chameleon Cafe ⊠Ⓜ *American*   27 | 17 | 25 | E

Northeast Baltimore | 4341 Harford Rd. (Montebello Terr.) | 410-254-2376 | www.thechameleoncafe.com

"Hurray!" cheer champions of this "treasure" in a Northeast Baltimore row house, a "top-flight" showcase for chef/co-owner Jeffrey Smith's "dedication" to "seasonal" gustation via an "elegantly prepared" New American menu accompanied by "excellent wines"; a "knowledgeable and attentive" team monitors the "simple" but "cozy" setting, and despite "all the buzz" over the "sublime dining", the "price is right."

Charleston ⊠ *American*   28 | 27 | 27 | VE

Harbor East | 1000 Lancaster St. (Exeter St.) | 410-332-7373 | www.charlestonrestaurant.com

"The hype is all true" at this "top-of-the-line" Harbor East "jewel" – rated No. 1 for Food, Decor and Service in the Baltimore Survey – which "raises the bar" with the "incomparable" Cindy Wolf's "stellar" New American cuisine, presented on a diner's-choice tasting menu paired with "outstanding wines"; the "impeccable" service and "sheer elegance" of the setting will "sweep you off your feet", so even if you "need to take out a second mortgage", "you won't care."

Cinghiale *Italian*   24 | 26 | 25 | E

Harbor East | 822 Lancaster St. (Exeter St.) | 410-547-8282 | www.cgeno.com

Charleston owners Cindy Wolf and Tony Foreman "work their magic" at this Harbor East Italian, where the "inspired" cooking, "highly attentive" service and "cosmopolitan" atmosphere go "so well together"; the "dressed-down" enoteca serves "quality meats and cheeses" from the in-house salumeria while the "more formal" osteria matches its "memorable" dishes with an "exceptional" wine list, and if it all comes at a "steep price", "you get what you pay for."

Di Pasquale's Marketplace ⊠ *Italian*   27 | 14 | 19 | I

East Baltimore | 3700 Gough St. (Dean St.) | 410-276-6787 | www.dipasquales.com

"One hundred percent authentic", this "family-run" Italian grocery in East Baltimore dispenses "awesome", "well-priced" deli faves (subs, "brick-oven pizza", "housemade lasagna", etc.) over the counter with "no fuss, no muss"; there's bare-bones seating for a "homey" lunch "in the neighborhood", but you "go for the great food not the atmosphere", so feel free to "take it home"; P.S. closes at 6 PM.

Faidley's Seafood ⊠ *Seafood*   27 | 10 | 17 | I

Downtown West | Lexington Mkt. | 203 N. Paca St. (Lexington St.) | 410-727-4898 | www.faidleyscrabcakes.com

"Go lump or go home" at this "legendary" Lexington Market "mecca for seafood devotees" that opened in 1886 and remains stuck in some sort of "miraculous time warp"; "you eat standing up" at high-top tables amid seafood counters, but since its "fantastic" "crab cakes (broiled please)" are the "standard by which all other Baltimore crab cakes are judged", few seem to care; P.S. "freshly shucked oysters" from its "excellent raw bar" make a "cheap lunch."

Helmand *Afghan*   26 | 20 | 23 | M

Mt. Vernon | 806 N. Charles St. (bet. Madison & Read Sts.) | 410-752-0311 | www.helmand.com

By "now a Baltimore landmark", this "unique" Mt. Vernon "treasure" is a "consistent" source of "out-of-this-world" Afghan "comfort food" ("don't miss" the pumpkin appetizer) that'll "please any palate" with its "nuanced spicing" of both "traditional meat" and "great vegetarian offerings", which incorporate fresh produce from its organic farm; with "personable" service and "fair prices", it's "naturally" "a popular spot", but "crowded" conditions don't deter legions of fans from "coming back for more."

Jack's Bistro ⓜ *Eclectic*   26 | 17 | 23 | M

Canton | 3123 Elliott St. (S. Robinson St.) | 410-878-6542 | www.jacksbistro.net

"Adventure" lovers who like to boast "you know what I ate last night?" mob this "guaranteed fun time" in Canton featuring "surprising"

Eclectic dishes with "ingredient combos that totally work" (chocolate mac 'n' cheese, "lots of sous vide"); "personable" service and a "charming" tavern setting are other pluses, though even devotees "wish the place were bigger"; P.S. closed Mondays and Tuesdays; food served until 1 AM.

Koco's 🛇Ⓜ *Pub Food*

| 26 | 11 | 22 | M |

Northeast Baltimore | 4301 Harford Rd. (bet. Overland & Weaver Aves.) | 410-426-3519 | www.kocospub.com

"It's huge, it's gigantic" . . . it's the "amazing crab cake" with "asteroid-sized lumps of meat" (though admittedly imported meat) at this "good ol'" Northeast Baltimore tavern; it's the wrong place if "you're looking for fancy" and the other pub grub is just "so-so", but prices that "won't break the bank", "attentive" service and a "down-to-earth" vibe have fans saying "bring a friend and chow down."

La Scala *Italian*

| 26 | 23 | 25 | E |

Little Italy | 1012 Eastern Ave. (bet. Central Ave. & Exeter St.) | 410-783-9209 | www.lascaladining.com

"Humongous portions" of "superb" Italian food *and* an "indoor bocce court"? "I'm so there" exclaim enthusiasts of this Little Italy "delight" where "everything's on the money", from chef-owner Nino Germano's "creative" cooking ("love the grilled Caesar salad") to the "old-school service" and "romantic" atmosphere; those who say it's "sure to impress" also "wish they could afford to go weekly."

Linwoods *American*

| 27 | 26 | 26 | E |

Owings Mills | 25 Crossroads Dr. (McDonogh & Reisterstown Rds.) | 410-356-3030 | www.linwoods.com

With its "well-heeled clientele" and "stylish" setting, there's a "New York feeling" in the air at this "long-term" Owings Mills "treat" that remains one of the region's "best and most consistent places"; chef/co-owner Linwood Dame's "luscious" New American fare puts "innovative twists on old favorites" ("this guy can cook!"), and while you may wish someone else were "paying the bill", a "charming staff" ensures the experience is "always superb."

Milton Inn *American*

| 26 | 27 | 25 | E |

Sparks | 14833 York Rd. (Quaker Bottom Rd.) | 410-771-4366 | www.miltoninn.com

"Still a winner after all these years", this "special occasion"–worthy "treat" tucked into a "romantic" Sparks inn (1740) lures locals and out-of-towners alike with "outstanding" New American fare and "superb wines" that are "nicely presented by attentive servers"; it's "rather pricey", but with an "elegant" ambiance enhanced by fireplaces, red brick and a flagstone patio for pre-dinner cocktails or dining, "there's a good reason why it's always crowded."

Peter's Inn 🛇Ⓜ *American*

| 27 | 18 | 22 | M |

Fells Point | 504 S. Ann St. (Eastern Ave.) | 410-675-7313 | www.petersinn.com

Perhaps "Baltimore's worst-kept secret", this "former biker bar" draws Fells Point foodies who vow it's "worth the wait" to sample its "short" "weekly menu" of "spectacular" New American cuisine and "great wines by the glass"; "friendly" servers navigate the "tight", "quirky"

FOOD | DECOR | SERVICE | COST

quarters featuring decor "right out of [your] father's basement", which somehow all seems so "hip" it begs the question "are you cool enough to eat here?"

Prime Rib *Seafood/Steak*
27 | 25 | 27 | VE

Downtown North | 1101 N. Calvert St. (Chase St.) | 410-539-1804 | www.theprimerib.com

In Downtown Baltimore, the "godfather of steakhouses" mixes "old-world elegance" with "just the right touch of film-noir decadence", live music and "dynamite food" – the "best slab-o-meat in town", "first-rate" crab and "huge" sides – to make each "expensive" meal an "event"; the "retro-classy" digs are attended by "tuxedoed waiters" (there's a business casual "dress code" for customers too), while the bar scene "will hurt your eyes if you're married."

Salt ⊠ *American*
27 | 22 | 25 | E

East Baltimore | 2127 E. Pratt St. (Collington St.) | 410-276-5480 | www.salttavern.com

Smitten surveyors "kinda love" this "top-notch" "neighborhood secret" crammed into a "tiny" East Baltimore row house, where a "reliable kitchen" turns out an "ever-changing menu" of "beyond-the-norm" New American fare; it's all washed down with "imaginative" cocktails and served by a "comfortably attentive" staff, and if "difficult parking" is a deterrent for some, most say "by all means, go."

Samos ⊠ ⊄ *Greek*
27 | 12 | 20 | I

Greektown | 600 S. Oldham St. (Fleet St.) | 410-675-5292 | www.samosrestaurant.com

They "come from miles away and wait for hours" to sample the "real-deal" Hellenic eats at this "well-priced" Greektown "institution", where chef-owners Nick and Mike Georgalas greet you with a "warm smile and open arms" and ensure no one "leaves unsatisfied"; it's "small, cramped" and "nothing fancy", but "quick" service and a BYO policy that "makes it even better" mean most "would go back in a flash"; P.S. "bring cash" and, on weekends, "your patience."

Sushi Sono ⊠ *Japanese*
26 | 21 | 24 | M

Columbia | 10215 Wincopin Circle (Little Patuxent Pkwy.) | 410-997-6131 | www.sushisonomd.com

"Who could ask for anything more?" ponder partisans of this somewhat "pricey" Japanese "Eden" in Columbia, where the "best sushi around" "takes your palate to new heights" and the sashimi and "cooked stuff" (shabu-shabu, "fabulous tempura") are "just as good"; an "attentive" staff and "attractive" quarters with "scenic views of Lake Kittamaqundi" offer further enticement.

Tasting Room ⊠ *American*
27 | 21 | 24 | E

Frederick | 101 N. Market St. (Church St.) | 240-379-7772 | www.tastetr.com

The "big windows let everyone see what you're eating" at this "sophisticated" New American, an "upscale" "gem" whose "fantastic" "seasonal" cuisine, "creative martinis" and vino off one of the "best wine lists for miles around" are "professionally" served "at a Frederick pace"; the decor has a "chic, modern" edge, but seating that's a "little cramped" means there's little "privacy" and no lack of "noise"; P.S. wallet-watchers can opt for "great lunch deals."

	FOOD	DECOR	SERVICE	COST

Tersiguel's *French*

26 | 23 | 26 | E

Ellicott City | 8293 Main St. (Old Columbia Pike) | 410-465-4004 | www.tersiguels.com

Francophiles "feel pampered" without the "stuffy French attitude" at this "charming" Ellicott City "winner", where chef-owner Michel Tersiguel's "outstanding" creations often include ingredients fresh from his farm; it's a "little pricey", and even a few *amis* consider the "cozy" historic house a bit "cramped", but all in all, it's "still a splendid experience after all these years."

Thai Arroy Ⓜ *Thai*

27 | 15 | 23 | I

South Baltimore | 1019 Light St. (bet. Cross & Hamburg Sts.) | 410-385-8587 | www.thaiarroy.com

Lines "often extend outside the door" for tables at this South Baltimore Thai, and for good reason: though portions are "massive", folks just "can't get enough" of its "exceptionally tasty" fare ("some spicy, some not"); a "lovely" staff oversees a dining room "small on space, huge on flavor", while a BYO policy that "makes it acceptable to have a 12-pack at your feet" also makes a "bargain" spot even "cheaper."

Thai Landing *Thai*

27 | 14 | 25 | M

Mt. Vernon | 1207 N. Charles St. (bet. Biddle & Preston Sts.) | 410-727-1234 | www.thailandingmd.com

"If you like your food spicy", consider this "above-average" Mt. Vernon Thai whose "authentic", "delicious" chow will prompt your taste buds to "send messages you've never heard before"; "service with a smile" outshines the nondescript decor, as do its "reasonable prices" and location "close to the Meyerhoff"; P.S. a post-Survey change in chef and ownership outdates the Food score.

Volt Ⓜ *American*

28 | 26 | 27 | VE

Frederick | Houck Mansion | 228 N. Market St. (bet. 2nd & 3rd Sts.) | 301-696-8658 | www.voltrestaurant.com

He lost *Top Chef*, but Bryan Voltaggio has a "winner" in this "electrifying" Frederick New American, where the "astonishing", "locally sourced" cuisine packed with "sensational flavors" is eclipsed only by the bounty of 'Table 21', at which the "culinary star" himself presents a "delectable" "21-course tasting menu" (the main dining room is à la carte); set in a "lovely" 1890 mansion awash in "modern" trappings and "over-the-top" service, it's "one of the best dining experiences" around – but "good luck getting a reservation"; P.S. the $20 lunch prix fixe and $15 bar lunch may be the "biggest bargains ever"; closed Mondays and Tuesdays.

Woodberry Kitchen *American*

26 | 26 | 24 | E

Hampden | 2010 Clipper Park Rd. (Clipper Mill Rd.) | 410-464-8000 | www.woodberrykitchen.com

It's in an "old foundry" west of Hampden, but there's no doubt chef/co-owner Spike Gjerde's "farm-to-table" New American "has been discovered" as it's Baltimore's Most Popular restaurant; expect "crowds" of "beautiful people" poring over an "ever-changing menu" of "stunning" fare made from "local, sustainable" ingredients, all paired with "interesting wines" and served by a "polished" staff; just know that the "rustic-urban" space is "noisy when full" and "reservations are a must"; P.S. a couple of casual spin-offs are planned nearby for early 2012.

Boston

TOP FOOD RANKING

	Restaurant	Cuisine
29	O Ya	Japanese
28	Oleana	Mediterranean
	La Campania	Italian
	Neptune Oyster	Seafood
	Lumière	French
	Hamersley's	French
	Uni	Japanese
	T.W. Food	American/French
	Menton	French/Italian
	Mistral	French/Mediterranean
27	L'Espalier	French
	Duckworth's	American
	Oishii	Japanese
	Craigie on Main	French
	Clio	French
	No. 9 Park	French/Italian
	Bergamot	American

Abe & Louie's *Steak*   26 | 24 | 26 | E

Back Bay | 793 Boylston St. (Fairfield St.) | 617-536-6300 |
www.abeandlouies.com

If you have an "über expense account", "you really can't go wrong" at
this Back Bay "landmark" serving "sensational steaks" and "equally
impressive everything else" in "huge portions", plus an "extensive
wine list" that offers many "reasonable prices"; "impeccable" "professional service" and "dark" "gentleman's-club" decor impart a "classic
feeling", but be prepared for "excessive decibel levels", particularly
from the "hot scene at the bar."

Bergamot *American*   27 | 23 | 26 | E

Somerville | 118 Beacon St. (Kirkland St.) | 617-576-7700 |
www.bergamotrestaurant.com

"Nuanced, creative" seasonal New American fare featuring "interesting
juxtapositions of tastes and textures" is "backed by a sound wine list"
and "well-trained, friendly" service at this "sophisticated but unpretentious", "wonderful addition" to Somerville; all in all, "prices are not
outrageous", although the "portions are on the smallish side" so big
appetites recommend you "get three courses or you may leave hungry."

Blue Ginger *Asian*   27 | 23 | 25 | E

Wellesley | 583 Washington St. (Church St.) | 781-283-5790 |
www.ming.com

"Highly creative" Asian fusion fare comes from this Wellesley destination's open kitchen, where "justifiably famous" chef Ming Tsai "actually cooks" when he's not "mingling with his guests"; "professional,
polished service" reigns, even though the "unpretentious" setting is
"packed" – you need to "make a reservation well in advance" or try for

the bar and its "more casual", "less expensive" but no less "intriguing menu"; P.S. "the foie gras shumai and the Alaskan butterfish may be the best appetizer–main course combination" ever.

Clio 🗷 *French*   27 | 26 | 26 | VE

Back Bay | Eliot Hotel | 370A Commonwealth Ave. (Mass. Ave.) | 617-536-7200 | www.cliorestaurant.com

"As interesting as ever", this "subdued", "luxe" "special-occasion destination" in the Back Bay's Eliot Hotel "sets the standard for contemporary French" fare with chef Ken Oringer's "cutting-edge" "edible art" composed of "unexpected textures with surprising flavors" and paired with an "exceptional wine list"; service strikes most as "attentive" and "knowledgeable" (though a minority finds it "pretentious"), and although it's "hyper-expensive" for "relatively small" portions, it's "well worth it" if you want to "eat like royalty."

Craigie on Main 🅼 *French*   27 | 23 | 26 | E

Central Square | 853 Main St. (Bishop Richard Allen Dr.) | Cambridge | 617-497-5511 | www.craigieonmain.com

"Formidable culinary presence" Tony Maws presents "unforgettable dining" at this "compelling" Central Square "destination" where "obsessive attention" to "local, sustainable" ingredients is obvious in his "luscious" French fare with "mind-boggling flavors"; "with all of this perfection, one might expect snobbery", but the staff's "seasoned professionals" are "hospitable" as they navigate the "lively", "unpretentious" setting, which includes a "fantastic bar" boasting "outstanding drinks" and an "excellent menu with pared-down prices" – but even the normally "costly" tabs are "worth every penny."

Duckworth's Bistrot 🅼 *American*   27 | 20 | 25 | E

Gloucester | 197 E. Main St. (Plum St.) | 978-282-4426 | www.duckworthsbistrot.com

Disciples of this "crown jewel" of Gloucester "love that you can order" half portions of chef Ken Duckworth's "sublime" New American fare, "so you can try more stuff" and "save money", just as with half pours from the "terrific wine list"; the "cute", "casual" setting – which is patrolled by a "knowledgeable staff" – is "small" and "popular" to boot, so "make sure you make a reservation, or you'll be eating elsewhere."

Hamersley's Bistro *French*   28 | 25 | 26 | E

South End | 553 Tremont St. (Clarendon St.) | 617-423-2700 | www.hamersleysbistro.com

"Bravo, Gordon!" cheer champions of this South End classic's "terrific" celebrity chef-owner, who's "almost always visible in the open kitchen" prepping "extraordinary" seasonal French bistro fare that includes the "to-die-for" signature roast chicken; the "country atmosphere" is "the epitome of grace and elegance", just like the "charming, low-key" but "efficient" servers, and while the meal is "expensive", the "outstanding wine list" showcases many "reasonable prices."

La Campania 🗷 *Italian*   28 | 24 | 25 | E

Waltham | 504 Main St. (bet. Cross & Heard Sts.) | 781-894-4280 | www.lacampania.com

"People come from far and wide" for this "transporting culinary experience" in Waltham, a "charming" "gem" creating both "inventive and traditional" "Italian country" dishes, "all splendid" and priced for those who "can afford luxury" (though the "staggering wine list" displays many "affordable" options); the "professional" staff is as "warm" as the "beautiful", "rustic" "farmhouse"–like setting, but just "make sure you have a reservation", "even for the bar."

Legal Sea Foods   *Seafood*   22 | 18 | 21 | E

Back Bay | Copley Pl. | 100 Huntington Ave. (bet. Dartmouth & Exeter Sts.) | 617-266-7775
Back Bay | Prudential Ctr. | 800 Boylston St. (Fairfield St.) | 617-266-6800
Park Square | 26 Park Plaza (Columbus Ave.) | 617-426-4444
Waterfront | Long Wharf | 255 State St. (Atlantic Ave.) | 617-227-3115
Harvard Square | 20 University Rd. (Eliot St.) | Cambridge | 617-491-9400
Kendall Square | 5 Cambridge Ctr. (bet. Ames & Main Sts.) | Cambridge | 617-864-3400
Chestnut Hill | Chestnut Hill Shopping Ctr. | 43 Boylston St. (Hammond Pond Pkwy.) | 617-277-7300
Peabody | Northshore Mall | 210 Andover St./Rte. 114 (Rte. 128) | 978-532-4500
Burlington | Burlington Mall | 75 Middlesex Tpke. (Rte. 128) | 781-270-9700
Framingham | 50-60 Worcester Rd./Rte. 9 (bet. Concord & Speen Sts.) | 508-766-0600
www.legalseafoods.com

Again voted Boston's Most Popular restaurant, this "trustworthy" seafood chain "reigns supreme" thanks to a "huge variety" of "consistently fresh" fish, not to mention the smarts to "adapt to changing times" with "innovative touches" (e.g. what may be the "best" gluten-free menu "in the world") while ensuring "solid value"; the decor of each branch is "different" (ditto the service, though staffers generally "know their stuff"), but when all is said and done, the "location doesn't matter" – "they're everywhere" because "they know what they're doing"; P.S. the sprawling new Seaport District destination offers a casual ground floor, a more formal second story, a rooftop lounge and an expanded menu featuring pizzas and pastas.

L'Espalier   *French*   27 | 27 | 27 | VE

Back Bay | 774 Boylston St. (bet. Exeter & Fairfield Sts.) | 617-262-3023 | www.lespalier.com

"If heaven were a restaurant", it would be this "regal experience" in the Back Bay, where chef Frank McClelland's "exquisite", "inventive" New French cuisine is "perfectly paired" with "outstanding wines"; though longtimers "miss" the "old-world charm" of the former brownstone, modernists dig the newish location's "sleek, modern" setting; meanwhile, everyone appreciates staffers who "treat you like a king" – but then again, "they should since you're paying a king's ransom" (it's "worth every penny"); P.S. the prix fixe lunch may be "the best midday deal in Boston."

Lumière   *French*   28 | 23 | 27 | E

Newton | 1293 Washington St. (Waltham St.) | 617-244-9199 | www.lumiererestaurant.com

Exhibiting "panache" plus a "real devotion to all things local, sustainable and green", "genius" chef-owner Michael Leviton presents New French fare as "art" (and with "wonderful wine pairings") at his "classy" "West Newton gem"; "impeccable service" makes it a "good choice for that special occasion", and while it's a "little pricey", it costs "less" than if it were located Downtown.

Menton   *French/Italian* | 28 | 27 | 29 | VE |

Seaport District | 354 Congress St. (A St.) | 617-737-0099 | www.mentonboston.com

Barbara Lynch's Seaport District "temple" of French-Italian gastronomy makes an auspicious Survey debut by earning the No. 1 scores for both Service and Decor thanks to its "unparalleled" staff and "elegant" setting; the "phenomenal" prix fixe-only cuisine, a "taste sensation", also "sets a new standard" as do tabs you may have to "mortgage your house" to pay – indeed, this ranks as Boston's "priciest restaurant."

Mistral   *French/Mediterranean* | 28 | 25 | 26 | VE |

South End | 223 Columbus Ave. (bet. Berkeley & Clarendon Sts.) | 617-867-9300 | www.mistralbistro.com

"Flashes of brilliance" illuminate this South End "legend" where dinner is an "event" thanks to chef Jamie Mammano's "imaginative", "sublime" French-Mediterranean cuisine paired with "glorious wines", "creative" cocktails and "terrific service"; an "elegant but not overly formal" aura permeates the "dramatic" high-ceilinged dining room and a "cool vibe" dominates the "chic bar" though it all comes at tabs that practically necessitate "a paycheck."

Neptune Oyster   *Seafood* | 28 | 20 | 22 | E |

North End | 63 Salem St. (Cross St.) | 617-742-3474 | www.neptuneoyster.com

A "pearl" "floating among red sauce" joints, this "classy", "divine" North End fishery specializes in "unreal lobster rolls", either "drenched with melted butter" or "New England–style with mayo", plus "superb raw-bar" selections and "creative seafood concoctions", which the "knowledgeable staff" can help pair with "interesting wines"; however, be prepared for "expensive" checks, "sardine-can digs" and a "no-reservations" policy that leads to "frustrating waits" – all "well worth it."

No. 9 Park   ☒ *French/Italian* | 27 | 25 | 27 | VE |

Beacon Hill | 9 Park St. (bet. Beacon & Tremont Sts.) | 617-742-9991 | www.no9park.com

"Meticulously prepared" French-Italian plates deliver "tastes and textures beyond compare" at chef Barbara Lynch's "elegant" flagship on Beacon Hill, where the "revelatory" meals are enhanced by "brilliant wine pairings" and service that goes "the whole nine yards"; you "won't get stuffed on the portions" and you'll likely get a jolt of "sticker shock", but it's "worth it" for a "joyful experience."

Oishii   Ⓜ *Japanese* | 27 | 17 | 22 | E |

Chestnut Hill | 612 Hammond St. (Boylston St.) | 617-277-7888 | www.oishiiboston.com

Sudbury | Mill Vill. | 365 Boston Post Rd./Rte. 20 (Concord Rd.) | 978-440-8300 | www.oishiitoo.com

Oishii Boston   ◑Ⓜ *Japanese*

South End | 1166 Washington St. (E. Berkeley St.) | 617-482-8868 | www.oishiiboston.com

"True artistry" is on display in the "extravagant", "sublime" sushi crafted at this trio of "vibrant Japanese gems" where the service is mostly "kind" and "attentive"; while the scene is "chic yet serene" in the South End, you're "confined as tightly as the maki" at the Chestnut Hill original (where there's "usually a wait") and the setting is a "sparse", "tiny, dark cave" in Sudbury, but whichever you choose, you might "need to sell some stocks" first – and it's "worth every penny."

Oleana *Mediterranean*

28	24	25	E

Inman Square | 134 Hampshire St. (bet. Elm & Norfolk Sts.) | Cambridge | 617-661-0505 | www.oleanarestaurant.com

"Exotic-spice" "guru" Ana Sortun makes "taste buds sing" at this Inman Square "diamond" where she weaves "layers of flavors" into "adventurous" Arabic-Mediterranean dishes that "emphasize locally grown" ingredients; the "enthusiastic servers" are "helpful with choosing a wine" from the "excellent" list, but just know that reservations are nearly "impossible to obtain" for the "cramped" but "warm" interior, while in summer, you have to "get there early" to score a table on the "lovely" patio, which doesn't accept bookings at all.

O Ya 🖪🅼 *Japanese*

29	23	27	VE

Leather District | 9 East St. (South St.) | 617-654-9900 | www.oyarestaurantboston.com

"Have you recently won a small fortune?" – then you have "the means" to enjoy this "cozy", unmarked izakaya in the Leather District, where "atomic" "bursts of texture and tastes" come from "every beautiful bite" of the "off-the-charts innovative" sushi, winner of Boston's No. 1 Food rating; suggestions from the "extensive sake list" by the "upbeat", "spot-on" staffers are just as "amazing" as the fare, but a caveat: even if you opt for the "luxurious" omakase and its "zillion tiny courses", it's possible you will still "leave hungry", as everything "comes in amuse-bouche portions" – nonetheless, it's an "unforgettable" meal.

T.W. Food *American/French*

28	22	27	E

Huron Village | 377 Walden St. (Concord Ave.) | Cambridge | 617-864-4745 | www.twfoodrestaurant.com

At this "extraordinary" Huron Village "hideaway", toque Tim Wiechmann's "sublime", seasonal New American–New French fare is "thoughtfully prepared" with local ingredients and "layers of complexity", then paired with wines from a "creative" list; the "casual", "minimalist" setting is "tight but charming" and conducive to "personal attention" from the "knowledgeable", "impeccable" staff, another element that makes it "worth the extra cost."

Uni *Japanese*

28	23	25	VE

Back Bay | Eliot Hotel | 370 Commonwealth Ave. (Mass. Ave.) | 617-536-7200 | www.cliorestaurant.com

"Exotic", "excellent", "expensive" are just some descriptors for the "impeccably fresh" sashimi prepared at this "cutting-edge" Ken Oringer sibling to Clio in the Back Bay's Eliot Hotel, where "stylish decor fills the cozy corners of the intimate dining area"; the "great attention to detail" in the "constantly changing" fare extends to the "huge cocktail list" as well as "fabulous" staffers who are adept at "suggesting something to make your eyes twinkle."

Chicago

TOP FOOD RANKING

Restaurant	Cuisine
29 Les Nomades	French
Alinea	American
Schwa	American
28 Arun's	Thai
Topolobampo	Mexican
Michael	French
Tallgrass	French
Tru	French
27 Blackbird	American
Oceanique	French/Seafood
Carlos'	French
Naha	American
Vie	American
Charlie Trotter's	American
MK	American
Katsu	Japanese
Everest	French
Sushi Wabi	Japanese
Frontera Grill	Mexican
Moto	Eclectic
Riccardo Trattoria	Italian

Alinea Ⓜ *American*   29 | 27 | 28 | VE

Lincoln Park | 1723 N. Halsted St. (bet. North Ave. & Willow St.) |
312-867-0110 | www.alinearestaurant.com

"World-famous for its vision and creativity", "genius" Grant Achatz's
"progressive" New American "gastronirvana" provides "amazing"
"avant-garde food" in a "labor-intensive" multicourse "wild ride" that
"incorporates all the senses" and includes cleverly "engineered" serving pieces ("acupuncture needles", "trapezes", "pillows", "branches",
"rubber tablecloths"); "*Get Smart* automatic doors" give way to the
"luxurious, minimalistic" Lincoln Park setting where a "professional"
staff (rated No. 1 for Service) provides "personal" attention "with
some humor", completing an "unforgettable", "shock-and-awe
experience" – albeit a "fiscally challenging" one that's certainly "not
for the faint of culinary heart"; P.S. "if you can afford it", choose the
"incredible wine pairings."

Arun's Ⓜ *Thai*   28 | 23 | 27 | VE

Northwest Side | 4156 N. Kedzie Ave. (bet. Irving Park Rd. & Montrose Ave.) |
773-539-1909 | www.arunsthai.com

"Who says Thai can't be upscale?" ask admirers of Arun
Sampanthavivat's "unforgettable" Northwest Side jewel where a "top-
notch" staff rolls out "exquisite" prix fixe meals composed of "unusual", "delicious little dishes" that "just keep on coming"; it's set in
"simple" digs, although more than a few "wish they'd upgrade the
space" to match the "splurge"-worthy prices.

	FOOD	DECOR	SERVICE	COST

NEW Aviary, The 🛇Ⓜ Eclectic

`-` | `-` | `-` | `E`

West Loop | 955 W. Fulton Mkt. (bet. Morgan & Sangamon Sts.) | 312-226-0868

Taking flight adjacent to sister restaurant Next, Grant Achatz's swanky bar/lounge makes an artful science out of eye-popping presentations, from the inventive molecular cocktails to the edgy, Alinea-inspired single bites of Eclectic fare; the airy West Loop setting features modern torchère lighting, undulating banquettes that form an operatic sea of waves and a standing area near the open kitchen.

Blackbird 🛇 American

`27` | `22` | `25` | `VE`

West Loop | 619 W. Randolph St. (bet. Desplaines & Jefferson Sts.) | 312-715-0708 | www.blackbirdrestaurant.com

The West Loop's "bold" "destination" "flagship of the [Paul] Kahan empire" flies an "outstanding", "ever-changing menu" that's "crafted in the finest tradition of New American" cuisine and coupled with an "unbelievable wine list" and "skillful service" in "sleek, stark" surroundings; while "priced for a special occasion", it delivers a vaunted "value-quality ratio" (wallet-watchers might "come for lunch"), and if the other "diners are so close you're practically wearing each other's clothes", the "high noise and energy level is part of the plan", so just "eat" and "talk later."

Carlos' French

`27` | `26` | `27` | `VE`

Highland Park | 429 Temple Ave. (Waukegan Ave.) | 847-432-0770 | www.carlos-restaurant.com

"Still near the top of the charts" after some 30 years, Highland Park's New French "destination" offers "amazing, approachable gourmet" cuisine and an "incredible, if pricey, wine list" accompanied by service "with grace and a sense of humor"; the "conversation-friendly", "intimate space" adds to the feeling of "understated elegance" (jackets are required), and while "you pay a premium", it's "perfect" for even the "most special of occasions."

Charlie Trotter's 🛇Ⓜ American

`27` | `25` | `27` | `VE`

Lincoln Park | 816 W. Armitage Ave. (bet. Dayton & Halsted Sts.) | 773-248-6228 | www.charlietrotters.com

Regulars revere "the original celebrity chef's palace of haute cuisine" as the "pinnacle" of "precision", where a "memorable" "three-hour homage" to New American "gastronomic bliss" "showcases flavors in new intensities and sometimes surprising combinations" alongside selections from an "encyclopedic wine list"; "formal", "professional service" befits the "staid" Lincoln Park setting, and though some patrons are "put off" by "pretense" and "petite portions", the faithful insist "go at least once in your lifetime", especially if you can "find someone with an expense account."

Everest 🛇Ⓜ French

`27` | `27` | `27` | `VE`

Loop | One Financial Pl. | 440 S. LaSalle St., 40th fl. (Congress Pkwy.) | 312-663-8920 | www.everestrestaurant.com

"High expectations" "reflect the name" of this Loop "special-occasion" French perched on the 40th floor of the Chicago Stock Exchange that surveyors hail as the "summit" for "sublime", "classic white-linen" dining on the "inventive menus" of Jean Joho; an "unbelievable" ("in size and price") "wine binder" enhances an experience that's completed with "pomp", "formal" service and a "view that seems to stretch to Iowa"; P.S. jacket suggested.

Frontera Grill 🗷 Ⓜ *Mexican*

| 27 | 22 | 23 | E |

River North | 445 N. Clark St. (bet. Hubbard & Illinois Sts.) | 312-661-1434 | www.fronterakitchens.com

"Magnificent" Mexican cuisine from celebrity chef Rick Bayless is a "revelation" at this River North "temple", voted Chicago's Most Popular and touted for its "bold", "complex flavors" ("he won *Top Chef Masters* for a reason"), "drinks as spectacular as" the fare and "colorful decor" with "museum-quality artwork"; the "crowds can be daunting" (it's mostly "first-come, first-served") but "it's worth the wait" to a "cultish following" that boasts "you have to believe Mexico is jealous" and calls the prices "totally reasonable"; P.S. "hint: sit at the bar for the same food but faster service."

Gibsons Bar & Steakhouse ● *Steak*

| 26 | 21 | 24 | E |

Gold Coast | 1028 N. Rush St. (Bellevue Pl.) | 312-266-8999
Rosemont | Doubletree O'Hare | 5464 N. River Rd. (bet. Balmoral & Bryn Mawr Aves.) | 847-928-9900
Oak Brook | 2105 S. Spring Rd. (22nd St.) | 630-954-0000
www.gibsonssteakhouse.com

"Waiters show you the slabs before they're cooked" at these "brash" city and suburban "speakeasy-styled steakhouses" serving "big", "succulent" steaks, "big side dishes" and "big desserts" at "big prices"; the "professional service" is "terrific" and "they pour a righteous drink", while the "people-watching" is peppered with "celebrities", "pro athletes", "cougars and sugar daddies" (especially in the "piano bar"), and if the Rosemont offshoot is "not quite the same" as the "Rush Street cornerstone", on the plus side, it's also open till midnight most nights; P.S. an Oak Brook outpost opened post-Survey.

Girl & The Goat *American*

| – | – | – | M |

West Loop | 809 W. Randolph St. (Halsted St.) | 312-492-6262 | www.girlandthegoat.com

Top Chef winner (and former Scylla chef-owner) Stephanie Izard is behind this midpriced West Loop arrival offering seasonal contemporary American sharing plates with Mediterranean influences, accompanied by Three Floyds brews on tap and Izard's own wine blend; the rustic-meets-industrial aesthetic mixes woods and vintage metalwork, and there's a long open kitchen, numerous seating options (including bar, lounge and outdoor) and, naturally, goat *objets d'art*; P.S. The Little Goat diner is in the works.

Katsu Japanese Ⓜ *Japanese*

| 27 | 16 | 23 | E |

Northwest Side | 2651 W. Peterson Ave. (bet. Talman & Washtenaw Aves.) | 773-784-3383

Fish fanatics "skip the tony and more-publicized sushi boutiques and head" to the Northwest Side's "hidden gem", the "best Japanese restaurant in Chicago" where "caring owners" offer the "freshest", "most delectable" seafood and "traditional" hot fare that's "often exquisite", accompanied by "attentive service" and an "excellent sake selection" in a "conversation-friendly", "elegant" atmosphere; cost is also "top of the line" but most maintain it's "worth the money."

Les Nomades 🚫Ⓜ *French*

29 | 27 | 28 | VE

Streeterville | 222 E. Ontario St. (bet. Fairbanks Ct. & St. Clair St.) | 312-649-9010 | www.lesnomades.net

"One of the last bastions of haute cuisine", the No. 1 for Food in Chicago is Streeterville's French "crème de la crème" of "very formal" "fine dining", where chef Chris Nugent's "sophisticated", "beautifully prepared and presented" fare "is en pointe" as is the "extremely attentive service" and "remarkable", "francocentric" wine selection; the "quietly elegant", "clubby townhouse" ("once a private dining club") is a "place out of time and space" with "white linens", an "upstairs fireplace" and "gorgeous flowers", and though it's prix fixe and "*très* pricey", it's "perfect for a special, romantic occasion."

Michael Ⓜ *French*

28 | 23 | 27 | VE

Winnetka | 64 Green Bay Rd. (Winnetka Ave.) | 847-441-3100 | www.restaurantmichael.com

Namesake chef and "personality" Michael Lachowicz is "always there, interacting with his guests" at this Winnetka "winner" where his "exceptional", "delicate and flavorful" New French fare with "spot-on wine pairings" is served in an "elegant but casual", "conversation-friendly" room by a staff that "works well together"; it's "pricey", but "worthwhile for celebrating, relaxing or rewarding a good client."

MK *American*

27 | 24 | 26 | VE

Near North | 868 N. Franklin St. (bet. Chestnut & Locust Sts.) | 312-482-9179 | www.mkchicago.com

It's continuing "kudos" for Michael Kornick's "classy", "happening" Near North haunt that's "stood the test of time" and still "shines" with "honest", "outstanding", "seasonal" New American cuisine "minus the fussiness"; expect "knockout desserts", a "stellar wine list" and "excellent service all around" in the "spare", "urban-cool", "renovated warehouse" space – in other words, it "meets high expectations" "from start to finish."

Moto 🚫Ⓜ *Eclectic*

27 | 23 | 27 | VE

West Loop | 945 W. Fulton Mkt. (Sangamon St.) | 312-491-0058 | www.motorestaurant.com

Simultaneously "serious and fun", Homaro Cantu's "amazing" West Loop Eclectic is ground zero for "molecular gastronomy", where "nothing looks like what it tastes like" when it comes to the "playful", "cutting-edge" creations; the "expensive" experience includes 10-course tasting menus, "phenomenal service", a "choice wine list" and "stark interiors" that "put the whole focus on the food", so even if a handful find that some of the "gimmicky" dishes "don't quite work", the "mind-bending" "originality" always makes up for it; P.S. it opened Ing in place of its more casual outpost, Otom.

Naha 🚫 *American*

27 | 24 | 25 | E

River North | 500 N. Clark St. (Illinois St.) | 312-321-6242 | www.naha-chicago.com

Locals find "the total package" at this "upscale" River North New American where chef/co-owner Carrie Nahabedian serves up "perfection on a plate" with a "world-class" yet "accessible" fusion of "contemporary styling" and "organic produce" at its "absolute peak";

beyond that, there's a staff that "anticipates your needs" and a "refined atmosphere" in a "cool, modern" space, so even those bothered by the "noise" "get over it" given the "spectacular" value.

NEW Next Ⓜ *Eclectic* — | — | — | VE

West Loop | 953 W. Fulton Mkt. (bet. Morgan & Sangamon Sts.) | 312-226-0858 | www.nextrestaurant.com

This highly anticipated follow-up to Alinea from über-chef Grant Achatz is built around a daring concept, offering themed tasting menus that change quarterly to reflect a different global cuisine and time frame – and equally unusual is the booking system, with diners buying 'tickets' priced on a sliding scale according to day and time; the high-style, modern West Loop setting includes a chef's table and a secluded VIP 'speakeasy', while the adjacent Aviary bar, with upholstered banquettes and torchère lighting, serves crafty cocktails and edgy bar bites.

Oceanique Ⓢ *French/Seafood* 27 | 22 | 27 | E

Evanston | 505 Main St. (bet. Chicago & Hinman Aves.) | 847-864-3435 | www.oceanique.com

Mark Grosz's "memorable", "magnifique" Evanston eatery offers some of the "best seafood in the city", serving "superb new fusion and old-school dishes" with "unique" "combinations of French and Asian flavors" along with a "fantastic wine list"; the "fancy", "formal" setting and "top-notch service" further elevate the experience (and the prices), but "you get what you pay for" here.

Riccardo Trattoria *Italian* 27 | 19 | 23 | E

Lincoln Park | 2119 N. Clark St. (bet. Dickens & Webster Aves.) | 773-549-0038 | www.riccardotrattoria.com

Dining at this "understated" Lincoln Park trattoria – the top-rated Italian in Chicago – "genuinely" "brings back trips to Italy" say insiders, who prefer to steer the "masses" away from their "tiny gem" offering "fantastic" "classic" and "seasonal" dishes delivered by a "personable", "on-point staff"; a "delightful", simple setting with wood tables further evokes the "unpretentious" "spirit of Tuscany" for a "bargain" of a "special" experience that fans long to repeat "again and again."

Schwa ⓈⓂ *American* 29 | 15 | 25 | VE

Wicker Park | 1466 N. Ashland Ave. (Le Moyne St.) | 773-252-1466 | www.schwarestaurant.com

Zealots call Michael Carlson a "god among men" for his "fascinating" New American cuisine with "bright, surprising flavors" and a "side of wit"; the prix fixe menu is "served by the chefs", adding to an "unforgettable" experience that unfolds in a "relaxed", "small" Wicker Park BYO storefront; though it's "not inexpensive", fans contend it offers a "wonderful value", and if a few gripe that this "quirky" place comes off as "too complicated" for its own good, the fact that you must "persevere" to "secure a reservation" proves they're outvoted.

Sushi Wabi *Japanese* 27 | 18 | 20 | E

West Loop | 842 W. Randolph St. (bet. Green & Peoria Sts.) | 312-563-1224 | www.sushiwabi.com

"Sushi snobs" regard this modern West Loop Japanese as "one of the best" spots to "belly up" for "inventive" maki ("it's like buttah"); just "plan to spend a few bucks", and keep in mind that "service lacks often" and tables in the "industrial"-looking setting afford little "privacy from your neighbors" – most notably during "prime time" when it's "crowded" and "high-energy (translate: loud)."

Tallgrass Ⓜ *French*   28 | 23 | 24 | VE
Lockport | 1006 S. State St. (10th St.) | 815-838-5566 |
www.tallgrassrestaurant.com
It's "well worth the drive from Downtown" gush groupies of this "relaxed", "romantic" French in a "beautiful" vintage building, where "decades of culinary experience" "shows" in the modern prix fixe–only menu; it's "still a value" after all these years, with a "knowledgeable" staff and "fantastic wine list" that's "extremely fairly" priced sealing its status as a "special night out" in the Southwest Suburbs; P.S. jackets are suggested.

Topolobampo Ⓢ Ⓜ *Mexican*   28 | 24 | 26 | VE
River North | 445 N. Clark St. (bet. Hubbard & Illinois Sts.) | 312-661-1434 |
www.rickbayless.com
"Converts" call Rick Bayless' "modern", "refined" River North standout "the best" "gourmet Mexican" "in the country", declaring the "remarkable" "regional" flavors "expensive but worth it"; the art-adorned, "white-tablecloth" setting – plus the "fine wine service" and a "skilled", "professional" staff – makes patrons "forget" preconceptions about "south-of-the-border" cuisine (just be sure to reserve "long in advance"); P.S. "value"-hunters might try the chef's "casual Frontera Grill" next door or grab a torta from nearby Xoco.

Tru Ⓢ *French*   28 | 27 | 28 | VE
Streeterville | 676 N. St. Clair St. (bet. Erie & Huron Sts.) | 312-202-0001 |
www.trurestaurant.com
Streeterville's jacket-required, "world-class" New French destination stays "true to its reputation" with "flawless" "super-luxury" tastings and famed, "expense account"–required "crystal steps of caviar"; while perhaps "a little stuffy", this "adult-only" go-to for "anniversaries" and "special occasions" is capped by a "wonderful wine selection", "serene", art-filled dining room and "extraordinary" service that resembles "heaven on earth."

Vie Ⓢ *American*   27 | 25 | 28 | VE
Western Springs | 4471 Lawn Ave. (Burlington Ave.) | 708-246-2082 |
www.vierestaurant.com
Locavores "drive from the city" and beyond to Paul Virant's "deservedly respected" New American "haven" in Western Springs, where "magical" dishes are crafted using "simple", "sustainable" ingredients (including house-"pickled garnishes" and "great charcuterie"); the "lovely" 1940s-era, French-inspired interior, the "wonderful" service and the high prices – though "lower than Downtown" – place it in the "special-occasion category", but admirers could "eat [here] every day"; P.S. Virant will divide his time between this flagship and Lincoln Park's Perennial Virant.

Dallas/Ft. Worth

TOP FOOD RANKING

Restaurant	Cuisine
29 Bonnell's	Southwestern
28 Saint-Emilion	French
French Room	American/French
Cacharel	French
Pappas Bros.	Steak
Teppo Yakitori	Japanese
Yao Fuzi	Chinese
Yutaka*	Japanese
27 Café Pacific	Seafood
Bijoux	French
Abacus	Eclectic
Nick & Sam's	Seafood/Steak
Lonesome Dove	Southwestern
Eddie V's	Seafood/Steak
Ellerbe	American
Fearing's	Southwestern
Lanny's Alta Cocina*	Eclectic
Tei Tei Robata Bar	Japanese
Nana	American
26 Stephan Pyles	Southwestern

Abacus ☒ *Eclectic* — 27 | 26 | 26 | VE

Knox-Henderson | 4511 McKinney Ave. (Armstrong Ave.) | Dallas | 214-559-3111 | www.kentrathbun.com

Chef Kent Rathbun's "top-tier" "culinary mecca" that's located in Knox-Henderson is once again voted Dallas/Ft. Worth's Most Popular restaurant, catering to a "who's who" of society types purveying "haute" Eclectic cuisine in "inspired presentations" (with many surveyors saying "the lobster shooters are a must"); additionally, all this fare comes served in a "sleek", cream leather–trimmed interior carried by an "impressive" staff that "really knows its stuff", so despite what some diners may call a bill that "hurts", for many it ranks as "close to perfect."

Bijoux ☒ *French* — 27 | 26 | 26 | VE

West Lovers Lane | Inwood Vill. | 5450 W. Lovers Ln. (Inwood Rd.) | Dallas | 214-350-6100 | www.bijouxrestaurant.com

Make sure to "prepare yourself" for a "top-of-the-line" "two-and-a-half-hour meal" at Scott Gottlich's "enchanting" West Lovers Lane destination that's located in Inwood Village and known for whipping up "heavenly" dishes of New French cuisine that many aficionados profess is "absolutely worth the splurge"; it all follows through with an "attractive", chandelier-lit interior and "impeccable", "unstuffy" service, so most surveyors conclude they certainly "couldn't recommend it more."

---

* Indicates a tie with restaurant above

Bonnell's 🗷Ⓜ *Southwestern*

| 29 | 26 | 28 | E |

Southwest | 4259 Bryan Irvin Rd. (Southwest Blvd.) | Ft. Worth |
817-738-5489 | www.bonnellstexas.com

"Master" chef, and "one of the nicest [guys] in town", Jon Bonnell is
behind this Southwest Ft. Worth "destination" that's rated No. 1 for
Food – with a rare 29 – in the Dallas/Ft. Worth Survey thanks to his
"brilliant" brand of "modern Texas cuisine" starring loads of "local
game" (elk tacos, anyone?); factor in "flawless" service and an "understated" Western-style setting – not to mention relatively understated prices – and you've got a "class act" all around.

Cacharel 🗷 *French*

| 28 | 26 | 27 | E |

Arlington | Brookhollow Tower Two | 2221 E. Lamar Blvd., 9th fl.
(Ballpark Way) | 817-640-9981 | www.cacharel.net

"First-class" all the way, this Arlington entry "overlooking the new
Cowboys dome" delivers true "fine dining", from the "marvelous"
French fare and steaks down to the "wonderful" Grand Marnier
soufflé; it's certainly not inexpensive, but with a "posh" cream-
colored setting and "charming" service, it's the "perfect spot for a
quiet, romantic dinner."

Café Pacific 🗷 *Seafood*

| 27 | 25 | 26 | E |

Park Cities | 24 Highland Park Vill. (Preston Rd.) | Dallas | 214-526-1170 |
www.cafepacificdallas.com

A Park Cities "institution", this "clubby" seafooder is where "elegant
ladies and dapper gents" savor "wonderful" dishes prepared "with
flair" plus some of the "best martinis in town"; it's all a bit "old school",
with "watchful, expert service" making for a "memorable" meal at
prices that well-heeled regulars can well afford; P.S. "tables are tough
to get on weekends", so reserve in advance.

Del Frisco's Double Eagle Steak House *Steak*

| 26 | 25 | 25 | VE |

North Dallas | 5251 Spring Valley Rd. (Dallas N. Tollway) | Dallas |
972-490-9000

Downtown Ft. Worth | 812 Main St. (8th St.) | Ft. Worth | 817-877-3999
www.delfriscos.com

"When you want to impress" – especially "on the company dime" –
this high-end chophouse chain, born in Dallas, fits the bill with
"top-flight steaks", a well-stocked wine cellar and "spectacular"
desserts; all branches thrive in "handsome" digs done up in "dark,
rich woods" with "lots of brass" making for a truly "consistent", if
somewhat predictable, experience.

Eddie V's Prime Seafood *Seafood/Steak*

| 27 | 26 | 25 | E |

Oak Lawn | 4023 Oak Lawn Ave. (Avondale Ave.) | Dallas | 214-890-1500
Cultural District | 3100 W. Seventh St. (Bailey Ave.) | Ft. Worth |
214-890-1500
www.eddiev.com

A "class act", this Austin-bred chainlet with links in Dallas offers a
"first-rate experience on all counts", from the "fabulous" steaks and
seafood (including "amazing fresh oysters" and crab) to the "professional" service and "modern", leather-trimmed quarters; given the
"expense-account" pricing, many seek out the "half-price apps" deals
during happy hour.

Ellerbe Fine Food 🅢🅜 *American*   27 | 21 | 22 | E

Hospital District | 1501 W. Magnolia Ave. (7th Ave.) | Ft. Worth |
817-926-3663 | www.ellerbefinefoods.com

Ft. Worth's increasingly "hip" Hospital District is home to this "very LA" venue spotlighting chef/co-owner Molly McCook's "highly imaginative" American cuisine rooted in "Southern" tradition and based on "local, seasonal" ingredients; factor in moderate prices and a "pleasant" converted gas station setting, and it's no wonder locals are lauding it as a "fabulous" "find."

Fearing's *Southwestern*   27 | 28 | 28 | VE

Uptown | Ritz-Carlton Hotel | 2121 McKinney Ave. (Pearl St.) | Dallas |
214-922-4848 | www.fearingsrestaurant.com

Smitten fans "have nothing but superlatives" for Dean Fearing's venue in Uptown's Ritz-Carlton Hotel, where "everything shines bright", from the "memorable" Southwestern meals to the "power-broker" clientele; "impeccable" service (including "tableside visits" from the man himself) in the "maze" of "beautiful" dining spaces elevates it to among "Dallas' finest" – if there's one place to "go bust", this is it.

French Room 🅢🅜 *American/French*   28 | 29 | 29 | VE

Downtown Dallas | Hotel Adolphus | 1321 Commerce St. (Field St.) |
Dallas | 214-742-8200 | www.hoteladolphus.com

It's "like eating at Versailles" at this "opulent" rococo showpiece in the landmark Hotel Adolphus Downtown, where the "luxurious" setting and "discreet" staff that "tends to you like royalty" help rank it No. 1 for Decor and Service in Dallas; factor in "superb", "sophisticated" French-New American cuisine and it all adds up to an "over-the-top" experience that's "close to perfection", and priced accordingly; P.S. jackets required.

Lanny's Alta Cocina Mexicana 🅢🅜 *Eclectic*   27 | 24 | 25 | E

Cultural District | 3405 W. Seventh St. (Boland St.) | Ft. Worth |
817-850-9996 | www.lannyskitchen.com

"Perfect for a date", this "beautifully appointed" Cultural District mainstay showcases "palate-pleasing" "Mexican-inspired" Eclectic plates from chef-owner Lanny Lancarte (a "maestro" in the kitchen); "personal" service and a "chic", "casually elegant" setting account in part for the "expensive" cost; P.S. the tasting menu with wine pairings is "highly recommended."

Lonesome Dove Western Bistro 🅢 *Southwestern*   27 | 23 | 24 | E

Stockyards | 2406 N. Main St. (24th St.) | Ft. Worth | 817-740-8810 |
www.lonesomedovebistro.com

Diners declare themselves "blown away" by celebrity chef-owner Tim Love's "modern takes" on cowboy cuisine ("love the buffalo!") at his "chic" Southwestern flagship in the Ft. Worth Stockyards; despite "splurge"-worthy pricing and a few "gaps in service", "out-of-towners" especially find it "hard to beat"; P.S. "reservations a must."

Lucia 🅢🅜 *Italian*   - | - | - | M

Oak Cliff | 408 W. Eighth St. (N. Bishop Ave.) | Dallas | 214-948-4998 |
www.luciadallas.com

Chef David Uygur (of the recently shuttered Lola) is generating quite a buzz with this new Oak Cliff Italian set in a '20s-era Bishop Arts building; expect a warm greeting, a rustic ambiance and excellent value for the caliber of cuisine, which focuses on the seasonal and artisanal with handcrafted salumi, breads and pasta; N.B. its popularity and tiny footprint (36 seats) make reservations a must.

Nana *American*

27 | 28 | 26 | VE

Market Center | Hilton Anatole Hotel | 2201 Stemmons Frwy., 27th fl. (Market Center Blvd.) | Dallas | 214-761-7470 | www.nanarestaurant.com

"High-quality dining in many senses" can be found at this "top-shelf" New American on the 27th floor of the Hilton Anatole in Market Center, offering "fantastic" views to accompany the "stellar" cuisine by chef Anthony Bombaci; thoughtfully curated Asian art on display and a "lovely" staff enhance the experience, justifying the "expensive" tabs.

Nick & Sam's *Seafood/Steak*

27 | 25 | 26 | VE

Uptown | 3008 Maple Ave. (bet. Carlisle & Wolf Sts.) | Dallas | 214-871-7444 | www.nick-sams.com

"You can feel the power" in this Uptown steakhouse known for "over-the-top" meals of "fabulous meat", seafood and "amazing sides"; the "dark", "old-fashioned" setting, brightened up by a "piano player in the kitchen", is the kind of place where regulars request their favorite table and "superb" waiter, so get in the swing and "bring the corporate AmEx or a Brinks truck."

Pappas Bros. Steakhouse 🗷 *Steak*

28 | 25 | 26 | E

Love Field | 10477 Lombardy Ln. (Northwest Hwy.) | Dallas | 214-366-2000 | www.pappasbros.com

Smitten carnivores swear "it doesn't get any better" than this Pappas family "flagship" in Dallas where the "luscious", "perfectly marbled" steaks "melt in your mouth"; the "memorable" meals are enhanced by "outstanding" wines, "fawning" service and a "lavish" 1920s-inspired setting – just "be prepared to shell out the big bucks."

Saint-Emilion 🗷🗹 *French*

28 | 26 | 28 | E

Cultural District | 3617 W. Seventh St. (Montgomery St.) | Ft. Worth | 817-737-2781 | www.saint-emilionrestaurant.com

"Always a winner for a special occasion" or "date night", this petite restaurant in Ft. Worth's Cultural District serves "amazing", "authentic" Gallic food "prepared with love and care" in a "romantic" country French setting; ever-present owner Bernard Tronche "oversees every little detail", ensuring "outstanding" service for an ultimately "high-end" experience; P.S. in addition to the prix fixe menu, they've added à la carte options.

Stephan Pyles 🗷 *Southwestern*

26 | 26 | 26 | E

Arts District | 1807 Ross Ave. (St. Paul St.) | Dallas | 214-580-7000 | www.stephanpyles.com

"Legendary", "charming" chef Stephan Pyles turns out another hit with this "must-do" Southwestern in the Arts District whose "rock-star" roster includes "spectacular" ceviche, "top-notch" turf items and an "impressive" wine list; though a few critics huff there's "too much hype", fans affirm the "vibrant" atmosphere, "stylish" decor and "wonderful" service all add to a "memorable experience" that's worth the big bucks; P.S. dine at the bar for a prime view of the kitchen in action.

Tei Tei Robata Bar Ⓜ *Japanese*
27 | **21** | **24** | **E**

Knox-Henderson | 2906 N. Henderson Ave. (Willis Ave.) | Dallas | 214-828-2400 | www.teiteirobata.com

Enthusiasts exalt the "uncompromising quality" of the "top-notch" sushi, "Tokyo"-style robata and "fantastic sake menu" at this Japanese "marvel" in Knox-Henderson; "everything is served elegantly and simply" in a contemporary, warmly lit space, though a few aren't so keen on the "scene", the "long wait" and the price/portion ratio.

Teppo Yakitori & Sushi Bar Ⓜ *Japanese*
28 | **22** | **27** | **E**

Greenville Avenue | 2014 Greenville Ave. (Prospect Ave.) | Dallas | 214-826-8989 | www.teppo.com

"Who knows how they get such fresh fish, but it's wonderful" attest admirers of the "brilliant" sushi, while grill-lovers laud the "stellar" yakitori by "chefs who take pride in their work" at this "comfortable" Japanese standout on Greenville Avenue; the slightly upscale tabs are further justified by a "knowledgeable" staff that always "recognizes" return customers.

Yao Fuzi Cuisine *Chinese*
28 | **24** | **25** | **M**

West Plano | 4757 W. Park Blvd. (bet. Ohio Dr. & Preston Rd.) | Plano | 214-473-9267 | www.yaofuzi.com

Customers "crave" the "exceptional" Shanghainese cuisine (featuring both "Americanized" dishes and "authentic" discoveries) at this "lovely" family-owned "gem" in a West Plano strip mall, a "big step above the typical joint" boasting a "calm, beautiful" ambiance along with "congenial" service; it's "not too expensive" either, making it a "top" choice all around.

Yutaka Sushi Bistro Ⓩ *Japanese*
28 | **21** | **26** | **E**

Uptown | 2633 McKinney Ave. (Boll St.) | Dallas | 214-969-5533 | www.yutakasushibistro.com

"Perfection in execution and presentation" sets apart this "popular" Uptown Japanese where "freaking genius" chef-owner Yutaka Yamato "makes everything look effortless" as he prepares the "finest" sushi and small plates; "warm service" and an adjacent sake lounge help ease the "waits" inside the "Lilliputian setting", and help the "pricey" tabs go down easier too; P.S. reservations accepted for six or more.

Denver Area & Mountain Resorts

TOP FOOD RANKING

	Restaurant	Cuisine
28	Fruition	American
	Frasca	Italian
	Matsuhisa	Japanese
	Splendido	American
	Mizuna	American
27	Sushi Sasa	Japanese
	Sushi Den	Japanese
	Rioja	Mediterranean
	L'Atelier	French
	Six89	American
	Del Frisco's	Steak
	Luca d'Italia	Italian
	Z Cuisine	French
26	Izakaya Den	Asian
	Grouse Mountain	American

Del Frisco's Double Eagle Steak House *Steak*

`27` `24` `26` `VE`

Greenwood Village | Denver Tech Ctr. | 8100 E. Orchard Rd. (I-25, exit 198) | 303-796-0100 | www.delfriscos.com

"Businessmen on expense accounts" join the "glitterati", e.g. "Broncos", at this Greenwood Village "power scene" known for its "generous" portions of "outstanding steaks", "impressive wine list" and "big bills"; a "knowledgeable, attentive staff" helps set a "relaxed" tone in the "warm, sumptuous" room, but be warned if you're seated close to the "hot bar": it's "sometimes too noisy"; P.S. there's also a "super" cigar lounge.

Elway's *Steak*

`24` `24` `23` `E`

Cherry Creek | 2500 E. First Ave. (University Blvd.) | Denver | 303-399-5353
Downtown Denver | Ritz-Carlton Denver | 1881 Curtis St. (19th St.) | Denver | 303-312-3107
www.elways.com

"Big John" "scores big" at this "always hopping" "place to meet and greet in Cherry Creek" (with a "sophisticated, welcoming" Downtown sibling), a "masculine", "classy environment" where "superb" servers present a "diverse menu" starring "flat-out outstanding", "beautifully seasoned slabs of grilled beef" alongside an "impressive wine list"; the "lively" bar scene is "truly spectacular", plus it offers its own "nightly special": "cougar"; P.S. though it's "expensive", "compared to the competition, prices are reasonable."

Frasca Food and Wine 🖾 *Italian*

`28` `24` `28` `VE`

Boulder | 1738 Pearl St. (18th St.) | 303-442-6966 | www.frascafoodandwine.com

"Believe the hype!" – this "beautiful little place" in Boulder is voted Colorado's Most Popular restaurant thanks to chef Lachlan Mackinnon-Patterson's "incredibly innovative", "ethereal" cuisine from the Friuli region of Northern Italy and "consummate host"/"outstanding sommelier" Bobby Stuckey's "killer wine list" and "unbelievable pairings"; it's "expensive", "yet feels like a bargain" considering it's such a "'wow' experience"; in fact, "the only flaws are the cramped seating" and "difficulty getting reservations", so if you haven't booked "the prescribed 30 days in advance", "go early and sit at the bar" or the salumi counter.

Fruition American
| 28 | 22 | 27 | E |

Country Club | 1313 E. Sixth Ave. (bet. Lafayette & Marion Sts.) | Denver | 303-831-1962 | www.fruitionrestaurant.com

"A not-to-be-missed adventure" sums up this "shining diamond" between Country Club and Capitol Hill, where chef Alex Seidel creates "innovative", "beautifully plated", "ever-changing" New American cuisine that earns Denver's No. 1 Food rating (and gets a boost from "excellent wine pairings"); the "tables are cramped" in the "tight quarters" ("plan ahead to get in"), but the "warmth" of "witty" host Paul Attardi and his "exceptional" staff creates a "cozy feel", which also helps to make the "expensive-side" tabs "seem more reasonable."

Grouse Mountain Grill American
| 26 | 24 | 24 | E |

Beaver Creek | Pines Lodge Beaver Creek Resort | 141 Scott Hill Rd. (Village Rd.) | 970-949-0600 | www.grousemountaingrill.com

Settle in for a "delightful" evening in the "elegant", "warm" dining room of Beaver Creek Resort's Pines Lodge, where "attentive" servers ferry "spectacular", "innovative" New American fare; or you might choose the "great piano bar" to listen to jazz (Wednesday–Sunday in season) while getting "Rocky Mountain high" via pours from the "dictionary-thick wine list" – just be warned: like the food, the vino's "exceptionally expensive" (but most find everything "worth it").

Izakaya Den 🅼 Asian
| 26 | 26 | 23 | E |

Platt Park | 1518 S. Pearl St. (Florida Ave.) | Denver | 303-777-0691 | www.izakayaden.net

"Just as good" as Sushi Den, this "fabulous" Platt Park offshoot is "a bit more creative", as it offers its "fantastic fresh fish" and "delicious rolls" alongside "innovative" Asian fusion "cooked small plates" boasting "amazing presentations and flavors" (there are "great cocktails" too, and everything's delivered by "accommodating" staffers); in addition, the "trendy" space is "bigger" than its "overcrowded" sibling, which "means less wait time" and an overall "more serene" experience.

L'Atelier French
| 27 | 24 | 25 | E |

Boulder | 1739 Pearl St. (18th St.) | 303-442-7233 | www.latelierboulder.com

"Clever" chef-owner Radek Cerny is "a master of creating inventive dishes" (with "impeccable sauces"), which are "beautifully presented" alongside an "extensive wine list" by "exceptionally attentive", "warm" staffers at this Boulder French with Eclectic influences; though "elbow-to-elbow", the "lovely", "little" digs feel "warm", and while it's somewhat pricey, the "gourmet lunches" are a relative "bargain."

Luca d'Italia 🈺🅼 Italian
| 27 | 21 | 26 | E |

Capitol Hill | 711 Grant St. (7th Ave.) | Denver | 303-832-6600 | www.lucadenver.com

"Another dazzling restaurant" from chef-owner Frank Bonanno (Mizuna), this "first-class tour of Italy" in "minimalist" Capitol Hill digs "impresses" with "delicious pastas" and "deftly prepared" secondi; the "warm" servers and sommeliers are "knowledgeable" to boot (the latter overseeing an "excellent wine list"), all of which conspires to create a "wonderful" "culinary adventure" that's "expensive" but "worth every penny."

Matsuhisa *Japanese*   28 | 22 | 24 | VE

Aspen | 303 E. Main St. (Monarch St.) | 970-544-6628 |
www.matsuhisaaspen.com

"Every bit as good" as famed NYC sibling Nobu, this "hip" spot in "see-and-be-seen" Aspen offers "exquisite presentations" of "phenomenal" sushi that's "worth every penny – and you will spend many of them"; a "professional staff" and a "wonderful" "Zen atmosphere" add appeal (that the main dining room's in a "basement keeps few people away, so book as early as possible"), plus there's an "amazing" upstairs bar whipping up "great saketinis that pack a punch."

Mizuna Ⓢ Ⓜ *American*   28 | 23 | 27 | E

Capitol Hill | 225 E. Seventh Ave. (bet. Grant & Sherman Sts.) |
Denver | 303-832-4778 | www.mizunadenver.com

"Another of Frank Bonanno's masterpieces", this "stellar" Capitol Hill New American "will knock your socks off" with its "innovative" dishes (consider the "heavenly tasting menu" with "great wine pairings", but definitely get the "legendary lobster mac 'n' cheese"); the environs are criticized for being "tight" and possibly "dated", but the "gracious", "impeccable service" helps to make it a "worry-free evening" that's "worth saving up for."

Rioja *Mediterranean*   27 | 24 | 25 | E

Larimer Square | 1431 Larimer St. (bet. 14th & 15th Sts.) | Denver |
303-820-2282 | www.riojadenver.com

"Every detail is executed to perfection" at this "hit" in "trendy" Larimer Square, from "master of taste and design" Jennifer Jasinski's "outside-the-box" Mediterranean cuisine (particularly the "to-die-for home-made breads and pastas") to the "outstanding service" to the "hip, urban", "glassware"-bedecked decor; there is "one beef" though: the "terrible acoustics", exacerbated by the fact that it's "usually crowded"; P.S. tabs "can be expensive", but the "decadent" brunch is a "great value."

Six89 Ⓜ *American*   27 | 21 | 26 | E

Carbondale | 689 Main St. (7th St.) | 970-963-6890 | www.six89.com

For "outstanding" "big-city food" at "'down-valley' prices", Carbondale foodies flock to this "charming" venue where chef-owner Mark Fischer turns out "seasonal, imaginative", "beautifully presented" New American fare in a "homelike setting"; add "a great range of wines for all tastes and budgets", "exceptional service" and "memorable summer patio dining", and it's easy to see why nonlocals deem it "worth the journey."

Splendido at the Chateau Ⓜ *American*   28 | 28 | 27 | VE

Beaver Creek | Beaver Creek Resort | 17 Chateau Ln. (Scott Hill Rd.) |
970-845-8808 | www.splendidobeavercreek.com

"It's like stepping into another world" at this "one-of-a-kind" "treat" in "posh Beaver Creek", where executive chef David Walford's New

American fare is a "brilliantly executed" "feast for the eyes and palate" (matched by "fantastic wines"); the "stratospheric prices" are easier to swallow given the "accomplished" service, "plush", European-style environs with a "fireplace and a piano" and "beautiful mountain views" – no wonder the smitten suggest it should be "renamed 'Perfetto.'"

Sushi Den *Japanese*

| 27 | 23 | 23 | E |

South Denver | 1487 S. Pearl St. (Florida Ave.) | Denver | 303-777-0826 | www.sushiden.net

Come "early" or endure a "painful wait" at the "sushi capital" of South Denver, which is "crowded" "no matter the day of the week" with "fashionable", "trendy" types indulging in "the freshest fish" ("all the usuals, plus many inventive" rolls), in addition to scads of "amazing" cooked fare; unsurprisingly, the "contemporary" room is "really noisy" and the checks are "expensive", but all in all, it's "well worth it."

Sushi Sasa *Japanese*

| 27 | 23 | 23 | E |

Highland | 2401 15th St. (Platte St.) | Denver | 303-433-7272 | www.sushisasadenver.com

"Artful" presentations of "sumptuous" "fish so fresh it's still quivering on your plate" is the deal at this Highland "heaven on earth", where sushi mavens suggest you go for "genius" chef-owner Wayne Conwell's "startlingly original omakase"; indeed, those with "adventurous palates" (not to mention deep pockets) "have a ball" in environs that are "modern", "upscale" and "intimate" (though less so after a post-Survey expansion, which most likely outdates the Decor score).

Sweet Basil *American*

| 26 | 23 | 24 | E |

Vail | 193 E. Gore Creek Dr. (Bridge St.) | 970-476-0125 | www.sweetbasil-vail.com

"End a powder day" at Vail's "extraordinary" "old faithful" that "lives up to its reputation" with "inventive", "exceptional" New American vittles boasting "bright, intense flavors", "excellent wines" and service with "not a whiff of pretension"; "ask for a window table" for "priceless views" of Gore Creek, or sit in the thick of things, soak up the "marvelous ambiance" and check out all the "interesting", lively diners "visiting their friends at the next table"; P.S. "lunch is wonderful, and more affordable than dinner."

Z Cuisine A Côté 🗷 Ⓜ *French*

| 27 | 22 | 22 | E |

Highland | 2239 W. 30th Ave. (Wyandot St.) | Denver | 303-477-1111 | www.zcuisineonline.com

"Highfalutin Francophiles" "can't believe" the "authentic", "gorgeous French feasts" served by a "knowledgeable staff" alongside "unpretentious wines" at this "adorable restaurant in the heart of Highland"; "sadly, it does not take reservations, seats only a handful of people" ("show up early" or "you risk dying of old age" waiting for a table), is open only Wednesday-Saturday and is "expensive" – but still, "it's worth the hassle."

Honolulu

TOP FOOD RANKING

	Restaurant	Cuisine
28	Sushi Sasabune	Japanese
	Hiroshi	Eurasian
	Alan Wong's	Hawaii Regional
	La Mer	French
27	Chef Mavro	French/Hawaii Regional
	Le Bistro	French
	Michel's	French
	Nobu Waikiki	Japanese/Peruvian
26	Orchids	Pacific Rim
	Hakone	Japanese
	Hy's	Steak
	Hoku's	Pacific Rim
	Roy's	Hawaii Reg.
25	Sansei	Japanese/Pacific Rim

Alan Wong's *Hawaii Reg.*   28 | 22 | 26 | VE

McCully | 1857 S. King St. (bet. Hauoli & Pumehana Sts.) | 808-949-2526 |
www.alanwongs.com

The place where "Hawaii Regional cuisine was born and still reigns",
Alan Wong's longtime standout garners Oahu's No. 1 Most Popular
honors thanks to "inspired" cuisine, an "exceptional" wine list and
"gracious" service that make it a "must when in Honolulu" for many,
including "President Obama"; you can "see the chefs work their
magic" in the open kitchen, and though some find the space otherwise
"pedestrian" and the location "hard to find", most agree the "heavenly
experience" is "well worth the effort" and "pricey" tabs.

Chef Mavro 🈺🅼 *French/Hawaii Reg.*   27 | 25 | 28 | VE

Moiliili | 1969 S. King St. (McCully St.) | 808-944-4714 | www.chefmavro.com
Though it "doesn't look like much from the outside", set on a "busy
corner" in Moiliili, George Mavrothalassitis' Hawaii Regional–French
standout offers "an evening not to be missed", featuring "perfectly
prepared" and "beautifully presented" dishes, "spot-on" wine pairings, "stellar" service and "elegant" decor; you'll pay a "hefty price"
(and still "walk out hungry" grouse some), but most agree the "memorable experience" is "worth every penny."

Duke's Canoe Club *American*   20 | 23 | 20 | M

Waikiki | Outrigger Waikiki | 2335 Kalakaua Ave. (bet. Duke's Ln. &
Kaiulani Ave.) | 808-922-2268 | www.dukeswaikiki.com

Like a "Hollywood version of Hawaii", this landmark at the Outrigger
Waikiki Beach makes you "feel the island spirit" thanks to "gorgeous" location and *Fantasy Island* setting adorned with pictures of
the eponymous surfing legend and assorted "beach boys"; "Hawaiian
singers" stroll among visitors and locals who "pretend they're on
vacation" as they knock back "killer" mai tais and tuck into "dependable" American pub grub served by a "friendly" (some say "ama-

teurish") staff – ok, maybe it's "noisy" and a little "touristy", but it's "still lots of fun."

Hakone M *Japanese*   26 | 23 | 26 | E

Waikiki | Hawaii Prince Hotel Waikiki | 100 Holomoana St. (Ala Moana Blvd.) | 808-944-4494 | www.princeresortshawaii.com

Even "guests from Japan" are "impressed" by the "excellent" buffet at this "higher-grade" Japanese in the Hawaii Prince Hotel in Waikiki, which offers a "wide array" of "authentic" dishes, including the "freshest sashimi and sushi", plus shrimp tempura that's "worth the price of admission alone"; service is "subdued" yet "outstanding", and the "quiet" setting offers a "fabulous view of Ala Wai" Harbor.

Hiroshi Eurasion Tapas *Eurasian*   28 | 23 | 27 | E

Restaurant Row | 500 Ala Moana Blvd. (bet. Punchbowl & South Sts.) | 808-533-4476 | www.hiroshihawaii.com

Two "masters", chef Hiroshi Fukui and sommelier Chuck Furuya, team up (together with restaurateur D.K. Kodama) at their "major-league" establishment on Restaurant Row, which has achieved "almost cult" status with its "inspired" Eurasian tapas featuring "locally grown products" and "fantastic" wine pairings from a "superb" list, plus "excellent" service in a "quiet, contemporary" setting; happy hour offers some "amazing" deals, and the occasional kaiseki dinners (reservations required) are a "great bargain."

Hoku's *Pacific Rim*   26 | 27 | 26 | VE

Kahala | Kahala Hotel & Resort | 5000 Kahala Ave. (Kealaolu Ave.) | 808-739-8780 | www.kahalaresort.com

"Stunning views" of the Pacific from an "oceanside" location and "elegant, contemporary" decor create a "romantic" tableau at the Kahala Hotel's "special-occasion" Pacific Rim establishment offering "topnotch" fare, including what some call the "best brunch on the beach in Oahu", and "exceptional" service; despite grumbles about "hotel prices" and "stuffy" taboos on "resort wear", most consider it an "excellent choice."

Hy's Steak House *Steak*   26 | 25 | 27 | E

Waikiki | Waikiki Park Heights Hotel | 2440 Kuhio Ave. (Uluniu Ave.) | 808-922-5555 | www.hyshawaii.com

Devotees promise an "unforgettable dining experience" at this "highend steakhouse" in the Waikiki Park Heights Hotel that's like a "gentlemen's eating club", with "superb" "white-glove" service from waiters in "tuxedos", "fabulous" steaks "cooked to perfection" and "tableside preparations of Caesar salads", plus retro "flambé desserts"; "overstuffed chairs", "leather booths" and a "Tiffany stainedglass ceiling" highlight the "formal", "throwback" setting, and while it's not cheap, many say it's "worth breaking the bank one time" for a "special occasion."

La Mer *French*   28 | 29 | 28 | VE

Waikiki | Halekulani | 2199 Kalia Rd. (Lewers St.) | 808-923-2311 | www.halekulani.com

"They make you feel like a big kahuna" at the Halekulani Hotel's "formal" French restaurant, voted Hawaii's No. 1 for Decor and Service, where you can hear the "sound of waves" and "Hawaiian music from the shore" in the "open-air room overlooking Waikiki Beach" as an "attentive" staff serves "amazing" Gallic cuisine with "subtle Asian accents" and selections from a "superb" wine list; sure, you'll "spend a fortune", but many insist it's "worth the splurge"; jackets required.

Le Bistro *French*

27 | 20 | 25 | E

Niu Valley | Niu Valley Shopping Ctr. | 5730 Kalanianaole Hwy. (Halemaumau St.) | 808-373-7990

Alan and Debbie Takasaki "make dining magic" at their Niu Valley "surprise for Francophiles", a "romantic retreat in a strip mall" where "balanced and beautiful" French cuisine "with Hawaiian flair" plus "excellent" service attract a "stimulating cross section of diners", including "lots of locals"; a few feel "cramped" in the "quiet, unassuming" space, especially when it gets "crowded", but just about all agree it's "worth a visit if not a detour."

Michel's *French*

27 | 27 | 27 | VE

Waikiki | Colony Surf | 2895 Kalakaua Ave. (Poni Moi Rd.) | 808-923-6552 | www.michelshawaii.com

For a "sumptuous" dining experience, "locals and tourists" alike head to this "legendary" Waikiki "warhorse" whose "beautiful location right on the beach" provides "unmatched" views of "awesome sunsets" and the "city lights" at night; "skilled, tuxedoed waiters do all sorts of tableside preparations" while serving "superb" Classic French cuisine in a "semi-alfresco" setting that makes "indoors seem like outdoors" – many just "don't want the evening to end" (or the check to arrive).

NEW Morimoto Waikiki *Japanese*

- | - | - | VE

Waikiki | Waikiki Edition Hotel | 1775 Ala Moana Blvd. (Hobron Ln.) | 808-943-5900 | www.morimotowaikiki.com

Iron Chef Masaharu Morimoto's newest venture in the posh Waikiki Edition Hotel showcases his signature Western-influenced Japanese cuisine, including a seven-course omakase menu, in a sleek, island-themed space by Thomas Schoos that features an open kitchen and a semi-private dining room enclosed in sheer curtains; you can take in views of the ocean and a nearby yacht club from the open-air lanai, which boasts plush sofas and two fire pits.

Nobu Waikiki *Japanese/Peruvian*

27 | 25 | 24 | VE

Waikiki | Waikiki Parc Hotel | 2233 Helumoa Rd. (Lewers St.) | 808-237-6999 | www.noburestaurants.com

"Nobu at his best" is how fans describe the "fabulous" Waikiki Parc Hotel outpost of his "far-reaching empire", where "creative", "memorable" Japanese-Peruvian fusion fare, including "superb" sushi, is served in a "beautiful space" teeming with "beautiful people" and a fair share of "local celebs and actors"; service is "excellent" if a "little stiff" to some, and though a few dissenters find the experience "not as mind-blowing as you'd expect" given the name and "price tag", by most accounts it's a "wow!"

Orchids *Pacific Rim*

26 | 28 | 27 | E

Waikiki | Halekulani | 2199 Kalia Rd. (Lewers St.) | 808-923-2311 | www.halekulani.com

A "magical setting" with "breathtaking views of Diamond Head" and what some call the "best Sunday brunch in all of Waikiki" are the highlights of this "classy" open-air Pacific Rim seafooder in the Halekulani Hotel, where you're regaled by the "sound of waves" and evening "live music on the lawn" in the "elegantly Hawaiian" room "overflowing with orchids"; the service is "friendly and gracious" while the "sophisticated" fare is "extraordinary", thus many concur it's "such a fine-dining experience, you hardly notice the price."

Roy's *Hawaii Reg.*   26 | 22 | 24 | E

Hawaii Kai | 6600 Kalanianaole Hwy. (Keahole St.) | 808-396-7697
Waikiki | Waikiki Beach Walk | 226 Lewers St. (Kalia Rd.) | 808-923-7697
www.roysrestaurant.com

Showcasing celeb chef Roy Yamaguchi's "modern mastery" of Hawaii Regional cuisine, this "high-end" nationwide chain (which originated with the Hawaii Kai location) earns the state's Most Popular honors thanks to "creatively prepared" fish, "unique" local specialties and other "fantastic" fare coupled with "excellent" service; if the decor is "looking a little too '90s" for some, that doesn't deter fans who say "every meal is a delight" and worth the "noise" and "crowds"; P.S. you "must have the chocolate molten lava cake."

Sansei *Japanese/Pacific Rim*   25 | 18 | 22 | E

Waikiki | Waikiki Beach Marriott Resort & Spa | 2552 Kalakaua Ave. (bet. Ohua & Paoakalani Aves.) | 808-931-6286 | www.sanseihawaii.com

"What a find" exclaim enthusiasts of this "popular" island chainlet where the Japanese and Pacific Rim fare – from "exceptional sushi" to "inventive" seafood and "killer cocktails" – "dazzles the palate"; "plan on a long wait" "even with reservations", as well as "noise" and iffy service at some locales, but you'll be rewarded by "chefs who love their work"; P.S. locals "get in line early" for the "fantastic" early-bird specials, when the place really gets "packed."

Sushi Sasabune ☒ *Japanese*   28 | 16 | 21 | VE

Ala Moana | 1419 S. King St. (Keeaumoku St.) | 808-947-3800 | www.sasabunehawaii.com

"You can definitely trust" Seiji Kumagawa to prepare an "absolutely amazing" omakase with "melt-in-your-mouth" fish "flown in that day" at this Ala Moana Japanese, voted Hawaii's No. 1 for Food; ok, those put off by "dictatorial" service (the chef "gets mad if you don't eat something") are "not quite comfortable" here, the decor isn't stellar and it may be the "priciest sushi on the island", but fans say it would be hard to find better "anywhere in the world."

Houston

TOP FOOD RANKING

	Restaurant	Cuisine
28	Le Mistral	French
	Kanomwan	Thai
	Pappas Bros.	Steak
	Mark's	American
27	Da Marco	Italian
	Chez Nous	French
	Masraff's	Continental
	Damian's	Italian
	Eddie V's	Seafood/Steak
	Tony's	Continental/Italian
	Glass Wall	American
26	Shade	American
	Indika	Indian
	Hugo's	Mexican
	Tony Mandola's	Seafood
	Vic & Anthony's	Steak
	Café Rabelais	French
	Au Petit Paris	French
	Morton's	Steak
	Ruth's Chris	Steak
	Del Frisco's	Steak
	Churrascos	S American

Au Petit Paris Ⓢ *French*   26 | 20 | 23 | E

Lower Shepherd | 2048 Colquitt St. (Shepherd Dr.) | 713-524-7070 | www.aupetitparisrestaurant.com

"*Très charmant*" purr fans of this Lower Shepherd "gem" famed for its "truly French" fare served in a rehabbed bungalow; whether it's "cozy" or just plain "cramped" is up for debate, though all agree it has a "homey", "pleasant" vibe, aided by a "welcoming" staff and prices that are moderate for the area.

Café Rabelais Ⓢ *French*   26 | 21 | 23 | M

Rice Village | 2442 Times Blvd. (bet. Kelvin & Morningside Drs.) | 713-520-8841 | www.caferabelais.com

"Tiny", "elegant" and oh-so-"very French", this "true bistro" in Rice Village features an ever-changing chalkboard menu of "terrific" Gallic cuisine complemented by "well-priced" wines; perpetually "packed" conditions mean it can get "a little noisy", but "attentive service" keeps the ambiance "charming."

Chez Nous Ⓢ *French*   27 | 22 | 23 | E

Humble | 217 S. Ave. G. (bet. Granberry & Staitti Sts.) | 281-446-6717 | www.cheznousfrenchrestaurant.com

Those who "don't mind driving out to Humble" are rewarded with this Gallic "gem" where "country French" cuisine is crafted using fresh-from-the-garden ingredients; "everything is first class", from the prices to the "professional" service and the "cozy" ambiance that's "old-fashioned in a good way" (think "your great aunt's living room"); P.S. jackets suggested.

Churrascos S American
26 | 22 | 24 | E

Lower Shepherd | 2055 Westheimer Rd. (Shepherd Dr.) | 713-527-8300
Southwest Houston | 9705 Westheimer Rd. (Gessner Rd.) | 713-952-1988
www.cordua.com

Offering a "different take on the Texas steakhouse", these South American grills from the Cordúa family furnish "über-flavorful" meats ("so tender you can cut them with a butter knife") capped with "excellent" cocktails and a "tremendous" tres leches cake for dessert; they're somewhat "pricey", but a "polished", "modern" look and "welcoming" hospitality mean they never fail to "impress."

Da Marco 🖂🅜 Italian
27 | 22 | 25 | E

Montrose | 1520 Westheimer Rd. (bet. Ridgewood & Windsor Sts.) | 713-807-8857 | www.damarcohouston.com

"Simply outstanding" praise patrons of chef/co-owner Marco Wiles' Montrose "classic" – and Houston's Most Popular restaurant – where a well-heeled crowd sups on "exciting", "sophisticated" Northern Italian cuisine in an "understated" former home; "yes, it's crowded, noisy and expensive", but service is "well tuned", if occasionally "rushed", and "the food never lets you down"; P.S. don't miss the "chalkboard specials."

Damian's Cucina Italiana 🖂 Italian
27 | 21 | 26 | E

Midtown | 3011 Smith St. (bet. Anita & Rosalie Sts.) | 713-522-0439 | www.damians.com

"Steady as she goes", this "old-school" Midtown Italian lures "business", "social" and theatergoing types with "consistently excellent" renditions of red-sauce favorites; a few find it "a little stuffy", but "excellent" service compensates and supporters swear "you can always count on it" for a special meal.

Del Frisco's Double Eagle Steak House Steak
26 | 25 | 25 | VE

Galleria | 5061 Westheimer Rd. (bet. Post Oak Blvd. & Sage Rd.) | 713-355-2600 | www.delfriscos.com

"When you want to impress" – especially "on the company dime" – this high-end chophouse chain fits the bill with "top-flight steaks", a well-stocked wine cellar and "spectacular" desserts; it thrives in "handsome" digs done up in "dark, rich woods" with "lots of brass" making for a "consistent", if somewhat predictable, experience.

Eddie V's Prime Seafood Seafood/Steak
27 | 26 | 25 | E

Memorial | CityCentre | 12848 Queensbury Ln. (I-10) | 832-200-2380
Upper Kirby District | West Ave. | 2800 Kirby Dr. (Westheimer Rd.) | 713-874-1800
www.eddiev.com

A "class act", this Austin-bred chainlet with links in Houston offers a "first-rate experience on all counts", from the "fabulous" steaks and seafood (including "amazing fresh oysters" and crab) to the "professional" service and "modern", leather-trimmed quarters; given the "expense-account" pricing, many seek out the "half-price apps" deals during happy hour.

	FOOD	DECOR	SERVICE	COST

Glass Wall ⓜ American
27 | 22 | 25 | E

Heights | 933 Studewood St. (10th St.) | 713-868-7930 |
www.glasswalltherestaurant.com

A "stunning mix" of "fresh", local ingredients turns up in the "sophisticated" New American dishes (think "higher-end comfort food") at this Heights "favorite" where the fare is bolstered by "daring", "spot-on" wine pairings from sommelier/co-owner Shepard Ross; add in "a simple, yet elegant" modern setting with an open kitchen, and "the only negative is the noise level"; P.S. the Food score does not reflect the departure of chef Lance Fegen.

Hugo's Mexican
26 | 22 | 25 | M

Montrose | 1600 Westheimer Rd. (Mandell St.) | 713-524-7744 |
www.hugosrestaurant.net

This upscale Montrose Mexican is known for its "sophisticated, nuanced" dishes plated with an "innovative, elegant twist"; the contemporary space is "loud", but "polished service" plus premium margaritas and plenty of "fine wines" keep most patrons happy; P.S. be sure to reserve ahead for Sunday's "fabulous brunch."

Indika ⓜ Indian
26 | 22 | 24 | E

Montrose | 516 Westheimer Rd. (Whitney St.) | 713-524-2170 |
www.indikausa.com

"Nouvelle" spins on traditional recipes distinguish this "delightful" lower Montrose Indian from chef-owner Anita Jaisinghani who sends out "beautiful", "bright-flavored" dishes, some with "enough spice to make you swoon"; an "upscale" contemporary setting, "knowledgeable" service and an "inspired" cocktail list are clues that it's "not cheap", but certainly "worth making a habit of."

Kanomwan ⓩ Thai
28 | 8 | 13 | I

Neartown | 736½ Telephone Rd. (Lockwood St.) | 713-923-4230

Gastronomes are known to gush over this Neartown BYO Thai (aka 'Telephone Thai') whipping up "fabulous" food at "unbeatable" prices; just bear in mind you'll have to "put up with" no-frills decor and endearingly "cranky" service.

Le Mistral French
28 | 26 | 25 | E

West Houston | 1400 Eldridge Pkwy. (Briar Forest Dr.) | 832-379-8322 |
www.lemistralhouston.com

"Spectacular" sums up this West Houston French rated the city's No. 1 for Food, where the Denis brothers roll out "beautiful" Provençal-accented plates and other Gallic dishes (the chocolate soufflé is a highlight) in a "lovely" white-tablecloth setting; prices are high, but "superior" service sets the stage for a "special meal."

Mark's American Cuisine American
28 | 27 | 27 | VE

Montrose | 1658 Westheimer Rd. (bet. Dunlavy & Ralph Sts.) |
713-523-3800 | www.marks1658.com

Housed in a "splendid" "old church" in Montrose, this New American from chef Mark Cox delivers a "heavenly" experience, with an "outstanding", "unfussy" menu based on seasonal ingredients, a "deep wine list" and service that's "unobtrusive", but always at the ready; indeed, even if the prices can feel a bit "hellish", most surveyors swear it's "not to be missed."

Masraff's ☒ *Continental*   27 | - | 25 | E

Galleria | 1753 Post Oak Blvd. (San Felipe St.) | 713-355-1975 | www.masraffs.com

"They take good care of their customers" at this family-owned "gem" where the "personal touch" shows in the "wonderful" Continental fare and coddling service; as for the bill, it's appropriately "expensive"; P.S. post-Survey, it moved to the Galleria, outdating the Decor score.

Morton's The Steakhouse *Steak*   26 | 23 | 25 | VE

Downtown | 1001 McKinney St. (bet. Fannin & Main Sts.) | 713-659-3700
Galleria | Centre at Post Oak | 5000 Westheimer Rd. (Post Oak Blvd.) | 713-629-1946
www.mortons.com

"Corporate types" clamor for the "massive" steaks and "wonderful" sides and wines at these "manly" Texas outposts of the nationwide chophouse chain; they're "consistent", from the "top-notch" service to the "dark", "noisy" settings and premium prices, and if some find them "nothing special", they're "rarely disappointing" either.

Pappadeaux *Cajun/Seafood*   22 | 19 | 20 | M
(aka Café Pappadeaux)

Medical Center | 2525 S. Loop W. (bet. Buffalo Spdwy. & Kirby Dr.) | 713-665-3155
Champions | 7110 FM 1960 W. (Cutten Rd.) | 281-580-5245
Galleria | 6015 Westheimer Rd. (Greenridge Dr.) | 713-782-6310
Memorial | 10499 Katy Frwy. (bet. Attingham Dr. & Town & Country Blvd.) | 713-722-0221
Northwest Houston | 13080 Hwy. 290 (bet. Hollister St. & Northwest Central Dr.) | 713-460-1203
Upper Kirby District | 2410 Richmond Ave. (Kirby Dr.) | 713-527-9137
West Houston | 12109 Westheimer Rd. (Houston Center Blvd.) | 281-497-1110
Stafford | 12711 Southwest Frwy. (bet. Hwy. 90A & Kirkwood Rd.) | 281-240-5533
The Woodlands | 18165 I-45 S. (Shenandoah Park Dr.) | 936-321-4200
www.pappas.com

Though it's "popular", opinions split on this "N'Awlins"-inspired chain; while it pleases the "masses" with "accessible" renditions of Cajun "classics", "value" pricing and portions that "guarantee leftovers", detractors dis "blah" fare and "cookie-cutter" "faux" Louisiana looks.

Pappas Bros. Steakhouse ☒ *Steak*   28 | 25 | 26 | E

Galleria | 5839 Westheimer Rd. (bet. Augusta & Bering Drs.) | 713-780-7352 | www.pappasbros.com

Smitten carnivores swear "it doesn't get any better" than this Pappas family "flagship" in Houston where the "luscious", "perfectly marbled" steaks "melt in your mouth"; the "memorable" meals are enhanced by "outstanding" wines, "fawning" service and a "lavish" 1920s-inspired setting – just "be prepared to shell out the big bucks."

NEW Philippe Restaurant +   - | - | - | M
Lounge ☒ *American/French*

Galleria | 1800 Post Oak Blvd. (Ambassador Way) | 713-439-1000 | www.philippehouston.com

Chef Philippe Schmit makes his much-anticipated return to the Houston dining scene with this slick, moderate-to-pricey Galleria-area hybrid of restaurant and lounge and American and French cooking traditions, featuring playful Gallic interpretations of Texan classics (e.g. spicy duck confit tamales, burgundy beef cheeks); the space features a first-floor zinc bar with its own menu, and a stylish industrial-contemporary upstairs dining room with contrasting light and dark hues.

Ruth's Chris Steak House *Steak*
26 | 23 | 25 | E

Galleria | 6213 Richmond Ave. (Greenridge Dr.) | 713-789-2333 | www.ruthschris.com

"Always a hit with the expense-account crowd", this "steadfast" chain "pampers" patrons with "thick", "buttery" steaks and "top-notch" service in "clubby" surroundings; it all adds up to a "quality" experience, though one with "few surprises, positive or negative."

Shade *American*
26 | 21 | 24 | M

Heights | 250 W. 19th St. (bet. Rutland & Yale Sts.) | 713-863-7500 | www.shadeheights.com

A pioneer in bringing "sophistication to the Heights", this "casually elegant" spot draws a "fab-looking" crowd for "fresh, flavorful", "not-overly-complicated" New American cooking; with an "efficient staff" and an "inviting" modern setting done up in neutral hues, the "only problem is the noise."

Tony Mandola's *Seafood*
26 | 21 | 25 | M

River Oaks | 1212 Waugh Dr. (Clay St.) | 713-528-3474 | www.tonymandolas.com

"Regulars abound" at this longtime seafooder in new River Oaks digs from the "ubiquitous" Mandola family mixing up "excellent" Gulf Coast-style classics, ultra-"fresh" oysters and a smattering of Italian standards; tabs are somewhat "pricey", but with an experience this "reliable", no one seems to mind.

Tony's 🅐 *Continental/Italian*
27 | 27 | 27 | VE

Greenway Plaza Area | 3755 Richmond Ave. (Timmons Ln.) | 713-622-6778 | www.tonyshouston.com

"La crème de la crème" of the local dining scene, this longtime Greenway Plaza charmer shows that Tony Vallone "hasn't lost his touch" with "top-notch" Italian-Continental cuisine made even better by a "four-star" staff and "stunning" art-filled setting, respectively rated tops for Service and Decor in Houston; though it certainly sets the "gold standard" in the area, many find "you need to be a regular" with deep pockets to best appreciate it.

Vic & Anthony's *Steak*
26 | 25 | 26 | E

Downtown | 1510 Texas Ave. (La Branch St.) | 713-228-1111 | www.vicandanthonys.com

This "high-end" Downtown steakhouse near Minute Maid Park "hits a home run" with "cooked-to-perfection" meats, "generous" sides and an "extensive" wine collection priced "for Enron executives who haven't been caught yet"; "elegant service" and a dark "modern bordello" setting increase the appeal – if you don't mind "having to empty your wallet", it doesn't get "much better than this."

Kansas City

TOP FOOD RANKING

	Restaurant	Cuisine
29	Justus Drugstore	American
28	Bluestem	American
	Michael Smith	American
27	Oklahoma Joe's	BBQ
	Le Fou Frog	French
	Capital Grille	Steak
	American	American
	Piropos	Argentinean/Steak
26	Extra Virgin	Mediterranean
	Starker's	American
	Jasper's	Italian
	Room 39	American
	Webster House	Eclectic

American Restaurant, The ⌧ *American*   27 | 24 | 27 | VE

Crown Center | 200 E. 25th St. (E. Pershing Rd.), MO | 816-545-8001 | www.theamericankc.com

"Celebrated chef" Debbie Gold "continues to serve up wonderful" New American cuisine "on the cutting edge" at this Crown Center "landmark" with a "fabulous skyline view", "extensive wine cellar" and "highly trained" staff; just "bring your gold card" and "dress well", though some suggest the dining room itself "needs a makeover"; P.S. lunch is offered the first Friday of every month.

Arthur Bryant's *BBQ*   25 | 12 | 17 | I

Kansas City, West | Legends at the Kansas Speedway | 1702 Village W. Pkwy. (Prairie Crossing), KS | 913-788-7500

18th & Vine | 1727 Brooklyn Ave. (18th St.), MO | 816-231-1123

Northland | Ameristar Casino Hotel Kansas City | 3200 North Ameristar Dr. (Birmingham Rd.), MO | 816-414-7474

www.arthurbryantsbbq.com

"Forget about Memphis and Texas": since 1930, this "real-deal" "BBQ heaven" in the Historic Jazz District has had "every segment of the KC community", "presidents and celebrities" queuing for "incredible sandwiches", "fabulous ribs" and "giant piles of fries"; true, the "disheveled" decor and "Army-mess-line" service is an "acquired taste" (not unlike its trademark "vinegary sauce"), but insiders insist it "can't be missed"; P.S. there are offshoots at the Kansas Speedway and Ameristar Casino.

Bluestem Ⓜ *American*   28 | 24 | 26 | E

Westport | 900 Westport Rd. (Roanoke Rd.), MO | 816-561-1101 | www.bluestemkc.com

For a "world-class meal", Westporters turn to this "true gem" from "culinary rock star" Colby Garrelts, whose "progressive" New American cuisine – crafted from "locally grown produce and meats" – is "fresh, balanced" and "beautifully presented"; enhanced by "informed service", it's "expensive" but "worth it", though a "comfy" adjacent bar that draws both "blue bloods and people in blue jeans" offers "substantial tastes at a fraction of the price."

Bristol Seafood Grill *Seafood*
`25` `25` `24` `M`

Downtown KCMO | Power & Light District | 51 E. 14th St. (Main St.), MO | 816-448-6007
Leawood | Town Center Plaza | 5400 W. 119th St. (Nall Ave.), KS | 913-663-5777
www.bristolseafoodgrill.com

They may be "as far from an ocean as you can get", but this "adult respite" in Leawood and its Downtown KCMO outpost feature a "constantly evolving" menu of "scrumptious" seafood prepared with "care and imagination"; a "superior staff" supplements the "elegant atmosphere", and while tabs can be "pricey", wallet-watchers fishing for deals note that lunch is a "real bargain."

Capital Grille *Steak*
`27` `26` `27` `E`

Country Club Plaza | Country Club Plaza | 4740 Jefferson St. (bet. W. 47th & 48th Sts.), MO | 816-531-8345 | www.thecapitalgrille.com

In this "steak town", "you have to be good" to succeed (especially if you're a "national chain") – and this Country Club Plaza destination "keeps pace" with "outstanding" chops and an "excellent wine list"; the "oaky" interior is "perfect for power dinners or special occasions" and overseen by a "professional", "pampering" staff, which makes it easier to swallow tabs that "aren't for the light of wallet."

Extra Virgin 🗷 *Mediterranean*
`26` `23` `24` `M`

Crossroads | 1900 Main St. (19th St.), MO | 816-842-2205 | www.extravirginkc.com

Michael Smith's "innovative" small plates – an "exceptional" mélange of Med flavors "geared towards adventurous diners" – "bring Europe to the Crossroads" at this "must-visit"; even better, the "bountiful libations" and "generous samples" of "haute cuisine without the haute attitude" (enjoyed in the "bar-centric" dining room or on the patio) can be had "without dropping a chunk of change."

Fiorella's Jack Stack *BBQ*
`26` `22` `23` `M`

Crossroads | Freight House | 101 W. 22nd St. (Wyandotte St.), MO | 816-472-7427
Country Club Plaza | 4747 Wyandotte St. (bet. 47th St. & Ward Pkwy.), MO | 816-531-7427
Overland Park | 9520 Metcalf Ave. (95th St.), KS | 913-385-7427
Martin City | 13441 Holmes Rd. (135th St.), MO | 816-942-9141
www.jackstackbbq.com

"KC BBQ goes upscale" "without losing its soul" at this "fab" foursome featuring "smokin' good" grub, like "burnt ends and beans"; even if the "lovely surroundings" make some "feel bad about eating with their fingers", they're still "noisy and crowded", which makes sense since they're voted the area's Most Popular restaurants.

Jasper's 🗷 *Italian*
`26` `22` `25` `E`

South KC | Watts Mill | 1201 W. 103rd St. (State Line Rd.), MO | 816-941-6600 | www.jasperskc.com

It's in a South KC "strip center", but step inside this "family-owned" "classic" and you'll feel like a "welcome guest in their home", and the "outstanding" Italian fare "makes it even better"; whether you're "entertaining out-of-town guests" or having a "romantic evening", it "never fails to please", especially if you nab a seat on the enclosed patio; P.S. thrifty types can nosh for "under $20" in the on-site deli.

Justus Drugstore: A Restaurant ⓜ American

| 29 | 21 | 25 | E |

Smithville | 106 W. Main St. (bet. Bridge & Mill Sts.), MO | 816-532-2300 | www.drugstorerestaurant.com

Even the "pickiest foodies" agree it's "worth the drive" to this Smithville "locavore heaven" to sample chef/co-owner Jonathan Justus' "exceptional" New American fare, which draws on "French and Napa influences" and earns the No. 1 Food rating for the KC area; there's also "attentive service with a leisurely pace" (so "don't go if you're in a rush"), "house-recipe cocktails" and a "pleasant", somewhat "funky" setting in an old drugstore, prompting partisans to proclaim "my prescription can be filled here anytime."

Le Fou Frog ⓜ French

| 27 | 20 | 24 | E |

River Market | 400 E. Fifth St. (Oak St.), MO | 816-474-6060 | www.lefoufrog.com

A "true cast of characters" "with a sense of humor" serves up "fantastic" French fare at this "charming" River Market bistro that simply "swirls with joie de vivre"; the "tiny" place is "crowded, noisy", "dark" and "not cheap", but no matter: it's "as close to France as you'll find in KC – and worth the investment."

Lidia's Italian

| 25 | 26 | 24 | M |

Crossroads | 101 W. 22nd St. (Baltimore Ave.), MO | 816-221-3722 | www.lidias-kc.com

"Still a favorite in KC", this Crossroads "mainstay" from celeb chef Lidia Bastianich offers "superb" Italian cuisine infused with "sublime flavor combinations" and complemented by "knock-your-socks-off" wines that are "easy on the pocketbook" (the food's "reasonably priced" too); you can "dine outdoors" and "watch the trains go by" (it's across from Union Station) or let the "exemplary" staff pamper you in a "gorgeous space" adorned with "magnificent" chandeliers and a towering "slate fireplace."

Michael Smith ⓩⓜ American

| 28 | 24 | 26 | E |

Crossroads | 1900 Main St. (19th St.), MO | 816-842-2202 | www.michaelsmithkc.com

"Pedigreed chef" Michael Smith "crafts dishes that are exciting, even daring" at his eponymous Crossroads New American, a "moderately expensive" "special-occasion spot" serving up "complex yet elemental" food "you can't make at home"; "much quieter" than adjacent sib Extra Virgin, it features "elegant" decor and "attentive" service, all the more reason to "eat here before New York kidnaps the place."

Oklahoma Joe's Barbecue ⓩ BBQ

| 27 | 15 | 19 | I |

Rosedale | 3002 W. 47th Ave. (Mission Rd.), KS | 913-722-3366
Olathe | 11950 S. Strang Line Rd. (119th St.), KS | 913-782-6858
www.oklahomajoesbbq.com

The "kitschy" "gas station location is part of the charm" of this KCKS "BBQ icon" that fuels 'cue-noisseurs with "championship-quality"

FOOD DECOR SERVICE COST

vittles, including some of the "best pulled pork in town"; it all comes with "order-it-pick-it-up" service, "long lines" and "reasonable prices"; P.S. the Olathe venue features a more traditional restaurant atmosphere.

Piropos *Argentinean/Steak* 27 | 26 | 25 | E

Northland | Briarcliff Vill. | 4141 N. Mulberry Dr. (Briarcliff Pkwy.), MO | 816-741-3600
Parkville | 1 W. First St. (West St.), KS | 816-741-9800 🖪 🅜
www.piroposkc.com

"Awesome steaks" with a "South American twist" make the cut at this "worth-a-trip" Argentinean venue in Northland; it's a "little expensive", but with "amazing service", "scrumptious desserts" and a "breathtaking view" of the skyline, just about everyone "wants to go back"; P.S. the Parkville branch opened post-Survey.

Room 39 🖪 *American* 26 | 21 | 25 | M

39th Street | 1719 W. 39th St. (bet. Bell & Genessee Sts.), MO | 816-753-3939
Leawood | Mission Farms | 10561 Mission Rd. (bet. I-435 & 103rd St.), KS | 913-648-7639
www.rm39.com

"Local from the stock in the saucepans to the art on the walls", this "small" "neighborhood gem" on "eclectic" 39th Street puts "considerable thought" into its "ever-changing menu" of "robust", "farm-fresh" American comfort food; "quaint" decor and "caring" staffers add to the allure; P.S. Leawood has less "atmosphere" but is still "worth a trip."

Starker's Restaurant 🖪 *American* 26 | 25 | 26 | E

Country Club Plaza | 201 W. 47th St. (Wyandotte St.), MO | 816-753-3565 | www.starkersrestaurant.com

"What a wine list" sigh sippers who frequent this "intimate" Country Club Plaza "treat" spotlighting the "creative" concoctions of chef-owner John McClure; perhaps prices for the "fresh", "seasonal" New American dishes run "in the high range", but "personal service" helps ensure you're in for a "special evening."

Webster House 🖪 *Eclectic* 26 | 27 | 25 | M

Crossroads | 1644 Wyandotte St. (17th St.), MO | 816-221-4713 | www.websterhousekc.com

Set on the second floor of a "converted schoolhouse" (with an antiques shop downstairs), this "sedate" Crossroads "destination" serves up "imaginatively prepared" Eclectic fare to everyone from "ladies who lunch" to culture vultures bound for the "opera or symphony"; if the "lovely" vintage furnishings and stained-glass windows are a "treat" for the eyes, "flawless service" makes it even better; P.S. a chef change occurred post-Survey, possibly outdating the Food score.

Las Vegas

TOP FOOD RANKING

	Restaurant	Cuisine
28	Joël Robuchon	French
	Todd's Unique Dining	Eclectic
	Steak House	Steak
	Raku	Japanese
	Sen of Japan	Japanese
	Guy Savoy	French
	Picasso	French
	L'Atelier/Joël Robuchon	French
27	Tableau	American
	Michael Mina	Seafood
	Lotus of Siam	Thai
	Le Cirque	French
	Prime	Steak
	Michael's	Continental
	StripSteak	Steak
	Del Frisco's	Steak
	SW Steakhouse	Steak
	Delmonico	Steak
	Nobu	Japanese
	Charlie Palmer	Steak

Aureole *American*   25 | 27 | 25 | VE

Strip | Mandalay Bay Resort | 3950 Las Vegas Blvd. S. (Hacienda Ave.) |
702-632-7401 | www.charliepalmer.com
The Vegas spin-off of the "NY original", this "dazzling" New American
in Mandalay Bay showcases the cooking of super-chef Charlie Palmer
served in "chicer than chic" digs by a "phenomenal" crew; even though
the cost of the meals (some areas are prix fixe only) is "expensive", no
one seems to notice given its much remarked upon "gimmick": a "majestic wine tower" where "James Bond"-ish gals in tight "cat-burglar"
outfits ascend to fetch your bottle, *Mission Impossible*-style.

Bouchon *French*   26 | 24 | 25 | E

Strip | Venetian Hotel | 3355 Las Vegas Blvd. S., 9th fl. (Sands Ave.) |
702-414-6200 | www.bouchonbistro.com
"As good as the Napa original", this "little bit of Paris" in the Venetian
from top toque Thomas Keller offers "lick-your-plate-clean" French
bistro cuisine in a "beautiful", Adam Tihany–designed setting; it's "expensive" and "you'll need a GPS" to find its ninth-floor nook, but payoffs
include "impeccable" service, "comfortable" vibes and a "delicious"
experience voted Most Popular in Vegas; P.S. breakfast is "a must."

Charlie Palmer Steak ⊠Ⓜ *Steak*   27 | 25 | 26 | VE

Strip | Four Seasons Hotel | 3960 Las Vegas Blvd. S. (Four Seasons Dr.) |
702-632-5120 | www.charliepalmer.com
"If it's Charlie Palmer, it has to be good", and this "elegant bastion of
all things bovine" in the Four Seasons is no exception, from the "lus-

cious" dry-aged steaks to the "top-notch" service and "superb" wine list; it's "pricey" enough that you may have to "go buffet the next night", but definitely "worth the treat."

Del Frisco's Double Eagle | 27 | 24 | 26 | VE |
Steak House *Steak*

East of Strip | 3925 Paradise Rd. (Corporate Dr.) | 702-796-0063 | www.delfriscos.com

"Double thumbs up" to this traditional steakhouse chain link east of the Strip, known for "wonderful slabs of meat", an "extensive" wine selection and "attentive" service; tinkling ivories set a "romantic" tone in the "worn" but "pleasant" dark-wood dining room, while regulars plant themselves at the "fun" bar with martinis so "large" they're difficult to drain "without falling off the chair."

Delmonico Steakhouse *Steak* | 27 | 24 | 26 | VE |

Strip | Venetian Hotel | 3355 Las Vegas Blvd. S. (bet. Flamingo Rd. & Sands Ave.) | 702-414-3737 | www.emerils.com

Another Emeril Lagasse "success story", this "quality" beef palace in the Venetian showcases "all the perks of fine dining", including a "gold-standard rib-eye", "unobtrusive" service and a "relaxed" atmosphere; still, surveyors split on the "austere", "cream-colored" setting: "subdued" vs. "not so hot."

Guy Savoy M *French* | 28 | 27 | 28 | VE |

Strip | Caesars Palace Hotel | 3570 Las Vegas Blvd. S. (Flamingo Rd.) | 877-346-4642 | www.caesarspalace.com

"Just like the one in Paris, only closer", this "fantabulous" New French in Caesars Palace offers a "once-in-a-lifetime experience" thanks to "transcendent" cooking, "stunning" decor and "flawless", "nicely paced" service from a staff that "does everything for you except chew the food"; *bien sûr*, you'll need "tons of cash" to settle the bill, but its Bubble Bar adjunct provides champagne and small plates for "relative bargain" tabs.

Joël Robuchon *French* | 28 | 27 | 28 | VE |

Strip | MGM Grand Hotel | 3799 Las Vegas Blvd. S. (Tropicana Ave.) | 702-891-7925 | www.mgmgrand.com

Nothing short of a "bucket-list dining experience" awaits in the MGM Grand at this New French "spectacle" from top toque Joël Robuchon, voted No. 1 for Food and Service in Vegas; "beautiful nights out" here include "high attention to detail" on the plate, similar "exceptional" consideration from the "classy" staff and an "opulent", lavender-and-cream setting; even though the "ultraexpensive" bill makes this a "once-in-a-lifetime" visit for some, devotees say it's hard to put a price on "absolute perfection."

Joe's Seafood, Prime Steak & | 26 | 22 | 25 | VE |
Stone Crab *Seafood/Steak*

Strip | Forum Shops at Caesars Palace | 3500 Las Vegas Blvd. S. (Flamingo Rd.) | 702-792-9222 | www.joes.net

"There's a reason" why this surf 'n' turfer in the Forum Shops at Caesars is "always packed": "gold standard"–quality chops and fish (i.e. those "out-of-this-world stone crabs"), delivered in "big", "masculine" digs by a "service-oriented" crew; even though it's "not cheap", most agree it supplies "great bang for the buck" and, unlike the Miami original, "they take reservations."

L'Atelier de Joël Robuchon *French* | 28 | 24 | 26 | VE |

Strip | MGM Grand Hotel | 3799 Las Vegas Blvd. S. (Tropicana Ave.) | 702-891-7358 | www.mgmgrand.com

"More relaxed" atmospherically and (slightly) cheaper than its fancy-pants next-door sibling, Joël Robuchon, this "marvelous" New French in the MGM Grand is best experienced from its "counter seats" offering an "entertaining view of the kitchen"; the "intricate", "small plate-format" meals are served at "twice the speed" of its neighbor, making it a natural for those who "care more about food and less about glamour."

Le Cirque Ⓜ *French* | 27 | 28 | 27 | VE |

Strip | Bellagio Hotel | 3600 Las Vegas Blvd. S. (Flamingo Rd.) | 702-693-7223 | www.bellagio.com

"Back on the upswing", this "wonderful transplant" imported from NYC to the Bellagio offers dining "perfection" via a "fantastic" New French menu accompanied by an "epic wine list"; "outstanding" service and Adam Tihany's "over-the-top" big-top decor further enhance the "special-occasion" vibe, making the "high-end" pricing palatable.

Lotus of Siam *Thai* | 27 | 12 | 21 | M |

East Side | Commercial Center | 953 E. Sahara Ave. (bet. Maryland Pkwy. & State St.) | 702-735-3033 | www.lotusofsiamlv.com

The "ugliest strip mall in America" is the unlikely site of this 25-year-old East Side "gem of gems", much acclaimed as the "gold standard" for some of the most "thoroughly authentic" Northern Thai food outside of Bangkok; its "massive menu" paired with a "fine Riesling collection" comes at a "reasonable price", leaving the "tasteless decor" and "jam-packed" conditions as the only sticking points; P.S. following a "recent expansion", it's somewhat "easier to get in."

Michael Mina *Seafood* | 27 | 25 | 26 | VE |

Strip | Bellagio Hotel | 3600 Las Vegas Blvd. S. (Flamingo Rd.) | 702-693-7223 | www.michaelmina.net

A "remarkable dining experience" awaits at this "civilized" seafooder in the Bellagio from the San Francisco chef, where the "attention to detail" is "wonderful" and the signature lobster pot pie "to die for"; granted, it's "ridiculously expensive" – "what isn't on the Strip?" – but compensations include "impeccable" service and an "elegant" setting.

Michael's *Continental* | 27 | 24 | 27 | VE |

South of Strip | South Point Hotel | 9777 Las Vegas Blvd. S. (Silverado Ranch Blvd.) | 702-796-7111 | www.southpointcasino.com

This "intimate", "out-of-the-way" Continental in the South Point Hotel is a "Vegas legend for a reason", starting with its "throwback" touches like "tableside preparations", "tuxedoed waiters" and ladies' menus sans prices; although it "costs an arm and a leg" to dine here, they "treat you like royalty" and the food is among the city's "finest."

Mon Ami Gabi *French* | 24 | 24 | 23 | E |

Strip | Paris Hotel | 3655 Las Vegas Blvd. S. (bet. Flamingo Rd. & Harmon Ave.) | 702-944-4224 | www.monamigabi.com

Outdoor tables with a "fabulous view" of the "Bellagio water show" make for "perfect people-watching" at this French steakhouse in the

Paris, "one of the Strip's finest sidewalk cafes"; what with the "good food", "affordable" rates and "fun" atmosphere, no wonder it's "always packed" – though some say "location is the major draw" here.

Nobu *Japanese* | 27 | 22 | 23 | VE |

East of Strip | Hard Rock Hotel | 4455 Paradise Rd. (bet. Flamingo Rd. & Harmon Ave.) | 702-693-5090 | www.noburestaurants.com
Sushiphiles undergo "out-of-body experiences" at this Hard Rock Hotel link of Nobu Matsuhisa's "phenomenal" Japanese empire, known for its "memorable" raw fish along with cooked dishes like the "must-order" miso black cod; high rollers go the "super-expensive" omakase route, while conversationalists bring a "hearing aid" and a "megaphone" to cope with the "loud" "party" atmosphere.

Picasso *French* | 28 | 29 | 28 | VE |

Strip | Bellagio Hotel | 3600 Las Vegas Blvd. S. (Flamingo Rd.) | 702-693-7223 | www.bellagio.com
"Fine art" meets "fine dining" at this "sublime" New French in the Bellagio, where chef Julian Serrano's "artful" presentations on the plate complement the "real Picassos" on the walls; the "bend-over-backwards" service is equally "memorable", while the "extraordinary" setting (voted Top Decor in Vegas) mimics a "magnificent art gallery" abetted by outdoor seats with "front-row views of the fountain show"; granted, the "only blue period here is after the bill arrives", but most concur the "sky-high" tabs are worth it for a "once-in-a-lifetime dining experience."

Prime Steakhouse *Steak* | 27 | 27 | 26 | VE |

Strip | Bellagio Hotel | 3600 Las Vegas Blvd. S. (Flamingo Rd.) | 702-693-7223 | www.bellagio.com
The name, the cuts of beef and the location in the Bellagio are all "prime" at this "first-class dining experience" via Jean-Georges Vongerichten, a "serious" steakhouse where the "glitzy" patrons are all treated like "winners, no matter what happens in the casino"; sure, the prices are "extremely high", but the chops are "cooked to perfection" and the chocolate-brown-and-Tiffany-blue setting is "stunningly beautiful", just like the view of the "fountain show" outside.

Raku ●☒ *Japanese* | 28 | 20 | 24 | E |

West Side | 5030 Spring Mountain Rd. (Decatur Blvd.) | 702-367-3511 | www.raku-grill.com
"Not a secret anymore", this "esoteric", sushi-free Japanese in a West Side shopping mall specializes in "amazingly authentic" small plates along with "fresh tofu", "homemade" soy sauce and robata grill items; it's a magnet for "cutting-edge foodies" (and off-duty chefs) given the "inexpensive" tabs, "charming service" and "late-night" hours.

Sen of Japan *Japanese* | 28 | 18 | 25 | E |

West Side | 8480 W. Desert Inn Rd. (Durango Dr.) | 702-871-7781 | www.senofjapan.com
"Strip fine dining without the Strip price tag" is yours at this "neighborhood" Japanese "favorite" on the West Side, where the sushi chef is so "creative" that regulars recommend you "go for the omakase"; "courteous" service and overall "high quality" round out the "enjoyable" picture.

Steak House *Steak*

28 | 20 | 25 | E

Strip | Circus Circus Hotel | 2880 Las Vegas Blvd. S. (bet. Desert Inn Rd. & Sahara Ave.) | 702-794-3767 | www.circuscircus.com

This "old-fashioned" steakhouse – accessed by "walking through the craziness of Circus Circus" – is a "carnivore's delight", with "wonderfully charred" chops served in a "clubby wood atmosphere" by an "attentive", "old-world" crew; fans say that "dollar for dollar", it's the "best value" on the Strip, and the "only reason to enter" the otherwise "low-rent" casino.

StripSteak *Steak*

27 | 23 | 25 | VE

Strip | Mandalay Bay Resort | 3950 Las Vegas Blvd. S. (Mandalay Bay Rd.) | 702-632-7414 | www.mandalaybay.com

The steaks are "poached in butter" before they hit the grill at this "upscale" Mandalay Bay steakhouse via Michael Mina that "stands out from the herd" with its "seared-to-perfection" chops and "even better sauces"; alright, the tabs are "exorbitant" and the acoustics "noisy", but overall it's an "A-1" entry in a "frightfully competitive" genre.

SW Steakhouse *Steak*

27 | 26 | 25 | VE

Strip | Wynn Hotel | 3131 Las Vegas Blvd. S. (bet. Desert Inn & Spring Mountain Rds.) | 702-248-3463 | www.wynnlasvegas.com

"Wonderful" steaks and a "dazzling" view of the "water show" from the patio are the hooks at this "special-occasion" chophouse in the Wynn, where the ambiance is "classy but not stuffy" and the service "super"; sure, it's "certainly not cheap" ("check current mortgage rates before making a reservation"), but many feel this "memorable" dining experience is "as good as it gets."

Tableau *American*

27 | 27 | 27 | E

Strip | Wynn Hotel | 3131 Las Vegas Blvd. S. (bet. Desert Inn & Spring Mountain Rds.) | 888-352-3463 | www.wynnlasvegas.com

A "great place to start the day", this "discreet, little-known" New American in the Wynn's south tower serves breakfast and lunch only in an "intimate" atrium setting with poolside views; the "soothing" atmosphere and "gracious" service lure a mix of "comped tourists" and "high-level execs", none of whom seem to pay much attention to the "above-average" prices.

Todd's Unique Dining 🗷 *Eclectic*

28 | 20 | 27 | E

Henderson | 4350 E. Sunset Rd. (Green Valley Pkwy.) | 702-259-8633 | www.toddsunique.com

Living up to its name, this "truly unique" Eclectic in Henderson is "as good as anything on the Strip", serving a "flavorful, well-prepared" menu washed down with an "extensive" selection of wine for an "economical" price; it may be "nothing to look at", but no one minds since hands-on chef-owner Todd Clore "actually presides over the kitchen."

Los Angeles

TOP FOOD RANKING

	Restaurant	Cuisine
29	Matsuhisa	Japanese
28	Angelini Osteria	Italian
	Asanebo	Japanese
	Mélisse	American/French
	Urasawa	Japanese
	Sushi Zo	Japanese
	Café 14	Continental
	Leila's*	Californian
	Providence*	American/Seafood
	Takao	Japanese
	Pizzeria Mozza	Pizza
27	Mori Sushi	Japanese
	Nobu Malibu	Japanese
	Sushi Nozawa	Japanese
	Jitlada	Thai
	Water Grill	Seafood
	Hamasaku	Japanese
	Saam/The Bazaar	Eclectic
	Spago	Californian
	Brandywine	Continental
	Hatfield's	American
	Osteria Mozza	Italian
	Piccolo	Italian
	Lucques	Californian/Mediterranean
	Bashan	American
	Katsu-ya	Japanese

Angelini Osteria Ⓜ *Italian*   28 | 18 | 24 | E

Beverly Boulevard | 7313 Beverly Blvd. (bet. Fuller Ave. & Poinsettia Pl.) | 323-297-0070 | www.angeliniosteria.com

LA's No. 1 Italian, this "splurge"-worthy Beverly Boulevard "treasure" "takes you to Tuscany" with chef-owner Gino Angelini's "delicious" fare, from "succulent" roast meats to "sublime" signature lasagna; add in a "charming" staff, and the "crammed", "cacophonous" space seems a "minor inconvenience" for such a "memorable" meal.

Asanebo Ⓜ *Japanese*   28 | 17 | 24 | VE

Studio City | 11941 Ventura Blvd. (bet. Carpenter & Radford Aves.) | 818-760-3348

"Celebs and foodies literally rub shoulders" at the "crowded" bar of this Japanese "standout" on Studio City's sushi row showcasing chef Tetsuya Nakao's "delectable", "top-end" creations "painstakingly constructed" from "extremely fresh" fish; though it thrives in a "no-frills" strip-mall setting, don't let appearances deceive you – the "steep" bills are not for the faint of wallet.

---

* Indicates a tie with restaurant above

	FOOD	DECOR	SERVICE	COST

Bashan ☒ *American* — 27 | 20 | 25 | E

Montrose | 3459 N. Verdugo Rd. (bet. Oceanview & Sunview Blvds.) | 818-541-1532 | www.bashanrestaurant.com

A "little treasure" hidden away "off-the-beaten-track" in Montrose, this New American delivers an "eating adventure" via chef Nadav Bashan's "fantastic", "ambitious" dishes fashioned from farmer's market ingredients; factor in "exceptional service", an "intimate" setting and prices deemed "reasonable given the caliber", and there's no doubt why locals feels so "lucky to have it" in their neck of the woods.

Bazaar by José Andrés, The *Spanish* — 27 | 27 | 23 | VE

Beverly Hills | SLS at Beverly Hills | 465 S. La Cienega Blvd. (Clifton Way) | 310-246-5555 | www.thebazaar.com

"The innovation is endless" at this "cutting-edge" "dining-as-theater" "adventure" in the SLS Hotel from chef José Andrés, where an "eager" staff sets out "daring but delicious" Spanish-inspired small plates so "avant-garde" you "feel like a judge on *Iron Chef*"; the "noisy", "extravagant" Philippe Starck–designed setting features various "wacky" "museumlike" rooms (including a patisserie that would make "Willy Wonka" proud), and even "the valet line is a scene", so although some say "overrated", for most it's well worth the "splurge."

Brandywine ☒ *Continental* — 27 | 20 | 26 | E

Woodland Hills | 22757 Ventura Blvd. (Fallbrook Ave.) | 818-225-9114

"Small in size, but grand in performance", this "fine-dining" room in Woodland Hills "impresses" with "delicious" Continental cuisine and "attentive" service overseen by a "charming" husband-and-wife team; even if some consider the French country decor a bit "dated", loyal fans find it hard to beat and well worth the drive "for a special occasion."

Café 14 ☒ *Continental* — 28 | 22 | 25 | E

Agoura Hills | Reyes Adobe Plaza | 30315 Canwood St. (Reyes Adobe Rd.) | 818-991-9560 | www.cafe-14.com

A "wonderful surprise" "right off the freeway", this Agoura Hills eatery presents "outstanding" Continental cuisine deemed "pretty fancy for a strip mall"; indeed, the low-key contemporary setting's not much to speak of, but service is "smart and respectful", and all "is forgotten" once "you taste the divine" food.

Hamasaku ☒ *Japanese* — 27 | 19 | 24 | E

West LA | 11043 Santa Monica Blvd. (Sepulveda Blvd.) | 310-479-7636 | www.hamasakula.com

"Swimmingly fresh" sushi and a "cornucopia" of "creative" rolls "named after celebs" headline an "adventurous" menu at this "superlative" West LA Japanese also offering a "kick-ass omakase"; though it's hidden behind a nondescript facade, it's a "favorite" for the "rich and famous", complete with "VIP" service and prices.

Hatfield's *American* — 27 | 25 | 26 | VE

Melrose | 6703 Melrose Ave. (Citrus Ave.) | 323-935-2977 | www.hatfieldsrestaurant.com

"Impeccable", "market-fresh" ingredients are transformed into "mind-blowingly delicious" New American dishes at this "exceptional" Melrose entry from husband-and-wife team Quinn and Karen Hatfield that "hits the mark every time" with "haute but not snobby" cuisine (including a "memorable" chef's tasting menu) served by a "knowledgeable" crew that "doesn't rush you"; the "modern" setting is "gorgeous" too, though "it helps to have a sugar daddy footing the bill"; P.S. a more casual iteration is opening on La Brea in 2012.

Jitlada Thai

27 | 11 | 17 | M

East Hollywood | 5233½ W. Sunset Blvd. (bet. Harvard Blvd. & Kingsley Dr.) | 323-667-9809 | www.jitladala.com

"Spicy, spicy, spicy" Thai food "scintillates the senses" at this "glorious" East Hollywood "go-to for adventurous foodies", offering not only "Bangkok fire" but a "multidimensional" "gastronomic" experience in a strip-mall "hole-in-the-wall"; service that can be "slow" "somehow adds to the authenticity and charm" and is elevated a bit by the staff's "awesome" recommendations.

Katsu-ya Japanese

27 | 13 | 19 | E

Encino | 16542 Ventura Blvd. (Hayvenhurst Ave.) | 818-788-2396
Studio City | 11680 Ventura Blvd. (Colfax Ave.) | 818-985-6976
www.katsu-yagroup.com

Admirers "never tire" of chef-owner Katsuya Uechi's Studio City "original" and its Encino offshoot, presenting "sublime" raw fish, "unique" cooked dishes and "can't-miss" "blackboard specials"; the "long lines", "crammed", "super-bland" rooms and "off-the-charts" noise levels are downsides, but if you can roll with it all, it's "incredible for the price."

Leila's ◧ Californian

28 | 20 | 26 | E

Oak Park | Oak Park Plaza | 706 Lindero Canyon Rd. (Kanan Rd.) | 818-707-6939 | www.leilasrestaurant.com

Sure, it's "hidden in an Oak Park shopping center", but "foodies" swear this upscale Californian is a "major player" on the strength of its "creative" entrees and "off-the-hook small plates" that pack an "amazing combination of flavors", complemented by an "extensive" wine list; the service is "superb" and the earth-toned decor is, well, "good enough", rounding out a pricey "treat" that is "absolutely worth the drive."

Lucques Californian/Mediterranean

27 | 24 | 25 | E

West Hollywood | 8474 Melrose Ave. (La Cienega Blvd.) | 323-655-6277 | www.lucques.com

"Superior in every respect", this "civilized" WeHo "destination" from "celebrated" chef/co-owner Suzanne Goin is a "foodies' delight" thanks to her "inspired" Cal-Med "creations" featuring "obscure, yet perfectly matched ingredients", plucked "fresh" from the "farmer's market", and a "fantastic wine list" assembled by co-owner Caroline Styne; "stellar service" and the "casually elegant space" set in "Harold Lloyd's carriage house" with a "charming courtyard" round out the "standout" experience, and while it's "pricey", the prix fixe Sunday suppers are a "bargain."

Matsuhisa Japanese

29 | 18 | 25 | VE

Beverly Hills | 129 N. La Cienega Blvd. (bet. Clifton Way & Wilshire Blvd.) | 310-659-9639 | www.nobumatsuhisa.com

The "original temple" that made "master chef" Nobu Matsuhisa "a household name", this Beverly Hills "masterpiece" regains LA's top title for Food in this year's Survey thanks to "superlative" sushi and "innovative", Peruvian-accented Japanese "works of art"; the "staff is amazing", while the setting is "simple" and "unassuming" relative to the "hype", and though the "bills have many digits before the decimal", most deem it a "must."

Mélisse ☒Ⓜ *American/French* | 28 | 26 | 27 | VE

Santa Monica | 1104 Wilshire Blvd. (11th St.) | 310-395-0881 | www.melisse.com

The *"ne plus ultra"* of French–New American cuisine, Josiah Citrin's Santa Monica "gem" is like a "trip to heaven and back" for "serious foodies" with its "top-notch" prix fixe menus and "brilliant wine pairings", "delivered with genuine hospitality" in an "intimate", "hushed" setting; sure, some find it "overpriced", and it leaves a few cold ("death by a thousand small, strange courses"), but most say if you're going to "splurge", this "transcendent dining experience" is "worth every $100."

Mori Sushi ☒ *Japanese* | 27 | 19 | 24 | VE

West LA | 11500 W. Pico Blvd. (Gateway Blvd.) | 310-479-3939 | www.morisushi.org

Afishionados advise "get the omakase" at this West LA Japanese, and sure, it'll cost "Mori of your money", but "it's worth it" for "exquisite" sushi made with the "freshest" seafood and "brilliant" specially grown rice, served on the chef's own "incredible handmade" ceramics; "warm" service and a room graced with "beautiful art" round out an experience so "sublime" that even "fish want to come here when they die."

Nobu Malibu *Japanese* | 27 | 20 | 23 | VE

Malibu | Malibu Country Mart | 3835 Cross Creek Rd. (bet. Civic Ctr. Way & PCH) | 310-317-9140 | www.noburestaurants.com

Though it's "much more low-key" than its West Hollywood sibling, this "relaxed" "neighborhood version" of the Nobu Matsuhisa brand in Malibu is still a "wonderful eating experience", as you "graze and gaze" at the "beautiful people" and "celebrities" who come for "superb" sushi and "amazing" Peruvian-accented Japanese dishes; "knowledgeable servers" "treat stars and regular patrons equally well", and sure, you'll need "money to burn", but many insist it's "worth it"; P.S. a move across the road from its present location is slated for spring 2012.

Osteria Mozza *Italian* | 27 | 23 | 24 | VE

Hollywood | 6602 Melrose Ave. (Highland Ave.) | 323-297-0100 | www.mozza-la.com

This "busy, energetic" Hollywood Italian from Mario Batali, Nancy Silverton and Joe Bastianich "lives up to the hype", conjuring "magic" in the form of "simple", "ethereal" dishes "executed exquisitely", a "fabulous" free-standing mozzarella bar and a "wine list thicker than the Bible"; given the "inspired" food, the occasional "attitude" from otherwise "smooth, professional service" is easy to overlook, just "bring your bankroll" and keep their number on redial – it's still "tough to get a rez."

Piccolo *Italian* | 27 | 22 | 24 | E

Venice | 5 Dudley Ave. (Spdwy.) | 310-314-3222 | www.piccolovenice.com

"Oh, what a meal!" marvel guests of this "phenomenal" "rare find" presenting "inventive, fantastic" Venetian food and carving out a "small sanctuary of sanity" in a "funky Venice location"; the "incredible" wine list, "romantic" atmosphere and "courteous" service by an Italian-speaking staff complete the "costly" yet "outstanding" experience, adding up to an "absolute delight."

Pizzeria Mozza ◐ *Pizza* | 28 | 19 | 21 | M |

Hollywood | 641 N. Highland Ave. (Melrose Ave.) | 323-297-0101 | www.pizzeriamozza.com

"Carbo load like a Roman god" on some of the "best pizza and antipasti" you've ever had at this "blast for the senses" in Hollywood (and now in Newport Beach), a "brilliant marriage of talents by Mario Batali and Nancy Silverton" resulting in food that diners "dream, lust and fantasize about"; an "inspired", "well-priced" wine selection and "exciting atmosphere" top off the meal, so even if there's "staff attitude", "tight" tables and "thunderous noise", "who cares?"; P.S. "reservations are a must unless you risk it and find a seat at the bar."

Providence *American/Seafood* | 28 | 25 | 27 | VE |

Hollywood | 5955 Melrose Ave. (Cole Ave.) | 323-460-4170 | www.providencela.com

Chef/co-owner Michael Cimarusti "rewards diners" with "spectacular presentations" of "inventive" seafood, with "stellar wine options" and an "exquisite cheese cart", at this "fabulous" New American in Hollywood; service is "beyond compare" and the "subtle" setting suits the "world-class" cuisine, so though it might "blow your budget", admirers say "go for the gusto" and order the tasting menu.

Saam at The Bazaar by José Andrés ⛫Ⓜ *Eclectic* | 27 | 26 | 25 | VE |

Beverly Hills | SLS at Beverly Hills | 465 S. La Cienega Blvd. (Clifton Way) | 310-246-5545 | www.thebazaar.com

"Designed to blow minds", this "extraordinary" Eclectic tasting room at The Bazaar in Beverly Hills presents 22 "sublime" bite-size courses by José Andrés, each one "adventurous" and "fulfilling in more ways than one"; "giddy diners" who also love the "skilled" service and "quiet luxury" of the Philippe Starck–designed space say bring an "open mind" and a "big fat wallet" – it's a "once-in-a-lifetime experience" that's definitely "worth the bucks."

Spago *Californian* | 27 | 25 | 26 | VE |

Beverly Hills | 176 N. Cañon Dr. (Wilshire Blvd.) | 310-385-0880 | www.wolfgangpuck.com

"Still exquisite" "after all these years" and voted LA's Most Popular, Wolfgang Puck's Beverly Hills haute "flagship" is a "mecca of Californian cuisine", where the "world-class kitchen" turns out "consistently superb" fare that "deserves all the raves it gets", and the "highly professional" staff "keeps the customers happy"; there are "celebrity sightings galore" in the "attractive, if overdesigned" room and "beautiful" patio, adding up to a "magical experience – with a bill to match."

Sushi Nozawa ⛫ *Japanese* | 27 | 8 | 17 | VE |

Studio City | 11288 Ventura Blvd. (bet. Arch & Tropical Drs.) | 818-508-7017 | www.sushinozawa.com

"Sushi places come and go", but Kazunori Nozawa's Studio City Japanese "stands the test of time" swear fans who swoon over his "purist" fin fare that's "as fresh as it gets"; "leave your mobile in the car" and "expect to wait" (no reservations), then once inside, "no talking", "do not even try to order rolls" (or brace for the "sternest gaze you'll ever suffer") and "just trust" the "master" to deliver "top-notch" creations that'll make you forget about the "stark lighting" and "zero ambiance."

Sushi Zo 🅢 *Japanese* | 28 | 15 | 21 | VE |

West LA | 9824 National Blvd. (bet. Castle Heights Ave. & Shelby Dr.) | 310-842-3977

"Omakase, omigod!" exclaim enthusiasts of this West LA Japanese "where the chef decides what you eat" and you "just sit back and let the good times roll" in the form of "heavenly sushi" (albeit at "out-of-this-world prices"); "zero atmosphere" is no problem for afishiona-dos, for whom its strip-mall location "next to a taco joint" "only adds to its otherworldliness."

Takao *Japanese* | 28 | 13 | 24 | VE |

Brentwood | 11656 San Vicente Blvd. (bet. Barrington & Darlington Aves.) | 310-207-8636 | www.takaobrentwood.com

This "unpretentious gem" in Brentwood "gives the sushi big guns a run for their money" with its "memorable" omakase and other "excep-tional", "authentic" Japanese offerings; there's "no annoying movie-star vibe" in the "unexceptional, small room", just "friendly, reliable" service and "inspired" dining, and sure, it's "not cheap", but most agree it's "worth it."

Urasawa 🅢🅜 *Japanese* | 28 | 23 | 28 | VE |

Beverly Hills | 218 N. Rodeo Dr. (Wilshire Blvd.) | 310-247-8939

A "culinary experience without peer outside of Kyoto or Tokyo", this omakase-only Beverly Hills Japanese showcases the "art" of "friendly wizard" Hiro Urasawa, whose "meticulous, warm" hospitality has earned it LA's No. 1 Service honors; "one-of-a-kind sushi and cooked dishes" are served in a "pristine, elegant" room, and while you may have to take out a "second mortgage" to foot the bill, most agree it's "worth it" for the "meal of the year – or a lifetime."

Water Grill *Seafood* | 27 | 24 | 25 | VE |

Downtown | 544 S. Grand Ave. (bet. 5th & 6th Sts.) | 213-891-0900 | www.watergrill.com

Even after the departure of popular chef David LeFevre, aficionados "don't get tired of going back again and again" to this Downtown des-tination for new toque (and *Top Chef* alum) Amanda Baumgarten's "magnificent" seafood, including "superior raw bar" offerings, and "excellent" wines; "thoughtful" service and an "elegant" atmosphere make it a popular option for "business lunches", an "overture for the theater" or "special occasions", the "high prices" notwithstanding.

Miami

TOP FOOD RANKING

	Restaurant	Cuisine
29	Naoe	Japanese
28	Palme d'Or	French
	Zuma	Japanese
	Palm	Steak
27	Il Gabbiano	Italian
	OLA	Pan-Latin
	Pascal's on Ponce	French
	Michy's	American/French
	Prime One Twelve	Seafood/Steak
	Nobu Miami Beach	Japanese
	Azul	European
	Matsuri	Japanese
	Michael's Genuine	American
	Hiro's Yakko-San	Japanese
	Joe's Stone Crab	Seafood
	Red	Steak
26	Oishi	Japanese/Thai
	La Dorada	Seafood/Spanish
	Francesco	Peruvian
	DB Bistro Moderne	French
	Osteria del Teatro	Italian
	Romeo's Cafe	Italian

Azul 🏛 *European* 　　　　　27 | 27 | 26 | VE
Brickell Area | Mandarin Oriental Hotel | 500 Brickell Key Dr. (SE 8th St.) | 305-913-8358 | www.mandarinoriental.com
This "favorite" in Brickell Key's Mandarin Oriental has welcomed a new chef who switched its menu from Med to Modern European with American and Asian accents (not fully reflected in the rating); cuisine aside, its "attentive but unobtrusive" service, "serious" wine list and "sleek" setting with "spectacular views" help make it a "special occasion" "delight" – "even if prices are close to those for nearby condos."

NEW DB Bistro Moderne *French* 　　26 | 25 | 25 | VE
Downtown | JW Marriott Marquis Miami | 255 Biscayne Blvd. Way (bet. SE 2nd & 3rd Aves.) | 305-421-8800 | www.danielnyc.com
Proof positive that NYC's Daniel Boulud is a "food god" is the "perfectly prepared" French fare at this "chic" yearling in Downtown's JW Marriott Marquis; service is "attentive" and the Yabu Pushelberg-designed space is "beautiful", so if you "can handle the tab", "what's not to like?"; P.S. don't miss the $32 sirloin, foie gras and truffle burger.

Francesco 🏛 *Peruvian* 　　　　26 | 17 | 23 | E
Coral Gables | 325 Alcazar Ave. (bet. Salzedo St. & SW 42nd Ave.) | 305-446-1600 | www.francescorestaurantmiami.com
According to fans, the "best ceviche in Miami" is to be found at this "first-rate" Peruvian in Coral Gables dishing up "expensive" but "con-

sistently amazing" seafood and other dishes, some "authentic", others with Italian touches; the small space gets "tightly packed" and the "decor could use a refresh", but the "owner is always on-site and it shows" in the overall "welcoming" vibe.

Hiro's Yakko-San ◐ *Japanese*   27 | - | 21 | M

North Miami Beach | Intracoastal Mall | 3881 NE 163rd St.
(Sunny Isles Blvd.) | 305-947-0064 | www.yakko-san.com

"Feel like Andrew Zimmern" sampling the "unusual" "izakaya-style" small plates and "inspired" sushi at this "adventurous" strip-center Japanese; a recent move to a "larger" North Miami Beach space outdates the Decor rating (folks say the modern setting, sporting a large sushi bar, is more "fancy" than the old address), but longtime fans are pleased it added lunch while retaining the same dependable service and "low" prices – especially during the late-night happy hour, 11 PM to close.

Il Gabbiano ◐☒ *Italian*   27 | 26 | 27 | VE

Downtown | One Miami Tower | 335 S. Biscayne Blvd. (SE 3rd St.) |
305-373-0063 | www.ilgabbianomia.com

From the antipasti to the after-dinner limoncello (both gratis), this Downtown sibling of Il Mulino in NYC exhibits "true Italian class"; expect an "inspired menu", "extensive" wine list, "stellar" service and "elegant" digs that extend to a "beautiful" outdoor terrace where diners can "gaze at Biscayne Bay or into their companions' eyes" – welcome distractions from tabs that reflect the "top-notch" quality.

Joe's Stone Crab *Seafood*   27 | 20 | 23 | VE

South Beach | 11 Washington Ave. (bet. 1st St. & S. Pointe Dr.) |
Miami Beach | 305-673-0365 | www.joesstonecrab.com

"Rob a bank, sell the house, [do] whatever it takes" to afford the "succulent" stone crabs that again make this "legendary" SoBe eatery Miami's Most Popular – though "the irony is that everything else on the menu is reasonably priced" and standouts like fried chicken and Key lime pie are equally "to die for"; "looong waits" and "rushed" service from "track-star" waiters racing through the "gigantic" space are the norm, but you can "avoid the madness" by heading to the recently "upgraded" takeout cafe; P.S. closed mid-May to mid-October.

La Dorada ◐☒ *Seafood/Spanish*   26 | 21 | 26 | VE

Coral Gables | 177 Giralda Ave. (Ponce de Leon Blvd.) | 305-446-2002 |
www.ladoradamiami.com

This Coral Gables Spaniard offers "elegant, wonderfully simple preparations" of seafood "flown in daily from the Mediterranean" – via "first-class airfare", judging by the cost; wallet-watchers say the "awesome" prix fixe lunch is a "great value", while "friendly service", a "good wine selection" and live music on weekends are further pluses.

Matsuri ☒ *Japanese*   27 | 20 | 21 | M

South Miami | 5759 Bird Rd. (bet. Red Rd. & SW 58th Ave.) | 305-663-1615

"Luscious" fish so "fresh" it "tastes like it swam into the restaurant" is the big lure at this longtime South Miami strip-mall mecca for "true sushi aficionados", but it also dishes up "good cooked items" (brush up on your kanji and "ask for the Japanese-language menu" for more "unique" offerings); the "austere" setting isn't always warmed by ser-

	FOOD	DECOR	SERVICE	COST

vice that can swing from "attentive" to "abrupt" – but "who cares with prices like this?"

Michael's Genuine Food & Drink *American* | 27 | 20 | 23 | E |

Design District | Atlas Plaza | 130 NE 40th St. (bet. 1st & 2nd Aves.) | 305-573-5550 | www.michaelsgenuine.com

The name of this "trendy" Design District "hot spot" is "a statement of intent which they deliver on" via chef-owner Michael Schwartz's "ambitious" yet "down-to-earth" small, medium and large plates of locally sourced New American "comfort" food, backed by "inspired" treats from "genius" pastry chef Hedy Goldsmith and a "well-considered" wine list; staffers can seem "a touch snooty" at times but their "efficiency", plus a "lovely" outdoor courtyard and "decent" prices, compensates.

Michy's Ⓜ *American/French* | 27 | 19 | 25 | E |

Upper East Side | 6927 Biscayne Blvd. (69th St.) | 305-759-2001 | www.michysmiami.com

Chef Michelle Bernstein is "at the top of her game" at this "pricey" Upper East Side "showcase" for her "novel takes" on New American–French "comfort food" (those with "commitment issues" can order multiple entrees in half portions); opinion diverges on the orange-and-blue decor – "funky" vs. "Aunt Mildred's living room" – but most applaud the staff's "attention to detail", including a "friendly" sommelier who's "genuinely interested" in suggesting "unique" pairings.

Naoe Ⓜ *Japanese* | 29 | 23 | 28 | VE |

Sunny Isles Beach | 175 Sunny Isles Blvd. (bet. Collins Ave. & Intercoastal Waterways Bridge) | 305-947-6263 | www.naoemiami.com

"I can't believe this exists in Miami" since it would be "outstanding even in Japan" gush fans of this "teeny" 17-seat Sunny Isles Beach star, rated the city's tops for Food and Service; Kevin Cory's "creative" omakase meals include a bento box "revelation" and "impossibly good" sushi, all presented with "warm", "personal" care by "charming" manager Wendy Maharlika; it's not cheap (price varies according to the day's offerings and how many courses you opt for), but it's so "worth it" – just book "well in advance" (two seatings, Wednesday-Sunday); P.S. it plans to relocate to Brickell Key in early 2012.

Nobu Miami Beach *Japanese* | 27 | 22 | 22 | VE |

South Beach | Shore Club | 1901 Collins Ave. (19th St.) | Miami Beach | 305-695-3232 | www.noburestaurants.com

"Beautiful fish and beautiful people" dazzle at this "über-hip" "pregame warm-up for SoBe's clubs", part of Nobu Matsuhisa's far-flung fusion empire renowned for its "incredible" Japanese-Peruvian cuisine crowned by "sushi to die for" (indeed, the bill alone "may kill you"); the space is "beyond minimalist compared to the rest of the Shore Club's glitz" and critics contend service is "not up to par with the prices", but "have a sake, chill" and "keep your eyes open – you'll be surprised who you might see."

Oishi Thai *Japanese/Thai* | 26 | 22 | 24 | E |

North Miami | 14841 Biscayne Blvd. (146th St.) | 305-947-4338 | www.oishithai.com

"Delicious" sushi and other "fabulous" Japanese fare shares billing with "exotic" Thai creations at this North Miami strip-maller, "admirably run" by a onetime Nobu chef; a "cool" modern Asian look, servers who "do everything they can to make for an enjoyable meal" and an optimal "quality/price ratio" further boost its appeal.

OLA *Pan-Latin*   27 | 22 | 25 | VE

South Beach | Sanctuary Hotel | 1745 James Ave. (bet. 17th & 18th Sts.) | Miami Beach | 305-695-9125 | www.olamiami.com

"Ceviche is king" at this "quiet" Pan-Latin respite from the "craziness of SoBe", offering a culinary "trip from Mexico to Argentina" courtesy of chef Douglas Rodriguez; set in the boutique Sanctuary Hotel well "off the main drag", it has a "trendy" yet "comfortable" vibe, a "thoughtful" wine list parsed by the "knowledgeable" crew and a "delightful" patio.

Osteria del Teatro *Italian*   26 | 18 | 24 | VE

South Beach | 1443 Washington Ave. (Española Way) | Miami Beach | 305-538-7850 | www.osteriadelteatromiami.com

"Incredible" Northern Italian cuisine takes *paesani* "back to the old country" at this "legendary" "white-tablecloth" "oasis of relaxation" "in crazy SoBe"; prices are "high" and quarters that some find "cozy" strike others as "uncomfortable, unless you're a sardine", but "sublime" wines and an "alert" staff that "anticipates your every move" help make it "a must."

Palm, The *Steak*   28 | 20 | 25 | VE

Bay Harbor Islands | 9650 E. Bay Harbor Dr. (96th St.) | 305-868-7256 | www.thepalm.com

"Top-quality meat cooked right", "great sides" and "strong drinks" are what you can expect "every time" at this Bay Harbor Islands outpost of the "quintessential NY steakhouse" chain; caricatures line the walls and "local bigwigs" fill the seats of the "clubby" environs, which are overseen by "old-school waiters" and host an "amiable bar scene", but it doesn't come cheap: "my credit card won't allow me near the place."

Palme d'Or *French*   28 | 27 | 27 | VE

Coral Gables | Biltmore Hotel | 1200 Anastasia Ave. (Columbus Blvd.) | 305-913-3201 | www.biltmorehotel.com

"The prize of Coral Gables, if not all of Miami/Dade, is this "superb" New French stunner where chef Philippe Ruiz "consistently outdoes himself" crafting "delectable" small plates matched by a "well-considered" wine list and "seamless" service in a "luxurious", "refined" setting; "not cheap" understates things, especially if you go all out and "stay the night" at the "beautiful" Biltmore for the "ultimate romantic evening."

Pascal's on Ponce *French*   27 | 20 | 25 | VE

Coral Gables | 2611 Ponce de Leon Blvd. (bet. Almeria & Valencia Aves.) | 305-444-2024 | www.pascalmiami.com

"Creativity abounds" in the "*magnifique*" New French cuisine at chef-owner Pascal Oudin's somewhat "unassuming" storefront bistro "just off the Mile" in Coral Gables; the setting is about as "small" as the bills are "big", but "first-rate" service and "soufflés so light that you won't gain a pound" help to explain why most surveyors find this destination "always a treat."

	FOOD	DECOR	SERVICE	COST

Prime One Twelve ☾ *Seafood/Steak* — 27 | 23 | 22 | VE

South Beach | 112 Ocean Dr. (1st St.) | Miami Beach | 305-532-8112 |
www.prime112.com

"Super sexy" yet "serious", this SoBe surf 'n' turfer dishes up "monstrous" portions of "amazing" food, but it's just as well known for hosting the "scene of scenes", with "Bentleys, Ferraris and Lambos" out front and "wannabes" "rubbing elbows" ("literally; they pack 'em in") with "movie stars", "sports legends" and "models" inside; downsides include "noise", "long waits", variable service and "black-card" tabs, but hey, "you'll have a story to tell."

Red, The Steakhouse *Steak* — 27 | 25 | 24 | VE

South Beach | 119 Washington Ave. (1st St.) | Miami Beach |
305-534-3688 | www.redthesteakhouse.com

As the name implies, this "classy" South Beach steakhouse is a true "red meat/red wine lover's paradise" with its "juicy", "velvety" Angus beef and "extensive wine collection" displayed behind a glass wall – though the "extravagant" price tags require a lot of green; "attentive" staff, a "cool ambiance" and a "stylish" "contemporary" look complete the "first-rate" experience.

Romeo's Cafe ⊠Ⓜ *Italian* — 26 | 19 | 26 | VE

Coral Way | 2257 SW 22nd St. (22nd Ave.) | 305-859-2228 |
www.romeoscafe.com

The "personal touch" is an art form at this "romantic" Northern Italian in Coral Way where "friendly" chef-owner Romeo Majano stops by each table to discuss "your tastes", then whips up "one amazing dish after the other" customized "just for you"; it's "on the pricey side" (four-course dinner for $60, six for $90; no à la carte) but that befits a "unique", "special-occasion" place; reservations are recommended.

Zuma ☾ *Japanese* — 28 | 27 | 24 | VE

Downtown | Epic Hotel | 270 Biscayne Blvd. (Brickell Ave.) | 305-577-0277 |
www.zumarestaurant.com

"Book way ahead" to secure a seat at Downtown's new "it" spot in the Epic Hotel because this European import (and "international sensation") is drawing throngs with its "Zen mastery" of modern izakaya-inspired Japanese fare plus sushi, robata grill items and more; "fabulous views" can be had from the terrace overlooking the Miami River, or you can just watch the "beautiful people" burning many "benjamins" in the "stunning" dining room and "vibrant" sake bar/lounge.

New Orleans

TOP FOOD RANKING

	Restaurant	Cuisine
28	Bayona	American
	Stella!	American
	Brigtsen's	Contemp. Louisiana
27	Clancy's	Creole
	Royal China	Chinese
	August	French
	Patois	American/French
	Bistro Daisy	American/Southern
	Herbsaint	American/French
	Commander's Palace	Creole
	Cochon Butcher	Cajun/Sandwiches
	Lilette	French
	Cypress	Creole
	La Boca*	Argentinean/Steak

Acme Oyster House *Seafood*   24 | 15 | 20 | M

French Quarter | 724 Iberville St. (bet. Bourbon & Royal Sts.) | 504-522-5973
Metairie | 3000 Veterans Memorial Blvd. (N. Causeway Blvd.) | 504-309-4056
Covington | 1202 N. Hwy. 190 (bet. Crestwood Blvd. & 17th Ave.) | 985-246-6155
www.acmeoyster.com

"Sit at the bar, chat with the shuckers" and savor "bivalve bliss" at this French Quarter "legend" that's "famous" for "briny" raw oysters (and "awesome" char-grilled ones) and "fried anything else"; the "tourists" can be a drawback, but "even the locals love" its "clean, cold" beauts, "frosty brews" and lively "banter" amid a "casual but electric" vibe bursting with "joie de vivre"; P.S. the Covington and Metairie off-shoots "lack the color" of the original but are still a "wonderful value."

August *French*   27 | 27 | 27 | VE

Central Business Dist. | 301 Tchoupitoulas St. (Gravier St.) | 504-299-9777 | www.restaurantaugust.com

"One of the best chefs in the country", John Besh "takes New Orleans cuisine into the future" while nurturing its "soul", turning "local ingredients" into "spectacular" New French dishes (with an "out-of-this-world" tasting menu option) at his flagship CBD "masterpiece"; "smart" service and "beautiful" surroundings with "tall brick walls" complete the "stellar" meal, so while the tab is "hefty", it's "oh-so-worth-it" – plus the weekday lunch lets you indulge for "a bit less cash."

Bayona ☒ *American*   28 | 26 | 26 | E

French Quarter | 430 Dauphine St. (bet. Conti & St. Louis Sts.) | 504-525-4455 | www.bayona.com

The "ever-amazing" Susan Spicer crafts "sublime" New American meals (with a Contemporary Louisiana touch) that "make your heart

---

* Indicates a tie with restaurant above

sing" at this "high-end" French Quarter "winner", voted No. 1 for Food in New Orleans – and "that's saying something" in a city where eating is a "way of life"; set inside a "lovely", "historic house" with "understated" ambiance, it boasts a "gorgeous" "tropical" patio, "top-notch" service and lunch that's a "true bargain" (featuring a "famous" duck sandwich), keeping it the "perennial choice" for an "unparalleled dining experience."

Bistro Daisy ⌧Ⓜ *American/Southern* 27 | 23 | 26 | E

Uptown | 5831 Magazine St. (bet. Eleonore St. & Nashville Ave.) | 504-899-6987 | www.bistrodaisy.com

"Exciting", "elevated" "regional cuisine" delights diners at this "diminutive" but "marvelous" New American–Southern by the "young" "husband-and-wife team" of chef Anton and Diane Schulte; its "unassuming" setting in a "handsomely renovated Uptown house" is "comfortable", the wine list "reasonable" and the service "engaging" and "accommodating", so regulars always feel "welcome and well fed."

Brigtsen's ⌧Ⓜ *Contemp. Louisiana* 28 | 23 | 28 | E

Riverbend | 723 Dante St. (Maple St.) | 504-861-7610 | www.brigtsens.com

"Sensational" Contemporary Louisiana cuisine by chef Frank Brigtsen and an "exemplary" staff overseen by wife and manager Marna keep this "converted shotgun house" in Riverbend "filled with locals", who rate it No. 1 for Service in New Orleans; the "homey" space is "tight", but most consider it worth the squeeze, the price and the "ride on the streetcar" for the "splendid" dinners with "unforgettable" pecan pie.

Clancy's ⌧ *Creole* 27 | 22 | 26 | E

Uptown | 6100 Annunciation St. (Webster St.) | 504-895-1111

A "who's who of New Orleans" stirs up a "vibrant" scene at this "traditional", slightly "pricey" Uptown "power hangout", "running into friends" and "swooning" over "superb" Creole "classics" (like smoked soft-shell crab) complemented by "generous drinks" and an "exhaustive" wine list; "hidden among family homes", its "out-of-sight" locale and "professional", "old-style" staff enhance its status as a "locals' darling", but stick to the "packed" downstairs, rather than the quiet, somewhat "dreary" upstairs, for prime "people-watching."

Cochon Butcher *Cajun/Sandwiches* 27 | 18 | 21 | I

Warehouse District | 930 Tchoupitoulas St. (bet. Andrew Higgins Dr. & S. Diamond St.) | 504-588-7675 | www.cochonbutcher.com

"OMG, just go!" exclaim "pork lovers" who "bring home the bacon", "load up on boudin" and even "go quackers" for the duck pastrami sliders, all prepared with the "highest integrity" and "Cajun flair", at this "temple of swine dining" by Donald Link – basically a "wine bar, meat counter and sandwich shop mashed together" under the same Warehouse District roof as Cochon; it's ideal for a "casual" lunch or "offbeat dinner" with "walk-up service", so "linger awhile" or simply "grab 'n' go" to indulge in a "primal" feast – "if you eat meat and don't visit while in New Orleans, you've blown it."

Commander's Palace *Creole* 27 | 28 | 27 | E

Garden District | 1403 Washington Ave. (Coliseum St.) | 504-899-8221 | www.commanderspalace.com

"Restored to her original splendor" (with "whimsical" touches in the "formal dining room"), this Garden District "grande dame" – once again voted Most Popular and No. 1 for Decor in New Orleans – is "always a celebration", whether for a "special evening" or "not-to-be-missed" Sunday jazz brunch "with the swells"; "superlative" Creole cuisine, "outstanding" service and "quintessential" Crescent City ambiance make it a "treat for the senses", and despite a little tutting that it's "touristy" and "expensive", few find fault with the "weekday special" of "25-cent martinis at lunch"; P.S. no shorts; jackets suggested for dinner.

Cypress ⍟Ⓜ Creole
27 | 20 | 24 | M

Metairie | 4426 Transcontinental Dr. (W. Esplanade Ave.) | 504-885-6885 | www.restaurantcypress.com

A "hidden treasure", this "upscale yet relaxed" "Metairie gem" provides "top-notch" contemporary Creole cuisine that "could go up against any" in the city; the food's "much better than the decor", but with the owners, chef Stephen and manager Katherine Huth, pouring on the "warm neighborhood" charm, those in the know "can't stay away."

Galatoire's Ⓜ Creole/French
27 | 26 | 27 | E

French Quarter | 209 Bourbon St. (Iberville St.) | 504-525-2021 | www.galatoires.com

"Bravo for tradition!" declare devotees of this "old-line" "national treasure" in the French Quarter, where "lunches live up to their raucous reputation" as "upper-crust, extravagantly dressed" guests dine on "superior" Creole-French fare (particularly the "fabulous" seafood) and often "drink their way right into dinner"; boasting "tuxedo-clad" waiters who "have been there for generations", and a "classic" main-floor dining room, replete with "black-and-white-checkered-tile", it's the "real deal" that's "ultra-New Orleans in every way"; P.S. jackets required after 5 PM and all-day Sunday; reservations only accepted upstairs.

Herbsaint ⍟ American/French
27 | 22 | 25 | E

Warehouse District | 701 St. Charles Ave. (Girod St.) | 504-524-4114 | www.herbsaint.com

Chef/co-owner Donald Link's "imaginative" yet "down-to-earth haute cuisine" "shines" at this "pleasurable" (and "not incredibly expensive") Warehouse District venue for "outstanding" New American–New French small plates and "terrific" Sazeracs, served by a "savvy" staff; though tables are "tight", the "light-filled room" affords a view of the "St. Charles streetcars", adding to the "rewarding experience."

La Boca ⍟ Argentinean/Steak
27 | 20 | 23 | E

Warehouse District | 857 Fulton St. (St. Joseph St.) | 504-525-8205 | www.labocasteaks.com

"Succulent", "unique cuts of meat", "incredible" fries and "sensual" gnocchi add up to "perfection" at this "authentic", upscale Argentinean steakhouse (a sib of RioMar) that inspires carnivorous "cravings"; a "reasonable wine list" and "huge" plates are a bonus, and while the Warehouse District space is "small", an "excellent" staff providing "personal" attention enhances the "wonderful meal."

Lilette ⍟Ⓜ French
27 | 24 | 24 | E

Uptown | 3637 Magazine St. (Antonine St.) | 504-895-1636 | www.liletterestaurant.com

Exactly "what a neighborhood restaurant should be", this "inviting" Uptown bistro "succeeds" with chef-owner John Harris' "ambitious"

French menu based on "stellar ingredients", served amid "chic" surroundings with "stamped tin panels on the ceiling"; "fantastic" drinks, "sumptuous" desserts and "knowledgeable" service round out the "delightful" (if "noisy") lunches and dinners, so most "love" joining in the "Paris-on-Magazine" scene.

Patois Ⓜ *American/French*

| 27 | 23 | 23 | E |

Uptown | 6078 Laurel St. (Webster St.) | 504-895-9441 |
www.patoisnola.com

"A top spot for serious foodies" (as well as *Treme* fans"), this "popular" "Uptown gem" by "cutting-edge" chef/co-owner Aaron Burgau presents "inspired", "deftly" prepared French–New American dishes that make for "magnificent" meals with "semi-casual neighborhood appeal"; add in "pleasing" brasserie-style digs, "outstanding martinis" and a "hip" yet "solicitous" staff tending to the "noisy" "thirtysomething" crowd, and many feel it defines the "new New Orleans."

Royal China *Chinese*

| 27 | 15 | 21 | I |

Metairie | 600 Veterans Memorial Blvd. (Aris Ave.) | 504-831-9633
"Fabulous dim sum" (served all day) and other "fresh", "incredible" dishes distinguish this affordable Metairie mainstay cooking up some of the "best Chinese in greater New Orleans"; "accommodating" owner Shirley Lee "knows everyone who comes in", so even though the plain old room "gets crowded", "warm, personal" service adds to the "remarkable value."

Stella! *American*

| 28 | 26 | 27 | VE |

French Quarter | Hotel Provincial | 1032 Chartres St. (bet. St. Philip & Ursulines Ave.) | 504-587-0091 | www.restaurantstella.com
"Star" chef-owner Scott Boswell takes "top-tier ingredients" and orchestrates a "culinary experience of epic proportions" with his "daring" New American dinners that "thrill", served with "expertise and style" at this "foodie" "destination" on a "quiet stretch of the Quarter"; the "intimate" room was refurbished post-Survey with exposed brick and a more contemporary design, and while the check remains "regal", most feel it's justified by the "unforgettable" meal.

New York City

TOP FOOD RANKING

	Restaurant	Cuisine
29	Le Bernardin	French/Seafood
	Daniel	French
28	Per Se	American/French
	Bouley	French
	Jean Georges	French
	Eleven Madison Park	French
	Sushi Yasuda	Japanese
	Annisa	American
	La Grenouille	French
	Peter Luger	Steak
	Marea	Italian/Seafood
	Gotham Bar & Grill	American
27	Blue Hill	American
	Gramercy Tavern	American
	Trattoria L'incontro	Italian
	Roberto	Italian
	Del Posto	Italian
	Danny Brown	European
	Mas	American
	L'Atelier/Joël Robuchon	French
	Picholine	French/Mediterranean
	Scalini Fedeli	Italian
	Milos	Greek/Seafood
	Café Boulud	French
	Saul	American
	Jean Georges' Nougatine	French
	Il Mulino	Italian
	Degustation	French/Spanish

Annisa *American*   28 | 24 | 27 | VE

W Village | 13 Barrow St. (bet. 7th Ave. S. & W. 4th St.) | 212-741-6699 | www.annisarestaurant.com

"A real grown-up's restaurant", Anita Lo's "quiet powerhouse" in the West Village delivers "superb", "upscale" New American cuisine with "elegant Asian inflections", "interesting wines" from "female vintners" and "impeccable" "pro" service; it all comes in "refreshingly minimalist" environs that "put the focus on the food", but are also "perfect for a special occasion."

Blue Hill *American*   27 | 23 | 27 | VE

G Village | 75 Washington Pl. (bet. MacDougal St. & 6th Ave.) | 212-539-1776 | www.bluehillfarm.com

"King of the locavore movement", "genius" chef Dan Barber produces "tantalizing", "brilliant meals" that "epitomize farm-to-table" at his "serene", "well-run" Village American; it "ain't cheap" but it's "utterly worth it" – especially given the "first-rate" service – but it's even more "frustrating" getting a reservation ever since "the Obamas stopped by."

	FOOD	DECOR	SERVICE	COST

Bouley *French* · 28 | 27 | 27 | VE

TriBeCa | 163 Duane St. (bet. Greenwich & Hudson Sts.) | 212-964-2525 | www.davidbouley.com

"Sublime from start to finish", David Bouley's "stunning" TriBeCa mother ship conjures "magic" with "nuanced", "flawless" French cuisine, a "glorious" setting and pro service that "borders on mind-reading"; it all makes for an "unforgettable" experience that's "worth" the steep cost – though the "greatest gift to Gotham gourmets" is its "leisurely" $55 five-course prix fixe lunch.

Café Boulud *French* · 27 | 24 | 26 | VE

E 70s | Surrey Hotel | 20 E. 76th St. (bet. 5th & Madison Aves.) | 212-772-2600 | www.danielnyc.com

UES "socialites" and "old-money" types collect at Daniel Boulud's "grown-up" standby where "everything's fab", from the "deluxe" French fare "expertly prepared" by chef Gavin Kaysen to the "pampering" service and "swank" setting; you'll "shell out" for such "luxury", but the "heavenly" $35 lunch prix fixe is a "bargain"; P.S. "go early and enjoy a drink" in the adjacent Bar Pleiades.

Daniel 🅧 *French* · 29 | 28 | 28 | VE

E 60s | 60 E. 65th St. (bet. Madison & Park Aves.) | 212-288-0033 | www.danielnyc.com

"When you want the best of everything", Daniel Boulud's "stately" East Side namesake delivers the goods, "perennially" inspiring "superlatives" for its "breathtaking" New French prix fixes, "stellar wine list" and "world-class service"; at the "zenith of formal" dining ("jackets required") with prices to match, it's "worth every centime" to "celebrate in style"; P.S. the slightly less "lavish" lounge menu is à la carte.

Danny Brown Wine Bar & Kitchen 🅜 *European* · 27 | 21 | 25 | E

Forest Hills | 104-02 Metropolitan Ave. (71st Dr.) | Queens | 718-261-2144 | www.dannybrownwinekitchen.com

Forest Hills locals boast this "off-the-beaten-path" find "rivals many in Manhattan" for "flair and flavor" with its "delectable" European cuisine, "simpatico service" and "classy" "bistro" quarters; devotees drawn to "first-rate" wining and dining at relatively "reasonable" prices are "so happy it exists."

Degustation *French/Spanish* · 27 | 20 | 25 | VE

E Village | 239 E. Fifth St. (bet. 2nd & 3rd Aves.) | 212-979-1012 | www.degustationnyc.com

"Sit at the counter and prepare to be wowed" at this "teeny" East Villager from Jack and Grace Lamb, where a tasting bar affords "ringside" seats as seemingly "choreographed" chefs create a "masterful" Franco-Spanish "small plates medley"; it's "pricey", but after the "blow-your-mind" performance, epicures have "absolutely no regrets."

Del Posto *Italian* · 27 | 27 | 27 | VE

Chelsea | 85 10th Ave. (bet. 15th & 16th Sts.) | 212-497-8090 | www.delposto.com

Like being "transported" to "Roma", this Chelsea "Italian masterpiece" from the Batali-Bastianich bunch is "in a class unto itself" with "rarefied" cuisine, "spectacular wines" and "psychic" "white-glove" service; it comes in an "opulent" "palazzo"-like space complete with "velvet curtains, marble floors", "dramatic stairs" and "even a piano player"; *certo,* "you pay dearly for the privilege", but you'll "relish every minute."

Eleven Madison Park ⊠ *French*   28 | 28 | 28 | VE

Flatiron | 11 Madison Ave. (24th St.) | 212-889-0905 | www.elevenmadisonpark.com

"Top of the line" even for Danny Meyer, this New French "experience" on Madison Square Park is "exquisite from beginning to end", matching chef Daniel Humm's "exhilarating" tasting menu–only cuisine with "world-class" service ("even the busboys have Cornell degrees") in a "majestic" "art deco" space; surveyors split on the "cryptic" new "sudoku"-card menu format ("an engaging adventure" vs. "precious"), and, of course, tabs are "in the stratosphere."

Gotham Bar & Grill *American*   28 | 25 | 27 | VE

G Village | 12 E. 12th St. (bet. 5th Ave. & University Pl.) | 212-620-4020 | www.gothambarandgrill.com

"Years of practice make perfect" at Alfred Portale's circa-1984 Village "landmark in fine dining" that remains "at the top of its game" with "magical" "skyscraping" New American cuisine, "marvelously orchestrated" service and a "spacious", casually "sophisticated" setting; the "unforgettable experience" is "well worth the final bill" – but if "money's tight" try the $25 "greenmarket lunch" (possibly "NYC's best deal").

Gramercy Tavern *American*   27 | 26 | 27 | VE

Flatiron | 42 E. 20th St. (bet. B'way & Park Ave. S.) | 212-477-0777 | www.gramercytavern.com

"Still a model" of New American dining "at its finest", Danny Meyer's "forever fabulous" Flatiron "destination" offers "inspired" "farm-fresh" cuisine from chef Michael Anthony via an "exemplary" staff that "glides you through the evening" in a "gorgeous", "refined"-"rustic" space designed to recall a 19th century New England tavern; yes, you "pay dearly" but it's resoundingly declared "worth it", so "beg for a reservation" in the prix fixe–only main room, or opt for the "lower-priced", à la carte, non-reserving front tavern room; P.S. the 22-seat private room is equally appealing.

Il Mulino ⊠ *Italian*   27 | 20 | 24 | VE

G Village | 86 W. Third St. (bet. Sullivan & Thompson Sts.) | 212-673-3783 | www.ilmulino.com

"For those who are starting the diet 'tomorrow'", there's this "old-world" Village Italian "must" where "almost-impossible-to-get" rezzies are rewarded with "amazing", "super-rich" Abruzzi-style dishes that just "keep rolling out" via "cheerful" "tuxedoed waiters" who try "to stuff you like a cannelloni"; a "big, hearty bill" and "really packed", "celeb"-studded room come with the territory, though "lunch is less hectic."

Jean Georges ⊠ *French*   28 | 27 | 28 | VE

W 60s | Trump Int'l Hotel | 1 Central Park W. (bet. 60th & 61st Sts.) | 212-299-3900 | www.jean-georges.com

Expect "brilliant everything" at Jean-Georges Vongerichten's "standard setter" in Columbus Circle, where the "transcendent" New French "works of culinary art" and "superior wines" are "exciting every time"; a "gorgeous", "soothing" modern space and "choreographed" pro service fully justify the "steep" bill, while the $38 prix fixe lunch remains one of the city's "best bargains."

Jean Georges' Nougatine *French*
27 | 24 | 25 | VE

W 60s | Trump Int'l Hotel | 1 Central Park W. (bet. 60th & 61st Sts.) | 212-299-3900 | www.jean-georges.com

"Less formal than Jean Georges but just as tantalizing", this "relaxed" front room provides "extraordinary" New French cooking and "personal" service, not to mention "floor-to-ceiling views of Central Park"; its $32 three-course prix fixe lunch may be the "deal of the century", but "business" types say it's "even better" for "not-crowded" breakfast or after-work drinks and snacks.

La Grenouille ⊠ *French*
28 | 28 | 28 | VE

E 50s | 3 E. 52nd St. (bet. 5th & Madison Aves.) | 212-752-1495 | www.la-grenouille.com

Just about "every superlative" applies to Charles Masson's "luxuriant" Midtown standard-bearer – the last (and best) of NYC's great classic French restaurants – from the "sublime" haute cuisine and "seamless service" to the "gorgeous floral displays" and overall sense of *"ancien régime* splendor"; now in its 50th year, this "time-tested" indulger of "expensive tastes" can be experienced at a "bargain" $36 lunch in the upstairs room; P.S. jackets required.

L'Atelier de Joël Robuchon *French*
27 | 25 | 26 | VE

E 50s | Four Seasons Hotel | 57 E. 57th St. (bet. Madison & Park Aves.) | 212-829-3844 | www.fourseasons.com

Super-toque Joël Robuchon's "artfully composed" Japanese-inflected French creations make for "world-class" dining at this very "refined" Midtowner in the Four Seasons whose seating chart includes a much-coveted counter offering a "fascinating" view of the "incredible talent" in the open kitchen; though a few cite "smaller-than-small" portions, "uneven" performance and "through-the-roof" pricing, most "feel like a king" here.

Le Bernardin ⊠ *French/Seafood*
29 | 27 | 28 | VE

W 50s | 155 W. 51st St. (bet. 6th & 7th Aves.) | 212-554-1515 | www.le-bernardin.com

"Formidable" is the consensus on this newly renovated, drop-dead "gorgeous" Midtown French seafooder via Maguy LeCoze and chef Eric Ripert, where the nuanced cooking is so "dazzling" that it's taken Top Food and Most Popular honors in our New York City Survey; "starchy" service, a "reverential" crowd and a "civilized" milieu combine for an "unforgettable" dining experience, and though the prix fixe–only menus come dear, the $70 lunch is a relative bargain; P.S. there's party space upstairs.

Marea *Italian/Seafood*
28 | 26 | 26 | VE

W 50s | 240 Central Park S. (bet. B'way & 7th Ave.) | 212-582-5100 | www.marea-nyc.com

Chef Michael White demonstrates "how a kitchen should be run" at this "sophisticated" CPS "stunner", voted NYC's No. 1 Italian thanks to a "scrumptious" seafood-slanted menu backed up with first-rate pasta and "flawless" service; the "glamorous", "celeb"-studded room burnishes the overall experience, but for best results, go on "someone else's dime" – this exercise in "sheer perfection" comes at a "titanic price", at least for dinner.

Mas ◗ *American*   27 | 24 | 27 | VE

W Village | 39 Downing St. (bet. Bedford & Varick Sts.) | 212-255-1790 | www.masfarmhouse.com

Achieving the "perfect harmony" of "comfort and cool", this West Village "sea of tranquility" showcases chef Galen Zamarra's "creative" yet "approachable" New American menu that's catnip for "Greenmarket food fanatics"; though "expensive", the "sophisticated", low-key setting emits enough "romance" to work for a "big date", while the "gracious" service and "excellent" food "encourage repeat visits."

Milos, Estiatorio ◗ *Greek/Seafood*   27 | 24 | 24 | VE

W 50s | 125 W. 55th St. (bet. 6th & 7th Aves.) | 212-245-7400 | www.estiatoriomilos.com

A "calm atmosphere and "airy", whitewashed setting bring "Santorini" to Midtown via this "glorious" Greek serving "picture-perfect" seafood "displayed on ice"; by-the-pound pricing makes for "second mortgage"-worthy tabs, so bargain-hunters stick to the appetizers.

Per Se *American/French*   28 | 28 | 29 | VE

W 60s | Time Warner Ctr. | 10 Columbus Circle, 4th fl. (60th St. at B'way) | 212-823-9335 | www.perseny.com

"Fine dining" is alive and well at Thomas Keller's "otherworldly" aerie in the Time Warner Center, a "destination restaurant if there ever was one", featuring "wonderfully orchestrated" French–New American meals; granted, the $295 prix fixe charge strikes some as "outlandish", but à la carte small plates are available in the salon, and there are the added perks of "classic" Central Park views and "second-to-none" service (fittingly rated No. 1 in this Survey); it's a "lengthy experience", but not that expensive on an hourly basis.

Peter Luger Steak House ⊄ *Steak*   28 | 16 | 20 | VE

Williamsburg | 178 Broadway (Driggs Ave.) | Brooklyn | 718-387-7400 | www.peterluger.com

A charter member of the "Zagat Hall of Fame", this "essential" Williamsburg "beef bastion" – voted NYC's Top Steakhouse for the 28th year in a row – is renowned for its signature "gold-standard" porterhouse, "superlative" sides and "righteous" burgers; sure, the "steaks are as aged as the waiters" (but fortunately "not as tough") and the "too bright", German tavern–style room is "less than exciting", though nonetheless it's "packed shoulder-to-shoulder every night"; "bring wads of cash" – it doesn't accept plastic.

Picholine *French/Mediterranean*   27 | 25 | 26 | VE

W 60s | 35 W. 64th St. (bet. B'way & CPW) | 212-724-8585 | www.picholinenyc.com

"Exquisite is the word" for Terrance Brennan's "elegantly restrained" "escape" near Lincoln Center, where "brilliant" French-Med cuisine capped by an "unparalleled" cheese course is enhanced by "perfect" service and "peaceful" surroundings; tabs that are "slightly cheaper than a trip to Paris" lend it "special-occasion" status, though "normal folk can live like kings" just sampling the "snacks at the bar"; P.S. check out the private rooms.

Roberto ☒ *Italian*   27 | 19 | 23 | E

Fordham | 603 Crescent Ave. (Hughes Ave.) | Bronx | 718-733-9503 |
www.roberto089.com

Chef Roberto Paciullo "regularly makes the rounds" at this Bronx
"treasure" near Arthur Avenue, a "culinary trip to Salerno" that
"stands with the best" for "exceptional" food plated in "generous
portions"; "excellent" service and "dark", atmospheric digs make it a
"real pleaser", but a "no-rez policy" and fervent "local following" may
mean "long waits."

Saul *American*   27 | 20 | 25 | VE

Boerum Hill | 140 Smith St. (bet. Bergen & Dean Sts.) | Brooklyn |
718-935-9844 | www.saulrestaurant.com

Chef-owner Saul Bolton's "inimitable style" is on full display at this
Boerum Hill storefront where "carefully crafted" New American
dishes "go toe-to-toe" with Brooklyn's best; "spot-on" service and
"minimalist" decor make the "Manhattan prices" more bearable.

Scalini Fedeli ☒ *Italian*   27 | 25 | 26 | VE

TriBeCa | 165 Duane St. (bet. Greenwich & Hudson Sts.) | 212-528-0400 |
www.scalinifedeli.com

Michael Cetrulo "scales the heights" at this TriBeCa Northern Italian
"revelation" for "exceptional" cuisine and wines dispensed by a "gracious" team in a "civilized", "vaulted-salon" milieu; the $65 prix fixe-
only dinner may seem a lot to some, but the deep-pocketed feel it
"could charge more and get away with it."

Sushi Yasuda ☒ *Japanese*   28 | 22 | 24 | VE

E 40s | 204 E. 43rd St. (bet. 2nd & 3rd Aves.) | 212-972-1001 |
www.sushiyasuda.com

It's true, "chef Yasuda has left the building", but this Grand Central-
area Japanese remains in "top form" with "ethereal" sushi sliced from
the "freshest fish known to man"; the blond wood-lined, "island-of-
serenity" setting distracts from the "skyrocketing" tabs, though the
$23 prix fixe is a "steal"; P.S. "reservations are imperative."

Trattoria L'incontro ☒ *Italian*   27 | 20 | 25 | E

Astoria | 21-76 31st St. (Ditmars Blvd.) | Queens | 718-721-3532 |
www.trattorialincontro.com

"As good as it gets" in Astoria and sometimes even "better than
Manhattan", this "first-class" trattoria features the "Midas-touch"
Italian cooking of chef-owner Rocco Sacramone; devotees don't notice
the "Midtown prices" and "Queens decor", mesmerized by the waiters' "memorized recitation" of a "telephone-directory" list of specials.

Union Square Cafe *American*   27 | 23 | 26 | VE

Union Sq | 21 E. 16th St. (bet. 5th Ave. & Union Sq. W.) | 212-243-4020 |
www.unionsquarecafe.com

Diners have an "emotional connection" with Danny Meyer's "senti-
mental-favorite" flagship off Union Square that "never gets old, just
better" thanks to its "full-flavored", "Greenmarket-fresh" American
cooking, "on-the-ball" service, stylish surrounds and that "camarade-
rie" at the bar; it's "lasted an eternity in restaurant time" – 27 years –
in part because "you can carry on a conversation" here.

Orlando

TOP FOOD RANKING

	Restaurant	Cuisine
28	Victoria & Albert's	American
	4 Rivers	BBQ
27	Del Frisco's	Steak
	Jiko	African
	California Grill	Californian
	Ravenous Pig	American
	Capital Grille	Steak
	Ruth's Chris	Steak
	Chatham's Place	Continental
26	Seasons 52	American
	Norman's	New World
	Le Coq au Vin	French
	K Restaurant	Eclectic
	Primo	Italian/Mediterranean
	Cítricos	Mediterranean
	Enzo's	Italian

California Grill *Californian*   27 | 26 | 26 | E

Magic Kingdom Area | Disney's Contemporary Resort, 15th fl. | 4600 N. World Dr. | Lake Buena Vista | 407-939-3463 | www.disneyworld.com

The view of the Magic Kingdom fireworks from the 15th-floor perch of this "festive" Contemporary Resort "fine-dining" option is "amazing", but "the real fireworks come from the open kitchen", producing "stunning" Californian fare and "yummy sushi" with a "sensational wine list" and "outstanding service"; even though it's "a bit pricey", it's still "one of the toughest tables to get" at Disney, so be sure to "book early."

Capital Grille *Steak*   27 | 25 | 26 | E

International Drive | Pointe Orlando | 9101 International Dr. (Pointe Plaza Ave.) | 407-370-4392 | www.thecapitalgrille.com

"For a special occasion", "business dinner or romantic getaway", locals and (particularly) "tourists" recommend this I-Drive iteration of the "clubby, classic" chain whose dry-aged "steaks are always cooked to specifications" and served in "generous portions" at a "big price" ("you get what you pay for"); factor in the "amazing wine list" and "outstanding" service, and you've got "no worries here."

Chatham's Place 🅢 *Continental*   27 | 23 | 27 | E

Bay Hill/Dr. Phillips | 7575 Dr. Phillips Blvd. (Sand Lake Rd.) | 407-345-2992 | www.chathamsplace.com

"If you can't get lucky after dinner here, you have no shot" wink inamoratos of this "romantic", "cozy, intimate" affair preparing "incredible" Continental "classics" in a virtually "hidden" Dr. Phillips location; "you can always count on excellence" from the "seasoned" staff too (concurrently "attentive" and "unobtrusive"), which, along with a "great wine list" and live guitar music on weekends, furthers its reputation as a "splurge" that "never disappoints."

Cítricos *Mediterranean*

26 | 25 | 26 | E

Magic Kingdom Area | Disney's Grand Floridian Resort & Spa |
4401 Grand Floridian Way (bet. Maple Rd. & Seven Seas Dr.) |
Lake Buena Vista | 407-939-3463 | www.disneyworld.com

"Too long" considered a "consolation prize" for folks who couldn't get into Victoria & Albert's next door, this "relaxed" Mediterranean in Disney's Grand Floridian is "enjoying the spotlight" thanks to "innovatively prepared" fare that "blows you away"; what's more, it's a "better deal for your money", with a staff that goes "above and beyond", "beautiful decor" and views of the "spectacular" Magic Kingdom fireworks display.

Del Frisco's Prime Steak & Lobster ☒ *Steak*

27 | 21 | 25 | E

Winter Park | 729 Lee Rd. (Alloway St.) | 407-645-4443 |
www.delfriscosorlando.com

"Poifect" cheer champions of this family-owned Winter Park chophouse's "clubby, masculine" "dark-wood-and-leather" decor "right out of the 1950s" and "tender steaks rushed from the kitchen still cooking on your lava-hot plate" by "attentive", "courteous" staffers "from a bygone era" (they convey "awesome lobster" too); prices are unsurprisingly "steep" for such an "upscale" experience, but for "an important business dinner" or a "special event", it "can't be beat."

Enzo's Restaurant on the Lake ☒Ⓜ *Italian*

26 | 23 | 24 | E

Longwood | 1130 S. Hwy. 17-92 (½ mile south of Rte. 434) | 407-834-9872 |
www.enzos.com

You'll feel like you're "eating inside your richest relative's house" at this Longwood Italian, a "romantic" "mainstay" "overlooking a pretty lake" ("remote but worth the trip"); the "delectable" dinners are preceded by "*magnifique*" antipasti, paired with "great" wines and ferried by "professional" servers, all of which adds up to a "memorable" experience that's doubly "wonderful" "if someone else is treating."

4 Rivers Smokehouse ☒ *BBQ*

28 | 16 | 21 | I

NEW **Winter Garden** | Tri-City Shopping Ctr. | 1047 S. Dillard St. (Colonial Dr.) | 407-474-8377
Winter Park | 2103 W. Fairbanks Ave. (Formosa Ave.) | 407-474-8377
www.4rsmokehouse.com

The "best brisket this side of Dallas" is the star, but all of the Texas-style barbecue is so "sublime", it could "convert a vegan" tease fans of this "runaway success" with locations in Winter Garden and Winter Park (and more on the way); even though it's almost "too popular", with "lines as long as any Disney ride" for the counter-served space with picnic table seating, "the wait is worth it" because the portions are "generous" and the price "doesn't break the budget."

Jiko – The Cooking Place *African*

27 | 27 | 27 | E

Animal Kingdom Area | Disney's Animal Kingdom Lodge |
2901 Osceola Pkwy. (Sherberth Rd. off Hwy. 192) | Lake Buena Vista |
407-938-4733 | www.disneyworld.com

You'll "leave roaring for more" at this "phenomenal" Animal Kingdom African offering "exotic flavors" "for the gourmand" and "one of the largest selections of South African wines" in the U.S., all "expertly explained" by the "friendly" staff; the "beautifully decorated" setting is made even more "stunning" by lights that "change from sunrise to sunset", and while it's true that tabs are generally "pricey", you're getting more than a meal here – you're getting an "amazing" "adventure."

K Restaurant 🖾 *Eclectic*
26 | 21 | 24 | E

College Park | 1710 Edgewater Dr. (bet. New Hampshire Dr. & Yates St.) | 407-872-2332 | www.kwinebar.com

"Like something you'd find in wine country", with a dining deck overlooking a backyard garden, this "funky" College Park Eclectic in a "remodeled home" features local "superstar" chef-owner Kevin Fonzo's "innovative, entertaining", "ever-evolving menu" filled with "fresh herbs and vegetables" grown on-site; prices are generally "reasonable", especially for the wines, of which the "personable", "informative" staff can "suggest great pairings."

Le Coq au Vin 🖾 *French*
26 | 20 | 25 | E

South Orlando | 4800 S. Orange Ave. (Gatlin Ave.) | 407-851-6980 | www.lecoqauvinrestaurant.com

A "country French jewel in an unlikely location" ("don't let the exterior fool you"), this "reasonably priced" South Orlando "classic" employs a "conscientious" staff to convey its "rich", "divine" "traditional" Gallic cuisine; servings are "large", but half portions are available to "save enough room" for the "magnificent signature soufflés", adding to a "wonderful experience" that, for most, isn't hampered by the "slightly outdated decor."

Norman's *New World*
26 | 27 | 27 | VE

South Orlando | Ritz-Carlton Orlando, Grande Lakes | 4012 Central Florida Pkwy. (John Young Pkwy.) | 407-393-4333 | www.normans.com

"A gastronomic experience you won't soon forget" awaits at this "gorgeous", "elegant" room in the Ritz-Carlton Grande Lakes, where "venerable and lauded" chef Norman Van Aken's "impressive", tropically influenced New World cuisine comes via "wonderful service"; gourmets "highly recommend ordering the tasting menu" to sample all of the "scrumptious" flavors, but even if you go à la carte, bear in mind it's "expensive."

Primo *Italian/Mediterranean*
26 | 25 | 24 | E

South Orlando | JW Marriott Orlando, Grande Lakes | 4040 Central Florida Pkwy. (John Young Pkwy.) | 407-393-4444 | www.grandelakes.com

"Primo is primo!" profess partisans of this "high-end" JW Marriott Grande Lakes locus where chef Melissa Kelly utilizes "seasonal ingredients", many from the "kitchen garden", in her "impressive" Italian-Mediterranean dishes; "wonderful" upscale-casual decor and "friendly, professional service" also earn accolades, but the resort is "out of the way" for many, so it's often saved "for special occasions", such as a "romantic weekend getaway."

Ravenous Pig 🖾🅼 *American*
27 | 23 | 24 | E

Winter Park | 1234 N. Orange Ave. (bet. Denning & Orlando Sts.) | 407-628-2333 | www.theravenouspig.com

"Creative" chef-owners James and Julie Petrakis' New American "comfort food", emphasizing "seasonal, local ingredients", is at once "gourmet" and "unpretentious", "pork-heavy" and "vegetarian"-friendly, "unique and sumptuous" at this "standout" Winter Park gastropub where the "friendly staff" is "helpful" in pairing the "appealing" wines, "great craft beers" and "wonderful cocktails"; "down to earth prices" are another reason it's "usually packed", so be sure to "make a reservation" or risk a "wait."

Ruth's Chris Steak House Steak

| 27 | 24 | 26 | E |

Bay Hill/Dr. Phillips | The Fountains | 7501 W. Sand Lake Rd.
(bet. Dr. Phillips Blvd. & Turkey Lake Rd.) | 407-226-3900
Lake Mary | 80 Colonial Center Pkwy. (County Rd. 46A) | 407-804-8220
Winter Park | Winter Park Vill. | 610 N. Orlando Ave. (Webster Ave.) |
407-622-2444
www.ruthschris.com

"Want to be treated like a celebrity?" – then head for these "elegant" Central Florida outposts of the national chophouse chain venerated for their "friendly", "solicitous service"; just as "outstanding" are the "sizzling", buttery steaks, which are complemented by "tempting, beautifully prepared" sides and "superb" wines, and while it "gets expensive since everything is à la carte", most deem it "worth every penny."

Seasons 52 American

| 26 | 26 | 26 | M |

Altamonte Springs | 463 E. Altamonte Dr. (Palm Springs Dr.) | 407-767-1252
Bay Hill/Dr. Phillips | Plaza Venezia | 7700 W. Sand Lake Rd.
(bet. Della Dr. & Dr. Phillips Blvd.) | 407-354-5212
www.seasons52.com

"Indulge without indulging" at this twinset of "pretty", "inviting" New Americans, which earn Orlando's Most Popular honors with their "flavorful", "sophisticated, health-conscious" seasonal fare, each item under 475 calories ("you won't be carrying out a doggie bag", but you will leave "pleasantly satisfied"); though opinions split on value ("reasonable" vs. "pricey") and atmosphere ("vibrant" vs. "too loud"), there are only cheers for the "knowledgeable", "pleasant" staff and "tons of wines by the glass"; P.S. "reservations are essential", as "walk-in wait times" can be "long."

Victoria & Albert's American

| 28 | 28 | 29 | VE |

Magic Kingdom Area | Disney's Grand Floridian Resort & Spa |
4401 Floridian Way (bet. Maple Rd. & Seven Seas Dr.) |
Lake Buena Vista | 407-939-3862 | www.victoria-alberts.com

"Add this to your bucket list", because chef Scott Hunnel's "magnificent" New American multicourse prix fixe, voted Orlando's No. 1 Food, is a "once-in-a-lifetime" "gastronomic" "blowout" (it's "extremely expensive", though "worth every penny"); "service fit for royalty", including a "personally inscribed" "keepsake menu", plus a "romantic" setting complete with harp music are "reminiscent of more elegant times", and the "out-of-this-world wine pairings" only add to "the most magical meal you can find in the Magic Kingdom"; P.S. "jackets are required for men", no children under 10.

Palm Beach

TOP FOOD RANKING

	Restaurant	Cuisine
28	Marcello's La Sirena	Italian
	Chez Jean-Pierre	French
27	11 Maple St.	American
	Captain Charlie's	Seafood
	Café L'Europe	Continental
	Casa D'Angelo	Italian
26	Abe & Louie's	Steak
	Trattoria Romana	Italian
	Café Boulud	French
	Chops Lobster Bar	Seafood/Steak
	Little Moir's	Seafood
	Capital Grille	Steak
	Flagler	Steak
25	Bluefin Sushi	Japanese/Thai
	Four Seasons	Seafood

Abe & Louie's *Steak*   26 | 24 | 25 | VE

Boca Raton | 2200 W. Glades Rd. (NW Sheraton Way) | 561-447-0024 |
www.abeandlouies.com

The bone-in fillet is "as good as it gets", the "sides are a great match"
and the wine list is "impressive" at this Boston-bred beef palace in
Boca favored for "power lunches" and "special occasions"; the
"clubby" environs are "comfy" and "well managed" by "experienced"
pros – "when you have a reservation for 8 PM, you sit down at 8 PM" –
so while it costs "big bucks", most feel it delivers big-time.

Bluefin Sushi *Japanese/Thai*   25 | 18 | 22 | M

Boca Raton | VPC Ctr. | 861 Yamato Rd. (Congress Ave.) | 561-981-8986 |
www.bluefinthaisushi.com

"First-rate sushi at a reasonable price" (try the "dynamite" lobster
bomb roll) accounts for the "popularity" of this "attractive", "modern"
Japanese outlet located in Boca Raton that's also known for turning
out "excellent", "inventive" Thai dishes elevated by "pleasant" service.

Bonefish Grill *Seafood*   22 | 19 | 21 | M

Lake Worth | 9897 Lake Worth Rd. (Woods Walk Blvd.) |
561-965-2663
Stuart | Stuart Ctr. | 2283 SE Federal Hwy. (Monterey Rd.) |
772-288-4388
Palm Beach Gardens | 11658 U.S. 1 (PGA Blvd.) | 561-799-2965
Boca Raton | Shops at Boca Grove | 21069 Powerline Rd. (bet. Glades Rd. &
W. Palmetto Park Rd.) | 561-483-4949
Boynton Beach | 1880 N. Congress Ave. (Gateway Blvd.) |
561-732-1310
www.bonefishgrill.com

"Just-out-of-the-water fish in many forms" "draws droves" to these
"delightful", "easygoing" seafooders ("hard to believe it's a chain");
"longish waits, even with a reservation" and "noise, noise, noise" are

balanced by "prompt and courteous" service and "competitive prices"; P.S. the "Bang Bang shrimp is bang-on."

Café Boulud *French* | 26 | 26 | 26 | VE |

Palm Beach | Brazilian Court Hotel | 301 Australian Ave. (Hibiscus Ave.) | 561-655-6060 | www.danielnyc.com

"Beautiful people" "break out their diamonds and gold" at this "un-Florida" "class act" in the Brazilian Court Hotel that's voted Palm Beach's Most Popular thanks to "sophisticated" French fare that "does Daniel [Boulud] proud", backed by "excellent" wines and a staff operating at "the peak of hospitality" in the "casually elegant" interior or on the "lush" terrace; sure it's "pricey", but the $20 prix fixe lunch and $25 weekend brunch are "bargains"; P.S. there was a post-Survey chef change.

Café L'Europe Ⓜ *Continental* | 27 | 27 | 27 | VE |

Palm Beach | 331 S. County Rd. (Brazilian Ave.) | 561-655-4020 | www.cafeleurope.com

"Bump elbows with the country's wealthiest people" at this "fine-dining icon" that's "still hitting all the right notes" after three decades with its "scrumptious" Continental cuisine, 2,000-bottle wine list and "superb" staff – rated tops in Palm Beach – that treats diners "like royalty"; add in an "old-world" setting filled with fresh flowers and "lovely" music via a "magical pianist", and even if tabs are "astronomical", it's "worth it."

Capital Grille *Steak* | 26 | 25 | 25 | VE |

Palm Beach Gardens | Legacy Pl. | 11365 Legacy Ave. (PGA Blvd.) | 561-630-4994
Boca Raton | Town Ctr. | 6000 Glades Rd. (St. Andrews Blvd.) | 561-368-1077
www.thecapitalgrille.com

"Where the elite meet to eat meat" sums up these chophouses that admirers deem a "cut above other national steak chains" – not just for their "perfect sear" but also for their "impeccable" service that ensures "everyone is treated like a VIP"; a "solid wine list", including many by the glass, and "clubby" "dark-wood" environs make for a "relaxing" time, so go ahead and "break the bank."

Captain Charlie's Reef Grill *Seafood* | 27 | 14 | 23 | M |

Juno Beach | Beach Plaza | 12846 U.S. 1 (bet. Juno Isles Blvd. & Olympus Dr.) | 561-624-9924

"Don't be put off by the dumpy strip-mall exterior" or no-reservation policy – this "wildly popular" Juno Beach seafooder is a "classic not to be missed" on account of "strikingly fresh fish" in "creative" preparations; "professional" service and a "large" list of wines "at ridiculously low prices" offset the "spartan surroundings and noise"; P.S. lunch is "less crowded" or try its takeout-oriented sib 3 Doors Up in the same strip.

Casa D'Angelo *Italian* | 27 | 22 | 24 | E |

Boca Raton | 171 E. Palmetto Park Rd. (bet. Mizner Blvd. & N. Federal Hwy.) | 561-996-1234 | www.casa-d-angelo.com

Chef-owner Angelo Elia's "outstanding" Northern Italian fare, including a "wide variety of homemade pasta", takes diners on a "delightful" "journey to Italy" without leaving Boca ; it's "expensive" (i.e. an excuse to "wear your Valentino") and tables are "a tad too cozy" in the "bustling" space, but "warm" service and a "wine room that has to be seen to be believed" help explain why it's "beloved" by many – reservations are highly recommended.

Chez Jean-Pierre Bistro ☒ French

28 | 22 | 26 | VE

Palm Beach | 132 N. County Rd. (bet. Sunrise & Sunset Aves.) | 561-833-1171 | www.chezjean-pierre.com

"*Mais oui*" exclaims the "very Palm Beach" crowd that flocks to this "family-run" "country kitchen" for chef Jean-Pierre Leverrier's "consistently awesome" French fare including "outstanding Dover sole" and profiteroles with "chocolate sauce worth drowning in"; the "elegant" space is lined with "unique" modern art and warmed by "attentive" service, and while it helps to have "money to burn", most say it "always delivers"; P.S. closed July through mid-August.

Chops Lobster Bar Seafood/Steak

26 | 25 | 26 | VE

Boca Raton | Royal Palm Pl. | 101 Plaza Real S. (1st St.) | 561-395-2675 | www.chopslobsterbar.com

From "excellent steaks" and "fabulous" "flash-fried lobster" to "top-notch" service, this "happening" Boca branch of an Atlanta-based surf 'n' turfer "rarely misses"; the full menu is offered in both the "clubby" steakhouse side and in the replica of NYC's famed Oyster Bar complete with vaulted, tiled ceiling, and there's a lively "bar scene" with live music most nights; of course, some balk at "billfold-fracturing" tabs, but most feel it's "worth it."

11 Maple Street ☑ American

27 | 22 | 25 | VE

Jensen Beach | 3224 NE Maple Ave. (Jensen Beach Blvd.) | 772-334-7714 | www.11maplestreet.net

This "out-of-the-way" New American in "funky" Jensen Beach is a place to "escape the hustle" while enjoying chef-owner Mike Perrin's "inventive" seafood-strong menu, featuring mostly small plates presented like "works of art" and "costing about the same"; set in a "quaint" "Old Florida house", it has a "lovely ambiance" and "friendly" staffers who are "knowledgeable" about the food and substantial wine list.

Flagler Steakhouse Steak

26 | 25 | 26 | VE

Palm Beach | The Breakers | 2 S. County Rd. (bet. Royal Palm & Royal Poinciana Ways) | 561-653-6355 | www.thebreakers.com

A bastion of "old Palm Beach dining", this "exceptional" steakhouse at The Breakers provides "impeccable" fare and "superb" service in an "elegant" "country-club" atmosphere with "lovely" views of the golf course; no surprise, it all "comes at a price", although lunch is comparitively "inexpensive."

Four Seasons – The Restaurant Seafood

25 | 26 | 26 | VE

Palm Beach | Four Seasons Resort | 2800 S. Ocean Blvd. (Lake Ave.) | 561-533-3750 | www.fourseasons.com

"It's the Four Seasons – that's all you need to know" aver fans who declare this "delightful" grande dame in Palm Beach is "hotel dining done right", from Darryl Moiles' "sensational seafood" to the "pampering" treatment; the "pretty" room is enhanced by water views, but be aware that "special evenings" like this "don't come cheap."

Kee Grill *Seafood/Steak*

24 | 21 | 22 | E

Juno Beach | 14020 U.S. 1 (Donald Ross Rd.) | 561-776-1167
Boca Raton | 17940 N. Military Trail (Clint Moore Rd.) | 561-995-5044

"Consistent quality and value" is the hallmark of this Boca–Juno Beach duo offering "finely prepared fish dishes" along with land-based options and "wonderful sides" like creamed spinach ("heaven in a ramekin"); the "tropical island" digs get "jammed" by an "older crowd" so "don't linger" because the staff, though "friendly", will "take the water glass out of your hand", leading insiders to recommend the "terrific" early-bird hour's more "relaxed pace."

Little Moir's Food Shack 🅢 *Seafood*

26 | 15 | 21 | M

Jupiter | Jupiter Sq. | 103 U.S. 1 (E. Indiantown Rd.) | 561-741-3626

Little Moir's Leftovers Café 🅢 *Seafood*

Jupiter | Abacoa Bermudiana | 451 University Blvd. (Military Trail) | 561-627-6030
www.littlemoirsfoodshack.com

Fish fanciers "queue up" at these "funky", "colorful" seafood "shacks" in different Jupiter malls for "a wide array" of "killer" Florida catch at "reasonable" prices; the original looks a bit "run-down" while the bigger Abacoa locale has a slightly "more grown-up atmosphere", but both have a "laid-back" charm enhanced by an "eclectic collection of craft beer" and "friendly" service.

Marcello's La Sirena 🅢 *Italian*

28 | 19 | 26 | VE

West Palm Beach | 6316 S. Dixie Hwy. (bet. Franklin & Nathan Hale Rds.) | 561-585-3128 | www.lasirenaonline.com

There are "no surprises" at this 25-year-old West Palm Beach "icon", just "unforgettable" Italian "soul food" – which rates as the No. 1 meal in the county – accompanied by a wine list full of "character" and "professional" service, making it perfect for "special occasions"; its "old-style, white-tablecloth" setting can get "crowded", but tables are in better supply if you "eat later than the senior set"; P.S. closed in summer.

Seasons 52 *American*

23 | 24 | 23 | E

Palm Beach Gardens | 11611 Ellison Wilson Rd. (PGA Blvd.) | 561-625-5852
Boca Raton | 2300 NW Executive Center Dr. (Glades Rd.) | 561-998-9952
www.seasons52.com

"Guilt-free" food (all items are under 475 calories) that "actually tastes exciting" – like "out-of-this-world" flatbreads and "cute" desserts in shot glasses – is the "unique concept" behind this "health-oriented but not health-nutty" chain featuring seasonal New American fare; "warm decor", "well-trained service", "interesting" wines and "active" bars with nightly live piano further explain why they're "very popular."

Trattoria Romana *Italian*

26 | 21 | 22 | E

Boca Raton | 499 E. Palmetto Park Rd. (NE 5th Ave.) | 561-393-6715 | www.trattoriaromanabocaraton.com

"Once you sample" the "terrific" "real Italian" food (including a "don't miss" antipasto bar) at this Boca "class act", "you understand why" it's always "crowded"; prices are "expensive" and the staff is said to "blatantly favor regulars", but on the plus side, a recent renovation added a "much needed" bar area serving cocktails, wine and *stuzzichini* that "make waits a lot more enjoyable."

Philadelphia

TOP FOOD RANKING

	Restaurant	Cuisine
28	Vetri	Italian
	Fountain	Continental/French
	Birchrunville Store	French/Italian
	Amada	Spanish
	Gilmore's	French
	Bluefin	Japanese
	Morimoto	Japanese
27	Talula's Table	European
	Bibou	French
	Little Fish	Seafood
	John's Roast Pork	Sandwiches
	Le Bec-Fin	French
	Lacroix	Eclectic
	Sovana	French/Mediterranean
	Savona	Italian
	Prime Rib	Steak
	Fond	American
	Matyson	American
	Restaurant Alba	American

Amada *Spanish*   28 | 24 | 25 | E

Old City | 217 Chestnut St. (bet. 2nd & 3rd Sts.) | 215-625-2450 |
www.amadarestaurant.com

"Ama-zing!" is how amigos describe Jose Garces' "contemporary"
Spaniard, voted Philly's Most Popular restaurant thanks to "elegantly
presented" tapas that "make your taste buds swoon", and while the
tabs can add up, many agree the "tasting menu is the best deal in Old
City"; "knowledgeable", "gracious" service and a "beautiful" ("perhaps
too dark") space add to the "incredible experience" you can share with a
"hot date" or "several friends" – be sure to book "months in advance."

Bibou Ⓜ⇗ *French*   27 | 18 | 26 | E

Bella Vista | 1009 S. Eighth St. (Kimball St.) | 215-965-8290 |
www.biboubyob.com

The "only thing missing is the Seine" at this cash-only BYO "jewel box" in
Bella Vista from Le Bec-Fin alum Pierre Calmels, who creates "beautifully rendered" French "masterpieces", and his "charming" wife,
Charlotte, who oversees "efficient" though "leisurely" service in an
"informal" setting; the "snug" space seats only 32, so before you "dust
off a great bottle of wine", keep in mind it's "hard to get a reservation" –
especially for the $45 Sunday prix fixe – now that the secret is out.

Birchrunville Store Cafe Ⓢ Ⓜ⇗ *French/Italian*   28 | 24 | 27 | E

Birchrunville | 1403 Hollow Rd. (School House Ln.) | 610-827-9002 |
www.birchrunvillestorecafe.com

Francis Trzeciak's "quaint" Franco-Italian BYO "hideaway" in a circa-
1898 Chester County store wows city folk and others with "magical"

cuisine that yields an "aha with every bite", served in a "relaxed" setting that exudes a "hands-on family-ownership feel"; it's a "little piece of heaven" all right – and some quip "you will think you drove that far" to get there (even the restroom is a "schlep") – but nearly all agree it's "more than worth" the trip (as long as you bring cash; no plastic); P.S. open Wednesday–Saturday, dinner only.

Bluefin 🍽Ⓜ *Japanese*   28 | 14 | 21 | M
Plymouth Meeting | 1017 Germantown Pike (Virginia Rd.) | 610-277-3917
"Don't just show up and hope for a table, it's not going to happen" at this "quality" Japanese BYO in a "dumpy" Plymouth Meeting strip mall, where suburban sushi "snobs" "fill themselves to the gills" with "spicy tuna sundaes" and other "phenomenal" offerings, served by an "over-the-top friendly" staff; most agree it's one of the "best around", and some lament "maybe if we hadn't told so many people, it would be easier to get a reservation."

Buddakan *Asian*   26 | 27 | 24 | E
Old City | 325 Chestnut St. (bet. 3rd & 4th Sts.) | 215-574-9440 |
www.buddakan.com
The "beautiful, cool people" expect a "sublime" experience and "get it every time" at Stephen Starr's "tried-and-true", "loud, loud, loud" Pan-Asian "winner" in Old City, where the "amazing" fare can "send you into a food coma", served by a "top-notch" staff in a "handsome", "trendy" setting; a few suggest "Buddha would be offended", for "there is nothing in moderation" here – including the prices, though most agree "taste trumps budget" at this "awesome" "wonder."

Fond 🍽Ⓜ *American*   27 | 18 | 26 | E
South Philly | 1617 E. Passyunk Ave. (Tasker St.) | 215-551-5000 |
www.fondphilly.com
Virtually all agree this "bright" BYO "star" in a "high-end storefront" on South Philly's "ever-growing East Passyunk strip" is a "can't-miss experience", thanks to Le Bec-Fin alum Lee Styer's "creative", "excellent" New American cuisine and Jessie Prawlucki's breads and desserts, for which "your mouth will keep thanking you"; "superb" service helps make up for the "noise", but "space is limited", so be sure to snag a reservation.

Fountain Restaurant *Continental/French*   28 | 28 | 28 | VE
Logan Square | Four Seasons Hotel | 1 Logan Sq. (Benjamin Franklin Pkwy.) |
215-963-1500 | www.fourseasons.com
"When you want to impress" someone, the Four Seasons' "swish" main room (No. 1 for Decor and Service in this Survey) is the "gold standard" for "luxurious" "power" dining, where Rafael Gonzalez's Continental-French cuisine will "blow you away", as will the "unparalleled" service "fit for a king and queen"; jackets are required and it'll "cost you more than three coins" in Logan Square's fountain outside, but most agree it's "worth every penny" and "calorie."

Gilmore's 🍽Ⓜ *French*   28 | 24 | 27 | E
West Chester | 133 E. Gay St. (bet. Matlack & Walnut Sts.) |
610-431-2800 | www.gilmoresrestaurant.com
You "always feel well cared for and well fed" at Peter Gilmore's "plush" French BYO "destination" in West Chester, where his "exquisite" "ep-

icurean delights" and "solicitous" service from a "professional" staff "add up to a first-rate" experience that transports you to "France" and "that little place in the valley that everyone whispers about"; it takes "three to four weeks' advance notice" to book a table in the "compact" townhouse space, but almost all agree it's "well worth the wait."

John's Roast Pork 🅱🍴 *Sandwiches*   27 | 7 | 17 | I

South Philly | 14 E. Snyder Ave. (Weccacoe Ave.) | 215-463-1951 | www.johnsroastpork.com

The top-rated sandwich shop in town occupies a "cramped" shack in South Philly, where groupies solve the "impossible decision" between the "best cheesesteak in town" and "equally outstanding" roast pork "with greens and provolone" by "getting both"; "surly service adds to the experience", and the only drawbacks are the "long lines" and "short hours" (until 3 PM or whenever the "bread runs out").

Lacroix at The Rittenhouse *Eclectic*   27 | 27 | 27 | VE

Rittenhouse | Rittenhouse Hotel | 210 W. Rittenhouse Sq. (bet. Locust & Walnut Sts.) | 215-790-2533 | www.lacroixrestaurant.com

"Classy with a capital C", this "magnificent" Rittenhouse Hotel venue is a "luxurious", "über-modern" showcase for "inventive", "awesome" Eclectic tasting menus, which are "matched with amazing views" of the square and "attentive" service from a staff that's "sometimes a little too eager to please"; the "$59 Sunday brunch" buffet and $24 lunch prix fixe, and the bar, are budget-friendlier slices of "foodie heaven"; P.S. a post-Survey chef change may not be reflected in the Food score.

Le Bec-Fin 🅱 *French*   27 | 27 | 27 | VE

Rittenhouse | 1523 Walnut St. (bet. 15th & 16th Sts.) | 215-567-1000 | www.lebecfin.com

"Save your calories for days" before heading to Georges Perrier's "gorgeous", "sense-seducing" Rittenhouse "institution", where the dress code may have been "relaxed" but not the kitchen's standards: expect "sublime" French cuisine "prepared to perfection" and enhanced by an "amazing dessert cart" and "impeccable" service; if a few think "time has passed" this "legend" by and quip that you have to "sell your kids" to pay the bill, most agree it's "world-class dining" that "everyone should experience at least once"; P.S. Le Bar Lyonnais, the bar beneath the restaurant, has been redone into a cocktail lounge called Tryst.

🆕 Little Fish *Seafood*   27 | - | 22 | E

Bella Vista | 746 S. Sixth St. (Fitzwater St.) | 267-455-0172 | www.littlefishbyob.com

Mike Stollenwerk's acclaimed seafooder – praised for serving "delectable", "original" dishes featuring "the freshed seafood in town" – relocated from South Philly to Bella Vista post-Survey; its BYO policy and "fantastic" Sunday prix fixe ("book way in advance") remain intact, but since it only added two seats, expect the same "super intimate", "sardine"-like conditions.

Matyson 🅱 *American*   27 | 19 | 24 | E

Rittenhouse | 37 S. 19th St. (bet. Chestnut & Ludlow Sts.) | 215-564-2925 | www.matyson.com

"Foodies" call this "classy" New American near Rittenhouse Square the "best BYO in the city", thanks to the "wonderful, creative" and "always changing" menu from Ben Puchowitz that is at once "consistent" and "refreshing"; the staff "feels like family", and while some chafe at the "forced intimacy" of the "small storefront" space and "noise" that'll have you "communicating in sign language", the majority deems it a "cut above the rest."

Morimoto Japanese   28 | 26 | 25 | VE

Washington Square West | 723 Chestnut St. (bet. 7th & 8th Sts.) | 215-413-9070 | www.morimotorestaurant.com

"Amazing", "pristine sushi", a "fascinating array" of cooked dishes and "top-notch" service all "dazzle" at this Japanese from Stephen Starr and *Iron Chef* Masaharu Morimoto, set in a "luminescent", "postmodern whale's belly of a space" in Wash West; besides maybe the "trippy" "phallic lamps" on the tables, the "only hindrance comes at the end" "on a little piece of paper" quip sticker-shocked surveyors, but "rest assured" it's worth it – especially if you "jump off the deep end" and try the "sublime" omakase tasting menu.

Osteria Italian   27 | 24 | 24 | E

North Philly | 640 N. Broad St. (Wallace St.) | 215-763-0920 | www.osteriaphilly.com

"Let your inhibitions go" at the Vetri gang's "industrial"-meets-"rustic" Italian in North Philly; it's "perfect" for a "date" or "celebratory night out" thanks to chef Jeff Michaud's "swoon-worthy" fare, which is backed by an "expansive" wine list and served by a staff that makes you feel "snuggled up in a warm, doughy embrace" in a room that's "full of energy"; while it's "not cheap", "easy street parking" (albeit in a "questionable" area) will save you some $$$.

Prime Rib Steak   27 | 26 | 26 | E

Rittenhouse | Radisson Plaza-Warwick Hotel | 1701 Locust St. (17th St.) | 215-772-1701 | www.theprimerib.com

You "feel like you're in a movie" at this "special-occasion" steakhouse in the Warwick, where a "fancy-shmancy", "'40s nightclub" tableau sets the stage for "caveman cuts" of "primo" beef, "large cocktails" and "tuxedo-clad" waiters who are "true professionals" (even when serving the "bargain" $39 prix fixe special); add "unobtrusive", "romantic" live piano music to the mix, and fans insist it's "all you need to feel that things will get better" in "tough economic times."

Restaurant Alba 🖂 Ⓜ American   27 | 22 | 24 | E

Malvern | 7 W. King St. (Warren Ave.) | 610-644-4009 | www.restaurantalba.com

A "mecca for seasonal locavores", Sean Weinberg's "open kitchen" in Malvern creates "amazingly creative" "Euro-style" New American "grill" dishes that are served by a "terrific" staff in a "micro"-sized, "rustic" setting; "you can't go wrong" with the Italian wine list from "small producers", but some who find it "pricey" in general complain the $15 corkage is "outrageous."

Savona Italian   27 | 26 | 26 | VE

Gulph Mills | 100 Old Gulph Rd. (Rte. 320) | 610-520-1200 | www.savonarestaurant.com

While Evan Lambert has freshened his "elegant" Italian "mainstay" in Gulph Mills, shrinking the "special-occasion" dining room, boosting the outside patio and expanding the bar, Main Liners still come for chef Andrew Masciangelo's "Rolls-Royce" cuisine "at Kia pricing"; the "informative" staff provides "superb", "consistent" service, while master sommelier Melissa Monosoff oversees a 1,000-bottle list housed in a "really cool wine cellar"; P.S. it recently started serving lunch.

Sovana Bistro ⓜ *French/Mediterranean* | 27 | 22 | 24 | E |

Kennett Square | 696 Unionville Rd. (Rte. 926) | 610-444-5600 | www.sovanabistro.com

"Competition for tables can be fierce" at Nicholas Farrell's French-Med bistro "gem" that's "worth the drive" to "horse country" outside Kennett Square, where he "knocks" the "socks off" "locavores" with "terrific" "presentations" of "amazing" dishes ("heavenly cheese plates", "gourmet pizzas") from his "100-mile menu"; the "warm" front-of-the-house provides "impeccable" service, while the servers are "knowledgeable", and even though it offers a "nice wine list", BYO is permitted with an $8 corkage.

NEW Talula's Garden *American* | - | - | - | E |

Washington Square West | 210 W. Washington Sq. (Walnut St.) | 215-592-7787 | www.talulasgarden.com

Aimee Olexy has brought the folksy aesthetic of her Talula's Table into Washington Square West with this indoor-outdoor garden paradise created in a partnership with Stephen Starr; the words of Alice Waters literally hang over the dining rooms, which brim with reclaimed materials, and the guiding principles include seasonal American fare and an outstanding cheese selection.

Talula's Table *European* | 27 | 20 | 26 | VE |

Kennett Square | 102 W. State St. (Union St.) | 610-444-8255 | www.talulastable.com

"Sure, you gotta wait a year" for a reservation (and show up at 7 PM sharp) at Aimee Olexy's BYO "foodie's paradise" in the back of a Kennett Square market-cum-takeaway, but fans insist it's "worth it" for the eight-course prix fixe (price varies by season), Euro-style "farmhouse-table dinners" for groups of eight to 12 people that are like "a wonderful homey dinner party" – except with "knowledgeable" servers; it's a "culinary adventure" that'll make even hard-core gourmands "cry uncle"; P.S. there's an invite-only kitchen table for two to eight guests.

Vetri ⓩ *Italian* | 28 | 23 | 27 | VE |

Washington Square West | 1312 Spruce St. (bet. Broad & 13th Sts.) | 215-732-3478 | www.vetriristorante.com

A "religious experience" is how devotees describe Marc Vetri's "splendid" Italian "splurge", rated No. 1 for Food in the city and deemed a sure way to "impress your date" (or anyone) thanks to its "quaint" Wash West brownstone setting, "polished" service, "wonderful" wine pairings and "sublime" $135 tasting menu (no à la carte); though most agree it's "worth every penny", you may want "a stiff drink just before the check arrives."

Phoenix/Scottsdale

TOP FOOD RANKING

	Restaurant	Cuisine
28	Kai	Eclectic
	Binkley's	American
	Quiessence	American
	Noca	American
27	Barrio Cafe	Mexican
	Tarbell's	American
	Eddie V's	Seafood/Steak
	FnB*	American
	Hana*	Japanese
	Vincent's on Camelback	French/Southwestern
	Vincent's Market Bistro	French
26	T. Cook's	Mediterranean
	Pizzeria Bianco	Pizza

Barrio Cafe Ⓜ *Mexican* | 27 | 19 | 23 | M |

Phoenix | 2814 N. 16th St. (Thomas Rd.) | 602-636-0240 | www.barriocafe.com

"This ain't yo' mama's Taco Bell" crow fans of chef-owner Silvana Salcido Esparza's "upbeat", "funky", "colorful" Southern Mexican spot in Central Phoenix, where the "innovative, superbly prepared" "haute" meals come with "fantastic" guacamole prepared tableside, an "amazing selection of tequilas" (around 200), "delectable margaritas" and "warm, attentive" service; its location in a "somewhat dicey area" doesn't prevent it from being "always crowded", and with no reservations accepted, "come early or come late or you certainly will wait."

Binkley's Restaurant Ⓢ Ⓜ *American* | 28 | 22 | 27 | VE |

Cave Creek | 6920 E. Cave Creek Rd. (Tom Darlington Dr.) | 480-437-1072 | www.binkleysrestaurant.com

"Every meal is a revelation" at "genius" chef-owner Kevin Binkley's "world-class" restaurant in an "aging strip mall" in "the boondocks" of Cave Creek, where the French-inspired New American fare is available in "elaborate", "cutting-edge" tasting menus whose "locally sourced" courses are "interspersed with tastings and palate-clearers that are equally imaginative" and "beautifully presented" by "polite" staffers; it may require "three hours" and "a second mortgage", but for a "wonderful treat for the soul and stomach", "it's worth every penny."

NEW Eddie V's Prime Seafood *Seafood/Steak* | 27 | 26 | 25 | E |

North Scottsdale | Scottsdale Quarter | 15323 N. Scottsdale Rd. (Greenway Hayden Loop) | Scottsdale | 480-730-4800 | www.eddiev.com

With a "fabulous new location" in the Scottsdale Quarter, this "glitzy" "desert oasis" "bustles all week" with "beautiful people" "young" and "older" sampling the "wide variety" of "succulent seafood" and "never-go-wrong" steaks that, while "expensive", are nonetheless "a

---

* Indicates a tie with restaurant above

good value"; "responsive service" is a plus, but "at peak hours", the "loud" din, especially from the "happening bar", can grate – though that's to be expected as the scene is as "hot" as "Arizona in July."

Fleming's Prime Steakhouse & Wine Bar *Steak*

26 | 24 | 25 | E

Chandler | 905 N. 54th St. (West Ray Rd.) | 480-940-1900
North Scottsdale | Market St. at D.C. Ranch | 20753 N. Pima Rd., Bldg. R (Thompson Peak Pkwy.) | Scottsdale | 480-538-8000
Scottsdale | 6333 N. Scottsdale Rd. (Lincoln Dr.) | 480-596-8265
www.flemingssteakhouse.com

"Perfectly aged beef" "cooked just right" may be the raison d'être for this "classy", "consistent" steakhouse chain, but respondents are equally enthusiastic about the "superb" wine program, featuring "100 wines by the glass", not to mention the "generous portions" and "obliging staff"; prices are "amped-up", so budgeters should consider the "killer happy-hour deals", including a burger that "can't be beat."

FnB Restaurant Ⓜ *American*

27 | 20 | 26 | E

Old Town | 7133 E. Stetson Dr. (Scottsdale Rd.) | Scottsdale | 480-425-9463 | www.fnbrestaurant.com

At this "teeny" "treat" in Old Town, "creative" chef-owner Charleen Badman "lovingly prepares" "magnificent" "farm-to-table" New American cuisine – served in "great portions for the money" with an "all-Arizona wine list" – while her partner, Pavle Milic, oversees the "impeccable service"; there are a few tables in the space with multi-colored floor tiles, but insiders suggest you "sit at the counter" to watch the "magic" – either way, "call far in advance for a reservation."

Hana Japanese Eatery Ⓜ *Japanese*

27 | 17 | 23 | M

Phoenix | 5524 N. Seventh Ave. (Missouri Ave.) | 602-973-1238 | www.hanajapaneseeatery.com

"Big pieces" of "reasonably priced" sashimi and "amazing sushi" made from "the freshest fish in town" keep this family-owned Japanese "neighborhood gem" in Phoenix "always crowded"; though the digs are "charmless" and "cramped", no one really minds, especially in light of the "friendly, efficient" service and no-corkage BYO policy; P.S. "for a real treat", "try the shabu-shabu on Sunday nights."

Kai Ⓢ Ⓜ *Eclectic*

28 | 27 | 29 | VE

Chandler | Sheraton Wild Horse Pass Resort & Spa | 5594 W. Wild Horse Pass Blvd. (Loop Rd.) | 602-225-0100 | www.wildhorsepassresort.com

"Prepare to be dazzled" by this "ultimate dining experience" in a resort restaurant on a Chandler reservation, where the "unique" Native American–inflected Eclectic fare earns Phoenix/Scottsdale's No. 1 Food rating – plus service is "remarkable", decor is "lovely" and views are "stunning", especially from the patio; it's "in the middle of nowhere" and "expensive", but for "special occasions", you "can't beat it."

Lon's at the Hermosa *American*

26 | 28 | 26 | E

Paradise Valley | Hermosa Inn | 5532 N. Palo Cristi Rd. (Stanford Dr.) | 602-955-7878 | www.lons.com

"Impress out-of-town friends", a "date" or "clients" at this "quintes-sential" "Arizona experience" in a "beautifully remodeled 1920s

Southwestern resort" in Paradise Valley, serving "exciting", "superb" New American cuisine in a "warm interior" and on an "extraordinary" patio with "mature trees, colorful flowers" and a fire pit; "gracious service" and an "admirable" wine list are two more reasons it's "a place you will go back to", one that's "extra nice if someone else is buying."

Noca ☑ American   28 | 20 | 24 | E

Camelback Corridor | 3118 E. Camelback Rd. (32nd St.) | Phoenix | 602-956-6622 | www.restaurantnoca.com

A "wonderful surprise in a strip mall", this Camelback Corridor spot creates "original", "exciting", "daily changing" New American savories that are so "ultradelicious", you'll "want to lick the plate" clean before the "personable staff" replaces them with the "fabulous" complimentary cotton candy; some find the decor "fairly blah", but "gracious owner" Eliot Wexler helps craft a "big-city vibe" that works for a "special occasion or just a nice night out" – "so long as you aren't strapped for cash."

P.F. Chang's China Bistro Chinese   22 | 22 | 22 | M

Chandler | Chandler Fashion Ctr. | 3255 W. Chandler Blvd. (bet. Chandler Village Dr. & Rte. 101) | 480-899-0472
Fashion Square | The Waterfront | 7135 E. Camelback Rd. (Scottsdale Rd.) | Scottsdale | 480-949-2610
Mesa | 6610 E. Superstition Springs Blvd. (Power Rd.) | 480-218-4900
North Scottsdale | Kierland Commons | 7132 E. Greenway Pkwy. (Scottsdale Rd.) | Scottsdale | 480-367-2999
Tempe | 740 S. Mill Ave. (bet.7th St. & University Dr.) | 480-731-4600
www.pfchangs.com

Though many voters are "not sure the Chinese would recognize" the "Americanized" Sino fare served at this chain, "who cares?" – it's "safe" and "scrumdiddlyumptious" enough to "please" "everyone", hence it earns Phoenix/Scottsdale's Most Popular restaurant rating; what's more, the price point is "reasonable", the setting is "classy" and the staff is "pleasant", so most forgive the sometimes "long waits to get in" and the "loud" "noise."

Pizzeria Bianco ☑☑ Pizza   26 | 19 | 21 | M

Downtown Phoenix | Heritage Sq. | 623 E. Adams St. (7th St.) | Phoenix | 602-258-8300 | www.pizzeriabianco.com

"Believe the hype" say surveyors of this "cult legend" in Heritage Square, which cranks out Neapolitan wood-fired pizzas so "extraordinary" (thanks in part to locally sourced ingredients), they could very well be the "best on the planet"; though you should prepare for a "long wait" ("absolutely worth" it) to get into the "quaint", brick-walled dining room at dinnertime, things have "greatly improved" now that hours have been "expanded" to include lunch, when "lines are almost nil."

Quiessence Restaurant &   28 | 26 | 25 | E
Wine Bar ☑☑ American

South Phoenix | Farm at South Mountain | 6106 S. 32nd St. (Southern Ave.) | Phoenix | 602-276-0601 | www.quiessencerestaurant.com

"Farmhouse meets gourmet" at this "bucolic", "romantic" "magnet for foodies" at the Farm at South Mountain, where the "sumptuous", "inventive", "constantly changing" New American fare is "beautifully presented" alongside "superb" wines in a "lovely, romantic" interior

	FOOD	DECOR	SERVICE	COST

and on a "wonderful" patio; "gracious", "professional service" abets the "unique experience", and while it's "expensive", "this is a place where you get what you pay for."

Tarbell's *American* | 27 | 22 | 26 | E |

Camelback Corridor | Camelback East Shops | 3213 E. Camelback Rd. (32nd St.) | Phoenix | 602-955-8100 | www.tarbells.com
Experience a "deft" "synergy of wine and food" at this "lively" Camelback Corridor "shining beacon" where "culinary celebrity" and oenophile Mark Tarbell pairs "wonderful" American fare with "fantastic" wines among "pleasant" trappings; he "runs a tight ship" in the service department too, with "helpful", "personable" staffers to attend to a crowd filled with "important people" – the kind who have no trouble paying slightly "high-end" tabs.

T. Cook's *Mediterranean* | 26 | 28 | 27 | VE |

Phoenix | Royal Palms Resort & Spa | 5200 E. Camelback Rd. (bet. Arcadia Dr. & 56th St.) | 602-808-0766 | www.royalpalmshotel.com
"Have anything, you'll love it all" assure acolytes of this Phoenix "jewel" in a "boutique resort" whose "exceptional" Mediterranean fare and "excellent wine list" are served by "stellar" staffers in "romantic" digs with "fireplaces everywhere" and "lush", "impressive grounds"; the "expensive" tabs are unsurprising given the "one-of-a-kind" "dining experience", but you need not "wait for a special occasion", what with the "incredible" breakfasts, lunches and brunches whose slogan could well be "same quality, lower price."

Vincent's Market Bistro *French* | 27 | 21 | 24 | M |

Camelback Corridor | 3930 E. Camelback Rd. (40th St.) | Phoenix | 602-224-3727 | www.vincentsoncamelback.com
There may be "no better deal in town" than this "adorable, little" French bistro by chef Vincent Guerithault, the "casual" sibling (and neighbor) to "venerable Vincent's on Camelback", where "delicious croissants" and other breakfast pastries and "mouthwatering" lunches and dinners (until 8 PM) come at "comparatively bargain prices"; although surveyors say they "hesitate to report" on its virtues since it's already so "hard to get into", they can't help shouting *"fantastique!"*

Vincent's on Camelback 🖪 *French/Southwestern* | 27 | 24 | 25 | E |

Camelback Corridor | 3930 E. Camelback Rd. (40th St.) | Phoenix | 602-224-0225 | www.vincentsoncamelback.com
"Year after year", this Camelback Corridor "institution" is "never a disappointment" thanks to chef Vincent Guerithault's "remarkable", "creative" "fusion of Classic French and Southwest cuisines" plus "gracious" service; the "deep wine list" pleases oenophiles, and if aesthetes lament "dated decor", most find the setting "romantic" and suited to "special occasions" as the "pricey" tabs suggest.

San Diego

Addison ⊠Ⓜ *French* | 27 | 28 | 28 | VE |

Carmel Valley | Grand Del Mar | 5200 Grand Del Mar Way
(Del Mar Meadows Rd.) | 858-314-1900 | www.addisondelmar.com
"When you want to be treated like a king or queen", this "foodie heaven" in Carmel Valley's Grand Del Mar Hotel "can't be topped" – it's No. 1 for Service in the San Diego Survey – and its "flawless" staff is matched by a "glamorous and romantic" setting; yes, it's a "splurge", but its "luxurious three-hour" extravaganzas featuring chef William Bradley's "impeccably prepared" New French fare and "stellar wines" make it the "crème de la crème" of "special-occasion destinations."

A.R. Valentien *Californian* | 26 | 26 | 25 | VE |

La Jolla | Lodge at Torrey Pines | 11480 N. Torrey Pines Rd. (Callan Rd.) | 858-777-6635 | www.arvalentien.com
The Lodge at Torrey Pines' "stellar" eatery proffers "divine" "farm-fresh" Californian cuisine – chef Jeff Jackson writes the menu daily around the market's best "local picks" – in a "beautiful Craftsman-style" setting with paintings by the namesake San Diego painter and boasts "exceptional views"; "impeccable service" completes the "romantic experience" for well-dressed "locals and visitors", who note you'd better "have enough space on your credit card" for the sizable bill – though it's resoundingly voted "worth the price."

Bud's Louisiana Café ⊠ *Creole* | 27 | 17 | 23 | I |

Kearny Mesa | 4320 Viewridge Ave. (bet. Balboa Ave. & Ridgehaven Ct.) | 858-573-2837 | www.budscafe.com
You can get "your bayou fix" ("garonteed!") at this "big" place in a Kearny Mesa "industrial park", whose "amazing" "real Louisiana food"

("excellent po' boys", "wonderful jambalaya") showcases the talents of chef-owner Bud Deslatte; its simple, "crowd-accommodating" digs and prices as friendly as the staffers draw an appreciative crowd of office and industrial workers from nearby businesses.

Donovan's Steak & Chop House Steak
26 | 24 | 25 | E

Gaslamp Quarter | 570 K St. (6th Ave.) | 619-237-9700
Golden Triangle | 4340 La Jolla Village Dr. (Genesee Ave.) | 858-450-6666
www.donovanssteakhouse.com

"Classic steakhouses", these palatial meateries in Golden Triangle and the Gaslamp are "solid contenders for best-for-carnivores honors" given the "died-and-gone-to-heaven" beef, "excellent wines", "attentive" service and "masculine ambiance" for "special occasions"; their mix of "beautiful" types and business folk don't wince at the "big check", but others note "the prix fixe will fill one up nicely for half the price."

El Bizcocho French
26 | 25 | 26 | VE

Rancho Bernardo | Rancho Bernardo Inn | 17550 Bernardo Oaks Dr. (Green East Rd.) | 858-675-8550 | www.ranchobernardoinn.com

"Consistently a favorite" known for its ultra-"attentive" servers who "make you feel like your happiness is the most important thing in the world", this legendarily "luxurious" dining room (where jackets are suggested) in the Rancho Bernardo Inn continues to deliver "beautiful", "elegant" French cuisine; all-around "cushy surroundings" including "grand piano" serenades mean it's perfect for a "romantic evening" or "special occasion", so "just forget about the bill and go for it"; P.S. the Food score doesn't reflect a recent chef change.

Farm House Café French
26 | 20 | 24 | E

University Heights | 2121 Adams Ave. (bet. Alabama & Mississipi Sts.) | 619-269-9662 | www.farmhousecafesd.com

"A real charmer" in up-and-coming University Heights, "amazing" chef-owner Olivier Bioteau's "tiny" "rustic French" hideaway makes diners "feel they've been invited into someone's home in the countryside" of France; its "impeccable" classics like "flat-iron steak frites" and "the best foie gras" (available seasonally) ferried by a cheerfully "attentive" staff make most feel its somewhat upscale prices offer serious "value", especially when the "reasonable wine list" is factored in.

George's California Modern Californian
26 | 25 | 26 | E

La Jolla | 1250 Prospect St. (bet. Cave St. & Ivanhoe Ave.) | 858-454-4244 | www.georgesatthecove.com

George Hauer's "upscale", trend-setting eatery above La Jolla Cove has been a "treasure on the foodie map" since 1984, thanks to star chef Trey Foshee's "outstanding" Californian cuisine that almost "outshines the unbelievable view" over the Pacific; "wonderful" service and a "superlative" modern space where "romance is always in the air" ensure it's a prime pick "for a special-occasion splurge" that "still ranks with the best dining experiences in town."

George's Ocean Terrace Californian
25 | 25 | 23 | E

La Jolla | 1250 Prospect St. (bet. Cave St. & Ivanhoe Ave.) | 858-454-4244 | www.georgesatthecove.com

Offering some of the "best rooftop dining in California", with "stunning views of La Jolla Cove" and "the Pacific crashing below", this "fabulous place for lunch" (dinner too) is voted San Diego's Most Popular restaurant; a "more affordable" though still "expensive" adjunct to George's California Modern downstairs, it offers chef Trey Foshee's "exceptional", "casual" Cal cuisine (fish tacos, black bean soup) in a "not-pretentious" setting manned by a "friendly, professional" crew; P.S. "make a reservation" or brave the "brutal wait."

Hane Sushi Ⓜ Japanese | 28 | 21 | 23 | E |

Bankers Hill | 2760 Fifth Ave. (bet. Nutmeg & Olive Sts.) | 619-260-1411
This Bankers Hill offshoot of Pacific Beach's Sushi Ota offers "amazing-quality fish" in "sushi experiences beyond belief", particularly if you decide to go for the "outstanding omakase" from chef-owner Roger Nakamura (a longtime protégé of Yukito Ota); "steady", "attentive" service and a "cool", "stylish" atmosphere take the sting out of "expensive" prices and "hard-to-find parking", ensuring most everyone "leaves happy."

In-N-Out Burger ● Burgers | 24 | 12 | 21 | I |

Kearny Mesa | 4375 Kearny Mesa Rd. (Armour St.)
Mission Valley | 2005 Camino Del Este (Camino Del Rio)
Carlsbad | 5950 Avenida Encinas (bet. Cannon & Palomar Airport Rds.)
Rancho Bernardo | 11880 Carmel Mountain Rd. (Highland Ranch Rd.)
Pacific Beach | 2910 Damon Ave. (Mission Bay Dr.)
Sports Arena | 3102 Sports Arena Blvd. (Rosecrans St.)
800-786-1000 | www.in-n-out.com
This "Southern California institution" with a "cult following" is "packed at all hours for a good reason": "best-on-planet" burgers, fries and shakes offered in "clean, upbeat" environs at a "reasonable price" (it's voted the No. 1 Bang for the Buck in San Diego); plus, there's "never service without a smile" here – no wonder out-of-towners plead "come to the East Coast!"

Market Restaurant & Bar Californian | 29 | 22 | 26 | E |

Del Mar | 3702 Via de la Valle (El Camino Real) | 858-523-0007 |
www.marketdelmar.com
"Culinary innovator" Carl Schroeder "makes magic" at his "hot spot" located near farms in Del Mar, where "fresh-as-can-be" ingredients "drive the ever-changing menu" of "sophisticated", "perfectly balanced" Californian "flavor explosions" that are rated No. 1 for Food in the San Diego Survey; a "killer" boutique wine list, "attentive, smart" staff and a "contemporary" interior featuring a "lively", "see-and-be-seen" atmosphere are other reasons it's roundly declared a "not-to-be-missed" experience fully "worth the splurge"; P.S. it also boasts a "top-notch sushi bar."

Mille Fleurs French | 26 | 25 | 25 | VE |

Rancho Santa Fe | Country Squire Courtyard | 6009 Paseo Delicias (Avenida de Acacias) | 858-756-3085 | www.millefleurs.com
If an "air ticket to Paris" is out of reach, there's always this "elegant country" retreat in Rancho Santa Fe, where "genius" chef Martin Woesle works "wonderful artistry" with New French cuisine, which is "served with panache" by a "top-notch" crew; it's just the place "when you want to impress", but "value" prix fixe options and bar menu notwithstanding, it helps to have a "sophisticated credit limit" – or better yet "others who are treating."

	FOOD	DECOR	SERVICE	COST

Morton's The Steakhouse *Steak*
26 | 24 | 25 | VE

Downtown | The Harbor Club | 285 J St. (bet. 2nd & 3rd Aves.) |
619-696-3369 | www.mortons.com
A steakhouse "standard-bearer", this Downtown link of the "big-ticket" chain offers "excellently prepared" cuts of beef and "grand sides" "served professionally" amid an "ambiance of wealth and class"; some find it a bit "staid" and wish they'd "lose the raw-meat presentation" and "high" wine pricing, but the many who love its "traditional" ways consider it "one of the best."

Nine-Ten *Californian/Eclectic*
27 | 22 | 24 | E

La Jolla | Grande Colonial | 910 Prospect St. (Girard Ave.) | 858-964-5400 |
www.nine-ten.com
At this "unpretentious" "gem" in La Jolla's "charming little" Grande Colonial Hotel, "remarkable" chef Jason Knibb uses "care and imagination" with "farm-to-table" ingredients, resulting in "nuanced", "first-class" Californian-Eclectic creations; a "first-rate wine list", "exceptional" service and "elegant" decor add up to a "special-occasion treat" considered well "worth the splurge"; P.S. wallet-watchers tout the "good-value" lunch and prix fixe options.

Pamplemousse Grille *American/French*
27 | 23 | 26 | VE

Solana Beach | 514 Via de la Valle (I-5) | 858-792-9090 | www.pgrille.com
"Don't shy away" from the "innovative experiments" whipped up by "top-drawer" chef-owner Jeffrey Strauss at this Solana Beach French–New American "standard"-setter, because "they always work" according to acolytes, who also cite "über-delicious" desserts and a "gasp-inducing" wine list; its "interesting" interior filled with "eclectic" art and a "cool" staff providing "pampering" service complete the "special-occasion-destination" experience, "with prices to match"; P.S. it's "located almost trackside" at Del Mar, so reservations are a must in season (July–September).

Paon *Californian*
26 | 23 | 27 | E

Carlsbad | 560 Carlsbad Village Dr. (bet. Roosevelt & Tyler Sts.) |
760-729-7377 | www.paoncarlsbad.com
At this "pleasantly unexpected" Carlsbad "winner", "wonderful" chef David Gallardo and many on staff came from the Golden Triangle's highly rated WineSellar & Brasserie – "and it shows" in its "fantastic", "creative", French-accented Californian cuisine, "connoisseur's wine list" ("let the sommelier choose") and "superb" pro service; factor in an "elegant" yet "laid-back" atmosphere, and it's "hard to improve" on the "solid all-around experience" here; P.S. there's a wine bar as well as an adjacent retail store, where bottles can be purchased for consumption in the dining room ($15 corkage).

Primavera Ristorante *Italian*
27 | 23 | 25 | E

Coronado | 932 Orange Ave. (bet. 9th & 10th Sts.) | 619-435-0454 |
www.primavera1st.com
Maybe it faces "tough competition" from newer Coronado restaurants, but this "gem" remains a "favorite" for "excellent" Italian "classics" like veal, osso buco and "wonderful" pastas – plus the chef "accommodates special requests and preparations"; its "formal" yet "comfy" white-tablecloth setting is matched by stellar service.

Sushi Ota *Japanese* | 28 | 15 | 20 | E |

Pacific Beach | 4529 Mission Bay Dr. (Bunker Hill St.) | 858-270-5670 | www.sushi-ota.com

The "phenomenal", "melt-in-your-mouth" sushi (including a "magnificent" omakase) from "skilled artist" Yukito Ota and his "hard-working" chefs at this Pacific Beach "locals' favorite" "isn't just a reason to eat in San Diego, it's a reason to move here" – "just ask all the Japanese customers" and other "worshipers" standing in "lines out the door"; though the "nondescript", "strip-mall" digs and occasionally "attitudinous" service make a few "want to get 'ota' here", most agree "this place is as good as it gets"; P.S. it's an especially "great value at lunch."

WineSellar & Brasserie ⓈⓂ *French* | 26 | 20 | 26 | E |

Sorrento Mesa | 9550 Waples St. (Mira Mesa Blvd.) | 858-450-9557 | www.winesellar.com

Though it's located in a Sorrento Mesa "tech park", this "professionally run" French "gem" located above one of Southern California's leading wine merchants is "pure bliss" for oenophiles, with its "spectacular" list of bottles and "no huge markups", plus "incredible pairings by the glass", complementing "talented" chef Matt Smith's "outstanding" cuisine; a "welcoming, soft and romantic" setting and "attentive" service add to the "remarkable experience."

Wine Vault & Bistro ⓈⓂ *Eclectic* | 27 | 21 | 25 | E |

Mission Hills | 3731A India St. (Washington St.) | 619-295-3939 | www.winevaultbistro.com

Aficionados are "consistently impressed" by this "well-kept secret" situated in a "cozy", "simple" second-story space in Mission Hills, where chef-owner Chris Gluck "does a terrific job pairing" "excellent", "fairly priced" wines with his "innovative" Eclectic cuisine to create "outstanding multicourse meals" delivered by an "awesomely friendly" staff within "relaxed" environs; it's only open Thursdays-Saturdays (with special wine events on other nights) and the menu changes daily, so check the website or subscribe to its newsletter to get the "nightly happening info."

San Francisco Bay Area

TOP FOOD RANKING

	Restaurant	Cuisine
29	Gary Danko	American
	French Laundry	American/French
28	Cyrus	French
	Manresa	American
	Aubergine	Californian
	Meadowood	Californian
	Acquerello	Italian
	Sushi Ran	Japanese
	Kiss Seafood	Japanese
	Chez Panisse	Californian/Mediterranean
	La Folie	French
	Masa's	French
27	Swan Oyster Depot	Seafood
	Sierra Mar	Californian/Eclectic
	Cafe La Haye	American/Californian
	Commis	American
	Marinus	Californian/French
	Chez Panisse Café	Californian/Mediterranean
	Canteen	Californian
	Erna's Elderberry	Californian/French
	Le Papillon	French
	Kokkari	Greek
	Boulevard	American
	Kaygetsu	Japanese

Acquerello ⓈⓂ *Italian*   28 | 25 | 27 | VE

Polk Gulch | 1722 Sacramento St. (bet. Polk St. & Van Ness Ave.) | San Francisco | 415-567-5432 | www.acquerello.com

"Like fine wine", this "grande dame" is "getting better with age" proffering "high-end Italian" prix fixes brought by a "well-honed" staff while pouring "the best pairings in town" in an "artful" setting in a "former church" off Polk Street; its "subdued" vibe and "aging clientele" are hardly hip, but judging from "the number of town cars arriving with people dressed to the nines" (jackets are suggested), this "ristorante" remains *"paradiso"* for "that special occasion" and "worth every coin."

Aubergine *Californian*   28 | 24 | 26 | VE

Carmel | L'Auberge Carmel | Monte Verde St. (7th Ave.) | 831-624-8578 | www.laubergecarmel.com

It's the "crème of Carmel" and "special in every way" gush groupies of this "charming", "intimate" Relais & Châteaux Californian turning out "absolutely exquisite" prix fixe meals "with wine pairings that will leave you talking for days" ferried by service "so good it raises the bar"; true, it also "pushes the envelope on price" and can be "a bit pretentious", but if you "don't come underdressed" (jackets suggested) and "bring several credit cards", "you'll be richly rewarded"; P.S. the arrival of a new chef might not be fully reflected in the Food score.

	FOOD	DECOR	SERVICE	COST

Boulevard *American*

27 | 25 | 26 | VE

Embarcadero | Audiffred Bldg. | 1 Mission St. (Steuart St.) | San Francisco | 415-543-6084 | www.boulevardrestaurant.com

"Power brokers", "celebrities" and "common folk" alike " count on" "a phenomenal meal" at Nancy Oakes' "iconic" Embarcadero "showstopper", where an "elegant" belle epoque setting with "lovely Bay views" provides a "marvelous atmosphere" for "heavenly" New American fare and "brilliant" wines; after nearly "20 years", it "keeps up with the newer, flashier joints" for that "big night out" (whether a "date or on business"), and while it's "a bit noisy", "pricey" and "difficult to get into", "once you are there", you're "treated like royalty" and it "never disappoints."

Cafe La Haye Ⓢ Ⓜ *American/Californian*

27 | 19 | 25 | E

Sonoma | 140 E. Napa St. (bet. 1st & 2nd Sts.) | 707-935-5994 | www.cafelahaye.com

"Everything works" at this "charming, tiny place off the Sonoma Square", from the "thoughtful menu" of "perfectly prepared" New American–"Californian comfort food" to the sips from the "winning wine list"; "topnotch" service and "great prices" make it highly "popular with locals", so "book ahead" because scoring a table is the "envy of Wine Country."

Canteen Ⓜ *Californian*

27 | 15 | 22 | E

Tenderloin | Commodore Hotel | 817 Sutter St. (Jones St.) | San Francisco | 415-928-8870 | www.sfcanteen.com

"Despite his expanding empire", Dennis Leary "continues to dazzle diners" at his "teeny-tiny" Tenderloin original producing "damn good" Californian dinners (including a Tuesday night prix fixe and "out-of-this-world" brunch) at a "surprisingly reasonable cost"; even with "well-trained" waiters, it's "not a place to impress a date", but the whole "retro seedy diner atmosphere" "is half the fun", as is having to "fight for a stool" at the counter to watch "the magic happening up close."

Chez Panisse Ⓢ *Californian/Mediterranean*

28 | 24 | 26 | VE

Berkeley | 1517 Shattuck Ave. (bet. Cedar & Vine Sts.) | 510-548-5525 | www.chezpanisse.com

Alice Waters' "legendary" Berkeley prix fixe "temple" remains the "ne plus ultra" of "fresh, local, organic" Cal-Med meals served with "no flash", just "gorgeous ingredients" "exquisitely handled", and continues to elicit "audible sighs" "night after night" in the "wondrous Craftsman wood" dining room with a "view of the open kitchen" "where it all started" (pilgrims can "request a tour"); the "superb" staff can seem "self-important", but the "integrity, vision and talent" behind this "gastronomic experience" is worth the effort and "investment."

Chez Panisse Café Ⓢ *Californian/Mediterranean*

27 | 23 | 25 | E

Berkeley | 1517 Shattuck Ave. (bet. Cedar & Vine Sts.) | 510-548-5049 | www.chezpanisse.com

To experience the "same care, creativity and commitment" to the "field-to-plate ethos" as at "the mother ship" downstairs "sans the sanctimonious airs" and "full expense", "it's worth the climb" – "on your hands, backward even" for a "relaxing lunch" or dinner at Alice Waters' à la carte cafe turning out "perfect pizza" and other "simple" Cal-Med "deliciousness" in a "lovely Craftsman setting" tended by a "well-trained" staff; best of all, you can still "take a tour of the kitchen."

Commis Ⓜ *American*

27 | 21 | 26 | VE

Oakland | 3859 Piedmont Ave. (Rio Vista Ave.) | 510-653-3902 | www.commisrestaurant.com

"Isn't Oakland lucky?" fawn "intense foodies" who relish "sitting at the counter" of this "unmarked" New American "hipster-haute" "jewel box" watching "gifted chef"-owner James Syhabout and crew "work like precision engineers" crafting "thought-provoking" molecular gastronomic prix fixes; the "subdued minimalist setting" is "not for everyone" and it's "tough to get a reservation", but "you definitely get your money's worth", from the "exotic" amuse-bouche to the "spot-on service."

Cyrus *French*

28 | 27 | 28 | VE

Healdsburg | Les Mars Hotel | 29 North St. (Foss St.) | 707-433-3311 | www.cyrusrestaurant.com

"The caviar and champagne cart" alone "is enough to convince" "starry-eyed" tourists and other "froufrou" fanciers that this New French Healdsburg "destination" is the place for a "blow-out fine-dining" dinner or Saturday lunch in otherwise "casual" Sonoma; you can "save yourself a ton of money" dining "à la carte in the bar", but chef Douglas Keane's "magnificent" prix fixes with "wine pairings" and "all the extras" proffered in a "gorgeous setting" with a near "1:1" "staff-to-guest ratio" are what gives other temples of "haute cuisine" "a run for their money."

Erna's Elderberry House *Californian/French*

27 | 28 | 27 | VE

Oakhurst | Château du Sureau | 48688 Victoria Ln. (Hwy. 41) | 559-683-6800 | www.elderberryhouse.com

"If you're going to Yosemite", "you must stop" at this "astounding" hotel eatery in Oakhurst, where "quintessential hostess" Erna "attends to every last detail" in an "elegant" dining room, proffering "spectacular" "multicourse gourmet" New French–Californian dinners; while "certainly pricey", it's "the height of perfection" (not to mention the "only option for a high-end meal" for miles); P.S. "if you really want to impress your lady-love", "stay overnight and indulge the rest of you at the super-pampering spa."

French Laundry *American/French*

29 | 27 | 28 | VE

Yountville | 6640 Washington St. (Creek St.) | 707-944-2380 | www.frenchlaundry.com

Like a "natural wonder", Thomas Keller's "rarified" stone "temple of gastronomy" in Yountville bedazzles surveyors with tasting menus of New American–French fare that "defies description" delivered with "service that borders on clairvoyant", creating an "absolutely amazing" "four-hour dream" evening or afternoon (Friday–Sunday) "of culinary theater" by a "master"; "it takes an act of God to snare a slot" and the "incredible" wine list looks to have "500% markup", but like a "Chanel suit", "if you have to ask" if it's "worth the money", you're "not worthy."

Gary Danko *American*

29 | 27 | 28 | VE

Fisherman's Wharf | 800 N. Point St. (Hyde St.) | San Francisco | 415-749-2060 | www.garydanko.com

Acolytes could "write a short story" on why Gary Danko's "highly sought-after gastronomic mecca" on the Wharf is again "Numero

Uno" for Food, Service and Popularity in the Bay Area Survey; to begin, "like your favorite" "little black dress", it's "perfect for any occasion", proffering "brilliant", customizable New American tasting menus and "stupendous wines" plus an "unequalled" cheese cart in a "gorgeous" room with service that "befits kings and queens" yet has a "refreshing lack of pretension" (you can also "eat at the bar"); in sum, where else can you pay "three- and four-digit prices" and "walk out feeling you more than got your money's worth"?

Kaygetsu Ⓜ *Japanese*   27 | 19 | 26 | VE

Menlo Park | Sharon Heights Shopping Ctr. | 325 Sharon Park Dr. (Sand Hill Rd.) | 650-234-1084 | www.kaygetsu.com

"Brilliant sushi and sashimi" ("served like little jewels" "and priced accordingly") and a "meticulously orchestrated" kaiseki menu that "changes every month" (order "in advance") are examples of the "delicate" "Japanese food done to ultimate perfection" at this "popular" Menlo Park place; add a "sake sampler" and the tab can really "mount", but "solicitous" service and a "sedate" "minimalist" setting that belies the "suburban strip-mall" location make it a "favorite splurge" of fin-atics.

Kiss Seafood 🅩Ⓜ *Japanese*   28 | 15 | 25 | VE

Japantown | 1700 Laguna St. (Sutter St.) | San Francisco | 415-474-2866

"You won't find chicken teriyaki" or "Americanized sushi" at this "superstar in Japantown", just "the chef and his wife" proffering "fantastic omakase" dinners comprised of the "freshest fish" and "amazingly subtle" "non-sushi items" in a reverent "tea ceremony style"; as it "seats only about a dozen people", calling it "intimate" is an understatement, but the owners are "so 'kawaii' (cute)" you just want to hug them" and the "extraordinary" meals are "worth every penny."

Kokkari Estiatorio *Greek*   27 | 26 | 25 | E

Downtown | 200 Jackson St. (bet. Battery & Front Sts.) | San Francisco | 415-981-0983 | www.kokkari.com

Fans muse that "if Odysseus" had made "his first stop" this "upscale" Greek estiatorio, "his travels" would surely have ended here among Downtown's "power-lunchers" and "luminaries" with their "limos" all "lined up outside", dining on "phenomenal", "rustic" yet "refined" meze and roasted meats from a "fireplace" spit that lends a "warm ambiance" to the "beautiful" rooms; "servers know their stuff and do their best to please" and the bar's a "lively" scene, proving that "after all these years", it's still "amazing all-around."

La Folie 🅩 *French*   28 | 25 | 27 | VE

Russian Hill | 2316 Polk St. (bet. Green & Union Sts.) | San Francisco | 415-776-5577 | www.lafolie.com

"One of the last bastions" of haute cuisine, chef-owner Roland Passot's "fouffy French" Russian Hill "grande dame" "has stood the test of time" as he "greets the customers" and presents "superb", almost "too beautiful to eat" tasting menus that are "as up to date" as the "elegant" "plush" setting; "from the amuse bouche" and "fabulous" wine pairings by "his brother George" to the "gracious" service that "recalls a bygone era", it "fits the (hefty) bill" "for that very special occasion"; P.S. the lounge next door serves "great apps" and cocktails.

Le Papillon *French*

27 | 25 | 26 | VE

San Jose | 410 Saratoga Ave. (Kiely Blvd.) | 408-296-3730 | www.lepapillon.com

"Masterfully prepared" New French fare is "pretty as a picture" and tastes just as "irresistible" at this "elegant" eatery that's "worth the splurge" for an "upscale" experience; never mind the "weird" location next to a San Jose strip mall, because the "cozy", "intimate" dining room is really "romantic", and "very fine" service enhances your "quiet tête-à-tête."

Manresa ☒ *American*

28 | 25 | 27 | VE

Los Gatos | 320 Village Ln. (bet. N. Santa Cruz & University Aves.) | 408-354-4330 | www.manresarestaurant.com

"Four-hour" meals filled with "inventions of which Edison would be proud" are turned out by "magician" chef-owner David Kinch at this "elegant", "experimental", "special-occasion" New American in Los Gatos that takes diners on "an unforgettable journey" via "Japanese-influenced" tasting menus featuring his own biodynamic produce; a "synchronized dance" of servers and sommeliers "bring it together" and "it may set you back" some serious coin, but it makes "true foodies' hearts skip a beat"; P.S. there's a new cocktail bar and lounge.

Marinus ☒ *Californian/French*

27 | 26 | 26 | VE

Carmel Valley | Bernardus Lodge | 415 Carmel Valley Rd. (Laureles Grade Rd.) | 831-658-3595 | www.bernardus.com

It's "a bit of a drive if you're not staying at the lodge", but "worth every mile" for some of the "best food on the Monterey Peninsula" swoon foodies who trek to this "elegant" "classic in Carmel Valley" to "be coddled" and "bask in the glow" of its "cheery fireplace"-lit "old-world ambiance"; chef Cal Stamenov's "exquisite" "*nouveau* French"-Californian tasting menu "is the star here", and for "special occasions when price does not matter", "let the sommelier guide you to wines perfectly paired to your dinner"; P.S. closed Monday and Tuesday.

Masa's ☒☒ *French*

28 | 24 | 27 | VE

Downtown | Hotel Vintage Ct. | 648 Bush St. (bet. Powell & Stockton Sts.) | San Francisco | 415-989-7154 | www.masasrestaurant.com

Acolytes "don't have a vocabulary with enough superlatives to describe the dining experience" at this venerable Downtown "destination"; if "not trendy", it's "stood the test of time" offering a "trifecta" of "incredible" "modern French" tasting menus that display "artistry" (with "top-notch" wine pairings), "complemented by perfect service" and an "elegant and quiet" "setting well suited for adults" (jackets are required); but unless you're "independently wealthy", the high tabs limit it as "a place for celebration."

Meadowood, The Restaurant ☒ *Californian*
(aka The Restaurant at Meadowood)

28 | 27 | 27 | VE

St. Helena | Meadowood Napa Valley | 900 Meadowood Ln. (Silverado Trail) | 707-967-1205 | www.meadowood.com

Tucked away past the "guarded entrance" of St. Helena's Meadowood resort, this "special-occasion" hillside hideaway "surrounded by trees" and croquet lawns is an "absolutely gorgeous setting" for dining on "exquisite" Californian tasting menus by chef Christopher Kostow at "the top of his game", matched by a "deep wine list" and delivered by a staff that anticipates "every need"; "an open and expansive" room and details such as "Riedel crystal" place it "a world away from the routine dining-out experience", though it's one "you'll pay dearly for."

Sierra Mar *Californian/Eclectic*

| 27 | 29 | 26 | VE |

Big Sur | Post Ranch Inn | Hwy. 1 (30 mi. south of Carmel) | 831-667-2200 | www.postranchinn.com

"Stellar views" of the Pacific "elevate the experience" at this "truly exceptional" "clifftop" "destination" – voted the Bay Area's No. 1 for Decor – in Big Sur's Post Ranch Inn, an "elegant" overlook with "walls of windows" that's "equally spectacular" for its "sophisticated" Cal-Eclectic cuisine, an "enormous" wine list and "personalized" service; "prices are also in the stratosphere", but "pampered" epicures consider it "well worth the splurge" (and lunch "on the terrace" is "memorable" too).

Slanted Door *Vietnamese*

| 25 | 22 | 21 | E |

Embarcadero | Ferry Bldg. Mktpl. | 1 Ferry Bldg. (The Embarcadero) | San Francisco | 415-861-8032 | www.slanteddoor.com

Although fans "still pine" for the old location "with the actual slanted door", Charles Phan's "high-energy", "high-end" Vietnamese "palace" on the Embarcadero "waterfront" remains "the king" for "irresistible" "Saigon-meets-SF" small plates and "perfect pairings" of "obscure wines" delivered by a "fast-moving" staff; the "minimalist" "gleaming glass" digs "aren't cozy", but the "spectacular" "views" and chews "wow", so while it's "noisy", swarming with Ferry "market tourists" and "impossible to get a rez", determined diners continue to "battle for a spot at the bar."

Sushi Ran *Japanese*

| 28 | 21 | 23 | E |

Sausalito | 107 Caledonia St. (bet. Pine & Turney Sts.) | 415-332-3620 | www.sushiran.com

The "cult following" drives "over the bridge" and spends "a week's wages" for "Japan-like sushi" that "tastes as though plucked from the sea seconds before hitting your chopsticks" and "gorgeous", "cooked" "kaiseki dishes" served by the "gracious hosts" at this Sausalito stalwart; "parking is a pain" and they "pack you in like on a Tokyo subway", but lunch is a "bargain" and the easier to get into "cute wine bar" with "outside seating" delivers a real "sake-to-me experience."

Swan Oyster Depot ⊠⇗ *Seafood*

| 27 | 13 | 23 | M |

Polk Gulch | 1517 Polk St. (bet. California & Sacramento Sts.) | San Francisco | 415-673-1101

"Fabulous" seafood "so fresh" that "you expect it to talk back" is the lure of this "no-frills oyster bar" and "humble fish market" in Polk Gulch that's been a "family-owned" "fixture" "for decades"; "scoring" one of the "rickety" stools at the "cramped" "marble counter" "has its price" – a "long line" "out the door" – but those who pay their dues and are "prepared to drop some serious coin" (cash only) will be made to "feel at home" by the "hilarious" "guys in fish-stained aprons" behind the bar; P.S. closes at 5:30 PM.

Seattle

TOP FOOD RANKING

	Restaurant	Cuisine
28	Cafe Juanita	Italian
	Paseo	Caribbean
	Mashiko	Japanese
	Spinasse	Italian
	Herbfarm	Pacific NW
	Rover's	French
	Corson Building	Eclectic
	Tilth	American
27	Nishino	Japanese
	Kisaku Sushi	Japanese
	Lark	American
	Shiro's Sushi*	Japanese
	La Carta de Oaxaca	Mexican
	Harvest Vine	Spanish
	Il Terrazzo Carmine	Italian
	Cantinetta	Italian
	Boat St. Cafe	French
	Salumi	Italian/Sandwiches
	Nell's	American
	Canlis	Pacific NW

Boat Street Cafe *French*
27 | 22 | 24 | M

Queen Anne | 3131 Western Ave. (Denny Way) | 206-632-4602 | www.boatstreetcafe.com

"Escape to France" at chef Renee Erickson's "unpretentious" lower Queen Anne bistro where the "fabulous" midpriced fare is served by a "brilliant" staff; antique posters of Babar the Elephant add to the "delightful" dinner setting with slate tables and candlelight, while the more "sparse" adjacent area serves lunch and weekend brunch.

Cafe Juanita Ⓜ *Italian*
28 | 24 | 27 | E

Kirkland | 9702 NE 120th Pl. (97th St.) | 425-823-1505 | www.cafejuanita.com

"Dazzled" fans "can't say enough" about the "superbly prepared" dishes chef-owner Holly Smith turns out at her "charming" Northern Italian "hidden" in Kirkland and rated No. 1 for Food in Seattle; set in a midcentury house with a "cozy fireplace", the dining room has a "romantic" feel and the "top-notch" staff is "knowledgeable", making for an experience that's "expensive" but "all-around outstanding."

Canlis 🄯 *Pacific NW*
27 | 28 | 27 | VE

Lake Union | 2576 Aurora Ave. N. (Westlake Ave.) | 206-283-3313 | www.canlis.com

"Opulent" cuisine and "exceptionally polished" service with a backdrop of "stunning Lake Union views" have put this "longtime favorite"

---

* Indicates a tie with restaurant above

of Seattle's "who's who" in a "class of one" since it opened in 1950 – only now chef Jason Franey adds his "own spin" to a "very contemporary" Pacific NW menu; the overall package of "civilized fine dining" and "wonderful ambiance" in a "perfect midcentury modern room" means "you'll pay dearly", but "they do it so well."

Cantinetta ☑ *Italian*　27 | 22 | 23 | M

Wallingford | 3650 Wallingford Ave. N. (bet. 36th & 37th Sts.) | 206-632-1000
Bellevue | 10038 Main St. (bet. 100th & 101st Aves.) | 425-233-6040
www.cantinettaseattle.com

Handmade pasta that "melts in your mouth" is a highlight of the "fabulous" Italian menu drawing Wallingford locals to this pricey yet "unassuming" Tuscan-themed "gem"; the "lively crowd" keeps the "cozy" room "packed" and "noisy", but a "pleasant staff that tries hard" "lets you forgive a little"; P.S. a mid-Survey chef change is not reflected in the Food score, and the Bellevue branch opened post-Survey.

Corson Building ☑ *Eclectic*　28 | 23 | 26 | VE

Georgetown | 5609 Corson Ave. S. (Airport Way) | 206-762-3330 | www.thecorsonbuilding.com

"Incredible" locavore prix fixe meals served "family-style" at "communal tables" draw "in-the-know diners" to Matt Dillon's Georgetown Eclectic "food mecca", where a kitchen garden (with chickens) and a "cool" old building conjure up the feeling of a "provincial home"; courses start with an "unpretentious introduction" from the chef and proceed with "extremely professional" service, so acolytes assess it's "worth every pretty penny"; P.S. closed Monday–Wednesday, à la carte Thursday and Friday.

Dahlia Lounge *Pacific NW*　26 | 24 | 25 | E

Downtown | 2001 Fourth Ave. (Virginia St.) | 206-682-4142 | www.tomdouglas.com

Local flavor wiz Tom Douglas' founding Downtown restaurant is "still buzz-worthy" after more than two decades, dishing out Pacific Northwest fare including "fabulous crab cakes" and "beyond heavenly" coconut cream pie; the "sultry" red dining room has "arty" touches like papier-mâché fish lamps and the staff is "first-class", so it's understandably "busy" – be sure to "reserve a table."

Harvest Vine *Spanish*　27 | 21 | 23 | E

Madison Valley | 2701 E. Madison St. (27th Ave.) | 206-320-9771 | www.harvestvine.com

Cognoscenti congregate at the copper bar to "watch the magic" as chefs prepare "fabulous" Basque tapas to "mix and match" with a "broad selection of Spanish wines" at this "romantic" Madison Valley casa; service is "knowledgeable" and the place is "always packed" (reservations are recommended) – just "watch what you're ordering because those small plates can add up."

Herbfarm ☑ *Pacific NW*　28 | 26 | 28 | VE

Woodinville | 14590 NE 145th St. (Woodinville-Redmond Rd.) | 425-485-5300 | www.theherbfarm.com

"Atop the bucket list" of sybaritic surveyors is the "amazing" evening of "serious dining" at this Woodinville wine country "destination" where "you're never sure what will come next" during the nine-course Pacific NW "extravaganza" of "pure perfection", complete with wines and "unparalleled service" that's rated No. 1 in the Seattle Survey; it all begins with a tour of the garden and afterward some "stay the night" in the suites, but be aware that you might need to "get a second job" to foot the bill.

Il Terrazzo Carmine ☒ Italian — 27 | 25 | 26 | E

Pioneer Square | 411 First Ave. S. (bet. Jackson & King Sts.) | 206-467-7797 | www.ilterrazzocarmine.com

Carmine Smeraldo makes everyone "feel like a regular" at his "suave" Pioneer Square Italian where the "stellar" fare is "sinfully delicious" and the "exceptional" staff is "warm and friendly"; the Florentine country setting "breathes power and elegance" and it's always full of "movers and shakers", so just remember to "bring the moolah" and "you will be happy."

Kisaku Sushi Japanese — 27 | 20 | 23 | M

Green Lake | 2101 N. 55th St. (Meridian Ave.) | 206-545-9050 | www.kisaku.com

At this "go-to" Japanese sushi spot in Green Lake, chef-owner Ryuichi Nakano transforms a "wide variety" of the "freshest seafood" into "classic and innovative" rolls and much-lauded omakase dinners; it's "always busy", so generally "attentive" service can get a bit "rushed", but prices are "reasonable" and it's "kid-friendly" – a welcome touch in this family-centric neighborhood; P.S. closed Tuesday.

La Carta de Oaxaca ☒ Mexican — 27 | 17 | 19 | I

Ballard | 5431 Ballard Ave. NW (22nd Ave.) | 206-782-8722 | www.lacartadeoaxaca.com

"It tastes like Mexico" say fans of the "spectacular" "authentic Oaxacan cuisine" at this "buzzing" Ballard cantina where the "affordable" "full-bodied" fare features "wow"-inducing mole and "even the salsa and chips are out of the ordinary"; though the "space can get a little cramped" with "long lines", a "friendly", "bustling staff" and margaritas that "hit the spot" ease "waits."

Lark Ⓜ American — 27 | 22 | 25 | E

Capitol Hill | 926 12th Ave. (bet. Marion & Spring Sts.) | 206-323-5275 | www.larkseattle.com

The "exceptional" menu "takes small plates to a new level" with "local, seasonal ingredients" at John Sundstrom's "rustic" New American on Capitol Hill's up-and-coming 12th Avenue; the wood-beamed room is "tasteful" and "intimate", and though some say it seems "expensive" because "you can't help" over-ordering, it's agreed "every bite's a winner"; P.S. though primarily a walk-in spot, it does accept same-day reservations.

Mashiko Japanese — 28 | 19 | 22 | M

West Seattle | 4725 California Ave. SW (bet. Alaska & Edmunds Sts.) | 206-935-4339 | www.sushiwhore.com

An "amazing assortment" of sustainable seafood "not to be had elsewhere" plus moderate prices equal lines and "a decent wait" at this "edgy", "inventive" West Seattle Japanese "joint"; afishionados sit at the sushi bar and order chef-owner Hajime Sato's "omakase to die for", and though the decor might be a mite "dated", scores have improved across the board.

Nell's *American*   27 | 22 | 25 | E

Green Lake | 6804 E. Green Lake Way N. (1st Ave.) | 206-524-4044 | www.nellsrestaurant.com

From a "superb", "innovative" menu featuring the likes of veal sweetbreads and grilled Mangalitsa pork, chef-owner Philip Mihalski cooks up "consistently first-rate" fare at his "beautiful" and expensive Green Lake New American; the "quiet setting" is conducive to conversation (some say "boring") and service is "elegant", so acolytes attest it's an experience "you can count on" all-around.

Nishino *Japanese*   27 | 23 | 25 | E

Madison Park | 3130 E. Madison St. (Lake Washington Blvd.) | 206-322-5800 | www.nishinorestaurant.com

"Supreme sushi" "sparkling with creativity" pleases the well-heeled patrons of this "mellow" Madison Park Japanese, where "beautiful" fish is fashioned into "traditional" and "contemporary" fare by Nobu-trained co-owner Tatsu Nishino; insiders "go omakase" and let the masters "do their work" in the "lovely", stylish room that's comfortable whether you're in "jeans or a suit", and don't mind a bill that's a "splurge."

Paseo ⌧ⓂⲆ *Caribbean*   28 | 9 | 16 | I

Shilshole | 6226 Seaview Ave. NW (62nd St.) | 206-789-3100
Fremont | 4225 Fremont Ave. N. (bet. 42nd & 43rd Sts.) | 206-545-7440
www.paseoseattle.com

"Magnificent" and "messy" Cuban sandwiches stuffed with "pork that melts in your mouth" practically "inspire poetry" at this "busy", wallet-friendly Caribbean duo; it may "run out of bread" and is "cash-only", but that doesn't stop fans from forming "lines out the door", especially at the "wee" Fremont original, though the newer Shilshole branch has "shorter" waits.

Rover's Ⓜ *French*   28 | 25 | 27 | VE

Madison Valley | 2808 E. Madison St. (28th Ave.) | 206-325-7442 | www.thechefinthehat.com

"Charming", "talented chef-owner" Thierry Rautureau "reinterprets" French cuisine in "gorgeous", "imaginative" dishes fashioned from the "finest Pacific Northwest ingredients" at his genteel Madison Valley house enhanced by "flowers, linens" and a "phenomenal staff" that exhibits the "right combination of proper and friendly"; while it's not cheap, degustation menus start at $59 and Friday lunches are a local favorite.

Salumi ⌧Ⓜ *Italian/Sandwiches*   27 | 11 | 18 | I

Pioneer Square | 309 Third Ave. S. (bet. Jackson & Main Sts.) | 206-621-8772 | www.salumicuredmeats.com

Hot sopressata sandwiches and salami from Gina Batali (Mario's sister) induce "OMGs" from surveyors who bow to this affordable Pioneer Square Italian "cured piggy product" shrine started by papa Armandino; though lines aren't quite as long as they once were at Seattle's "worst-kept secret", there's still a "wait" – but plan ahead and you can book a lunch party in the private back room.

Shiro's Sushi *Japanese*

27 | 15 | 23 | E

Belltown | 2401 Second Ave. (Battery St.) | 206-443-9844 | www.shiros.com

"Master" Shiro Kashiba's Pacific Northwest–inspired Japanese is "pitch-perfect" and poised to "expand your sushi comfort-zone" boast Belltowners who call the omakase at the 11-seat sushi bar a "life-altering experience"; a "knowledgeable staff" helps explain "traditional delicacies", and though it's "pricey", there's "no attempt to be cool or trendy" – plus "if you're lucky", you'll spot a celebrity.

Spinasse *Italian*

28 | 22 | 23 | E

Capitol Hill | 1531 14th Ave. (bet. Pike & Pine Sts.) | 206-251-7673 | www.spinasse.com

"Fabulous" Piedmont cuisine and "light-as-a-feather" handmade pasta are the "real deal", channeling "little joints in Italy" for patrons of this Capitol Hill "gem" offering à la carte and family-style-tasting menus; toque Jason Stratton keeps the rustic quarters "buzzing with energy", including the seats at the chef's counter offering a "wonderful kitchen view", and it's all deemed "well worth the cost"; P.S. for a quick bite, hit Artusi, the aperitivo bar next door.

Tilth *American*

28 | 21 | 25 | E

Wallingford | 1411 N. 45th St. (International Ave.) | 206-633-0801 | www.tilthrestaurant.com

Eco-savvy chef Maria Hines dishes out "wonderful, inventive" locavore fare in "surprising preparations" tailored to both "vegans and carnivores" at her organic-certified Wallingford New American; a "welcoming", "knowledgeable" staff and a "cheerfully informal" Craftsman bungalow setting are more reasons fans "would eat here every day if [they] could afford it", plus weekend brunch is a "delight."

NEW Walrus & the Carpenter 🅐 *American/Seafood*

– | – | – | M

Ballard | Kolstrand Bldg. | 4743 Ballard Ave. NW (bet. 17th Ave. & Shilshole Ave.) | 206-395-9227 | www.thewalrusbar.com

Don't let the oyster bar designation fool you – while this Ballard seafood sibling of the Boat Street Cafe is luring seafood lovers with its freshly shucked bivalves, it's also dishing out midpriced New American dinners and desserts, craft cocktails, wine and microbrews; the hip digs pack in all ages at the zinc bar and simple tables that ring the walls, and the smart money shows up early to snag a seat.

Wild Ginger *Pacific Rim*

25 | 23 | 22 | E

Downtown | Mann Bldg. | 1401 Third Ave. (Union St.) | 206-623-4450
Bellevue | The Bravern | 11020 NE Sixth St. (110th Ave.) | 425-495-8889
www.wildginger.net

Once again Seattle's Most Popular, this "classy" Downtown and Bellevue duo proffers "pricey" "one-of-a-kind" Pacific Rim fare including "imaginative" dishes with housemade sauces and a specialty of "fragrant roasted duck on cloudlike buns"; Bellevue's weekend dim sum brunches add to the appeal, and though the bustling, "sleek" dining rooms hold hundreds of diners, "reservations are a must."

St. Louis

TOP FOOD RANKING

	Restaurant	Cuisine
28	Niche	American
27	Stellina	American/Italian
	Sidney St. Cafe	American
	Trattoria Marcella	Italian
	Tony's	Italian
	Paul Manno's	Italian
26	Dominic's	Italian
	Pappy's	BBQ
	Annie Gunn's	American
	Atlas	French/Italian
	Crossing	American
	Pomme	American/French
	Chez Léon	French
	Al's	Seafood/Steak
	Harvest	American
25	Roberto's Trattoria	Italian
	Giovanni's on the Hill	Italian

Al's Restaurant 🅢🅜 *Seafood/Steak*   `26` `20` `25` `VE`

Downtown | 1200 N. First St. (Biddle St.) | 314-421-6399 |
www.alsrestaurant.net

Take a "trip back in time" via "large portions" of "wonderful" chops
and seafood ferried by "outstanding" "waiters in tuxedoes" at this
"quiet" Downtown "tradition", which features a bar done up like
"an old river boat"; the great expense (you won't know it "until the
bill arrives" because there are "no prices to be found" on the
menu) makes it a "once-a-year place" for some, while others "stay
away" because the neighborhood's "not great" and the men's-club
decor "needs a revamp."

Annie Gunn's 🅜 *American* .   `26` `21` `24` `E`

Chesterfield | 16806 Chesterfield Airport Rd. (Baxter Rd.) | 636-532-7684 |
www.anniegunns.com

"Never misfiring", this "loud", "crowded" and "dark" far West County
"slice of heaven" matches "excellent" chef Lou Rook's "creative side
dishes" with his "delectable", "just-a-little-left-of-familiar" American
mains ("fabulous meats" are the specialty, as the restaurant was
"birthed from the adjacent Smokehouse Market"); just know that it's
not cheap and you "definitely need reservations on weekends", and if
you seek quiet (away from the "lively bar"), ask for the year-round
enclosed sun room.

Atlas Restaurant 🅢🅜 *French/Italian*   `26` `20` `26` `M`

Forest Park | 5513 Pershing Ave. (bet. De Baliviere Ave. & Union Blvd.) |
314-367-6800 | www.atlasrestaurantstl.com

Aim your compass north of Forest Park for this "quaint", "charming
bistro" where the "tantalizing" French-Italian dishes are "consistently

superb" and filled with "seasonal treats" (don't "shrug off" dessert – the "butterscotch pudding is a masterpiece"); the staffers "see that everything runs smoothly" as they provide the "loyal clientele" with "excellent value"; P.S. ratings don't reflect a post-Survey change of ownership and chef.

Chez Léon Ⓜ French — 26 | 24 | 24 | E

Clayton | 7927 Forsyth Blvd. (Central Ave.) | 314-361-1589 | www.chezleon.com

"There's something about it that makes me happy" smile supporters of this "authentic" Central West End bistro where a "skillfully executed menu" is paired with "faithfully French decor" that's "so charming, you feel like you're in Paris"; the "lively, inviting atmosphere" comes complete with "fantastic service", sidewalk seating and a pianist on Fridays and Sundays, so "order the Grand Marnier soufflé" and "settle in for the evening"; P.S. the prix fixe menu is a "great value."

Crossing, The Ⓢ American — 26 | 20 | 24 | E

Clayton | 7823 Forsyth Blvd. (Central Ave.) | 314-721-7375 | www.fialafood.com

"Flexible and appealing multicourse tasting menus" – available with "expertly matched" pours from an "intelligent wine list" – make "ambitious" chef-owner Jim Fiala's "intimate" Clayton New American (with "inventive" seasonal French and Italian influences) "more affordable"; the "fine-dining" experience is abetted by "attentive service", but belied by digs with "no pizzazz."

Dominic's Ⓢ Italian — 26 | 23 | 27 | E
The Hill | 5101 Wilson Ave. (Hereford St.) | 314-771-1632
Dominic's Trattoria Ⓢ Italian
Clayton | 200 S. Brentwood Blvd. (Bonhomme Blvd.) | 314-863-4567
www.dominicsrestaurant.com

"Exquisite service" is the hallmark of this "fine Italian eatery on The Hill", where tuxedo-clad staffers ferry "fantastic", "pricey" fare amid "lovely", "formal" surroundings; a modernist minority deems the whole experience "dated", but most folks appreciate it as a "tradition" for "special occasions" or just dinner with friends – and "leave wanting more"; P.S. the Clayton branch was not surveyed.

1111 Mississippi Ⓢ Californian/Italian — 24 | 24 | 23 | M

Lafayette Square | 1111 Mississippi Ave. (Chouteau Ave.) | 314-241-9999 | www.1111-m.com

"Challenge your palate" at this "gastronomic adventure" in Lafayette Square, where "flavor combinations you would never imagine come together flawlessly" on a "reasonably priced" Italian menu boasting "fresh local ingredients" and "Californian influences"; the multitiered setting in a "restored brick" warehouse manages to be "chic but not stuffy" (ditto the "charming", "capable" staff), and while it's often "crowded" and "noisy", the patio is always "delightful."

Giovanni's on the Hill Ⓢ Italian — 25 | 22 | 25 | E

The Hill | 5201 Shaw Ave. (Marconi Ave.) | 314-772-5958 | www.giovannisonthehill.com

"Chosen by presidents and Oprah", this "regal, formal" "celebration" "landmark" on The Hill employs "impeccable" waiters in tuxedos to convey its "spectacular" "gourmet Italian" fare; the "large portions" may necessitate "elastic-banded pants", but you'll "leave weighing what you came in" – the "day's pay" "removed from your wallet" evens things out.

Harvest ☑ American | 26 | 21 | 25 | E |

Richmond Heights | 1059 S. Big Bend Blvd. (Clayton Rd.) | 314-645-3522 | www.harveststlouis.com

"As its name implies", this Richmond Heights New American utilizes "creative ingredients" from "local purveyors" in its "exceptional", "always evolving" cuisine (there's also a "delicious" spa menu); "gracious service", "great midweek deals" (it can be "a bit pricey" at other times) and "amazing bread pudding" yield bushels of praise, but the "update"-ready "1993 Santa Fe" decor reaps little acclaim.

Niche American | 28 | 24 | 26 | E |

Benton Park | 1831 Sidney St. (I-55) | 314-773-7755 | www.nichestlouis.com

At this "trailblazer" in "historic Benton Park", "gifted" chef Gerard Craft's "adventurous", "exquisite" New American cuisine – voted No. 1 in St. Louis – "tantalizes" with "inspired combinations" of "local ingredients"; you'll "feel sophisticated" just stepping into the "cosmopolitan", "minimalist" digs, but don't come without a reservation, because "space is at a premium" (the fee, conversely, "isn't all that expensive"); P.S. feel free to ask a "savvy" server to recommend a "triumphant" dessert.

Pappy's Smokehouse BBQ | 26 | 16 | 21 | I |

Midtown | 3106 Olive St. (Cardinal Ave.) | 314-535-4340 | www.pappyssmokehouse.com

"Unbelievably succulent" meats, sides that are "not an afterthought" and "reasonable prices" draw pit fans to this Memphis-style Midtowner (never mind the "sparse decor"), voted the No. 1 BBQ spot in the nation; on "most days", the line "winds throughout the entire restaurant", but "quick", "friendly" staffers "keep things moving" – just "be sure to arrive early", 'cause "when the smoker empties", the place closes.

Paul Manno's ☒ Italian | 27 | 18 | 25 | E |

Chesterfield | 75 Forum Shopping Ctr. (Woods Mill Rd.) | 314-878-1274

It's "tucked away in an unassuming strip mall", but "man oh man", the Italian "food far outshines" the location at this "spectacular little place" with "Rat Pack–era" decor in Chesterfield; even though it's "always crowded", "noisy" and the "tables are close together", "excellent host" Paul and his "incredible" staff make everyone feel at ease.

Pomme ☒ ☑ American/French | 26 | 23 | 25 | E |

Clayton | 40 N. Central Ave. (bet. Forsyth Blvd. & Maryland Ave.) | 314-727-4141 | www.pommerestaurants.com

"For a romantic dinner" in Clayton, lovebirds glide into this "intimate", "quiet, sophisticated bistro" with "dark lighting, brick walls and dramatic artwork", where chef-owner Bryan Carr whips up "ever-changing" New French–New American plates that "taste like they were sent from heaven"; the portions may be a "bit skimpy for the price", but "fair" fees can be found on the "great" *carte du vin*; P.S. "for a more casual night", "try the Pomme Cafe and Wine Bar" two doors down.

	FOOD	DECOR	SERVICE	COST

Roberto's Trattoria ⓈⓂ Italian
25 | 20 | 23 | M

South County | Concord Plaza | 145 Concord Plaza Shopping Ctr. (bet. Baptist Church Rd. & Lindbergh Blvd.) | 314-842-9998 | www.robertosstl.com

A "secret well-kept from many", this "simply decorated" trattoria in a South County strip mall offers "wonderful", "authentic" Italian fare paired with "decent wines"; "friendly, professional service" and "reasonable prices" are two more reasons it's "worth the effort to find."

Sidney Street Cafe ⓈⓂ American
27 | 24 | 26 | E

Benton Park | 2000 Sidney St. (Salena St.) | 314-771-5777 | www.sidneystreetcafe.com

The "cozy", brick-lined setting is just as "perfect for romance" or a "special occasion" as it is for "casual" dining at this New American "jewel" in Benton Park, voted St. Louis' Most Popular restaurant; "talented" chef Kevin Nashan's "knock-your-socks-off" fare (a bit "expensive" but prices are "fair" for the quality) is "written on tabletop chalkboards" and "described with wit and accuracy by the able staff" – just "make reservations well in advance" to experience it.

Stellina ⓈⓂ American/Italian
27 | 18 | 21 | I

South City | 3342 Watson Rd. (bet. Arthur & Hancock Aves.) | 314-256-1600 | www.stellinapasta.com

There's "always something new" to try at this South City American-Italian, which gets high marks thanks to "fabulous homemade pastas" featuring "seasonal, local ingredients", plus "marvelous sandwiches, salads" and "decadent desserts", all at "fair prices"; surveyors also say the "service is impressive"; P.S. a post-Survey expansion nearly doubled the seating and added a bar, outdating the Decor score.

Tony's Ⓢ Italian
27 | 25 | 28 | VE

Downtown | 410 Market St. (B'way) | 314-231-7007 | www.tonysstlouis.com

There's "none other like this" "venerable" Downtown "gem" that manages to "hit new highs, year after glorious year", with "service as if for nobility" and "outstanding" "gourmet Italian cuisine"; some say the "fancy" setting's frozen in "1985", yet it remains a "go-to for special occasions"; P.S. don't forget to "bring your trust fund."

Trattoria Marcella ⓈⓂ Italian
27 | 20 | 24 | M

South City | 3600 Watson Rd. (Pernod Ave.) | 314-352-7706 | www.trattoriamarcella.com

"Trot to the Trat as fast as you can" for "to-die-for lobster risotto" (a daily "off-menu special") and other "spectacular" Italian fare – but "make a reservation" first, because the "comfortable", "casual" South City setting is "packed every night" with a "loyal following"; the "knowledgeable staff" garners its share of praise, but prices that are an "absolute steal" "for the quality" get the heartiest applause.

Washington, DC

FOOD	DECOR	SERVICE	COST

TOP FOOD RANKING

	Restaurant	Cuisine
29	Marcel's	Belgian/French
	Inn at Little Washington	American
	Komi	American/Mediterranean
28	CityZen	American
	Rasika	Indian
	Makoto	Japanese
	Eve	American
	Citronelle	French
	Palena	American
27	L'Auberge Provençale	French
	Prime Rib	Seafood/Steak
	Obelisk	Italian
	Tosca	Italian
	Corduroy	American
	L'Auberge Chez François	French
26	2941 Restaurant	American
	Blue Duck Tavern	American
	Minibar	Eclectic
	Central Michel Richard	American/French
	Ray's The Steaks	Steak
	Sushi Taro	Japanese
	Kinkead's	Seafood

Blue Duck Tavern *American*

| 26 | 24 | 25 | E |

West End | Park Hyatt | 1201 24th St. NW (bet. M & N Sts.) | 202-419-6755 | www.blueducktavern.com

"Lucky ducks" are "cosseted" by a "marvelous" staff at this "outstanding" West End New American destination, a "farm-to-table" "delight" spotlighting chef Brian McBride's "innovative" "comfort cuisine" – including "perfect french fries" topped off with "wickedly scrumptious" apple pie; plus, add in "atmospheric" decor both "inside and out" (sit near the "fountain on the terrace") and prices that are "reasonable for the quality", and, yes, it's "all it's quacked up to be."

Central
Michel Richard 🖎 *American/French*

| 26 | 21 | 23 | E |

Penn Quarter | 1001 Pennsylvania Ave. NW (11th St.) | 202-626-0015 | www.centralmichelrichard.com

"Stylish, great food, fun, exciting, chic" – chef Michel Richard's "genius" makes it all come together at this Penn Quarter "gem", a "bustling" New American–French brasserie where "comfort food gone way beyond your imagination" comes with "polished" service in an "airy California atmosphere"; yes, the "hopping bar scene" and "high-energy" dining room can be "noisy" ("sit in back" by the open kitchen), but "amazing" meals for "prices you can afford" quiet most skeptics.

Citronelle 🅂Ⓜ *French*

(aka Michel Richard Citronelle)

Georgetown | Latham Hotel | 3000 M St. NW (30th St.) | 202-625-2150 | www.citronelledc.com

28 | 25 | 26 | VE

"If heaven had its own dining room", it might look a lot like Michel Richard's "exquisite" Georgetown New French, where the "master chef's" "joie de vivre" still inspires each plate, and a "stunning" wine list and servers who "make you feel special" add to the "unforgettable memories"; naturally, tabs are "up there", but that's the price of "culinary nirvana" (the lounge menu is a bit "more limited" and a bit easier on the wallet); P.S. for a "special splurge, eat at the chef's table."

CityZen 🅂Ⓜ *American*

SW | Mandarin Oriental | 1330 Maryland Ave. SW (12th St.) | 202-787-6006 | www.mandarinoriental.com

28 | 27 | 28 | VE

Scoring a "trifecta" of near "perfection on all fronts", this "first-class" New American in the Mandarin Oriental showcases chef Eric Ziebold's "creative brilliance" in a "sleek and sensual" setting with "top-tier" servers and a "fantastic" sommelier; from the "intriguing" six-course tasting menu to the "heavenly mini–Parker House rolls", it's a "transformational experience" that's "worth every penny"; P.S. "smaller" three-course prix fixes in the more casual bar ($50) and dining room ($80) are likewise rife with "delectable delights."

Corduroy 🅂 *American*

Mt. Vernon Square/Convention Center | 1122 Ninth St. NW (bet. L & M Sts.) | 202-589-0699 | www.corduroydc.com

27 | 24 | 25 | E

Chef Tom Powers' "remarkably sophisticated" New American cuisine has finally found its "niche" – and it's virtually "outside the Convention Center door" in a townhouse that provides an "elegant", "conversation-conducive" setting for his "creativity"; a "well-priced wine list" that's "thorough without being overwhelming" and a "professional" staff complement the "powerful" cooking, while an "underutilized" upstairs bar provides a "perfect retreat", along with a three-course prix fixe (a $30 "steal").

Eve, Restaurant 🅂 *American*

Old Town | 110 S. Pitt St. (bet. King & Prince Sts.) | Alexandria, VA | 703-706-0450 | www.restauranteve.com

28 | 25 | 27 | VE

"Hitting on all cylinders", this "magical" Old Town New American proffers a choice of "unforgettable" experiences: an "ambrosial" nine-course romp in the "serene" tasting room, or a "gastronomic extravaganza on a smaller scale" in the "hip" bistro and lounge; chef/co-owner Cathal Armstrong "coaxes the best" from his "superb ingredients" (including "vegetables from the garden in back") and "impeccable" staff – from the "mesmerizing mixologist" to the "knowledgeable" sommelier – so naturally devotees deem it well "worth the splurge"; P.S. the $14.98 weekday bar lunch "is a steal."

🆕ᴱ🆆 Fiola 🅂 *Italian*

Penn Quarter | 601 Pennsylvania Ave. NW (entrance on Indiana Ave. bet. 6th & 7th Sts.) | 202-628-2888 | www.fioladc.com

- | - | - | M

At this much-anticipated Penn Quarter Italian trattoria, chef-owner Fabio Trabocchi offers midpriced, approachable versions of the exquisite cuisine served at his erstwhile Tysons Corner stunner, Maestro; the beautiful redo of Le Paradou's spacious digs, modeled on a posh Italian villa, boasts dramatic spiral chandeliers, an elegant bar lounge and an alfresco courtyard.

Inn at Little Washington *American* | 29 | 28 | 29 | VE |

Washington | Inn at Little Washington | 309 Middle St. (Main St.), VA | 540-675-3800 | www.theinnatlittlewashington.com

From the "truffle popcorn to the last lick of the sorbet sampler", there's "brilliance in every bite" at Patrick O'Connell's "magical" New American in the Virginia countryside; once again, its "drop-dead gorgeous" setting and "irreproachable" staffers who strive for "perfection in every detail" bring it the No. 1 rating for Decor and Service in the DC Survey – no surprise to those who happily dip into their "life's savings" to "savor" this "exquisite experience"; P.S. "stay the night to keep the fairy tale going."

Kinkead's *Seafood* | 26 | 22 | 24 | E |

Foggy Bottom | 2000 Pennsylvania Ave. NW (I St.) | 202-296-7700 | www.kinkead.com

"Consistency reigns supreme" at chef-owner Bob Kinkead's piscatorial "aristocrat" in Foggy Bottom, offering "sparkling seafood" "served with style" in a "surprisingly large" space designed to "encourage private conversations" among its "movers-and-shakers" clientele; "you pay a lot, but you get a lot" at this "first choice for a VSD (very special dinner)", but value-seekers can head to the "friendly" downstairs bar/cafe for "lighter fare" and lighter tabs.

Komi ☒Ⓜ *American/Mediterranean* | 29 | 22 | 28 | VE |

Dupont Circle | 1509 17th St. NW (P St.) | 202-332-9200 | www.komirestaurant.com

"Way out of the box and over the top" describes the "dazzling" "food adventure" at chef-owner Johnny Monis' "intimate" Dupont Circle "star", where a *degustazione* "marathon" of "intricate" Med-American courses – from "delectable bite-sized morsels" to "gourmet goat" – are matched "beautifully" with "esoteric wines"; "unpretentious" servers provide a "seamless experience from the front end to the kitchen", and if the "price is high and choices minimal", few dispute it "delivers on the 'wow' scale."

L'Auberge Chez François Ⓜ *French* | 27 | 26 | 27 | VE |

Great Falls | 332 Springvale Rd. (Beach Mill Rd.), VA | 703-759-3800

Jacques' Brasserie Ⓜ *French*

Great Falls | 332 Springvale Rd. (Beach Mill Rd.), VA | 703-759-3800 www.laubergechezfrancois.com

A "five-star" drive down "winding country roads" to Great Falls, VA, sets the mood for an "exceptional experience" at this "French classic" nestled in "gorgeous" surroundings; it's "not as glitzy" as some, but after "professional, caring" servers deliver multiple courses of "rich" Alsatian fare and wine from a "list that'll blow you away", most are won over by its "old-timey elegance" that harks back to a "more relaxed era" – and at a price that makes it a "bargain compared with Downtown" restaurants lacking its enduring "charm"; P.S. more affordable fare is now offered à la carte at dinner downstairs in the comparatively casual and cozy Jacques' Brasserie.

L'Auberge Provençale *French*

27 | 25 | 25 | VE

Boyce | L'Auberge Provençale | 13630 Lord Fairfax Hwy. (Rte. 50), VA | 540-837-1375 | www.laubergeprovencale.com

"An hour or so outside the city but a world away", this "beautiful" Boyce "getaway" is a "romantic" (and "expensive") fireplace-filled retreat for "lovers of fine food" and the "great outdoors"; "delectable" French tasting menus, an "extensive" wine list and "divine" service make it a "treasure" for a "special" meal, but for a truly "amazing" experience, "stay the night" and have breakfast too.

Makoto ☑ *Japanese*

28 | 20 | 25 | VE

Palisades | 4822 MacArthur Blvd. NW (U St.) | 202-298-6866

"As authentically Japanese as you can get", this "intimate" Palisades kaiseki specialist reaches the "pinnacle of quality" with an "adventurous" chef's menu showcasing eight to 10 courses of "exquisite" "works of art" accompanied by "geishalike service"; "delicate" sushi also figures in a "fabulous experience" that's "like leaving the country for the night" (you'll even trade your shoes for "slippers" on entry), so despite "limited room" and seating on hard "wooden boxes" it's "totally worth" the premium price.

Marcel's *Belgian/French*

29 | 26 | 28 | VE

West End | 2401 Pennsylvania Ave. NW (24th St.) | 202-296-1166 | www.marcelsdc.com

"Master" chef Robert Wiedmaier "orchestrates" culinary "miracles" at this West End Belgian-French "class" act, where the "superlative" cuisine (e.g. the "famous", foie gras–enriched boudin blanc) earns the No. 1 Food rating in the DC Survey; "stellar service" and a "romantic" Provençal setting (that was recently refreshed) enhance an "exceptional" performance that justifies "dropping serious cash" and putting in "extra treadmill time"; P.S. the pre-theater deal includes complimentary car service to the Kennedy Center.

Minibar ☑ *Eclectic*

26 | 21 | 24 | VE

Penn Quarter | 405 Eighth St. NW, 2nd fl. (bet. D & E Sts.) | 202-393-0812 | www.minibarbyjoseandres.com

You can "expect the unexpected" from "magician" José Andrés, so "do whatever it takes to score" one of the six $150 seats at his tiny Penn Quarter Eclectic "chef's tasting" five nights a week in part of the former Café Atlántico space; it's an "incredible" 30-bite "science class" dealing in "molecular gastronomy" that may be "America's closest approximation" to an "el Bulli experience", thus fans are happy about the rumored expansion in 2012; P.S. ratings include votes for its erstwhile parent.

Obelisk ☒☑ *Italian*

27 | 20 | 27 | VE

Dupont Circle | 2029 P St. NW (bet. 20th & 21st Sts.) | 202-872-1180

"Balanced perfection" is the keystone of this "tiny" Italian prix fixe "treasure" off Dupont Circle, where "well-chosen wines" complement a "never-ending feast" of "inventive" fare that "changes daily" and is "special without being showy"; it comes at a "surprisingly reasonable cost" given the "quality" and the "high level of service", so "bring a special friend for a fine, long evening" – just be sure to "make reservations" and "go hungry."

Palena *American* | 28 | 21 | 24 | E |

Cleveland Park | 3529 Connecticut Ave. NW (bet. Ordway & Porter Sts.) | 202-537-9250 | www.palenarestaurant.com

"Exemplary" chef-owner Frank Ruta conjures "meals that fire on all cylinders" at his Cleveland Park New American, where diners "savor every morsel" of "wonderful and imaginative" French-Italian–inspired prix fixe selections in an "old-world" dining room staffed by "cordial, attentive" servers; post-Survey, the "absolute steal" casual cafe portion has been expanded to the adjacent light-filled space and fitted out with a marble bar and wood-burning grill, further elevating what may be the "city's top burger" and making it easier to "snag a seat" for expanded lunch and dinner menus.

Prime Rib ⑤ *Seafood/Steak* | 27 | 25 | 27 | VE |

Golden Triangle | 2020 K St. NW (bet. 20th & 21st Sts.) | 202-466-8811 | www.theprimerib.com

In DC's Golden Triangle, the "godfather of steakhouses" mixes "old-world elegance" with "just the right touch of film-noir decadence", live music and "dynamite food" – the "best slab-o-meat in town", "first-rate" crab and "huge" sides – to make each "expensive" meal an "event"; the "retro-classy" digs are attended by "tuxedoed waiters" (there's a business casual "dress code" for customers too), while the bar scene "will hurt your eyes if you're married."

Rasika ⑤ *Indian* | 28 | 25 | 25 | E |

Penn Quarter | 633 D St. NW (bet. 6th & 7th Sts.) | 202-637-1222 | www.rasikarestaurant.com

"Does anyone really not rave about the food?" at this Penn Quarter "winner", where "intensely flavorful" Indian dishes take palates on "wondrous culinary journeys" that have dreamers wishing for an "extra stomach" (for the likes of "crispy" fried spinach that "Popeye would kill for"); "deft" servers who "appear to enjoy" their jobs and a "glittering" (if "noisy") atmosphere bolster its status as one of DC's "best restaurants – without 'best restaurant' price tags"; P.S. a second location is planned for the West End in early 2012.

Ray's The Steaks *Steak* | 26 | 15 | 21 | E |

Clarendon | Navy League Bldg. | 2300 Wilson Blvd. (Wayne St.), VA | 703-841-7297

At this "classic" "carnivore's paradise" in Clarendon, meat mavens opt for "consistently rockin' steaks", "educated servers" and "bargain pricing" over posh amenities – and, true to form, its 2009 move to "bigger digs allowed for reservations" but "no decor (but you're not paying for it)"; while some "don't understand the hype" over things like "free sides" and "reasonable" wine, they're vastly outnumbered by those who say it's "all about good quality at a good price."

Sushi Taro ⑤ *Japanese* | 26 | 20 | 22 | E |

Dupont Circle | 1503 17th St. NW (P St.) | 202-462-8999 | www.sushitaro.com

Following a "stunning redesign" and the installation of a "more authentic" Japanese menu, this Dupont Circle East destination offers kaiseki dinners that will "bowl you over" in a "sleek" (not "cozy") setting, plus "exotic" sushi prepared at an intimate "chef's table"; while vocal vets are "sad" to see "no California rolls in sight" and "expensive" tabs at what used to be a "Tokyo-style" haunt, at least the $12.95 "bento box lunch" is a "steal."

Tosca ⌂ *Italian*

27 | 23 | 26 | VE

Penn Quarter | 1112 F St. NW (bet. 11th & 12th Sts.) | 202-367-1990 | www.toscadc.com

Celebrated for its "quiet elegance" and "divine" Italian cuisine paired with wines to "match every dish and taste", this Penn Quarter "standout" is lined with "power players" at lunch and "romantic" sorts at night – because "no matter whom you bring here", its "seasoned" pros make the "experience special"; "understated" decor (some say "boring") completes the package, one with "pricey" tabs tempered by a "bargain" $38 pre-theater prix fixe deal; P.S. "try the chef's table in the kitchen."

2941 Restaurant ⌂ *American*

26 | 27 | 26 | VE

Falls Church | 2941 Fairview Park Dr. (I-495), VA | 703-270-1500 | www.2941.com

Enter past a "shimmering" koi pond and you'll discover "lush views" of a "tranquil" garden and lake from this "top-flight" New American's "impressive" dining rooms, whose "floor-to-ceiling windows", "artisan lighting and huge mirrors" belie its Falls Church office park locale ("who knew?"); the "exquisite" French-accented fare from chef Bertrand Chemel is presented with "polished" professionalism, making it a "special-occasion favorite", and while "being treated this well" is "not inexpensive", there are "good deals" at the bar.

2 Amys *Pizza*

25 | 16 | 19 | I

Cleveland Park | 3715 Macomb St. NW (Wisconsin Ave.) | 202-885-5700 | www.2amyspizza.com

Making "pizza like God intended" (or at least with the Naples pizza association's "blessing"), this "always crowded" Cleveland Parker proffers "sublime" "wood-fired, heat-blistered" pies that vie with its "fantastic charcuterie" as reasons to "battle hungry stroller-wielding" families for space in its "hectic" white-tiled premises; since grown-ups can seek refuge on the "lovely patio" or in the "well-stocked" wine bar and "quieter" upstairs dining room, the vast majority agree that "although wait times are 2 often 2 long", the place is "not 2 be missed."

Zaytinya ● *Mediterranean/Mideastern*

25 | 23 | 21 | E

Penn Quarter | Pepco Bldg. | 701 Ninth St. NW (G St.) | 202-638-0800 | www.zaytinya.com

Foodies "worship" at José Andrés' "cathedral of Eastern Mediterranean" flavors in the Penn Quarter, a "sleek", "airy" space "oozing hipness" and offering a "dazzling array" of "fascinating small plates" covering "Greece to Lebanon with all stops in between"; it's "loud, brash" and "always crowded", but staffers who "keep it real", a "user-friendly wine list" and tabs that "won't suck the money out of your wallet" help make it the Most Popular restaurant in the DC Survey – and render reservations "indispensable."

Wine Vintage Chart

This chart is based on a 30-point scale. The ratings (by U. of South Carolina law professor **Howard Stravitz**) reflect vintage quality and the wine's readiness to drink. A dash means the wine is past its peak or too young to rate. Loire ratings are for dry whites.

Whites	95	96	97	98	99	00	01	02	03	04	05	06	07	08	09	10
France:																
Alsace	24	23	23	25	23	25	26	22	21	22	23	21	26	26	23	26
Burgundy	27	26	22	21	24	24	23	27	23	26	26	25	26	25	25	-
Loire Valley	-	-	-	-	-	-	-	25	20	22	27	23	24	24	24	25
Champagne	26	27	24	25	25	25	21	26	21	-	-	-	-	-	-	-
Sauternes	21	23	25	23	24	24	29	24	26	21	26	25	27	24	27	-
California:																
Chardonnay	-	-	-	-	22	21	24	25	22	26	29	24	27	23	27	-
Sauvignon Blanc	-	-	-	-	-	-	-	-	-	25	24	27	25	24	25	-
Austria:																
Grüner V./Riesl.	22	-	25	22	26	22	23	25	25	24	23	26	25	24	25	-
Germany:	22	26	22	25	24	-	29	25	26	27	28	26	26	26	26	-

Reds	95	96	97	98	99	00	01	02	03	04	05	06	07	08	09
France:															
Bordeaux	25	25	24	25	24	29	26	24	26	25	28	24	24	25	27
Burgundy	26	27	25	24	27	22	23	25	25	23	28	24	24	25	27
Rhône	26	22	23	27	26	27	26	-	26	25	27	25	26	23	27
Beaujolais	-	-	-	-	-	-	-	-	-	27	25	24	23	28	25
California:															
Cab./Merlot	27	24	28	23	25	-	27	26	25	24	26	24	27	26	25
Pinot Noir	-	-	-	-	-	-	26	25	24	25	26	24	27	24	26
Zinfandel	-	-	-	-	-	-	25	24	26	24	23	21	26	23	25
Oregon:															
Pinot Noir	-	-	-	-	-	-	-	26	24	25	24	25	24	27	24
Italy:															
Tuscany	25	24	29	24	27	24	27	-	24	27	25	26	25	24	-
Piedmont	21	27	26	25	26	28	27	-	24	27	26	26	27	26	-
Spain:															
Rioja	26	24	25	22	25	24	28	-	23	27	26	24	24	25	26
Ribera del Duero/ Priorat	25	26	24	25	25	24	27	-	24	27	26	24	25	27	-
Australia:															
Shiraz/Cab.	23	25	24	26	24	24	26	26	25	25	26	21	23	26	24
Chile:	-	-	-	-	24	22	25	23	24	24	27	25	24	26	24
Argentina:															
Malbec	-	-	-	-	-	-	-	-	25	26	27	26	26	25	-